Crackup

Crackup

*The Republican Implosion and the Future of
Presidential Politics*

SAMUEL L. POPKIN

OXFORD
UNIVERSITY PRESS

OXFORD
UNIVERSITY PRESS

Oxford University Press is a department of the University of Oxford. It furthers the University's objective of excellence in research, scholarship, and education by publishing worldwide. Oxford is a registered trade mark of Oxford University Press in the UK and certain other countries.

Published in the United States of America by Oxford University Press
198 Madison Avenue, New York, NY 10016, United States of America.

Library of Congress Cataloging-in-Publication Data
Names: Popkin, Samuel L., author.
Title: Crackup : the Republican implosion and the future of
presidential politics / Samuel L. Popkin.
Description: New York, NY : Oxford University Press, [2021] |
Includes bibliographical references and index.
Identifiers: LCCN 2020049817 (print) | LCCN 2020049818 (ebook) |
ISBN 9780190913823 (hardback) | ISBN 9780190913847 (epub)
Subjects: LCSH: Republican Party (U.S. : 1854–) | United States—Politics and government—21st century. |
Trump, Donald, 1946–
Classification: LCC JK2356.P725 2021 (print) | LCC JK2356 (ebook) |
DDC 324.2734—dc23
LC record available at https://lccn.loc.gov/2020049817
LC ebook record available at https://lccn.loc.gov/2020049818

DOI: 10.1093/oso/9780190913823.001.0001

1 3 5 7 9 8 6 4 2

Printed by LSC Communications, United States of America

To the next two generations:
My children Lucy and David,
their spouses Seth and Paige,
and my grandchildren Sadie and Henry

Contents

Acknowledgments

The constant support and invaluable feedback of my wife, Susan Shirk, made this book possible. Throughout our marriage she has filled our lives—and those of our children and grandchildren—with love and joy. I dedicated my last book to her and now I am dedicating this book to the next two generations of the family we have made together. Even while building UC San Diego's 21st Century China Center and writing her own foundational books, she has contributed to my work with understanding and constructive criticism. I cherish her and look forward to the day when we can resume traveling together. In the meantime, though, it's my turn to ease her way while she finishes her latest book.

Writing this book was only possible because my editor, Dave McBride, and my agent, Jill Marsal, believed so strongly in this project. For ten years Jill has read my chapters with an eagle eye for clarity and logic. Even with increased management responsibilities at Oxford University Press, Dave found the time to give smart, incisive feedback. After Donald Trump's election, it would have been all too easy to dismiss the premise of a Republican Party crackup. I am grateful that they both gave me unwavering support, and I hope this book justifies their trust.

My work on the ways changes in campaign finance and new media options transformed parties and politics only came together in a book because Gabriel Greene, the director of artistic development at La Jolla Playhouse, cared enough about this project to once again find time to help me. As a dramaturg, he kept my structural focus squarely on the Republican Party and off the sideshows. In addition to feedback and good cheer, Molly Schneider provided extraordinary assistance by organizing more than 10,000 newspaper and magazine articles so that I could quickly search and cite them while tracking unfolding issues or connecting the pieces of the stories. I was also fortunate for Francesca Lupia's essential help; she provided fresh, sharp eyes, and ensured that my citations backed my text, and that the references weren't too obscure for readers whose political awareness begins with 9/11 or the Great Recession. Huchen Lu and Zoe Nemerever created my tables.

I am equally indebted to fellow academic researchers. My study of the distinctive ways national politics plays out differently in the House, the Senate, and the White House was aided by years of conversations and feedback from Matt McCubbins, Gary Cox, and Roger Noll. Professors Frances Lee, Andrew Clarke, and Sarah Binder were also helpful at critical junctures by e-mail and with timely articles for the *Monkey Cage*, the *Washington Post's* political science blog. Gary Jacobson has perfected the art of finding clear, straightforward ways to see the changes in relations between national and local issues in congressional elections. Thad Kousser helped me understand state legislatures and the critical role governors play in trying to connect the realities of managing government with how national legislators deal with the laws and regulation of campaign finance.

When I was an undergraduate at MIT, Howard Rosenthal introduced me to the ways modern research methods could help us address pressing social issues. All of political science owes a debt of gratitude to him and his former students and coauthors Nolan McCarty, Adam Bonica, and Keith Poole for their work on political polarization and the growth of wealth inequality in America.

What we owe each other as a country depends upon who we are and how much we trust government. My colleagues Tom Wong and Marisa Abrajano have helped many of us understand the complexities of immigration and the current stalemate over those who have lived and worked in America for decades. Michael Tesler and Shanto Iyengar have made sense of the ways race and media interact in a country where people can vote for an African American presidential candidate in one election, and then vote for a person who denies his predecessor was eligible to even run in the next. Chris Baylor and James Guth helped me decipher the complex maze of religious mobilization from Jimmy Carter onward. Arthur Lupia and Marc Hetherington have drawn attention to two distinct aspects of trust and political decision-making; both helped me understand the value of eroding trust in government, and how that makes it harder for governments to regulate tobacco, pollution, or coal. Raymond La Raja warned us of the dangers lurking in anti-party campaign finance reforms. Nancy Rosenblum placed the low regard for political parties in perspective and helped me explain why they are a necessary virtue, not a necessary evil.

At a moment when the work of journalists has been dangerously diminished or villainized, reporters have risen to the occasion, refusing to be cowed. Calling journalism the "first draft of history" understates the depth and value of the hundreds of books and articles I cite. In all my years in national politics there have never been so many insightful analyses from so many perspectives. I relied on so many writers that I cannot hope to list them all. Jane Mayer's *Dark Money* is the gift that keeps on giving; it showed me the supreme irony and peril of a world where billionaires celebrate Ayn Rand's world of great men who do it all on their own, while quietly forming a cartel to control state and national legislation. Tom Edsall has chronicled the ways that austerity and race have been changing our politics for over thirty years and has consistently managed to incorporate a vast array of scholarly research into his work. Besides her never-ending line of stories about President Trump, Maggie Haberman gets my vote as the "Most Valuable Tweeter." Her comments on stories or tweets invariably connect the dots or flesh out the story. Jonathan Tilove was an invaluable window on Texas politics; perhaps the greatest compliment I can pay him is that he made it possible to smile while reading about Ted Cruz. Besides his own illuminating articles, Dan Balz developed a team of younger reporters ready to carry on at his level for decades.

I am particularly grateful to friends and family members who read early drafts. Richard Thaler encouraged me to turn an early chapter into a book and nudged me to clarify my reasoning. David Popkin and Paige St.Clair Fitzgerald found time for detailed comments on my arguments and order of presentation. James Hamilton, Robert Kaiser, Jill Lepore, Arne Westad, Barney Frank, Sandy Lakoff, Pamela Ban, Henry Kim, Abby Weiss, Peter Gourevitch, and Len Chazen all read chapters and corrected errors both factual and grammatical. And perhaps the most important piece of advice came from Peter Goldman, who always reminded me of the *Newsweek* mantra: be sure there are enough signs pointing to the candy store.

Introduction

In 2016, a businessman so discredited that he could no longer get a casino license or borrow money from an American bank was elected president of the United States of America. How did this happen? How could Donald Trump—armed only with a barebones campaign operation, a few powerful slogans, and almost complete ignorance of any policy issues—manage to beat a field of prominent, well-funded GOP governors and senators—and then win the presidency?

It is easy to mock, ridicule, or scorn the former president as if he alone were the problem. But blaming Donald Trump for being exactly the kind of person he showed himself to be in the campaign is as comforting and easy as it is self-defeating. As Jill Lepore wrote of the press baron William Randolph Hearst, "Hating some crazy old loudmouth who is a vindictive bully and lives in a castle is far less of a strain than thinking about the vulgarity and the prejudices of his audience."[1]

Trump's rants about President Barack Obama, race, and immigration were an important part of his appeal. But they are insufficient to explain his extraordinary accomplishment. Conflicts over race and immigration are often cited as the primary reasons for the Republican Party's current divisions. But while such tensions are certainly present, they are not new to the country, and they were more violent and more present in daily life in other periods of the last century.

So what brought us to this moment? As I argue in this book, what *is* new is the collapse in trust of Congress and the inability of the political parties to respond to voters' concerns. Hardly a day goes by without columnists, disaffected Republicans, and Democratic politicians attacking the GOP for failing to defend the Constitution, cooperate with allies, or protect elections from foreign meddling. If the party were capable of these actions, there would not have been a president like Donald Trump.[2]

The Anna Karenina Principle

To paraphrase the opening line of Leo Tolstoy's *Anna Karenina*, successful political parties are all alike, but every unsuccessful political party is unsuccessful in its own way. The geographer and historian Jared Diamond, explaining the development of human societies, used Tolstoy's famous observation, this "Anna Karenina Principle," to explain why searches for single causes of success are so misleading. In so many human endeavors, he showed that "success actually requires avoiding many separate possible causes of failure."[3]

A successful political party is a coalition in which there is peaceful coexistence between its diverse groups, and candidates from the party can compete and win at both the state and national level. All it takes for a party to turn from comity to carnage is a breakdown of the truce among its major groups.

Trump is a symptom of a much larger and more insidious issue plaguing the Republican Party, one that began well before him and may last well after him. During his years in real estate, Donald J. Trump had proven himself an expert in profiting from distressed properties, and the Republican Party, rife with dissensus, certainly fit the bill; after years of overpromising and underperforming, Republican voters became disillusioned with the GOP establishment.[4]

"Outsider" candidates win support when citizens lose faith in the ability of elected representatives to fulfill their promises and solve problems. Trump campaigned as someone untainted by responsibility for Washington's stalemates, claiming his alleged business success meant he could cut through legislative obstacles the way Alexander the Great had undone the mythical Gordian knot with a single stroke of his sword.

The single most important reason that the United States ended up with an anti-party president—one who, upon accepting the nomination of his party, proudly proclaimed "I alone can fix it"—is the collapse of Republican leadership in the House and Senate. That was the straw that broke the elephant's back. It was unlike any break the party had experienced in over a century. This was not the doing of inept or unqualified leaders. Rather, it was an institutional failure that occurred when the chosen leaders no longer had the power necessary to form consensus within their caucuses.

Someone as ill-prepared and improbable as Trump could only win the GOP nomination because the party had already cracked up into uncompromising groups with incompatible demands, and had alienated so many of its voters that no Republican leader or politician had the credibility to exploit Trump's record of broken promises, betrayals, and shady deals.[5]

Crackups—by which I mean a breakdown of cohesion within a party that prevents its leaders from developing realistic, *achievable* goals they can deliver on when they control the White House and majorities in the House and Senate—are an inevitable feature of the American federal system. They can endure for many election cycles, because the parties' diverse groups are always jockeying among themselves for power. There will always be conflicts between voting blocs, donors, and party elites that make it hard for a party to compete well enough to win the presidency and legislative majorities.

This Republican crackup is different from past crackups, however. This is the first time—for the Democrats or the GOP—that no group within the party could create a synthesis of old orthodoxies and new realities that altered the party's direction enough to build a new consensus. This is the first time that a candidate with virtually no support from established leaders won a party's nomination, let alone the presidency. The Republicans imploded to the point that no candidate offering a defense of their traditional stands could come close to winning the nomination for president.

I want to make it clear from the start that this crackup is not a one-time failure of the Republican Party; Democrats have no reason to gloat and feel immune to a similar fate. Democrats were so badly split over social issues and redistributive government programs that they only controlled the White House for four out of twenty-four years between Lyndon Johnson and Bill Clinton. When the next rift occurs, they will be just as susceptible to the factors that led to the current GOP crackup.

In this book, I argue that Donald Trump is symptomatic of the problems facing both parties. Ongoing changes in social and commercial media, combined with campaign finance reforms, are at the heart of the Republican crackup—and of future potential crackups in both parties. From now on, whenever there is a serious internal rift, parties will be prone to capture by a presidential candidate with no support from its leaders. Unless major reforms occur, both parties are vulnerable to legislative factions big enough to block compromise but too small in numbers or extreme in their demands to develop realistic policies that could garner majority support within the party.

Changes in social media and an expansion of the forms of commercial media have raised the number of issues voters follow and lowered the standards of reporting from many news sources. These changes make it easier for individual politicians to find audiences and build personal reputations at odds with their party's brand. In the 1960s, the main way for a senator to get a national television audience was by chairing a hearing so important that people tuned in. That gave party leaders control over national exposure; a senator had to earn respect and trust before being selected.

Today, it often seems that there are as many channels and programs as there are politicians in Washington. In 2008, the political consultant Ed Rollins observed how easy it was to start a campaign without ever becoming a "serious candidate with serious solutions." All one had to do to raise several million dollars was go on television and say something "outrageous . . . throw a hand grenade."[6] Thanks to the growth of social media and the rise of low-budget commentators at the expense of costly investigative reporting, there are also more ways to degrade the credibility of expertise and devalue inconvenient facts.[7]

Misguided campaign finance reforms and Supreme Court rulings over the last twenty years have limited the ability of political parties to raise money directly, while at the same time removing all limits on independent spending by corporations and wealthy individuals. These rulings paved the way for billionaires with pet issues to build their own lavishly funded political organizations outside of party control, allowing them to operate behind the scenes and spend millions on advertisements while legally hiding the source of funds for the ads.

Moving the money away from parties has changed politics in America, weakening House and Senate party leaders and making it harder to pass legislation critical to their party's supporters. When a party's congressional leaders lack the leverage to bring the extremes of the party together, the system breaks down.

We are living with the unintended consequences of these changes, most prominently the Bipartisan Campaign Reform Act of 2002 and *Citizens United v. Federal Election Commission* (known, respectively, as McCain-Feingold and *Citizens United*). These changes in the fundamental rules of campaign finance are the result of an inadvertent synergy between the progressive quest for a government cleansed of party bosses, big money, and interests deemed "special," on the one hand, and the anti-government determination of social and economic conservatives to make government smaller and less progressive, on the other. The combination has stripped the major parties of most of their power to enforce any collective responsibility on their legislative colleagues, or upon a president from their own party.

How *Crackup* Came to Be

This book began in 2013 as an additional chapter for a second edition of my earlier book, *The Candidate: What It Takes to Win—and Hold—the White House*. I wanted to elaborate on an important theme: the tactics that aspiring presidential candidates deploy to alter their party's brand and become president.

The questions I faced demanded a lengthier examination than a chapter would allow, and it soon turned into a much bigger project focusing on the changing nature of intraparty battles in general, and the current crackup of the Republican Party in particular.

Several of those questions involved Senator Ted Cruz. During President Obama's second term, whenever I gave a lecture, someone would ask me, "Is Hillary Clinton going to win in 2016?" I always responded, "It depends on how much damage Ted Cruz does to the Republican Party."

I considered Cruz the key to the 2016 election—partly because he was the most entrepreneurial and politically creative Republican senator, but mostly because he was using the Senate in a brazenly self-serving manner; he seemed determined to be known as the bravest and purest one of all, regardless of the damage he inflicted on his party. Why were Senate Republicans walking on eggshells and letting Cruz get away with his stunts?

Cruz was a polished Supreme Court litigator who clerked for Chief Justice William Rehnquist. His SCOTUS victories marked him as a star-in-the-making, suggesting a bright future in a courtroom, a governor's mansion, or perhaps even the White House. Why, then, did he decide to run for president without building on his strengths? Why did he come to Washington as the destructive Mr. Hyde, and not the refined Dr. Jekyll?

I also had questions about Congress. The Republican-controlled House passed sixty-seven bills to repeal Obamacare during its namesake's administration, safe in the knowledge that the president would veto their attempts. Yet in 2017 they had unified control in Washington without any plan for how to replace Obamacare. Were they merely playacting the entire time during Obama's presidency? This was the most visible demonstration of moon-promising bravado without a realistic policy to fulfill their promise. However, it was not as damaging as the factional fights among representatives and senators.

Whenever there is a surge of new representatives or senators, the freshman class pushes for changes in the direction of their party as they work their way into their party's leadership system and committees. After the 2010 midterm election, some conservative Republican representatives who had previously aligned themselves with the "Tea Party" movement coalesced into a party within the party. This faction eventually became the Freedom Caucus, a faction too narrow to lead but big enough to block the majority. How did the insurgents maintain a distinct identity without ever offering feasible policies of their own?

Soon thereafter, Republican members of the House, and then the Senate, began using weapons inside their party that in the past had been deployed only against the opposition. Incumbent senators and representatives raised money to unseat their colleagues in primaries, forced government shutdowns to dramatize pet issues, and employed obscure legislative tactics to humiliate their own party's House or Senate leader—solely for personal media coverage. These maneuvers highlighted the reality that some party members cared more about the size of their faction than about the ability of their party to legislate or bargain with the other party's president.[8]

The Freedom Caucus blocked any compromise with their Republican colleagues, scoring publicity for themselves while claiming—in defiance of all logic and history—that total victory could be achieved. The end result of that continuous overpromising was a loss of confidence in party leadership among voters that tainted their opinions of Republican presidential candidates with government experience. Donald Trump's history of bankruptcies, relations with organized crime, and praise of dictators were well known, but voters still preferred a candidate unsullied by close relations to a perpetually ineffectual party. (Cruz, the only person who had a chance against Trump, devoted his four years in Washington to demeaning, disparaging, and undermining the party leadership to signal clearly that he was not part of the party establishment.)

Weak Parties Enable Strongman Rule

After President Trump was sworn in, there were ominous forecasts of an inevitable "stress test for the Constitution" that his presidency would pose. The real stress test, however, was for the Republican Party. A president can be checked and balanced if, and only if, Congress acts to control defiance of the rule of law. Would Republicans—in unified control of Congress, but disunited as a party—be capable of constraining the president?

When Gary Cox and Barry Weingast examined 150 years of executive constraint and electoral accountability, they found that "the health of legislatures is more important than the health of elections" for stable economic growth. In a system with low constraint of the executive, there is more cronyism and corruption, and it shows up in the number of investments whose values plummet or soar when there is a transition in power.[9]

There is nothing self-evident or intuitive about the fact that the British Parliament or the American Congress, each comprising several hundred self-interested members, should produce a more stable and transparent government and support more rapid economic growth than would be possible in a government run by a single self-interested executive. If it were obvious, we would not see reruns of the fantasy that a single strong, determined person could do it all.

Strongman rule rarely ends well, and it never lives up to its promise. A strongman is subject to influence by a few, whereas a legislative process draws upon input from many. When one person dominates the political system, access to that person becomes crucial, and whoever has the leader's ear has a chance to receive special benefits. Strongmen leaders, be they authoritarian or democratic, become isolated, paranoid, subject to flattery, and prone to caring more about loyalty than competence. In contrast, when a legislature votes on whether to pass a law that changes the rules, all of the diverse opposing interests have a chance to enter the fray and compete over benefits, blocking many of the most egregious possible actions in the process.[10]

In the Trump era, we are undergoing a version of the same crisis that led to the creation of parliaments and the end of monarchical rule centuries ago. The president used his delegated powers, in effect, to reverse-engineer democracy and increase the power of the unitary executive—actions which will almost surely continue to shape our political system long after Trump's exit from the Oval Office.

All legislation requires give and take within the parties, which is only possible when party leaders have the authority to make the final judgments on who is given more and who is given less. Those decisions are always somewhat subjective, because so many intangibles are involved, but they invariably give the legislators from the most partisan districts or states less than their voters want in order to protect the more vulnerable politicians upon whom the party's majority status depends.

A political party can only act responsibly when legislative leaders have the resources necessary to punish and reward party members and build consensus on the legislation that is central to the party brand. When parties stand together, voters can connect their vote to the government's policies. This is hardly a new point, but it has become even more important in the last twenty years. As Morris Fiorina wrote in 1980, and again in 2002, "The only way collective responsibility has ever existed, and can exist given our institutions, is through the agency of the political party; in American politics, responsibility requires cohesive parties."[11]

And yet parties are given relatively little respect as institutions. Nancy Rosenblum's dissection of the "ceaseless story of antipartyism" in the United States shows how little concern political theory and political science have devoted to the importance of parties. "Any concession to parties and partisans," she notes, is "pragmatic, unexhuberant, unphilosophical, grudging."[12]

Indeed, as the New York Times literary critic Jennifer Szalai ruefully wrote:

> Politicization is the last refuge of the scoundrel. To "politicize" something—hurricanes, intelligence, science, football, gun violence—is to render it political in a way that distorts its true meaning. That, at least, seems to be the reasoning of those who use the term as an insult: We adhere to pristine, unadulterated facts and call for unity; they politicize those facts for partisan gain and divide us even more.[13]

Politicization, Szalai adds, sometimes functions as shorthand for everything wrong with our current political moment. But America's problems are due to the breakdown of parties, not an excessive politicization of issues by the parties.[14]

The only way problems, ideals, and demands can be turned into accomplishable goals is though successful politicization, and that always entails compromise and bargaining. Rosenblum's central insight, missed by many reformers, is that parties do more than respond to or reflect the passions and demands of the voters; they also construct legislative debate and bargaining by drawing "politically relevant lines of division."[15]

An issue does not become an issue just because people tell pollsters they are concerned about it. The passion, anger, and frustration that lead to demands for action reduce change to slogans people can chant, put on a bumper sticker, or wear on a pin. But those slogans or chants don't include the steps needed to effect the change. If they did, the Gordian knot would already be cut.

From a party's point of view, an issue is important if it confers benefits to some groups within the party without alienating others. Bargaining and trade-offs are always necessary, and the more passionate the demands, the more necessary is the bargaining. The process is always messy because it requires coalitions of legislators with diverse interests to build a majority for all the steps.

Since the 1960s, reforms intended to cleanse the political system and make politicians more responsive to voters have had the consequence of weakening the ability of legislative leaders to reach intraparty consensus. Democracy requires compromises about principles, but it can be hard to defend principled compromise against charges of weakness and betrayal—and even harder when trust in the government and parties is absent.[16] While principled compromise has become harder than ever to achieve, we blame the parties for undesirable outcomes, even as we put the solutions outside their control.

American parties have never been like corporations. There is no CEO who can enforce cooperation among party elites. No party executive can compel a candidate to withdraw for the sake of another candidate, fire a legislator who threatens the party's brand name, or prevent billionaire donors from funding disruptive candidates who promote divisive issues. With weakened party leaders and unlimited, unregulated spending by outsiders, critical decisions shift from public view to "shadow parties" responsible to no one but a few wealthy donors.[17]

With these observations, we begin to see how we ended up where we are today. The consequences of party crackups are not simply political; they also directly impact the health of our economy, our society, our citizens. As I write this, the US death toll from COVID-19 has surpassed 350,000, and the number of domestic cases has crossed twenty million. In the first year of this pandemic, there were more American deaths than all four years of World War II battles.[18] While the end of 2020 saw the stock markets at or near record highs, the holiday season for many was more like Charles Dickens's *A Christmas Carol*. The Bureau of the Census's December surveys of the pandemic's impact recorded that one in eight Americans were struggling to obtain enough food, and one in three had difficulty paying their ordinary expenses. Twenty million persons lost jobs due to business slowdowns and closings; 5.9 million were out of work with COVID symptoms, or caring for someone with COVID symptoms; and 6.8 million were out of work because their children's schools were closed or online.[19] None of this was foreordained in a country with the world's greatest scientists and most advanced capacity for medical research.

And all this would have been avoidable if the party controlling the White House had been able to adapt its priorities to deal with the crisis.

What Is the Right Time to Change?

Unfortunately, adapting a party's strategies and priorities—even in a time of apparent crisis—is far easier said than done. As a party's stand on an issue becomes difficult for many politicians to defend, these politicians will argue that the party must change its position or lose the next election. But for whom is that stand indefensible, and at what cost? What should be the party's priority: control of governors' mansions, the House of Representatives, the Senate, or the White House? The interests of presidents, senators, representatives, and governors are different enough that changes necessary to control one branch often impede or undermine attempts to control the other branches.

Politicians will also always disagree on whether the current problem is a temporary aberration or a permanent shift. As climate scientists and economists know, it is difficult to sway people to make immediate changes to prevent an eventual crisis. In a federal system, it is particularly difficult to distinguish between momentary growing pains and a crisis that will lead to massive fissures; between an issue affecting only one region or demographic group and an emerging change in the national consensus; between the ever-present conflicts between representatives, senators, governors, and presidential candidates, and conflicts that might damage all of them. Supreme Court decisions can transform state issues into national issues; wars and economic crises can turn yesterday's conventional wisdom into today's nonsense; and every generational shift changes social norms. So many events can end the peaceful coexistence within a political party, and the multiple and overlapping conflicting interests within a party can persist for years before enough of its members can agree on how to rebrand and unify the party.

Indeed, the current Republican crackup has been in the making for nearly two decades. In 2003, during a fierce Democratic primary battle, former president Bill Clinton remarked wistfully that in every campaign, Democrats want to fall in love with a candidate, while Republicans just "fall in line."[20] At the time, that view—organized Republicans and disorganized Democrats—seemed correct. In 2000, after all, the GOP had settled on Texas governor George W. Bush as its candidate without much acrimony or disaffection, while Democrats were still brawling over whether Al Gore should have been more liberal or more moderate.

But, as we will see, even as Clinton spoke about Republican harmony, the GOP was quietly entering the most fractious period either party had gone through since the 1960s, leading directly to where we are now.

1

The Last Republican President?

In late 1998—two years before the 2000 presidential election and eighteen months before the parties would coronate their nominees at their national conventions—Republican Party leaders already had their man.

It was after the midterm election in November, during the Republican Governors Conference in New Orleans, that party officials began the informal process of vetting potential presidential candidates. They were anxious about the 2000 election; the last four years had been a bewildering series of triumphs and setbacks. The GOP had won control of the House of Representatives in 1994, followed by a Senate majority in 1996. Then, their attempt to impeach President Bill Clinton for perjury and obstruction of justice backfired with voters. For the first time in 174 years, the president's party had gained in the midterm. In addition, the two senators leading the impeachment trial were voted out of office, and Speaker of the House Newt Gingrich and his chosen successor Bob Livingston both had to resign when their own affairs were exposed.

As the party leaders began their deliberations in New Orleans, no one doubted that a governor—as someone untainted by the disarray in Washington—would be the best presidential candidate in 2000. Republican strategist Mike Murphy described the meeting:

> "Who's gonna run?" And then they all look around at each other warily, and they begin this process of selection. [Tom] Ridge [of Pennsylvania] can't go because he's pro-choice. Tommy Thompson [of Wisconsin] can't go because he can't raise any money. [John] Engler [of Michigan] can't go because he's not charismatic enough. . . . The only guy left standing in the room when they got done canceling each other out was [George W.] Bush.[1]

In 1999, as the 2000 primary season was in its nascent stage, Republican Party chairs flew to Texas to meet with the "bad-boy," born-again former governor, and son of the forty-first president. Afterward, one official recalled, "Everybody was happy . . . we were like pigs in shit."[2]

Bush turned out to be the last candidate for at least twenty years—and possibly longer—to win the nomination of a unified Republican Party. Twelve years after his re-election, the party seemed so irrevocably divided that he confided to close friends, "I'm worried that I will be the last Republican president."[3]

Gradually and Then Suddenly

Breakdowns in party unity often happen in two phases, "gradually and then suddenly," as a Hemingway character explained bankruptcy in *The Sun Also Rises*. Rudiger Dornbusch would later repurpose Hemingway's words to describe a common pattern of national economic breakdown: "The crisis takes a much longer time coming than you think, and then it happens much faster than you would have thought."[4]

Implicit in Murphy's summary of that New Orleans meeting in 1998 were three critical criteria for a Republican presidential candidate in 2000: support from religious conservatives, the talent to sell a conservative vision of the country's future, and the ability to raise the massive amounts of money now needed to win the nomination—which meant supporting tax cuts for big donors.

Left unspoken was a fourth essential attribute, one too sensitive to discuss openly: the ability to avoid collateral damage from commitments popular with some voters that would alienate many others. With public opinion veering away from Republican Party orthodoxy on several fronts, who would best be able to navigate the needs of the base without estranging enough independent voters to make winning a general election impossible? Religious conservatives, fiscal conservatives, and defense hawks all wanted policies that they could get from the GOP only as long as they could support each other's goals. But their marriage of convenience, which Ronald Reagan had officiated back in 1977, was strained to its near-breaking point.

It was getting harder for the party to appeal to social and religious conservatives without turning off less-religious and secular voters, especially as attitudes toward contraception and abortion moved to the left. It was also becoming more difficult to promote tax cuts for the wealthy without alarming older voters about the future of Social Security and Medicare.

Bush looked like the one candidate that could hold the party together. Long before New Orleans, Bush's longtime strategist, Karl Rove, had been maneuvering behind the scenes to connect Bush to the key players and critical constituencies within the Republican Party, privately reassuring conservatives of all stripes of the governor's bona fides.[5]

Bush's pre-primary outreach was devised to make as many private promises as possible without public commitments on complex issues. He knew better than to hamper his own general election chances, and the critical interest groups to whom he catered were reassured enough to refrain from loud public demands during the primaries. If Bush won and failed to deliver, they could sit out his re-election campaign.

One of the most powerful GOP activists, the anti-tax champion Grover Norquist, privately recounted the governor's overtures:

> Bush went to every piece of the coalition and said, "I know you want to be left alone on guns. Deal." "I know you want to be left alone on taxes. Deal." "Property rights? Deal." "Home schooling? Deal." Went to everyone and got 'em signed up or neutralized, including me, two years before the election.[6]

The Doomsday Button

Once primary voting began, it took Bush less than a month to gain certain victory—and yet the process foreshadowed ongoing conflicts between party elites and Republican voters. Without a covert, mud-slinging attack on Senator John McCain's character, Bush might not have won the nomination.

McCain, lacking Bush's establishment money and deep ties to evangelicals and social conservatives, skipped Iowa (the first primary battleground) altogether. Instead, he hunkered down in New Hampshire, riding through the Granite State in his bus, the "Straight Talk Express."

That left Iowa as a battle between Bush and Steve Forbes, the wealthy heir to the magazine that bore his name. As in 1996, when Forbes spent $37 million on a failed, quixotic run for president, the centerpiece of his 2000 campaign was a flat tax. Bush had already privately assured Republican leaders that he supported tax cuts on the upper-income groups whose taxes had risen under the Clinton administration; he and Rove prepared a preemptive tax cut to blunt the impact of Forbes' message.

It worked, though not as well as he'd hoped. In a state where the Republican primary caucus is dominated by voters mobilized through their churches, the born-again Bush managed only 41 percent of the vote, against Forbes's 31 percent. The support for Forbes's large tax cuts among conservative primary voters *and* the widespread support for protecting middle-class entitlements—Medicare and Social Security—were on a collision course. Republican voters, like all others, wanted more government than they were willing to pay for.

New Hampshire signaled more trouble for Bush and the conservative core of the party. McCain's independence, candor, and heroism attracted moderate Republicans and independents. In contrast to Bush's well-documented checkered past, no one doubted the character and honor of a man who had endured years of torture in North Vietnamese captivity, refusing to accept an early release in exchange for denouncing the war—and even trying to hang himself to ensure he didn't crack under torture.

Despite the money and media Bush dumped into the state, McCain won the New Hampshire primary with 49 percent to Bush's 30 percent. National coverage flourished for McCain, and ordinary voters poured money into his campaign. Over the next few days, McCain's campaign took off. In the critical South Carolina primary that followed New Hampshire, McCain jumped from 20 points behind Bush to virtually tied in less than a week.[7]

Bush was saved by the primary calendar—and the religious right. With McCain soaring in the polls, Bush pushed "the doomsday button" and his lieutenants sent out word to "take the gloves off." Ralph Reed, a top Christian Coalition operative, may have looked like a choir boy, but in private he liked to boast: "I paint my face and travel at night. You don't know it's over until you're in a body bag."[8]

The Christian Coalition had tied their fate to Bush's, and they delivered. McCain was ambushed with waves of dishonest attacks, some of which were even spread by his Republican colleague (and Senate Majority Leader) Trent Lott.

Some smears could not be pinned directly on Bush—notably the waves of phone calls claiming that the McCains' adopted Bangladeshi daughter was actually his biological child, or the letters and e-mails sent to South Carolina voters from Richard Hand, a Bible professor at Bob Jones University, alleging that "McCain chose to sire children without marriage."[9]

Other attacks, however, were orchestrated by the campaign itself. With Bush standing at his side, the chairman of the National Vietnam and Gulf War Veterans Coalition told a campaign audience that McCain had "come home and forgotten us." At McCain rallies, Bush supporters told people that McCain was not a war hero, and was secretly pro-choice.[10]

Bush triumphed in South Carolina, effectively stopping McCain's surge. Neither the Arizona senator nor any of his staff ever forgot the dishonest attacks, or that Bush had silently stood on the stage when McCain's war record had been impugned. Conceding the South Carolina primary, McCain said, "I will not take the low road to the highest office in the land. . . . I want the presidency in the best way, not the worst way."[11]

Bush had won support from the moneyed Republican donor class and anti-government conservatives with his program to cut taxes, but he had to adapt quickly during the general election campaign to deal with the fiscal achievements and economic growth of the Clinton presidency.

At his 1998 State of the Union address, Clinton announced that the federal government would actually run a budget surplus—the first since 1969. That budget surplus meant double trouble in the campaign for "W," the nickname used to distinguish the governor from his father, President George H. W. Bush. First, it countered the Republican argument that a tax cut was necessary to balance the budget. Second, when Clinton announced the surplus to an unusually large national audience—many of whom had tuned in to hear if he would refer to the just-breaking story of his affair with Monica Lewinsky—he proposed that the country should use the surplus to "save Social Security first."

Bush's polling made clear that his tax cuts were his least popular proposal with swing voters. As the Democratic nominee, Vice President Al Gore, pointed out that his opponent would give more money to the top 1 percent of the country than to education, health care, and defense combined, Bush downplayed his tax cuts and focused on his plans for saving Social Security and improving education.[12]

Once the Supreme Court issued its ruling in *Bush v. Gore* and confirmed Bush's general election victory, it was imperative for the president-elect to firm up his legislative base before moving ahead. He was well aware that the Democrats would pounce if any splits developed among Republicans.

Rove believed that the two parties were at a point where they had "exhausted their governing agendas," and was determined to create a new synthesis. Solidifying the base was the first stage of Bush and Rove's plan to make the GOP the majority party.[13]

Before he was even inaugurated, Bush was hit with demands—in most cases, more extreme than his own plans—from religious leaders and anti-government conservatives, all of whom wanted to be first in line to get their rewards before the well ran dry or conflicts flared up.

Bush's (relatively) bloodless anointment as leader of the Republican Party did nothing to minimize the cracks within the GOP. The minute he had to actually follow through publicly on his private promises to one group, there was open resistance from other parts of his coalition. There was an ever-widening regional divide over the rights of women and gays; a split between affluent and moderate-income voters over whether to cut taxes or protect the safety net; and divides between younger, more educated voters and older Republicans over the role of government in environmental regulation.

Even when national public opinion shifts, politicians do not easily change long-standing positions if it makes it harder for them in their district or state. Actually changing the party's agenda meant confronting members of Congress uninterested in bending their personal reputations and pledges for the good of the president and the party.

Legislative Ambition versus Presidential Success

When George W. Bush won in 2000, it gave the Republicans their first unified national government since 1954. He now faced conflicts between legislative ambition and presidential success; in every area, the president had to deal with newly energized Republican representatives more concerned about maintaining their own individual power than a national majority for the president.[14]

When Republicans won control of the House in 1994, it capped a long, slow shift in the balance of power between the parties. Thereafter, either party was capable of winning or losing control of the House or Senate in every election. Frances E. Lee, for the Senate, and Adam Bonica and Gary Cox, for the House, have shown how near-parity between the two parties after 1994 changed the nature of bipartisanship. When every district mattered, politicians had less ability to separate from their party brand in campaigns, so the incentives for any legislator to work with the other party dwindled.[15]

Bush enjoyed Republican majorities in both the House and Senate, but there were still problems. For one thing, nearly every Republican in Congress—not to mention the president himself—had signed "The Pledge."

This was the brainchild of Grover Norquist, hailed by Newt Gingrich as "the single most effective conservative activist in the country." Norquist's avowed goal was to cut the federal government so much he could "drown it in the bathtub." That meant cutting taxes as much as possible, no matter how much it affected popular programs like Social Security or Medicare.

He used his weekly breakfast meetings in Washington to create what he called the "Leave Us Alone" coalition. For Norquist, the ideal citizen was "the self-employed, homeschooling, IRA-owning guy with a concealed-carry permit . . . because that person doesn't need the goddamn government for anything."[16]

Norquist's Americans for Tax Reform created the "Taxpayer Protection Pledge" in 1986, and signing it—thereby committing "to oppose any and all tax increases"—became a litmus test for Republican candidates, as well as Democratic candidates running in red-leaning districts.

Once a politician commits to an absolute principle like Norquist's, any concession becomes a sign of weakness—or even "an admission of depravity." For Norquist, deficits were never a reason to increase taxes; they were evidence more cuts in spending were needed.[17]

"'No Compromise,'" the late Nobel Prize–winning economist Thomas Schelling wrote, "is a great battle cry but usually a poor strategy." While absolute positions are generally a bad strategy for political parties, the pledge proved to be a brilliant move for Norquist, who equated any bipartisan legislation with "date rape."[18]

Within a month of Bush's inauguration, the challenges of balancing commitment and compromise became clear as the Republican-led Congress began legislating a major tax cut aimed at upper-income taxpayers. Bush's proposal called for $1.6 trillion worth of cuts over ten years, while many Democrats and some Republican senators wanted no more than $1 to $1.2 trillion, so that more would go to Medicare, education, and infrastructure.

Republican dissent was quickly squelched. When GOP Senator Jim Jeffords of Vermont publicly stated his displeasure that the tax cut meant cutting support for special education, Andrew Card, Bush's chief of staff, went on Vermont Public Radio and argued that Jeffords should support the president's agenda, not special education. Another senator told the *New York Times* that the tax cut was the Bush administration's "crown jewel," and Jeffords was trying to steal it, like "the Pink Panther."

Despite the White House's efforts, Republicans could not push the $1.6 trillion cut through. The Senate bill moved $450 billion from tax cuts to education and debt reduction, and it passed 65–35, with the support of fifteen Democrats.[19]

Bush's tax cut rewarded his upper-income supporters but did nothing about his pledge to protect Social Security. As governor of Texas, he'd believed that anyone living in the United States, legal citizen or not, needed education for the good of all. Using conservative ideas to promote general social welfare, however, did not place protecting entitlements or special education ahead of cutting taxes as much as possible.[20]

Theology versus Science

Even before Bush had taken office, the religious right made it clear that they wanted a say in cabinet appointments, the results of which were guaranteed to cause him trouble among younger voters and educated, secular voters.

Norquist had been working with religious conservatives within the party for years, and evangelicals were a critical part of his coalition. In the 1990s, Norquist's evangelical allies had been content to prioritize tax cuts above social issues such as abortion and homosexuality, with Reed claiming that a disproportionate focus on such issues had "limited [the] effectiveness" of the Christian Coalition.[21] Now, however, its leaders were ready to flex their muscles and mobilize for their core moral issues. As a result, Bush was hamstrung in planning the transition and assembling his cabinet.

Bush's first choice for attorney general, Montana governor Marc Racicot, was torpedoed by the combined forces of Norquist and religious conservatives for the sin of trying to extend hate-crime laws to cover sexual orientation after the gruesome murder of Matthew Shepard in Wyoming.[22] After futile attempts to find an acceptable, pragmatic nominee, Bush was pushed to nominate John Ashcroft. As Missouri attorney general, Ashcroft had opposed a voluntary integration plan for St. Louis; as a senator, he had knowingly distorted the record of a Black state Supreme Court justice to block his nomination for the federal judiciary. He supported the right of schools to fire gay teachers and opposed abortion for victims of rape or incest. After a five-week battle, Ashcroft was confirmed, 58–42.[23]

The religious right's growing influence also came to the fore in the brewing controversy over stem cell research. Embryonic stem cells held great medical promise for people with spinal cord injuries, type 1 diabetes, and many other life-threatening diseases. Destroying an embryo for its stem cells, however, was opposed by the Catholic Church and many conservative evangelical leaders. The issue was so contentious that stem cells became the subject of Bush's first national address to the country, in which he responded to the moral issue while skirting a fight between science and theology: the government would only fund research with existing lines of stem cells to prevent the destruction of any more embryonic cells for research.[24]

The economic moves to the right on tax cuts and the attempts to roll back the previous decade of progress on reproductive rights, education, and the environment prompted three Republican senators—John McCain, Lincoln Chafee, and Jim Jeffords—to consider leaving the Republican Party. With the Senate composed of fifty Democrats and fifty Republicans, any defection would tip the balance in the Democrats' favor.

After mulling the move, Chafee decided to wait. Then, while McCain and his aides were negotiating with Senate Minority Leader Tom Daschle, Jeffords broke with the GOP, ending six years of Republican Senate control.[25] Jeffords's bombshell decision took the heat off of McCain. Instead of switching parties, he became "the magic ingredient in any legislative deal." His name on proposed legislation was as important as support from the party's Senate leaders, as other senators grew leery of Bush's social policies and tax cuts.[26]

McCain and his wife were suddenly invited to dinner with the president and Laura Bush at the White House. It was just the four of them—and two food tasters, McCain joked. This did not heal the grudges McCain held after the GOP primary, but his sudden rise in status did quell his impulse to leave the party.[27]

Bush Hits "the Trifecta"

By Labor Day of his first year in office, Bush was floundering. He had managed to pass his tax cuts, but his party had lost their Senate majority and he was receiving poor marks for his economic management. The dot-com tech bubble had burst, the economy was sliding into recession, and Enron's bankruptcy had exposed the poster child for energy sector deregulation as a villainous fraud.

The events of one day—September 11, 2001—transformed Bush from a weak president into a wartime leader upon whom people depended for security. His popularity rating topped 90 percent—breaking the record his father had set after Operation Desert Storm in 1991—and stayed in the 80s for over a year. In the words of political science professor Gary Jacobson, Bush was now judged as "the defender of the nation against shadowy foreign enemies rather than as a partisan figure of dubious legitimacy." Congress, too, enjoyed a surge in approval, viewed as "the institutional embodiment of American democracy rather than as the playground of self-serving politicians addicted to petty partisan squabbling."[28]

Prior to the attacks, Bush's 2000 campaign pledge to honor the sanctity of the Social Security funds—popularly called a "lockbox"—morphed into a conditional pledge of sanctity with three exceptions: "recession, war, or a national emergency." Just like that, the conditional had become factual. "Lucky me," Bush grimly joked after 9/11. "I hit the trifecta!" With a national crisis and an immediate need for increased defense spending, promises to strengthen Social Security and Medicare were deferred while Congress debated how to fund the war.[29]

It is hard for an opposition party to salute a popular commander-in-chief while criticizing a war. Democrats were thus painted into a corner, and the war in Afghanistan gave Republicans a modest electoral gain in the 2002 midterm election—a major break with the historical regularity of midterm losses for the president's party. The net gain of two senators and eight representatives restored Senate control to the GOP and gave Bush a bigger cushion in the House—but no help in addressing the middle-class safety net.

In 2003, as soon as the new senators and representatives were sworn in, Bush pushed for another tax cut, again concentrating on capital gains and dividends. With the invasion of Iraq about to begin, and the growing sense that the military effort in Afghanistan would be long and costly, some senators balked at increasing the deficit for the benefit of the wealthy. McCain and Chafee, among others, refused to vote for any tax cut during the war, while several other Republican senators pushed for a more modest cut.

For the first time in American history, however, there was serious support *during wartime* for cutting taxes. House Majority Leader Tom DeLay declared that "nothing is more important in the face of a war than cutting taxes," and the anti-tax Club for Growth ran ads equating opposition to the tax cuts with France's opposition to the war.[30] Vice President Dick Cheney was even more blunt. "Reagan proved deficits don't matter," he told a dumbfounded Treasury Secretary Paul O'Neill. "We won the midterms. This is our due."[31]

Despite Cheney and DeLay's enthusiasm, Bush's tax cuts had never been popular, and they were getting even harder to defend. In 2003, the tax cuts for the top 1 percent of the country totaled more than the cuts for the bottom

60 percent; the following year, they would total more than cuts for the lower *80* percent. The inflation-adjusted median income of men had not risen substantially in more than thirty years; the country's growth in average income was due entirely to the growth in incomes among the top few percent. Thus, the rich were getting richer while most of the country was losing ground financially.[32] Voters who wanted the government to leave them alone still wanted their Social Security and Medicare, and the Bush tax cuts did nothing to persuade older voters that they would be better off if these programs ended or were privatized.

Moving the Money Moves the Party

In the time since he'd flirted with changing parties, John McCain had been busy: he'd worked to close loopholes in gun legislation, pushed for a patient's bill of rights, and—most impactfully of all—teamed with Democratic senator Russ Feingold to tackle campaign finance reform. Their well-intentioned, reform-minded legislation would have devastating consequences for political party organizations and bipartisanship. Driving money out of the parties fueled the rise of uncompromising single-issue candidates, increased the power of lobbyists, and weakened party leaders in both the House and Senate.[33]

The McCain-Feingold bill, officially called the Bipartisan Campaign Reform Act, attempted to end the power of major donors to influence candidates and parties, and remove the advantage enjoyed by men like Bush and his deep-pocketed connections. The premise of the legislation was that organizations and persons donating unlimited amounts to political parties distorted politics by giving them undue influence compared to small donors and ordinary citizens. The bill put strict limits on the amounts that could be donated to parties, as well as limits on ads broadcast by corporations and unions.

Naturally, the bill provoked opposition. Its constitutionality was challenged in a suit by Republican senator Mitch McConnell, who argued against shifting money away from the parties. Other critics joined the suit, arguing the change would make politics more extreme and less accountable.[34]

Before the Supreme Court hearing, the *New York Times* published an editorial urging passage of the law. A prime specimen of a pious, naïve, and wrong fantasy about money and politics, the editorial scoffed at the idea that parties would be weakened by the legislation, claiming the law could "cleanse our democracy of the poison of huge special-interest campaign contributions."[35]

Instead, the legislation ended up *increasing* the power of large donors. Beforehand, as longtime GOP operative Scott Reed noted in a *Wall Street Journal* interview, "when you wanted to run for Congress, you had to head to Washington to meet national party leaders and seek their help." Once McCain-Feingold became law in 2002, the help—and money—came increasingly from outside the parties.[36]

Unable to get meaningful campaign funds through their party, lawmakers were turning directly to lobbyists. Not only could lobbyists personally donate $4,000 ($2,000 in the primary and $2,000 in the general election), they could also be installed as the treasurers of a legislator's pet political action committee (PAC)—and thereby raise additional money from their clients. Lobbyists would organize breakfasts, lunches, and dinners for members of committees that handled legislation of interest to their clients; some lobbyists served as the treasurer of twenty or more PACs.[37]

McCain-Feingold strengthened ideological purists at the expense of the compromisers within parties, as candidates could raise money faster from major donors unbeholden to the broader interests of the party as a whole.[38] "Money, like water, will seek its own level," scholars Sam Issacharoff and Pamela Karlan prophesied in 1999. "The price of apparent containment may be uncontrolled flood damage elsewhere."[39]

Now donors could push harder for their ideal policy, instead of the policy that worked best for the party. They could also spend money on anonymous attacks on their enemies and hide the motives behind an ad.[40]

In 2000, before the legislation, the two major parties aired two-thirds of all presidential ads. In 2004, the first post-reform election, the ratio dropped to just over one-third, and the party share of political funding of campaigns has continued to decline since. The law had a particularly potent, trickle-down effect on state parties, since the national party's own resources were curtailed.[41]

New Laws, Bigger Loopholes

By 2004, 527s and 501s—groups so named because of the IRS codes under which they were formed—and "dark money" contributions started to play a bigger role in elections. (Section 527 of the IRS code allows tax-exempt spending on issues as long as there is no explicit advocacy for or against electing a candidate. Section 501 is where "social welfare" organizations reside; they are tax-exempt and don't have to divulge their donors.)

While there were ostensible limits on how much money could be spent, there were also loopholes. The rule of thumb for nonprofit groups was that no more than half their budget could be spent on influencing elections, so these groups developed shell games to make it appear that only 49 percent of their budgets were spent on political ads. Group A would donate its original money to Group B, which would then donate to a third group that would give it back to the original group. That made the group's budget appear to be twice the size of the original donations, allowing them to spend 98 percent of the original anonymous donations to influence elections—hence the term "dark money."

Accountability, intraparty compromise, and the parties' individual brands were weakened—unintended consequences of a misguided ritual of purification. As a result of McCain-Feingold, money gushed to groups supposedly unaffiliated with any candidate, usually to attack other candidates, and almost always hiding the source of the funds.

A donor's motive is one of the single most important cues voters have when evaluating ads, and now this information was effectively withheld. The ad would show the name of the group, often artfully chosen to mask its motives—like "Californians for Good Schools and Good Jobs," a group solely funded by Phillips 66, a Texas oil company. And even when the donors were *eventually* disclosed in filings with the IRS, the process of learning their identity was time-consuming and difficult.[42]

The balance of power thus shifted from parties to donors. In the 2004 election, forty-six people donated more than one million dollars each to Section 527 organizations, and at least eight hundred super PACs installed lobbyists as their treasurers. These committees spent $525 million, more than the combined total raised by Bush and Senator John Kerry, his Democratic opponent.[43]

Campaign standards suffered as well. While campaigns have always included innuendo, dog whistles, grossly exaggerated claims, and deception, these allegedly "independent" groups were free to push the boundaries ever farther. There was, after all, no affiliated candidate or party that could be called upon to defend their ads. Defenders of McCain-Feingold say these groups were not an *intended* consequence of the legislation, but they were nonetheless a *predictable* consequence. The legislation moved money and shifted power from party organizations to groups that were less accountable for the accuracy and tenor of their ads.[44]

The most remembered and controversial ad of the 2004 election was by a group called "Swift Boat Veterans for Truth." Three wealthy Texas supporters of Bush donated $9.5 million to produce a video questioning the legitimacy of the Purple Hearts, Bronze Star, and Silver Star Kerry had earned in the Vietnam War. The video's disputation of his heroism, bravery, and rescue of wounded comrades under fire was deceptive, dishonest, and contradictory to the official military records. It also diverted Kerry's campaign from its intended issue agenda.

Though he was actively campaigning for Bush, McCain forcefully denounced the attacks on Kerry's service—as did fellow Republican senator and Vietnam veteran Chuck Hagel—but the rebuttals got a fraction of the coverage received by the attack. The "swiftboating" of Kerry—as dishonest attacks would thereafter come to be known—foreshadowed the ways in which wealthy individuals and opportunistic zealots across the political spectrum could now make poorly substantiated or fabricated attacks that no candidate or party would be willing to put their name on. The Bush campaign's top lawyer, Benjamin Ginsberg, was a paid consultant to the Swift Boat Veterans for Truth—a completely legal move that showed how easy it was for campaigns and "uncoordinated" PACs to stay close.[45]

Bush's Hollow Victory

Republican leaders rejoiced after Bush's 2004 re-election victory. Bush had won 51 percent of the popular vote, and the GOP controlled a majority of the House, Senate, and governor's mansions. "Republican hegemony," the prominent conservative commentator Fred Barnes crowed, "is now expected to last for years, maybe decades." The leading theorist of political realignments, Professor Walter Dean Burnham at the University of Texas, agreed—as long as Republicans kept "playing the religious card along with the terrorism card."[46]

But like the proverbial canary in a coal mine, danger signs of serious, ongoing, and irreconcilable conflicts were emerging in the Republican Party. Fresh from the euphoria of election night, the institutional power of the Republican Party establishment proceeded to implode.

In his second term, Bush wanted to attract young voters with Social Security reform, and use immigration reform to win support from the growing Hispanic population. He was unsuccessful on both counts.

When Bush ran for Congress in 1978, the centerpiece of his failed campaign was Social Security privatization, allowing workers to put some of their payments into stocks and bonds. Otherwise, he said, "Social Security will be bust in ten years."[47] Privatization was the Holy Grail of economic conservatives and libertarians, but their goal was not providing security for the elderly. "Social Security is the soft underbelly of the welfare state," Stephen Moore, the former president of the Club for Growth, now argued. "If you can jab your spear through that, you can undermine the whole welfare state."[48]

Ken Mehlman, Bush's re-election campaign chair, freshly installed as the head of the Republican National Committee, enthusiastically promoted privatization as a way to attract younger voters, the group most enthusiastic about stock markets and most concerned about the program's future.[49]

But the quest to end middle-class entitlements like Social Security and Medicare flopped badly. To be sure, growing deficits and stagnant wages made the arguments about short-term danger plausible, and the campaign for partial or full privatization began with half the country already believing they would not get their benefits. The devils in the many details, however, were impossible to overcome if the bottom line was to make the changes without any new taxes on the rich. If young people put some of their Social Security funds into the stock market, where would the money come from to pay older retirees? The large and influential American Association of Retired Persons (AARP) had supported Bush's Medicare extension, but it now loudly opposed his plan.

The only plan that had strong national support was to raise the Social Security tax ceiling. Among Democrats, Republicans, and independents, 60 percent of each group was willing to tax all income (not just the first $90,000 of earnings) to protect Social Security, and 68 percent of Democrats and half of Republicans opposed cutting benefits for anyone. The Republican establishment, however, was not on the same wavelength as their base.[50]

Fighting to protect their tax cuts by privatizing the safety net without raising taxes before the deficit exploded, Republicans resurrected the promise of a lockbox. Instead of a metaphorical lockbox protecting guaranteed government Social Security funds, the new Republican pitch was for personal, private lockboxes—usually called an IRA. The idea bombed despite the endorsement and cheerleading of Congressman Paul Ryan, Federal Reserve chair Alan Greenspan, Senator Jim DeMint, and conservative columnists at the leading national newspapers.[51]

Within three months, two-thirds of the country disapproved of Bush's handling of Social Security. The actual crisis point of benefit cuts was farther away than Republicans had stated, and when it became clear that, with the money diverted into the stock market, there would be massive short-term costs involved to pay older workers and current retirees, the plan was dead. By mid-June, 80 percent of the country still believed in a government obligation to provide a decent standard of living for the elderly—especially those with a low income—and nearly two-thirds of respondents in national polls still supported raising the cap on income subject to the Social Security tax.[52]

Around the same time as the GOP's privatization plans were failing, so too were Bush's promises of immigration reform. Conservative talk radio outlets began to circulate rumors about terrorists crossing the border from Mexico and "Minutemen" conducting vigilante border patrols. Bush's commitment to closing the border and preventing future illegal immigration was not seen as credible. When Bush's advisors met with Republican congressional representatives, "people were booing and hissing." Any mention of legalization, let alone citizenship, was so radioactive that the president's preferred formulation evolved to a vague aim of "bringing workers out of the shadows."

On the basis of his firebrand opposition to immigration, Representative Tom Tancredo of Colorado became a conservative star; eighty members of the House identified themselves as members of Tancredo's anti-immigration caucus, a five-fold increase from 2001.[53] Grover Norquist—a loud supporter of immigration reform, since it would not raise taxes—warned that Tancredo was "the face of the Republican Party losing elections for the next 20 years," and proposed "sending Tancredo to Guantanamo."[54]

Inside the Republican caucus, House Majority Leader Tom DeLay—whose nickname, "The Hammer," was well-earned—played the key role in ending any hope of resolving the crisis. He pushed an anti-immigration agenda and told his colleagues and lieutenants that border security should be the only priority, steamrolling the comprehensive approach favored by Speaker Dennis Hastert and James Sensenbrenner, the committee chair handling the legislation. [55]

DeLay's Money Machine

In addition to smashing any chance at immigration reform, "The Hammer" was at the center of a major congressional scandal that would undermine his party's standing.

The introduction of presidential primaries in the early twentieth century was supposed to weaken the power of political bosses and restore "power to the people." While it certainly accomplished the former, it also increased the power of well-organized, well-financed groups like the National Rifle Association, the Christian Coalition, and Norquist's Americans for Tax Reform. They could arrange events, raise money, and recruit staff for candidates willing to support their cause. And nobody in Congress benefited more—for a while—than Tom DeLay.

As soon as Republicans gained power in 1994, they moved to turn the Washington lobbying industry into a GOP political machine. DeLay, working with Norquist, Ralph Reed, and lobbyist Jack Abramoff, created his own personal power base with brutal efficiency.

Once McCain-Feingold pushed money out of the parties, men like Abramoff—who could connect congressional representatives with lobbyists and money—were essential. DeLay made a point of telling anyone with any interest in government contracts or legislation how close he was to Abramoff. At a time when a top-tier lobbying firm might bill $20 million a year, Abramoff and his covert lobbying partner, former DeLay aide Michael Scanlon, managed to bill over $82 million in three years to Indian tribes concerned about protecting their casinos. In one two-year period, 2003–2005, former aides to DeLay brought in over $45 million in fees to lobbying firms. Former aides to Hastert brought in just $2.1 million.[56]

DeLay's dash for cash turned into a major scandal involving playing the religious card on behalf of casinos. The size and ruthlessness of the lobbying and influence peddling eventually made headlines when their shell games were exposed. Particularly noteworthy were the ways they used Christian organizations to mobilize voters to block new casinos, thereby protecting the profits of other tribal casinos from competition.

A *Time* magazine cover had once called Reed "The Right Hand of God," but he now had a hand out for money to start his run for statewide office in Georgia. Reed could not openly accept money from casinos in exchange for his support, so Abramoff donated funds to Norquist, who then donated to Reed's organizations.

This dark money had to be hidden, Abramoff wrote, because "[w]e do not want opponents to think that we are trying to buy the tax payer [*sic*] movement." And Reed would have had little value as a Christian conservative opposing a casino if people knew he was being paid by a rival casino.[57]

In the end, John McCain wielded a bigger hammer than DeLay. When the first stories about the shakedown of Indian tribes appeared, McCain, chair of the Senate Indian Affairs Committee, pounced on the issue to raise his own profile before his 2008 run for president. "One of the founding fathers of Indian gaming" and a gambler himself, McCain could now exact revenge on Reed, who was a leader in the covert campaign to smear McCain in 2000, and DeLay, whose notions of honor and service were offensive to the Arizona senator.[58]

The final fallout from the scandal totaled twenty-one persons who pled guilty or were convicted in court, including two White House officials, one House representative, and nine current or former congressional aides. Abramoff was convicted of conspiracy, wire fraud, and tax evasion, and spent four years in prison. Neither Reed nor Norquist were indicted, but Reed's goal of becoming Georgia's governor evaporated. DeLay's reputation never recovered from his involvement with Abramoff, their many lavish golfing trips, or the $500,000 salary he paid his wife to work on his campaign.[59]

Instead of cleansing the parties, McCain-Feingold had made the money system even dirtier and less transparent than when corporations could give openly. Corporations, in fact, gave less money under the new rules. Many were wary of giving money to new groups that might connect their corporate brand with controversial positions that offended stockholders or customers.[60]

Katrina Washes Out the GOP

As if scandals weren't enough, Hurricane Katrina followed in August 2005. The death, devastation, and destruction along the Gulf of Mexico—compounded by the inept mismanagement of the crisis by the Federal Emergency Management Agency (FEMA), headed by someone with no disaster relief experience—became a vivid symbol of governmental failure and national decay.

In the 2006 midterm elections, Republicans lost control of the House and Senate, going from 232 representatives to 202, and from 55 senators to 49.

Democratic turnout jumped 25 percent from the 2002 midterm, while Republican turnout dropped 4 percent. The costly, brutal occupation of Iraq was dragging on, the deficits were exploding, and the GOP's attempts to pass unpopular legislation on immigration and entitlements had been unsuccessful.

Once the Democrats regained control of Congress in 2007, their first bills laid bare how the GOP had favored corporate and business supporters at the expense of voters concerned about their paychecks. For seven years, Republicans had used their majority power to block bills proposing minimum wage increases. This was important to powerful, moneyed interests, including the National Chamber of Commerce and the National Federation of Businesses. Now the politicians were forced to take a public stand and choose between their donors and voters.

In the first two weeks, the Democratic Congress raised the minimum wage, reduced interest rates on student college loans, expanded stem cell research support, and managed to strengthen ethics rules. It was, journalist Thomas Edsall noted, a dramatic display of "basic competence and authority after four decades of defeat and division, whether in the majority or minority."[61]

The GOP Brand Collapses

The institutional power of the Republican Party was collapsing. Splits on science, religion, and economics were getting harder to paper over. The wealthy got major tax breaks, while nothing was done about stagnant wages or shoring up Social Security. David Frum, a former Bush speechwriter, pointed out that one of the most popular moves Bush had made for moderate-income voters was adding a prescription drug benefit to Social Security—a policy that conservatives, especially the activists, despised. Republicans were on the less popular side on environment, healthcare, and education.

Throughout Bush's presidency, the language of the Republican Party had changed to emphasize "freedom" instead of "liberty." Liberty implies a system of rules, with restraint and order. Freedom, linguist Geoffrey Nunberg observed, generally means "the absence of personal or psychological encumbrances." This was in keeping with the themes of the "Leave Us Alone" mindset: fewer regulations and lower taxes.[62]

But most of the coalition didn't want to leave others alone. They didn't want people to live in communities where stem cell research was an issue of science, not theology; or where birth control and abortion were medical procedures, not sins; or where assault rifles signified danger, not freedom. The Leave Us Alone world only wanted to be left alone some of the time; they welcomed government assistance when disaster or enemies struck, or when they retired.

Bush's pitch for "compassionate conservatism" meant developing programs to get people back on their feet (like drug rehabilitation and prisoner reentry) and a reformed immigration system. But most Republican lawmakers had signed Norquist's pledge and were not interested in spending money on compassion. When Jim Towey, Bush's director of faith-based initiatives, talked with representatives about the programs, "[t]heir eyes would glaze over, like, 'Why are you talking to me about this?'" When Bush talked to them, Towey added, they told him, "All this stuff about poor people, immigrants, refugees—this is how Democrats talk."[63]

Compassionate conservatism took a backseat to slashing taxes. In his first four years, Bush cut the dividend tax rate from 38.6 percent to 15 percent, and capital gains from 20 to 15 percent. Along with the other tax cuts and loopholes, the federal tax on investment income was 9.6 percent, while the federal tax on wages averaged 23 percent. The beneficiaries of these cuts rewarded him amply by donating to his re-election campaign; seven of the top ten employers of Bush contributors were Wall Street firms.[64]

The failure to privatize Social Security foreshadowed growing tension within the GOP over entitlements. Elderly, middle-class, and working-class Republicans counted on programs that the wealthy wanted to slash to protect their tax cuts. In retrospect, Karl Rove realized that starting Bush's second term with privatization killed immigration reform: "The sequencing was off. If we had done immigration first, it would have passed." After trying to shrink the safety net, bringing in more persons to share what little help the government was willing to give people was a nonstarter.

Peter Wehner, head of Bush's Office of Strategic Initiatives, saw the changes. After 2005, he said, "Our base was changing. Some of it was tied to 9/11. Some of it was tied to economic insecurity. Some of it was tied to a sense of lost culture for a lot of people on the right."[65]

Bush, too, saw the warning signs early on in his second term. "He told his closest advisors he was worried about protectionism, isolationism, and nativism taking root, especially among Republicans," Tim Alberta wrote. " 'These -isms,' Bush said, 'are gonna eat us alive.' "[66]

As the 2008 primaries loomed, the future once again looked grim for the party. At the end of January, Tom Davis, a rising star in Congress, announced he was retiring. Davis was no backbencher; he ran the Republican Congressional Campaign Committee (RCCC) from 1998 to 2002, and was so successful and respected that the party chair promoted him over more senior colleagues to chair the Committee on Government Reform. When someone so respected and promising decides to leave the House, it is a warning sign of pending trouble.

In May, Davis followed up with a blistering memo in which he observed that the party's brand "is in the trash can," and "if we were a dog food, they would take us off the shelf."[67] Things were so bad, Davis noted, that companies once solidly behind the GOP, like big drug companies, UPS, FedEx, and government contractors, were now donating to Democrats for protection. Even prominent Republicans who were now lobbyists, like Bob Livingston— who was poised to become the Speaker of the House when he resigned over his affair with a lobbyist during the Clinton impeachment hearing—and J. C. Watts, a prominent African-American representative who had co-chaired Bob Dole's presidential campaign, were also donating to Democrats. In addition, 73 percent of Americans thought the country was on the wrong track, while only 15 percent thought the country was on the right track.

Seldom does a politician's diagnosis stand up as well as the Davis memo. Six months before the election, he saw no easy way to turn the party around. The chasm between urban and rural areas of the country had been widening since at least 2000. Moderate Republicans were being defeated by Democrats, giving more power to religious and social conservatives, and fewer connections to newly emerging industrial elites with international supply chains and ethnically diverse work forces. Changing campaign finance regulations were pushing the party to the right and turning compromise and bipartisanship into four-letter words. There were more and more ways for candidates to make waves and raise money, and party leaders were finding it even harder to hold their colleagues in line on legislation.

The echoes from that New Orleans meeting in 1998 were still resonating: How to rebuild? Who could lead the party forward? This time, though, a nominee's ascension would be far from bloodless.

2

Young Guns and Billionaires

On November 4, 2008, Barack Hussein Obama was elected the forty-fourth president of the United States of America, defeating John McCain by nearly ten million votes. The surge in voter turnout for the new president generated countless stories about the new electorate and progressive social transformation: more minority voters, a more tolerant younger generation, and the possibility of a post-racial America.

Standing apart from the mainstream media's self-congratulatory euphoria was a more realistic assessment of Obama's victory, courtesy of the satirical online site *The Onion*: "Black Man Given Nation's Worst Job," the headline read. "In his new high-stress, low-reward position," the article continued, "Obama will be charged with such tasks as completely overhauling the nation's broken-down economy, repairing the crumbling infrastructure, and generally having to please more than 300 million Americans and cater to their every whim on a daily basis."[1]

As inspiring a candidate as many considered Obama to be, the precipitous collapse of the Republican brand was a major underlying factor in his victory. The state-by-state vote totals that Democratic presidential candidate John Kerry received in 2004 would have been enough in 2008 to win the election: at least 3.5 percent of the voters who chose President George W. Bush either voted for Obama or stayed home in 2008.[2] (See Appendix, Table 1.)

McCain had managed to win the Republican nomination without committing to anti-tax or anti-gay policies, but he couldn't unite the party and get its organizational and financial support against Obama until he yielded. He switched sides and announced support for offshore drilling and the teaching of intelligent design. He even disowned the immigration bill he had written and supported the "enhanced interrogation" methods that had been used on him as a prisoner of war in Vietnam. The maverick senator who once swore that he would never "take the low road to the highest office in the land" became a candidate of the religious right and Grover Norquist, forced to share the podium with a running mate at home on the low road.[3]

When McCain declared that he wanted to make the Bush tax cuts he had long opposed permanent, Norquist acknowledged it was a "big flip-flop. . . . But I'm happy he's flopped." James Dobson, the founder of Focus on the Family, had vowed he would never support McCain, and was one of the religious leaders threatening to mobilize the delegates to the Republican Convention to overturn his first choice, centrist Democrat Joe Lieberman, for vice president.

Without the enthusiastic support of the leaders of the religious right, Bush would not have won in 2000 or 2004. But he had not fulfilled their demands after his re-election, and they were pushing for a stronger, more credible commitment than mere lip service. When McCain gave in and chose Alaska governor Sarah Palin instead of Lieberman, Dobson proclaimed he'd "never been so excited about a ticket in my life."[4]

McCain's compromises revealed the divides between social conservatives and economic conservatives. Conservative religious groups cared more about protecting their theology from changing interpretations of individual rights than they cared about defense, trade, or foreign relations. They were also comfortable with the types of intolerant racial undertones that McCain had never stomached before—and that set off alarms among Obama's supporters.

Peter Hart, who was conducting a series of focus groups for the Annenberg Center, told Thomas Edsall that in every focus group that year, participants raised the possibility that Obama would be assassinated. During the primary race between Senator Hillary Clinton and Obama, attitudes about interracial dating were correlated to voters' preferences between the two candidates, and these attitudes also predicted which Democrats and independents voted for Senator McCain. And after Obama's victory, opposition to intimate relations between the races became related to party preferences—after a long period in which race relations and the desire to keep the races apart socially was not important for party identification.[5]

Palin could drive crowds to an angry frenzy with racial dog whistles like "I am just so fearful that [Obama] is not a man who sees America the way you and I see America." Palin's presence on the ticket forced McCain to detour from the high road; he needed her supporters to have any chance to win. Sometimes he went quietly along with the crowds yelling epithets about Obama—"Traitor!" "Off with his head!" "Kill him!"—before pushing back.

McCain's reputation for honor was so strong that it was assumed almost universally that the attacks on Obama was all Palin "going rogue." In fact,

McCain's campaign strategists had decided that they needed to try to raise doubts about Obama's American sensibility and commitment. The McCain campaign ran ads suggesting that Obama had been "disrespectful to Governor Palin"—an old Southern way of suggesting the need to put the (Black) man back in his place—and Georgia representative Lynn Westmoreland told his voters that Obama was "uppity."[6]

When Palin went after Obama and his relationship with Weather Underground founder William Ayers—"This is not a man who sees America as you and I do—as the greatest force for good in the world. This is someone who sees America as imperfect enough to pal around with terrorists who targeted their own country"—she was reading a script she had been sent by Nicole Wallace, the former White House communications director for George W. Bush, now serving as a McCain spokeswoman.[7]

Palin's inexperience and rhetoric drove away some of McCain's strongest supporters, including his old allies in the defense and foreign relations communities and veterans of the Reagan and Bush administrations— among them one of McCain's heroes, General Colin Powell. McCain eventually was unable to acquiesce to his campaign's attempts at character assassination. When a woman at one event called Obama an untrustworthy Arab, McCain turned white and then stammered, "No, ma'am. He's a decent family man."[8]

Nothing McCain could have done, however, would have removed the angry racial undertones from the reaction of so many to Obama. Palin was a grim foreshadow of the fears unleashed by Obama and his millions of supporters—of every color—that threatened cultural and religious conservatives. Despite years of opposition from evangelicals and the economic albatross of the Great Recession, McCain received more votes in 2008 than Bush received in 2004 in ten of the eleven states in the former Confederacy.

White opposition to Obama was particularly strong in areas where there once had been cotton plantations; these were areas with the strongest support for segregation and ongoing efforts to disenfranchise African American voters. Not surprisingly, these were also the areas with the most inequality between races, and where the highest percentage of whites said they did not trust the federal government.[9]

Obama could occasionally joke, as he did at the 2008 Al Smith Dinner in New York, that "I got my middle name from somebody who obviously didn't think I'd ever run for president." But his middle name was relentlessly used to illustrate his foreignness, as proof that he was a Muslim, or at least someone not really "American."[10]

Obama's race obscured the extent of the Republican decline. If he had been a white Democrat with the same policies, he would have been expected to win a far larger share of the vote, given the abysmal state of the Republican brand and the collapse of the economy under Bush. As Michael Tesler summarized:

> Dozens of studies show that out-group antagonisms—measured by racial resentment, anti-Black stereotypes, opposition to intimate interracial relationships, ethnocentrism, anti-Muslim attitudes, and even living in areas with many racist Google searches—were significantly stronger predictors of opposition to Obama in 2008 than they had been in prior elections or than they would have been if John McCain had faced Hillary Clinton instead of Barack Obama in the 2008 election.[11]

Race was an unavoidable issue for the president. No matter what he did, there was an assumption for many that he was doing it more for minorities than for whites. For the next eight years, these resentments racialized evaluations of everything Obama did and said.[12]

Bigger Money, Smaller Tent

As divided as the GOP may have been, its donors could at least agree on their opposition to Obama. For the first time since McCain-Feingold, "the full force of conservative wealth in America [was] mobilized by a common enemy."[13] Before Obama was sworn in, Republican legislators and their wealthy donors were organizing to block his goal of universal healthcare and prevent spending to revive the perilous economy, rescue the auto industry, or provide relief for mortgage holders.

The industrialists Charles and David Koch had been trying to launch a grass-roots "counter-establishment" movement for years. McCain-Feingold opened the door for wealthy individuals and corporations to create organizations where their identities could be kept from the public.[14] In 2003, when the reforms took effect and wealthy donors could no longer contribute large sums directly to political parties, the Koch brothers created a network of like-minded millionaires and billionaires, with a minimum contribution that reached $100,000 a year by 2008. Depending on their specific concerns, attendees contributed additional funds to umbrella organizations like Americans for Prosperity, or to separate projects related to redistricting, state regulations, minority outreach, healthcare, etc.[15]

With Obama as president, the Kochs had lucked into an ideal situation for furthering their plans. First, Bush's financial bailout staved off the total collapse of the financial system, so they could oppose aid for homeowners and any stimulus spending to revive the economy without risking their own fortunes. Second, the president was African American. While Obama wanted to get the two parties to work together and develop a consensus on both economic recovery and healthcare, many Republican voters were un- likely to ever trust or respect him; they would suspect that any program he proposed was designed to help minorities at their expense.

Well before the financial crisis, the Kochs began organizing to stop "cap-and-trade legislation" designed to limit carbon emissions after the Democratic-led House passed such a bill in 2007. That bill died in the Senate, but they saw the growing awareness of climate change as a threat to their energy businesses. Now they could work with their network to take on the structure and organization of the federal government, not just address spe- cific legislation and regulations.

In 2008, the Kochs' political advisor, Richard Fink, told them that if they wanted to stop Obama and the "progressive tide," doing it right meant "the fight of their lives"—one that was "going to get very, very ugly." Charles and David, heirs to the second-largest family fortune in America (behind only Walmart founder Sam Walton's), were ready to "resort to extraordinary po- litical measures." Most amazing of all, they'd leave no fingerprints.[16]

Among the attendees at the Koch's 2009 summit were eighteen billionaires worth a combined $214 billion, most of whom had had run-ins with the gov- ernment over pollution, insider trading, tax evasion, and other assorted ac- tivities that only the ridiculously rich could afford to attempt.[17] The highlight of that year's summit was a debate about the path forward for the Republican Party following the market meltdown, the collapse of the Bush presidency, and Obama's election. Two starkly different options were debated by the Senate's two most conservative lawmakers: South Carolina's Jim DeMint and Texas's John Cornyn.

Cornyn, a former jurist and a serious legislator, believed that you needed a big tent to win the power to govern; compromise thus signified neither be- trayal nor weakness. DeMint, in contrast, viewed outreach and a big tent as dilutions of pure conservatism; his mantra was that "thirty Republicans who believed in something [were better] than a majority who believed in nothing."

No one at that summit was interested in incremental changes when they could fight for total victory. After McCain-Feingold, there was no longer any way a political party could control insurgents and force them to broaden their narrow interests to reflect those of the whole party, or to accept an incremental step rather than go for broke.[18]

As Congress worked through the complexities of the Affordable Care Act (ACA), already derisively labeled "Obamacare" by its opponents, the spigot for wealthy donors willing to spend tens of millions in political campaigns was about to open even wider.

In January 2010, the Supreme Court issued a ruling in favor of "Citizens United," a conservative nonprofit group that had been barred from showing an anti–Hillary Clinton movie. After a series of intricate judicial maneuvers, the Court loosened the constraints on independent expenditures and applying the First Amendment to corporations. In federal, state, and local elections, corporations and wealthy individuals could now spend any amount they wished without voters ever learning who had donated the "dark money."

This further tilted power away from official party organizations and toward factions within the parties who could write big checks in support of their pet issues and causes. "When the money flows through a different channel, the party ends up with a different center of gravity," wrote Heather K. Gerken and Joseph Fishkin. "It means some voices count more inside the party than they did before—and other voices count less."[19]

When a financial catastrophe loomed in September 2008, it required tortuous bipartisan negotiations between a Democratic Congress and a Republican president to stave off total ruin. Congress voted to spend hundreds of billions of dollars to prevent a collapse of the financial system. Wealthy bankers and Wall Street financiers benefited at once, while ordinary people lost their jobs, homes, and pensions. This infuriated legislators in both parties.

Now Democrats controlled both the White House and Congress, and they were forced to bear the onus of more unpopular, poorly understood spending to move the economy off life support. The new president faced what his strategist David Axelrod called "a potential disaster of epic proportions." An immediate, massive stimulus bill was necessary to avoid calamity. At first, Republican legislators were sympathetic and willingly offered heartfelt suggestions for ways to spend the money. A high-ranking Republican on the transportation committee even suggested high-speed rail.[20]

Then DeMint attacked the stimulus as a "trillion-dollar socialist experiment," while Koch-linked groups unleashed an advertising blitz—full-page ads in major newspapers—reinforcing that criticism. Researchers at Koch-funded think tanks challenged Obama's credibility, showing by their disagreement with him that not all experts agreed that a stimulus was necessary. A week after the ads ran, the House Republican caucus agreed that they would oppose any stimulus spending.[21]

The Kochs' and DeMint's national crusade against "socialism" had Republican legislators watching their backs. DeMint introduced a Senate amendment to the stimulus bill, replacing all the stimulus spending (even for infrastructure and public schools) with tax cuts. The amendment failed to pass, but all but five Republican senators endorsed it.[22]

DeMint was not done. He then warned Republicans that some of the standard boilerplate language in Obama's stimulus bill was an attack on religion. Armed with a legal document produced at evangelist Pat Robertson's American Center for Law and Justice, he claimed that students could not meet in dorm rooms to pray together in buildings built with stimulus funds. The nonpartisan Poynter Journalism Institute's PolitiFact labeled the charge false, noting that the same language had already been upheld repeatedly by the Supreme Court.[23]

There was never any war on religion. There was, however, a war against redistribution that had been escalated by changes in campaign finance, which were both moving the GOP to the right and weakening the resources of party leaders trying to build consensus within the House and Senate.

The stimulus bill eventually passed the House with no Republican votes, and just three GOP votes in the Senate. Republican representatives got the bonus without the onus. Not taking a difficult vote would help prevent them from getting attacked in primaries, yet over the next two years, half of all Republican representatives applied for money for their districts—even for green, energy-efficient technologies they'd publicly dismissed as inefficient and unnecessary.[24]

Orchestrated Spontaneity

Before the Obama stimulus bill passed, plans were underway for a national movement to block mortgage relief for homeowners. The major conservative talk radio figures were quietly receiving major retainers from conservative organizations, and websites were registered and ready to go live. Their cue would be an attack on homeowners in distress, blaming them—not the banks or investors—for the recession. The goal was moving the GOP to the right, replacing Democrats and moderate Republicans with anti-government conservatives.

The day after the stimulus bill passed, CNBC commentator Rick Santelli launched into an infamous tirade on CNBC's *Squawk Box*. The featured guest that day was Wilbur Ross, a Koch ally who criticized government plans to provide mortgage relief to homeowners about to lose their homes. Santelli apparently agreed; his rant went viral on YouTube within hours:

> How about this, Mr. President. . . . Why don't you put up a website to have people vote on the Internet as a referendum to see if we really want to subsidize the losers' mortgages? [. . .] This is America! How many people want to pay for your neighbor's mortgages that has an extra bathroom and can't pay their bills? Raise their hand! President Obama, are you listening?[25]

Santelli's message was clear: directing government aid to homeowners was "promoting bad behavior," not saving the economy. After he finished, Ross congratulated Santelli "on your new incarnation as a revolutionary leader."[26]

Within hours of the broadcast, a previously registered but inactive website, ChicagoTeaParty.com, was up and running with a video of Santelli's call to action; by then, the video was already up on the Drudge Report. The next morning a manual, "How to Organize Your Own 'Tea Party' Protest," was online at FreedomWorks, the website of former Texas congressman and House Majority Leader Dick Armey, who had been supported by the Kochs.[27]

Journalists Mark Ames and Yasha Levine had reported from Russia for years, and these seemingly extemporaneous moves felt similar to the fake "grass-roots" movements that the Kremlin frequently created. Santelli, they found, was a frontman for the launch of a carefully timed, organized effort involving the Koch brothers to block changes in healthcare, government spending, and environmental regulation. While there were organizations with no connections to the Koch network, there were multiple ties between Koch-funded groups and groups that arose "spontaneously" across the country in the days after the rant. The Kochs couldn't control the disparate groups of zealots, ordinary concerned citizens, libertarians, and social conservatives, but they assumed that anti-Obama and anti-Obamacare opposition would slow Obama and block Republican cooperation.

The brothers had been trying for years to provoke the kind of fervor embodied by the "Tea Party," secretly financing term-limits initiatives to weaken incumbents (particularly when Democrats controlled state legislatures) and increase the power of outside money. They were poised to capitalize.[28]

Within two months, a national movement was off and running. Tea Party groups were channeling and organizing around the same impulse that had launched Ross Perot's 1990s third-party campaigns: anxiety about America's growing diversity. They supported increased spending on Medicare and Social Security and opposed spending on food stamps and welfare. For many, support for the Tea Party stemmed from a general opposition to spending on people—neither white nor Christian—who they believed were threatening the country's identity.[29]

Blaming "the losers" was an easy way to rationalize self-preservation. In reality, many people losing their homes were victims of crippled local economies. Plummeting home values made it nigh-impossible for millions of unemployed and underemployed families to sell homes worth less than the mortgage, so they couldn't easily move if they found work elsewhere.[30] Santelli's rant about extra bathrooms and frivolous spending ignored the growing wealth inequality and the declining wages of more than half of the country. All of the growth in earning since that time had been concentrated in the top tenth of the country. More than half of all families in the country did not have enough savings to cover three weeks of earnings.[31]

The geographic variations in disruption, and the growing power of groups opposed to government efforts to deal with the people in distress, diminished the capacity of the government to respond to the crisis and grapple with groups trying to block action, whatever the future consequences. FreedomWorks was in a position to guide and nurture the politically inexperienced volunteers who were anxious to stop Obama. They supplied organizers for "Porkulus" rallies against the stimulus bill that most economists—liberal or conservative—believed was essential to preventing a depression after 2008.

Americans for Prosperity (AFP) and other conservative groups quietly funneled money, directly and indirectly, toward endorsements and promotion of their ideas. They targeted their outreach toward TV and radio personalities like Rush Limbaugh, Mark Levin, Sean Hannity, and especially Glenn Beck, the man whom nearly 25 percent of Tea Party identifiers trusted more than anyone else in politics, according to large national surveys. Hannity,

Beck, and Limbaugh each received over a million dollars a year from conservative group sponsorships.[32]

Michael Harrison, editor of *TALKERS*, a trade publication for talk show advertisers, pointed out that the conservative talk radio stars sold their air time and endorsements like "people who broadcast from used car lots or restaurants." As long as it didn't hurt their ratings, they were open for business.[33]

AFP, like FreedomWorks, was instrumental in molding many—though far from all—disparate Tea Party activists into a more focused whole. It underwrote and organized training seminars and conventions, provided logistical support for rallies, and funded candidates.

Professionals like Peggy Venable, a political operative who had worked for the Kochs for more than fifteen years, were important for shaping the movement and making it more palatable to a broad audience. At a Tea Party training session titled "Texas Defending the American Dream," Venable told five hundred trainees they could do something about Obama's "socialist vision for this country." The job of AFP, she explained, was to educate activists on policy details, and give them "next step training" and lists of officials to target.[34]

Old-Fashioned Racism Returns

Organizers from the Koch network worked to broaden the Tea Party's appeal by curtailing the overt racism and anti-abortion language that would alienate suburban voters. The core thrust of the national organizers working behind the scenes was message discipline. Racism was a major motivator for many of the activists, but subtle, coded racism was often more persuasive then the old-fashioned, crude racism of the 1950s. Organizers urged volunteers to avoid all religious and racial issues and focus on forcing the government to cut spending and reduce the national debt: "Bring your 'Don't Tread on Me' signs, and bring your healthcare signs," advised a Tea Party organizer at a fundraising event. "Please leave your anti-abortion signs at home. Please leave your anti-Obama signs at home."[35]

They had limited success. As Amy Fried and Douglas Harris wrote, trying to channel paranoia and suspicion is "an imprecise art." The crude language from talk radio played on diversity to raise distrust of Obama's programs. From Election Day on, Rush Limbaugh called Obama "Santa Claus," claiming that the stimulus bill was "reparations." Using a Black dialect, Limbaugh said "he's gon' cut this country down to size, he's gon' make it pay for all its multicultural mistakes that it has made, its mistreatment of minorities." Glenn Beck asked his audience, "Have we suddenly transported into 1956 except it's the other way around? . . . Does anybody else have a sense that there are some that just want revenge? Doesn't it feel that way?"[36]

Meanwhile, Sarah Palin was ready to capitalize on her new celebrity status with social conservatives, seizing on one particular (and particularly innocuous) detail of the ACA. All fifty states already had legislation allowing people to have end-of-life directives specifying their decisions for doctors to follow; the ACA simply covered the cost of discussing one's directives with a physician. Palin twisted this facet into a claim that the law created "death panels" to decide who would live and who would die:

> The America I know and love is not one in which my parents or my baby with Down Syndrome will have to stand in front of Obama's "death panel" so his bureaucrats can decide, based on a subjective judgment of their "level of productivity in society," whether they are worthy of health care. . . . Such a system is downright evil.[37]

Even in a year dominated by massive distortions and lies, Palin's "death panel" claim earned PolitiFact's "Lie of the Year" award. Palin's claim originated with Patients First, an Americans for Prosperity group that warned local audiences that the law mandated physician-assisted suicides: "Hitler issued six million end of life orders—he called his program the final solution. I kind of wonder what we're going to call ours." Palin got the credit, while the Kochs and Frank Luntz, a well-connected conservative pollster who developed the phrase, remained in the background.[38]

Obama was in a difficult bind; race was media catnip. Confronting the racist slurs risked raising the stereotype of the "angry Black man," making it even easier for talk radio luminaries like Limbaugh and Beck to assert that his policies were revenge for slavery. Appearing to dismiss the criticisms as racism could enrage those with genuine concerns. Instead, Obama chose to continue the focus on coalition-building for his legislation, making a national address to Congress to lay out the goals of the ACA.[39]

That speech before Congress, however, is remembered less for anything Obama said than for two words uttered by a Republican congressman. Just after Obama addressed the baseless rumors that the bill would cover undocumented immigrants, South Carolina representative Joe Wilson jumped up and shouted "You lie!" Notwithstanding the charged, vitriolic state of polarized debate and old-fashioned racism, Wilson's behavior stunned both parties' legislators.[40]

In the new world of campaign finance, Wilson's outburst was rewarded. In the four congressional campaigns since Wilson first ran for Congress in 2002, he'd raised an average of $1.1 million; he raised nearly $5 million for his next campaign.[41]

"For two centuries, the South has feared a takeover by blacks or the feds," Maureen Dowd wrote in a grim assessment of the divisive reaction to the president. "In Obama, they have both." Lest anyone think Dowd was engaging in hyperbole, Georgia congressman Paul Broun compared Obamacare to "The Great War of Yankee Aggression" during a congressional debate.[42]

Moving the Party

The year 2010 marked the first time that conservative groups spent more money in primary campaigns against incumbent GOP representatives and senators than against Democrats in the general election. Former Oklahoma Democratic congressman Dan Boren summarized the mindset of the big donors: "No one's saying, 'Here's $50 million for a good compromise.'"[43]

In 2010, and again in 2012, three quarters of all super PACs were at the ideological extremes of the parties. The money continued to pour in. In 1980, only one donor gave more than a million dollars to political campaigns (adjusted to 2012 value). In the 2011–12 election campaigns, 155 persons contributed more than a million dollars—and one couple, Sheldon and Miriam Adelson, contributed more than $100 million.[44]

Republicans could now find financial support for more extreme policies and more aggressive tactics. When the big donations had gone directly to the parties, former Speaker Dennis Hastert explained, it had "kind of a homogenizing effect," bringing candidates together around middle-of-the-road solutions.[45] With so much money outside the party, leaders could no longer exert as much moderating influence.

No one exemplified how the shift in national political options changed the country and the Republican Party better than South Carolina senator Jim DeMint, whom an admirer once nicknamed the "leader of the Huns." And no issue exemplified DeMint's tactics like his attack on Obamacare.

In 2006, Massachusetts governor Mitt Romney passed a healthcare plan with a mandate requiring everyone in his state to buy health insurance. During a celebration of the bill's passage at the Heritage Foundation—the right-wing think tank at which the basic ideas of the plan had originated— DeMint praised Romney's use of a "conservative idea" to prevent free riders from taking advantage of the healthcare system. The Heritage Foundation, instrumental in the plan's construction, hailed the mandate as "a two-way commitment between government and citizen."[46]

The Heritage Foundation plan was, in fact, the best way to cut spending without a single-payer, government-managed system, and its mandate was an essential component. Without it, no plan could guarantee coverage for people with preexisting conditions when they changed jobs or moved. Even Newt Gingrich supported the Heritage plan and its mandate at one point.[47]

Obamacare had cribbed its required mandate from Romney's (and the Heritage Foundation's) own plan, but that wasn't enough to prevent DeMint's conservative principles from shifting; it was now more important to eliminate the insurance mandate he had once praised than to prevent free riders. And for the billionaires and multimillionaires opening their checkbooks for groups like FreedomWorks and Americans for Prosperity, such a two-way commitment was no longer acceptable.

Now DeMint could raise funds to move the party farther to the right; there was enough money available to allow him to target any incumbent in primaries if he deemed them insufficiently conservative. Even if they won, the incumbents would remember that moderation was costly. Throughout 2010, he traveled the country "demonizing conservatives who he says aren't conservative enough, helping nominate candidates more interested in throwing grenades than in passing legislation, and belittling compromise."[48]

The Uncompromising Republican Wave

In the 2010 midterms, Republicans gained a net of sixty-four congressional representatives, giving them a 242–193 majority in the House. With or without McCain-Feingold, the GOP would have made major gains in 2010; first-term presidents historically suffer congressional losses in their first midterm election. Midterm waves are generally followed by turbulence within the victorious party as the new cohort overestimates their power in a divided government, fails to enact sweeping change, and eventually merges into the party mainstream.

This cohort was different. As Obama's strategist David Axelrod described it, the Tea Party was "a grassroots citizens' movement brought to you by a bunch of oil billionaires." He was correct that much of the training, infrastructure, and money came from persons connected to the Koch network.

But the new wave was a group that Lisa Disch showed was a "white citizenship movement," with ideas that only partially connected with legislation or the Koch's goals. Their intense visceral distrust of Obama and his spending on "others" obscured their willingness to spend money on the entitlements their constituents valued, even if it meant taxing the wealthy.[49] The changes in spending that weakened the party and unleashed big donors changed the fundamental character of the wave, turning compromise into heresy—and dividing the party further.

Republicans picked up six seats in the Senate, leaving them with forty-seven senators. The GOP might have gained control of the upper chamber as well, were it not for several fringe candidates whose extreme or bizarre comments received national attention and cost the party everywhere. Neither the RNC, the Koch network, nor anyone else had managed to recruit candidates angry enough to attract Tea Party voters without alienating more moderate or educated voters. In Delaware, Christine O'Donnell—who equated masturbation with adultery and did not know what the First Amendment was—must surely have been the only Senate candidate in history to claim, "I'm not a witch." In Nevada, Senator Harry Reid nearly lost to Sharron Angle, who championed a Scientologist plan to give massages to prisoners.[50]

Senate candidates in other states did not have to take stands on topics like masturbation, witchcraft, or Scientology. But failed Colorado Senate candidate Ken Buck's quotes defending extreme versions of party orthodoxy—such as his opposition to abortion even in cases of rape and incest, and his view of Social Security as an unconstitutional, "horrible policy"—caused damage to other candidates who had to comment on his statements. Without funding and support from Jim DeMint and other groups pushing for farther-right candidates, the GOP would likely have won in Colorado.[51]

Fox News provided no help to party leaders or establishment groups; it was focused on ratings and revenue, not election results or legislation. Senate Majority Leader Mitch McConnell wanted Trey Grayson, a sophisticated and personable banker, to be his fellow Kentucky senator. Fox, however, granted massive airtime to Grayson's primary opponent, Rand Paul, a libertarian ophthalmologist whose father, Ron Paul, was a gadfly Republican congressman and serial presidential candidate for both the Libertarian and Republican parties.

Rand Paul belonged to a medical association advocating voluntary vaccinations, wanted to abolish the Federal Reserve Board, and opposed the 1964 Civil Rights Act because, he said, requiring businesses to serve everyone was not the government's proper role. He declared his candidacy on Glenn Beck's show, did his fundraising via his father's mailing list of people who supported a return to the gold standard, and appeared regularly on the show of conspiracy theorist Alex Jones.[52]

Media competition between Fox, conservative talk radio, and powerful websites like the Drudge Report, Breitbart, and Newsmax meant a ratings bonanza for the Tea Party. For someone like McConnell, Rand Paul was closer to O'Donnell's witchcraft than to conservative orthodoxy. He called Roger Ailes to complain that Grayson was not being given time to make his case. Despite their friendship, Ailes was unwilling to help: Rand Paul was a "better draw." Once again, an establishment candidate was bested by an outsider who despised legislative compromise and was good for ratings.[53]

Divided They Flail

Nearly two years earlier, on the night of the Obama's inauguration, the pollster Frank Luntz held a dinner with Newt Gingrich and some of the next generation's emerging conservative stars. Luntz—who had devised the wildly successful "Contract with America" that fueled the GOP's 1994 congressional victory—had a strategy to guide conservatives back to power.[54]

Luntz had a high level of credibility, based both on his results and the people who hired him. He had helped Koch Industries develop a combative approach to global warming, starting with devising a less threatening name—climate change—and an artfully worded pledge that killed Republican support for any regulation of emissions involving taxes or fines, which included both cap-and-trade regulation and direct carbon taxes and fines. He'd since also developed the playbook for opposing Obamacare, coining phrases that fed directly into pervasive doubts and fears of the ACA.[55]

Luntz's plan was simple. From day one of the Obama administration, Republicans would use their control of the House as a "spear point," utilizing hearings and legislative debates to jab Obama relentlessly and vote against his spending bills. Then they would capture the House by campaigning against the unpopular spending.

Republican dominance in the 2010 midterms was step one in Luntz's plan. Now, after winning the midterms, they would use their subpoena power to attack the administration, while blocking new programs or tax increases.[56] Leading the attack were the "Young Guns"—Representatives Paul Ryan, Kevin McCarthy, and Eric Cantor—so named because of the title of their coauthored 2010 book. Cantor focused on taxes and was on the leadership ladder, Ryan was the budget wonk, and McCarthy was the strategist. Together, they argued that the leaders of the party "betrayed its principles" by increasing spending and raising the deficit.

Despite the planning, 2011 ushered in six years of constant brinksmanship driven by conflicts within a divided Republican Party. The changes in campaign finance, and the emergence of major donors and groups like members of the Koch network and the Club for Growth, had changed the game.

Bipartisan cooperation required consensus within parties on what mix of gains and concessions is worthwhile. No such deals were possible when groups within the party preferred all-or-nothing posturing and attacked dissenters in primaries.

Most of the freshman class had been recruited, financed, and trained by outside groups like FreedomWorks, Tea Party groups, or Americans for Prosperity. For many of them, purging the party of RINOs—"Republicans in Name Only"—was more important than growing the party. They thought anyone who supported the bank bailout was a RINO until proven innocent, never minding—or realizing—that the Koch brothers and AFP had quietly supported the bailout when the economy was in freefall.[57] .

Nearly all the new freshmen joined the Republican Study Committee (RSC), doubling its size so that it included two-thirds of House Republicans. The RSC had been active since the 1970s as the place where conservative Republican legislators developed strategies for bargaining with moderate colleagues.

Trying to strengthen his power as speaker in 1995, Gingrich had killed funding for the group. The move backfired, strengthening the RSC at the expense of the party. Its 164 members pooled resources and paid dues: $2,500 for a freshman, $5,000 for representatives, and $10,000 for the Steering Committee members. In addition, they allied themselves with the Heritage Foundation and relied on the think tank's staff and other outsiders for analyses of legislation and help in recruiting members.[58]

A Grand Bet Blocks the Grand Bargain

It was easy for the GOP to agree that Obamacare should go. It was impossible for them to do so without controlling the two-thirds of the House and Senate required to override a presidential veto. Many of the Tea Party House members, however, were willing to shut down the government anyway. Some of them didn't understand the implications of a such a gambit, and others didn't care about the aftermath as long as they showed their willingness to fight a righteous battle.

Speaker John Boehner wanted to avoid battles that would hurt the party, but he could not control the gung-ho freshmen or stop his colleagues from furthering their careers at the expense of the GOP's chances of defeating Obama in 2012. The members of the new Tea Party–dominated class of Republican freshman representatives were determined to honor their pledges above all else. The top items for their first year were to repeal the Affordable Care Act and cut $100 billion from the budget by removing every discretionary bit of spending or program Obama had added.[59]

Cutting all the new spending was as unrealistic as ending Obamacare. Much of the spending in the healthcare bill was spending authorized through legislation, meaning it could only be stopped with new legislation that required Senate approval and the president's signature. To add insult to injury, the nonpartisan Congressional Budget Office reported that repealing Obamacare would add $230 billion to the deficit over the next decade and reduce the number of insured Americans by 32 million.[60]

The result was a series of trivial bills designed to look like promises kept. Before the year ended, the House passed fourteen bills containing provisions to change, alter, or kill Obamacare, but the results were "much ado about nothing," minor tweaks or provisions that never made it through the Senate. The only leverage left for the Republican Congress was the ultimate threat: shutting down the government by refusing to raise the debt ceiling.[61]

At an orientation session for most of the eighty-seven new Republican members of Congress, Luntz had praised the new members when all but four said they would vote against raising the debt ceiling. "Good for you," Luntz said, "because your base is going to kill you if you vote to raise the debt ceiling."[62]

While experienced legislators knew that a shutdown could be damaging for the party, the freshman representatives were undeterred by the disastrous outcomes of the Newt Gingrich shutdowns of 1995 and 1996. Nor did it faze them that their pledge to roll back new Obama spending to 2008 levels evolved into a doubly erroneous simplification. Equating a rollback to 2008 levels with cutting $100 billion was based on a preliminary Obama budget that was never submitted. Moreover, the current fiscal year would be half over when their budget was passed, so their original intent actually meant cutting just $32 billion. After promising $100 billion, many freshmen feared settling for $32 billion would make them look like RINOs.

In April 2011, Republicans headed off a shutdown at the last minute with a seven-week stopgap measure to keep the government open, but the posturing continued. In May, severe tornados and storms hit five Southern states, and Republicans insisted that the billions for disaster relief first be offset by cuts elsewhere in the budget—violating a precedent.[63]

After the first two debt-ceiling fights, Boehner wanted to find a deal that kept his party out of trouble until *after* the upcoming presidential election. In June, Boehner started working privately with Vice President Joe Biden on a "grand bargain" to pass a debt ceiling increase without a shutdown. But such a bargain required both parties to make painful concessions.

On July 1, the Treasury Department announced that the government would run out of funds in early August without another debt ceiling increase. When Boehner showed a tentative deal to Cantor on July 21, Cantor rejected it, preferring a shutdown to any deal that threatened his support among the freshman representatives or his anti-tax reputation. Meanwhile, Democrats were insisting on some new taxes as part of any bargain.[64]

Instead of a grand bargain, Ryan Lizza wrote, Cantor steered the Republicans to a "grand bet." In exchange, Democrats had offered some painful changes to entitlement eligibility, student loans, and other programs dear to their base. Cantor's view was that increasing the debt limit was just as big a concession as cutting the safety net: "I don't think the White House understands how difficult it is for fiscal conservatives to say they are going to vote for a debt-ceiling increase," he said.[65]

The $4 trillion grand bargain included taxes and spending cuts, but Cantor wanted only a smaller bargain with no tax increases, which was too one-sided a deal for the Democrats.[66] Cantor understood the perils of a default but was unwilling to challenge the Republican Study Committee. And Jim Jordan, the RSC chair, was unwilling "to support a bipartisan compromise that might actually pass."[67]

Many of the RSC members were running scared. They knew they would get hammered by Democrats for trying to cut Medicare, and now they were getting attacked by Grover Norquist and other groups for not fighting for more spending cuts. Then a leaked e-mail revealed that Jordan's RSC executive director, Paul Teller, was secretly identifying wavering members of Congress for outside groups to target with ads and threats to fund primary opponents. Jordan apologized to the entire party, but the damage was done.[68]

Jordan's tactical escapades left the party in a far worse situation. After two weeks debating proposals that had zero chance of becoming law, the party could not agree to accept the compromise Speaker Boehner negotiated with the White House. An agreement was finally reached on August 1 that guaranteed no more showdowns before the 2012 election. If a bipartisan committee couldn't agree on budget cuts, there would be automatic cuts in spending, half from domestic programs and half from defense. This left the Democrats in better shape to protect domestic programs that the compromise, but it guaranteed more opportunities for Jordan and his allies to raise money and make headlines.[69]

As Boehner had feared, the ongoing brinksmanship over the budget hurt his party, keeping the spotlight on Republicans' unwillingness to raise taxes on the very wealthy, or to spend any money on stimulus or jobs. Only 20 percent of the public thought Republicans had a plan to deal with jobs and unemployment, and 69 percent thought the GOP favored the rich.[70]

The Pre-primary Obstacle Course

Obama was vulnerable, but Republican voters had little confidence in party leadership as the campaign opened. Mitt Romney was the front-runner, but with the weakest numbers in any recent Republican nomination campaign; only 17 percent of likely primary voters supported him.[71]

Romney's strategy was to focus on the weak economy, while minimizing social issues. "Our whole campaign is premised on the idea that this is a referendum on Obama," said Stuart Stevens, Romney's strategist. "The economy is a disaster, and Obama is uniquely blocked from being able to talk about jobs."[72]

Romney described Obama as a well-intentioned but "out of his depth" president who doesn't get "what makes America work." That message—that Romney's success as a businessman gave him special knowledge that politicians didn't have—was precisely why Romney was the opponent Obama feared most.[73] That well-crafted message, however, was undermined by the hard-edged approaches Romney—like McCain before him—was forced to adopt in order to survive the primaries and satisfy the demands of various groups within his own party.

Like an army moving across the countryside, a campaign can only stay on course if it can prevent ambushes and avoid diversionary actions. In the new campaign finance environment, it was harder than ever for a front-runner to avoid positions far from the mainstream in the primaries. And Romney's strategy had two big obstacles: a religion problem and a billionaire problem.

The Tea Party House members were mainly from the South or rural, religious areas in the Midwest and West. Many of them were pushing social positions that Romney explicitly wanted to suppress—divisive views that played well in their parts of the country but were poison elsewhere. They supported Senate and House challengers with stringent pro-life positions, and cheered candidates echoing their views.

By 2012, the Koch network was powerful enough to challenge mainstream candidates on global warming or government spending. Transgressors of their new orthodoxy rushed to repudiate their sins as the GOP campaigns were launched.

Minnesota governor Tim Pawlenty was the first sinner to convert when he renounced his support of cap-and-trade legislation to reduce emissions: "I've said I was wrong. It was a mistake, and I'm sorry. . . . I don't try to duck it, bob it, weave it, try to explain it away. I'm just telling you, I made a mistake."[74] The progressive former Utah governor Jon Huntsman then did a triple flip, abandoning his past support for cap-and-trade legislation and emissions controls, the economic recovery act, and Obamacare.[75]

Later that year, Mitt Romney also changed his mind on climate. He started his campaign in 2011 stressing the need to reduce emissions. By the fall, however, he'd become a climate skeptic. In between, he had begun to woo the Kochs for financial support against Obama.[76]

The Ryan Budget Litmus Test

The Koch network wanted more than a pledge on spending and taxes, and now they had an actual federal budget as a litmus test for prospective candidates: Paul Ryan's "Path to Prosperity."

Ryan's "remarkable talent for radiating good intentions" and his fervent belief that Social Security was no longer the third rail of American politics made him a rock star among major conservative donors. The Koch network put their resources behind his budget—a radical overhaul that aimed to control the deficit by shrinking the social safety net and cutting taxes for the wealthy. They knew it wouldn't pass the Senate, but once House Republicans passed it, Ryan's budget would be the starting point for the 2012 party platform.[77]

Ryan had introduced versions of this budget as his party's alternative to the Democratic majority budget in 2007, 2008, 2009, and 2010. Each time, at least 20 percent of his own party voted against it. When he introduced the Koch-backed 2011 version, 98 percent of Republicans voted yes, and the budget passed—without a single Democratic vote.[78]

The toxicity of the budget immediately altered the national political environment. That very afternoon, Kathy Hochul, a young unknown Democrat running for an open congressional seat in a special election in upstate New York, goaded her well-known opponent, Jane Corwin, into saying she would vote for the Ryan budget. The moment Corwin endorsed the Ryan budget, Hochul's campaign took off.[79]

As Hochul's numbers closed in on Corwin's, Republicans panicked. The freshmen held a press conference, complaining that harsh Democratic rhetoric harmed the chances of finding a middle ground. In *New York* magazine, Dan Amira skewered the ploy, joking that the Democratic response was two letters long: "F" and "U."[80]

Five weeks after the House passed the Ryan budget, Hochul won in the most conservative district in New York. In just over a month, she had soared from fifteen points down to a ten-point victory by talking nonstop about Medicare, an expensive entitlement program that was nevertheless considered worthwhile by 70 percent of Tea Party voters. House Minority Leader Nancy Pelosi took her cue, vowing that the top three issues in the fall election would be "Medicare, Medicare, and Medicare."[81]

The "grand bet" was not paying off, yet Ryan remained a hero to the Koch network. His fellow Young Gun, Eric Cantor, urged him to run for president. Ryan demurred, but he was interested enough to test his appeal. He ran ads that summer in Iowa, defending his budget and urging primary candidates to endorse it.[82]

Super PAC Money Changes Campaign Strategy

"Campaigns don't usually end because candidates give up," Romney campaign strategist Stuart Stevens wrote, "they end because they run out of money." In the new world of outside finance and super PACs, more money provided longer campaigns for candidates with no chance of winning. That made it harder for viable candidates to stay clear of commitments popular on the fringe of their party.

Dark-horse candidates who mobilize passionate minorities have always been a problem for candidates with a realistic chance of victory in November. Now fringe candidates could make a showing without local organizations or support within the party. All it took to run was a few newsworthy lines, a billionaire willing to fund a super PAC, and a media outlet to reach voters.

Koch network members were not the only billionaires trying to make a difference. Others were willing to support candidates, backing their pet issues regardless of how few votes they pulled or how nonexistent their chances were of winning the nomination. Candidates who would have been nonstarters in the past, like Newt Gingrich and former senator Rick Santorum, were kept afloat by billionaire donors. Neither Gingrich nor Santorum had any support from former colleagues or any local organization or staff. But Gingrich had $20 million from Sheldon and Miriam Adelson, and Santorum had more than $2 million each from Foster Friess, an evangelical Christian, and William Dore.[83]

In March, Republican Indiana governor Mitch Daniels, a successful executive with a strong record on moral issues, tried to head off the growing preoccupation with fringe social issues by calling for a truce. Daniels's plea, aimed at redirecting the primary's focus to addressing the economic crisis so important to most voters, was both prescient and futile.[84]

Debate Audiences Become the Message

Conservative media magnified the disarray in the party. Fox News and talk radio covered candidates for ratings, regardless of the plausibility of their candidacies. The distinction between political power and media profits was painful for Republican leaders like Representative Tom Cole, a solid conservative who lamented Fox's market share-driven conservatism as "playing to the prejudice of their audiences or reinforcing them—as opposed to engaging in enlightened and intellectual debate."[85]

After 2008, the RNC had decided that they would hold more primary debates to increase exposure to the party's message and candidates. The 2012 cycle saw twenty debates, some sanctioned and organized by the party with various outlets—five on the Fox Network, three on CNN—and some organized directly by Tea Party groups, many of which mortified Republicans trying to update the brand and attract young voters and independents. "The thinkers and the operatives cringed," Jonathan Martin observed, "at the umpteen debates and carnival-like procession of candidates with little chance of landing in the Oval Office."[86]

The change backfired. The audience, not the candidates, became the message—and it was not a message party leaders wanted. In one debate, Rick Perry received the loudest cheers when he bragged about presiding over the most executions of any governor; in another, when the moderator asked whether a man without insurance should be allowed to die, the audience rang with approving whoops. In a third debate, the audience booed a gay soldier asking a question via satellite from active duty in Iraq.

The candidates' messages were hardly any better. Santorum, who had famously asserted that legalizing sodomy would justify polygamy and incest, now claimed that the US military's "Don't Ask, Don't Tell" policy—which prohibited discrimination against closeted LGBT military personnel while barring openly gay, bisexual, or lesbian members from serving—was a special privilege for gays that should be repealed. Congresswoman Michelle Bachmann contended that if same-sex marriage were allowed, public schools would be "forced to start teaching that same-sex marriage is equal, that it is normal and that children should try it."[87]

The Establishment's Last Gasp

Between entertainment media, free-wheeling billionaires, and committed social conservatives, there was no way for Romney to stay on his chosen path. By the end of 2011, he had been forced to reverse his previous positions on global warming, stem cell research, abortion, and funding Planned Parenthood. And the national healthcare plan based on the same model as his Massachusetts plan? Romney now declared it to be "bad law, bad policy, and . . . bad for America's families."[88]

When the primary voting began in early January 2012, Romney edged out Santorum in the Iowa caucuses and won New Hampshire easily. His early success panicked the religious right. Despite Romney's suspect capitulation, they wanted someone in the White House who would vigorously defend their values and fight secularism. Membership in their religious organizations— not to mention church attendance and the number of baptisms—had been declining for a decade, and support for gay marriage and abortion was growing, particularly among young voters.[89]

At the same time, they were growing stronger within the party. There were now ninety-four Republican House members from the eleven states of the former Confederacy, an area in which the Christian Coalition had been steadily gaining valuable local power within the Republican Party. (See Appendix, Table 3.)

As presidential primaries gained force after the post-1968 reforms, presidential candidates built primary organizations separate from the local party, weakening local party organizations in much of the country. Christian Coalition leaders used their church networks to move in to the depleted organizations. Christopher Baylor charted their approach to gaining control:

> Their less fiery peers lacked the patience and intensity to learn tedious party rules and organize against them for unpaid positions. Once in place, they screened candidates for beliefs and helped likeminded candidates with media attention and access to their networks.[90]

Evangelical leaders met before the South Carolina primary, determined to unify religious conservatives behind one candidate. But which one—Newt Gingrich or Rick Santorum? On the one hand, Gingrich had been married three times, and his current wife, Callista, had been his mistress for six years. On the other hand, Santorum was a devout Catholic—"a Catholic missionary who happens to be in the Senate," one former aide said.[91]

After two days "fueled by prayer and passionate speeches" and three rounds of ballots, the leaders voted to endorse Santorum. But even though the group claimed there was a "strong consensus" for Santorum, only 89 of roughly 150 attendees backed him. Twenty-five stuck with Gingrich and the others abstained.[92] Several days later, in the state with the highest proportion of evangelical voters, their handpicked candidate lost badly in South Carolina to the thrice-married Southerner who had converted to Catholicism for his current wife.

Fueled by the Adelsons' largesse, Gingrich went after Obama as "the food stamp president" who hated work, while his super PAC spent millions of dollars on ads attacking Romney for his slash-and-burn maneuvers at Bain Capital. Gingrich's victory alarmed party leaders. They could not unite on budgets, immigration, abortion, or much of anything beyond tax cuts. But they did agree that Gingrich would be a disaster as the nominee—and if he actually beat Romney in the upcoming Florida primary, the candidate most likely to defeat Obama would be grievously wounded before he had the chance to do so.

Bob Dole, who had endorsed Romney, released a statement exhorting his colleagues to "take a stand before it is too late." With Gingrich at the head of the ticket, there would be "an adverse impact" on all down-ticket Republicans. "Hardly anyone who served with Newt in Congress has endorsed him," Dole continued, "and that fact speaks for itself."[93]

With Gingrich subdued, Romney eventually wrapped up the nomination, finally overcoming Santorum in the Midwestern primaries. Yet Romney won only 42 percent of all votes cast in the primary, and with the focus now on the general election, he faced both young voters who weren't attracted to old orthodoxy on government, climate, or sexuality, and older voters who valued Medicare. Santorum had made it impossible for Romney to maneuver around the rights of the unborn, and Gingrich did a better, more credible job of attacking him as a job-cutting corporate raider than any Democrat could have done.

Obama Divides and Conquers

In the general election, Stuart Stevens had little choice but to run Romney's campaign as if the economy were the only issue. They had no way to counter Obama and neutralize the "diversionary" social issues where they were on the losing side. But Obama was not about to let Romney campaign solely on the one issue he could compete on.

In May, the president announced his personal support for same-sex marriage. Republican pollster Jan van Lohuizen rushed out a memo to warn Republican officials that support for gay rights was accelerating among voters of every age and party, and that every year new voters (who were most likely to approve) were entering the electorate and replacing the older voters who were least likely to do so. Romney had to tread lightly. He adhered to his conviction that marriage was between a man and a woman, but did not oppose a same-sex couple's right to adopt, and avoided any attacks on gays in the military.

A month later Obama acted on immigration, giving protection to the group known as "Dreamers," allowing young Hispanics who were in school, high school graduates, or US military veterans to stay in the US temporarily and work legally.

Romney had attacked Rick Perry in the primary for granting undocumented Hispanic immigrants in-state college tuition in Texas. But when asked if he would repeal Obama's Dream Act, all Romney could say was that he would "look at that setting as we reach it." Later, he added that Obama's action was a "stop-gap measure" when the country needed a long-term solution. What that long-term solution was, Romney didn't—and couldn't—say.[94]

The party was so divided that they could not agree upon defensible policy alternatives to Obama's declarations and administrative orders. The best they could do was attack unpopular Obama moves as unconstitutional or "political," and blame him for the sluggish economy.

In August, Romney picked Paul Ryan as his running mate, a choice designed to energize Tea Party supporters who doubted the sincerity of Romney's conservatism. Now the Republican establishment, the party base, the Tea Party congressional delegation, and the Koch network were on board.[95]

Stevens opposed the pick, leery of having to defend the Ryan budget. It didn't take long for Stevens's worst-case scenario to unfold. Two hours after Romney announced his pick, the National Republican Congressional Committee sent out a memo on how to minimize the most dangerous aspects of the budget: "Do not say: 'entitlement reform,' 'privatization,' 'every option is on the table,' . . . Do say: 'strengthen,' 'secure,' 'save,' 'preserve,' 'protect.' "[96] In Ryan's acceptance speech at the Republican National Convention, his criticisms of Obama administration policies— including Obamacare's changes to reimbursement procedures, which had saved $700 billion and were endorsed by Ryan himself in his own budget—were swiftly condemned as hypocritical and riddled with inaccuracies by liberal pundits and conservative media alike.[97] When the Obama campaign called out Ryan's convention speech and the Romney campaign's ads about welfare reform as "blatantly false," Romney's pollster, Neil Newhouse, responded with the now infamous line, "We're not going let our campaign be dictated by fact checkers."[98]

Public polls showed no convention bump for Romney, but the campaign was still confident. If their voter turnout assumptions were correct, Romney was ahead. They expected white turnout to be higher—and minority participation lower—than in 2008. The Koch organizers were in the field along with the RNC and state parties. Karl Rove was spending $300 million on advertisements, and Romney's crowds were enthusiastic and fired up. Even as public polls showed Obama ahead in crucial battleground states, the race was always close.

And then Mother Nature made one of the more extreme, irrational aspects of the Ryan budget headline news across the country. Tropical Storm Sandy—later upgraded to a hurricane—devastated parts of the Northeast, causing massive flooding and power outages, and prompting Chris Christie and Bob McDonnell—two of the four governors that had been vetted as potential candidates by the Koch brothers—to warmly embrace Obama's response to the disaster.

Hurricane Sandy wiped out much of the New Jersey coastline, and Christie publicly and effusively thanked Obama for flood relief, personally touring the damaged areas with him. Facing political troubles in his home state, Christie was eager to work with the president and distance himself from the candidate certain to lose in his state.[99]

McDonnell, the head of the Republican Governors Association and a passionate defender of the Ryan budget, recoiled from that budget's proposed cuts to FEMA, the agency now saving Virginia from a "Frankenstorm" crisis. McDonnell praised Obama for his "direct and personal" approach and said Virginia was "very grateful" for a response that was "incredibly fast."[100]

In a stroke of irony, an extreme weather event of the kind becoming more frequent due to climate change handed Obama—whose attempts to address man-made climate change had earned scorn and opposition from the GOP—political vindication.

Election Night 2012

From Republican Party leaders to right-wing talk show hosts to the two men whose names were on the top of the ticket, November 6, 2012, was a moment of supreme optimism: Mitt Romney was going to win the presidency that evening. He had ended the campaign as "Moderate Mitt," not as the straitjacketed candidate of the Republican primary. As Romney's campaign plane returned to Boston after a last mad dash through battleground states, he told reporters he had "just finished writing a victory speech.... It's about 1,118 words." There were no what-ifs or uncertainty. The fireworks had been ordered.[101]

By 10:00 p.m. on election night, as conservative analysts at other networks described Obama's victory as a "repudiation of the Republican Party" (Alex Castellanos, CNN) and called for intraparty "soul searching" (Nicole Wallace, ABC), Fox News steadfastly refused to call Ohio—and thus the election—for the incumbent.[102]

Both Roger Ailes and Karl Rove—who had raised $325 million for his super PAC, Crossroads America, to help elect Romney and down-ballot Republicans—believed the exit polls were skewed in favor of Obama. "Liberals like to share their feelings," Ailes told his Decision Desk staffers, "and conservatives work, so they don't vote until later." Until midnight, Rove held on to the idea that Ohio was too close to call.[103]

After the loss had sunk in, Ailes consoled himself with the thought that "if Romney wins, it's good for the taxpayers. If Obama wins, it's great for our ratings." He had achieved his first goal of building a major conservative network, but that network undermined his second goal of electing a conservative president by providing national platforms for many of the extreme views that were destabilizing the party.[104]

"To see what is in front of one's nose," George Orwell wrote, "needs a constant struggle." It was inconceivable to Ailes and Rove that the Republicans' triumph in 2010 would not translate to presidential success in 2012.[105]

Democrats had now received more votes than Republicans in five of the last six presidential elections. Republican Party leaders had failed to find common ground to unite social and economic conservatives, while growing the party's base amid rising inequality. As long as obstructionists were rewarded by wealthy outsiders, and anyone who wanted efficient government instead of much smaller government would be attacked in the primaries, Republicans couldn't develop internal consensus and deal with the president.

In the 1990s, despite bitter conflicts between the parties, Republicans managed to work with President Clinton on welfare reform, form a balanced budget agreement, and end with a government surplus—all while trying to impeach the president. When 2011 ended, Senator Lindsey Graham concluded that progress on conservative goals through bipartisan cooperation was something they could only dream of now.[106] Intraparty fissures, already stark at the beginning of Obama's first term, had deepened. How long could they hold together entirely by opposing Obama, without any plans of their own?

3

Ted Cruz Crashes the Party

Election Night 2012 left conservative stalwarts bereft. "I went to bed last night thinking we've lost the country," the conservative radio talk show host Rush Limbaugh told his audience. "I don't know how else you look at this."[1] It was a stunning reversal from a man so powerful that he was made an honorary member of the Republicans' caucus when they took power in 1994. Back then, he'd been so bullish on the future of the GOP that he'd advised the lawmakers to "leave some liberals alive so we can show our children what they were."[2]

Mitt Romney's respected pollster, Neil Newhouse, assumed minority turnout would be slightly less than 2008, and that undecideds would break for the challenger. In fact, minority voters were a *higher* proportion of the electorate (26.3 percent) than in any past election. "It's unbelievable," a top Romney aide said. "Somehow they got 'em to vote."[3]

The Republicans' problems with their own base were as serious as their problems with a changing electorate. Declining white Republican turnout, not increasing minority turnout, was why Romney lost. The standard pro-business, low-tax message was not rousing once-reliable Republican voters; two million white voters who had voted in 2008 stayed home in 2012. The same state-by-state total of votes won by John Kerry *eight years earlier* in 2004 would have won the 2012 election with 284 electoral votes, just as Kerry's 2004 vote would have won in 2008. (See Appendix, Table 2.) To compound the problem, young voters turning eighteen were more socially liberal and less anti-government than the older voters who were dying.[4]

Heather Higgins, a conservative activist and former *Wall Street Journal* columnist, summed up the core issue: "[Most Americans] believe Republicans . . . cannot be trusted to care about cutting spending in a way that is remotely concerned about who it hurts, and are retrograde to the point of caricature on everything else."[5]

During the campaign, Romney had been recorded at a private fundraiser dividing the electorate into the 53 percent who were makers and the

47 percent who were parasitic takers. That distinction had become popular in conservative media since the day Obama was elected, and echoed Limbaugh's constant reference to the president as Santa Claus. Four years into Obama's presidency, the kind of racially coded rhetoric and appeals to Obama's "otherness" that had troubled observers on the 2008 campaign trail had become commonplace in conservative circles.

Romney's explanation for the increased minority turnout also echoed that standard conservative line: Obama won with "gifts" like healthcare or amnesty to "certain demographics." His analysis might have comforted his supporters, but it showed how out of touch the party was with its own base.[6]

Stunned by Obama's decisive victory, the Republican National Committee (RNC), the House and Senate Republican caucuses, the Republican Governors Association, and the Koch brothers' network of wealthy anti-government donors each met to chart their separate paths forward.

The party was in trouble and everyone knew something would have to change. But who would be willing to change their demands? What could the party do about well-funded outside groups that supported extreme candidates in primaries to punish insufficiently zealous incumbents? And how could the party discourage candidates from sounding like Rush Limbaugh or a Fox News analyst to build a following, when that was where so many of their voters turned for commentary?

The Republican Party lived in a new media world, where people like Limbaugh, Ann Coulter, and Fox News commentators such as Laura Ingraham assured their audiences that principles need never be compromised, and government was guilty until proven innocent. In this modern world of dark money and new media, no one understood how much damage could be inflicted on the party by congressional representatives and senators who were willing to savage colleagues in service of their political ambition. Thanks to the new Texas senator, Ted Cruz, a political firebrand out for himself no matter the cost, they were about to find out.

Whenever a zealous faction in the House is willing to force their party into passing extreme legislation, Sarah Binder pointed out, the party's leaders can only go along with their far-side group if their Senate counterparts serve as their firewall—a check and balance within the party to squash any outlandish bills sent to them by the lower chamber. Cruz was about to breach the firewall and bring Tea Party madness into the Senate.[7]

The RNC's Barbour Report

In the wake of the 2012 election, the RNC set up a blue-ribbon panel, the Growth and Opportunity Project, to make recommendations on how to expand the party beyond its white, middle-aged base. Its report identified areas where change was needed, but was vague about how to remove the barriers to expanding the party. The review panel, chaired by Republican strategist and Mississippi RNC committee member Henry Barbour, also demonstrated the depth of intraparty divisions and the threat posed by conservative groups friendly to, but not of, the party.

The GOP was trying to come to grips with a shift in the political terrain that neither party had fully grasped. The McCain-Feingold reforms had weakened the ability of legislative leaders in the House and Senate to manage legislation and protect the party brand. Wealthy donors who wanted "undiluted" policies opposed the compromises within and between parties that were necessary for partial progress toward party goals.

The report acknowledged the power of the Koch network, without using any names, and carefully noted that while they were a valuable asset, "a lot of centralized authority in the hands of a few people at these outside organizations is dangerous." The RNC panel hoped to persuade the Kochs to be more open to "empowering local conservative leaders to help rally voters behind the best conservative candidates," which was "a much more effective approach than anyone in Washington trying to dictate our primaries." In other words, they were asking the Kochs not to supplant and marginalize the party.[8]

In addition to indicating the depth of the party's internal divisions, the RNC's report also highlighted the changing demographics of the country, and the growing social tolerance of the electorate:

> If Hispanic Americans hear that the GOP doesn't want them in the United States, they won't pay attention to our next sentence . . . our Party's position on immigration has become a litmus test, measuring whether we are meeting them with a welcome mat or a closed door.
>
> [Mitt Romney] lost voters younger than 30 by 5 million votes . . . the Party is seen as old and detached from pop culture . . . we must change our tone—especially on certain social issues that are turning off young voters.
>
> 40 percent of female voters are single . . . Obama won single women by a whopping 36 percent.[9]

What the commission dared *not* say revealed the deeper divisions within the party. It did not identify which "certain social issues" were turning off younger voters and single women. They did not mention their positions against abortion (even for rape victims), same-sex marriage, climate change, or even evolution, as nothing *could* be said that all the major factions within the party would agree on.

For Republican leaders—if not their base—the least contentious way out of their demographic predicament was immigration reform, which would allow the GOP to once again capture the 30–40 percent of the Hispanic vote they'd enjoyed during the Reagan years and in 2004 with George W. Bush. Had Romney received 40 percent of the Hispanic vote, his strategists concluded, he could have carried Florida, Virginia, Ohio, Colorado, New Mexico, and Nevada.

Immigration reform would also buy them time to deal with conflicts over even more divisive issues like gay marriage, abortion, and sex education. And it was no small point that Sheldon Adelson, the Kochs, and the majority of the biggest donors were supportive of immigration reform. So were the National Chamber of Commerce, Rupert Murdoch, Grover Norquist, and major Catholic and evangelical groups.[10]

The big obstacle to bringing back Hispanic voters, of course, was the anti-immigration voters the party depended upon to win. The party had tried—and failed—to pass immigration reform in 2005, and Mitt Romney had won the 2012 primary by campaigning against citizenship or any regular status for undocumented people living in the United States. "Part of the party knows exactly who they are," warned Republican pollster Steve Lombardo, "and they don't want to move from a very rigid and defined identity."[11]

The Koch Network

While the Koch network agreed with the GOP establishment in supporting immigration reform, there was a limit to their loyalty. They had no interest in adapting their goals to help the party if it meant spending $50 million on a compromise or accepting new taxes as part of a grand bargain. "Our mission is to advance a free society that helps people improve their lives," said Marc Short, the president of the nonprofit group that ran the Koch network, "not to prop up or defend the Republican Party."[12]

The brothers' network was developing all the organizational, technical, policy, recruitment, fundraising, and turnout capacities of a political party. Their projected budget for the 2014 midterms was $125 million—more than the combined 2012 fundraising totals for the House and Senate Campaign Committees of either party.[13]

The Republican Party did not have the Kochs' financial power, speed, or ability to spend millions at the drop of a hat, and the Kochs were not about to sit idly by if any politician defied their issue positions. They were not interested in a bigger tent if it meant diluting their definition of pure conservatism.

The RNC report acknowledged the danger of so much power concentrated in a few hands, but there was nothing the party could do. Steve Schmidt, a veteran of several Republican administrations and a key member of the 2008 McCain team, was frank about the effect of hugely wealthy donors turning presidential campaigns into "an ideologically driven ecosystem . . . If you have a single person responsible for your nomination, you owe them every-thing." Needless to say, that was the whole point.[14]

While the Kochs lost nationally in 2012, their deep pockets and the ability to deploy their money and staff rapidly produced breakthroughs with long-term benefits. They moved far ahead of Democrats in state after state thanks to a program called REDMAP, which helped fund efforts to take control of state governments and state supreme courts. This bottom-up approach not only benefited the party on the state and local levels, but also had gigantic—and lasting—implications for national races down the line.

Once a decade, legislative maps are redrawn in most states based upon the US Census results. By investing in staff and technology to take advantage of all Republican legislative successes in 2012, the Koch network caught Democrats napping and delivered a gift that would keep on giving for the next ten years: complete control of redistricting—and therefore, more favor-able electoral boundaries—in states with four times as many total electoral votes as those controlled by Democrats.[15]

The Kochs had spent hundreds of millions of dollars on turning the GOP 180 degrees on climate change and creating an infrastructure to train and guide many of the Tea Party organizers. They spent untold millions on influencing state legislation to limit restrictions on the energy industry, and many more millions on foundations and think tanks. Dollar for dollar, the $30 million spent on REDMAP was their most effective investment. Before the McCain-Feingold reforms, the DNC and the RNC would have been deeply involved with—and influential in—redistricting. Now, compared to the Koch network, the state party organizations were underfinanced and behind the technology curve.[16]

At the same time, the Kochs moved to find higher-quality conservative candidates—with fewer foot-in-mouth problems—to finally knock the Democrats out of their Senate majority. In 2012, as in 2010, certain Republican Senate candidates lost winnable races due to offensive comments. Richard Mourdock and Todd Akin, both running in solidly conservative states with strong religious traditions, caused migraines for Republicans nationwide when they waded into the question of whether abortion should be allowed in cases of rape. Mourdock opined that any pregnancy resulting from rape was "something that God intended," while Akin pushed back against the premise of the argument altogether, claiming that "[i]f it's a legitimate rape, the female body has ways to try to shut that whole thing down."[17] (Comments like these prompted Karen Hughes, a counselor and communications director for former president George W. Bush, to write, "If another Republican man says anything about rape other than it is a horrific, violent crime, I want to personally cut out his tongue."[18])

To find better candidates, the Kochs decided to devote more resources to Senate primaries and added a new organization to their network to train and groom candidates. Then they brought six of the most promising to meet with major donors—one of whom, a little-known state representative in rural Iowa named Joni Ernst, likened the training and network exposure she received to Eliza Doolittle's transformation.[19]

At the 2013 meeting of their network, they held sessions for donors on how to defeat candidates from the rowdier Tea Party groups who were likely to lose in a general election or make progress even harder to achieve in Washington if they did get there.[20] The Koch brand was becoming toxic to Democratic activists, but the intricate ways donors could legally move money and hide donors' names (and motives) from voters gave the Kochs an important advantage over past political hit-and-run groups. As Nick Confessore explained:

> Not unlike a political version of Cayman Islands banks, the networks allow political strategists to sidestep regulations and obscure the source of funds. Campaign contributions that would be banned or restricted in one state can be sent to a state where the rules allow money to flow more freely, often scrubbed of the identity of the original donor. Some groups work behind

the scenes to orchestrate "money bombs" of smaller contributions from hundreds of different donors, allowing the groups to provide candidates with large doses of cash—fingerprint-free—even in states with low contribution limits.[21]

The Republican Congressional Retreat

Chastened by the damage the Ryan budget had caused in the last election, Speaker John Boehner and his leadership team tried to convince their colleagues to repair the party brand and help elect a Republican president in 2016. That meant convincing the Tea Party class of 2010 that more than just total opposition to Obama was necessary.

The 2013 Republican congressional retreat featured a dinnertime speech titled "Using Adversity to Our Advantage by Working Together," delivered by Erik Weihenmayer, the first blind man to scale the peak of Mount Everest. The Republicans' problems were even more basic than that; they couldn't agree on what their goals were. Paul Ryan, Eric Cantor, and Kevin McCarthy—the much-heralded Young Guns—now looked like the gang that couldn't shoot straight.

Congressional representatives, particularly those from the South and rural areas, worried more about primary challenges from the right than about winning the November general election. After the 2012 election, 98 of the 234 Republicans representatives in Congress, or 42 percent of the Republican caucus, were from the eleven former Confederate states and leaned conservative on both social issues and domestic spending. (See Table 3.)

Once again, the Republican leadership called for patience to avoid getting bogged down in unwinnable fights, or obstructing proposals like immigration reform. A chastened Ryan warned that Obama would "try to get us to fight with each other—to question each other's motives—so we don't challenge him. We have to be smart. We have to show prudence."[22]

Still, congressional posturing continued. In an unusual New Year's Day session, after twenty years of blocking any tax increases whenever they were the majority congressional party, Republicans had to let Boehner send a bill containing a tax increase to the floor. Ryan joined Boehner in voting for the bill, but Cantor, McCarthy, and two-thirds of House Republicans voted no. The bill passed because 90 percent of the Democrats backed the president. Once again, Cantor had protected his connection to the economic conservatives and let Boehner take the heat.[23]

The Tea Party class of 2010 still believed that Congress had the power to force the president to veto his signature accomplishment, the Affordable Care Act, by threatening a government shutdown—despite the damage the last showdown had done to their party. The respected political analyst Charlie Cook warned them that, without compromise, it would be hard to win a Senate majority. They were undeterred; protecting their standing at home and avoiding primary challenges was more important than winning the Senate or the presidency.

The result was the growth of a "Vote No and Hope for Yes" coalition, a group totaling one hundred Republican House members. They regularly voted against debt ceiling legislation and other necessary but unpopular bills, while hoping or praying the legislation would pass anyway and prevent certain disaster. There was no easy way to persuade them that not defaulting on the debt was more important than stopping Obamacare or defunding Planned Parenthood.[24] Gingrich sounded the same theme to the party throughout the year. Repealing the ACA alone was inadequate: "We have to be able to explain to people what we would do to make your life better," he said.[25]

Obamacare was no longer a promise; it was a reality. Tea Party members could not offer a conservative alternative because the ACA itself was a conservative plan. There was no way to guarantee insurance to persons with preexisting conditions unless there was a mandate. But "attacking Obamacare worked at election time," so they were willing to perpetuate the "fiction."[26]

From the perspective of many representatives, this relentless opposition paid off better than party building, even if it did grievous damage to their party's presidential candidates. As Republican pollster and strategist Bill McInturff pointed out, presidential politics were relatively insignificant to most of them. They cared more about electing governors and scoring good talk radio coverage than they did about electing a Republican president. Governors who controlled redistricting after the 2010 census could give them safer districts, and talk radio loved absolutist, no-compromise stands.[27]

Senators

The disarray in the Senate was growing. Republican senators from battleground states—particularly states with large urban areas—had to find ways to defeat primary challengers from the right without alienating the moderate Republican women they would need in the general election.

Republican senators were uncertain how much power the Tea Party and groups like the Club for Growth, FreedomWorks, and the Koch network had, and which incumbents they would attack next. What position on which issue might next become a sign of inadequate conservatism?

The defeat of an ordinary United Nations Convention—one identical to the law of the land—showed how nervous even the most experienced, popular senators were. In December, the former Senate leader, presidential nominee, and World War II veteran Bob Dole visited the Senate to make a plea for passage of the United Nation Convention on the Rights of Persons with Disabilities, which every American veterans' group, from right to left, overwhelmingly supported.

The innocuous treaty, modeled on existing and entirely noncontroversial US disabilities laws, was denounced by Rick Santorum and Glenn Beck as "a United Nations world-government conspiracy to kill disabled children." After that onslaught, only eight Republican senators (none of whom represented a Southern state) voted for the treaty. It did not pass.

Even Lamar Alexander and Lindsey Graham, two sophisticated senators with international perspective, voted against the treaty; both were up for reelection in 2014 and were unwilling to challenge the deep-pocketed Heritage Foundation or local Tea Party groups.[28]

Most of the GOP's victorious senators, like the representatives, took solace from what Ramesh Ponnuru, a senior editor at the *National Review*, described as "pleasing illusions." "They knew that Romney lost, and they knew that they won," Ponnoru wrote, "and that was about all they knew."[29] They blamed Romney for not being conservative enough, which was comforting—and wrong. Romney received more votes statewide than twenty-five of the thirty-three GOP candidates running for the Senate; only one Republican senator, Dean Heller in Nevada, won in a state that Romney lost.

Governors

Republican governors were paying a steeper price for their party's unwillingness to deal with the growing number of people needing assistance to survive. Unlike congressional representatives, they couldn't pass the buck; they had states to run, and budgets that included education, public safety, health, transportation, and parks. Thanks to the Great Recession of 2008, wage stagnation and unemployment were cutting state revenues, and the National Home Price Index was down more than a third since 2005. The working poor were losing ground economically.[30]

Republican governors were also dealing with their party's cuts in federal spending on healthcare, education, highways, and infrastructure. They needed disaster relief from FEMA to manage their responsibilities, in direct contrast to House members who could duck blame for the details buried in a budget like Ryan's.

Republicans, in the words of Louisiana governor Bobby Jindal, had to stop being "the party that simply protects the rich so they get to keep their toys," and start addressing the problems of ordinary people. But the party could do little if the rich were willing to spend a lot of money on primary challenges to Republicans who wanted other people to be able to afford any toys.[31]

Tennessee governor Bill Haslam tried to explain to representatives how much trouble governors like him had with unemployment, declining wages, and reduced taxes. He didn't get very far, because he couldn't protect most of them from primary challenges. "If you're in a seat that's 80 percent Republican, you don't see the pendulum swinging by very fast," he said.[32]

Nine Republican governors—even some that had been invited to meetings of the Koch network—began laying the groundwork to work with the Obama administration and participate in the Medicaid expansion of Obamacare, in some cases over the opposition of Republican-controlled state legislatures.[33]

Ohio governor John Kasich was willing to defend his action before the wealthy donors of the Koch network. Invited to speak to them after the Medicaid expansion began, he told the crowd exactly what he had been saying in Ohio in public:

> I don't know about you, lady. But when I get to the pearly gates, I'm going to have an answer for what I've done for the poor . . . I know this is going to upset a lot of you guys, but we have to use government to reach out to people living in the shadows.[34]

Twenty Koch donors walked out on Kasich. He was never invited back.[35]

In a further sign of Republican apostasy, governors wanted to require online giants like Amazon and eBay to pay state sales taxes. Small businesses everywhere saw people who would come in, look at merchandise, and then order online to avoid sales tax. Tea Party senators, under pressure from small businesses, were willing to buck Grover Norquist and outside money groups when they had strong support at home. The governors' argument—that taxing Internet sales was not a new tax at all, but simply ending tax avoidance by online shoppers—started to gain currency.[36]

Many governors were willing to go even further, including tax increases in any bargain to cut the growing cost of entitlements. People were hurting, millions had lost their jobs or homes, and wages were down. The pressure to raise the quality of life in their states, including through tax increases, was on.

Rubio versus Cruz

By election night in 2012, candidates were already laying down markers for 2016. Two of the most prominent were Florida senator Marco Rubio, elected in 2010, and newly elected Texas senator Ted Cruz. Both knocked off establishment favorites in their Senate primaries, both were Cuban Americans, and both had been supported by Tea Party organizations. Other than ambition, they had nothing else in common.

Rubio wanted to repair the breach in the party and expand support among younger voters and immigrants. Cruz wanted to widen the breach and persuade Tea Party supporters and evangelicals that he could deliver more for them than anyone else by avoiding compromises and bipartisanship.

Cruz was one of the few politicians championed by the Tea Party and religious right who had political and intellectual accomplishments of the highest order—including a Supreme Court clerkship with Chief Justice William Rehnquist and, as Texas solicitor general, several victories in defense of social conservatism before the Supreme Court.

He was the first person with the oratorical skills and intelligence to exploit the new possibilities available to a ruthless senator. His strategy took advantage of the ways that campaign finance reforms had weakened party leaders in the Senate and House. He planned to promote himself at the expense of the party, using tactics that had not been available to past senators running for president.

Cruz's goal was to win the presidential nomination by becoming, literally, a party of one. His strategy depended upon Republican legislative failure. Passing any legislation requires compromises—what Jim DeMint had reviled as diluted conservatism.

Rubio wanted to raise his profile by resolving the immigration impasse. No one thought that persuading anti-immigration voters would be easy. His strategy required legislative success, and that depended tactically on a party establishment still influential enough to help him.

On February 7, 2013, a month before the RNC released its report highlighting the importance of winning back Hispanic voters, *Time* magazine's cover was a portrait of Marco Rubio. The optimistic headline emblazoned across the page read, "The Republican Savior." Pro-immigration-reform Republicans were counting on the Florida senator to break the immigration stalemate.[37]

Nine months after Rubio graced *Time*'s cover, the magazine named Cruz one of ten finalists for the 2013 Person of the Year, an honor eventually given to Pope Francis.[38] *Time* stated:

> Love him or hate him he is a vision of the future. . . . The faux filibuster to "defund Obamacare" waged by [Cruz] made him so unpopular with his fellow Republicans . . . that they might have made him walk the plank—except that the GOP's approval ratings were sinking so fast that even the plank was underwater.[39]

Marco Rubio: A Leader, Not a "Sombrero on the Elephant"

Even before he reached the Senate in 2010, Marco Rubio was a national asset to his party. In 2005, when he became the first Cuban American Speaker of the Florida House of Representatives, the Voice of America, the overseas news service of the US government, beamed his speech around the globe.[40]

Rubio was prized for his oratory and ability to make conservative values come alive through his biography. Dan Gelber, then the Democratic Party's minority leader in the Florida Legislature, had a saying about Rubio's sincerity and impact on crowds: "Young women swoon, old women pass out, and toilets flush themselves." When the two men made their farewell addresses to the state legislature on the same day, Gelber was stunned to see his wife weeping during Rubio's story of his life in America as a first-generation Cuban American.[41]

From early in his career, the Republican elite had high hopes for Rubio. During his 2010 Senate run, the Conservative Political Action Conference (CPAC) named him a keynote speaker. (In contrast, when Ted Cruz ran for the Senate in 2012, he was invited to CPAC only to introduce Donald Trump.) Shortly after Rubio was sworn in as a senator, he was invited by Nancy Reagan to speak at the Reagan Library. After his speech, Republican insider and intellectual Jack Pitney sang his praises: "Two words: vice president." To Pitney, Rubio seemed "a serious policy maker," as opposed to "the warm-weather version of Sarah Palin."[42]

Kevin Madden, a long-time Romney insider, was just as positive: "He's someone with an Hispanic heritage who's beloved by the conservative base of the party and he has been elected statewide in a crucial electoral battleground." Both Karl Rove and Mitch McConnell unsuccessfully urged the Romney campaign to select him for vice-president.[43]

As soon as Romney conceded in November 2012, Rubio called on his party "to broaden their tent and improve their outreach . . . to people in minority and immigrant communities who are trying to make it." He didn't intend to become a token Latino, the person whose name appeared on everyone's vice-president list in order to prove the party was inclusive. He understood, as a Latino strategist told Jonathan Martin, that simply "putting a sombrero on the Republican elephant" wouldn't solve the party's problems.[44]

Rubio saw himself as a bridge between the establishment and the anti-immigration, anti-government Tea Party, and he was wary of absolutism. When he got to Washington, he kept links to the Tea Party but avoided their extreme demands. When pressed to join the Senate's Freedom Caucus, Rubio diplomatically declined; if the Tea Party were captured by politicians, he explained, "[i]t's gonna lose its effectiveness . . . the real power of the Tea Party comes from its ability to drive the debate and the issues from the grassroots up, as opposed to from the politicians down." When Cruz, already known as a Tea Party hardliner, made several pilgrimages to Washington to seek endorsements for his 2012 Senate race, Rubio made sure he was always busy, and had his staff meet with Cruz instead.[45]

Many of the leaders and senators from states with large Hispanic populations wanted a conservative solution to the immigration impasse, and that had always been part of Rubio's appeal. If he didn't push for inclusion, he would lose much of his value to the establishment and most major donors. Since he had championed a way for undocumented immigrants to remain in the US without citizenship, he could never be considered an absolutist against immigration reform; he had to find a way to convince hardline opponents of reform that some form of legal status was better than the current "de facto amnesty" status of 11 million undocumented immigrants.

By the end of 2012, Rubio was the biggest draw in the Republican Party. He was tapped to deliver their response to Obama's 2013 State of the Union Address, as part of an attempt to repackage their identity before they had even changed their policies. Rubio's message was that the Republican Party was not solely the party of rich white guys. "I didn't inherit any money from [my parents]," he said, "but I inherited something far better—the real opportunity to accomplish my dreams."[46]

Sen. Ted Cruz, R-Tea Party?

After Ted Cruz's Senate victory speech in 2012, reporters wondered whether he would be "Sen. Ted Cruz, R-Texas, or Sen. Ted Cruz, R-Tea Party." His victory was hailed as an eleven on a ten point scale: the Tea Party's first "ready for prime time" senator. He had taken on one of the most powerful state-level Republican establishments in the country—and won.

In the bloody 2012 Senate primary between Cruz and Lieutenant Governor David Dewhurst, the Texas establishment—Governor Rick Perry, Senators John Cornyn and Kay Bailey Hutchison, and all but one Republican state senator—endorsed Dewhurst, who spent more than $25 million of his personal fortune in the primary. Cruz, who had never held elected office, was supported by the Tea Party, the Club for Growth, Freedom Works, and iconic figures from the Goldwater and Reagan campaigns like Phyllis Schlafly, Edwin Meese, and Richard Viguerie.[47]

After Cruz defeated Dewhurst, the establishment endorsed him, but he offered them no olive branch. His gratitude was instead directed to Sarah Palin, Senators Jim DeMint, Rand Paul, and Mike Lee, and Fox Network commentator Sean Hannity.[48]

No one boasted more of ideological purity—and was more "obviously tactical"—than Cruz, who was "always maneuvering to stay at the front of the parade." One of his favorite lines to contrast his political courage with the fecklessness of other politicians was, "We were all taught in biology that invertebrates can't walk upright, but politicians disprove that every single day."[49]

Cruz refused to tell reporters if he would support his fellow Texan senator for a Senate leadership position. Asked whether he considered Cornyn a warrior against federal spending, he damned his colleague with faint praise, saying only, "He has been an important leader."[50]

From the day he arrived in Washington, Cruz was running for president. His strategy was to dominate the Tea Party wing; work to be the second choice of the evangelical and libertarian parts of the party, pick up those voters once their favored candidates faded, and eventually go one-on-one with whomever dominated the establishment side of the party.

His father was an important player in the strategy. Pastor Rafael Cruz was a fiery orator who condemned homosexuality as a plot against the family and regularly spoke on platforms alongside preachers who called for punishing unrepentant homosexuals with death. While Pastor Cruz was drawing crowds of evangelicals, talking their talk and praising his son, Senator Cruz concentrated on the main target: Tea Party supporters.[51]

Cruz did everything he could to show that he was purer than any other Republican. His stunts put other Republicans at risk in their home states and made party leaders look cowardly. And no one could stop him. "No U.S. Senate debut in memory has so teemed with tumult and controversy," wrote the *Austin American-Statesman*'s chief political writer, Jonathan Tilove.[52]

Within six weeks, Cruz was giving speeches at Republican dinners all over the country, a beacon to activists who wanted to push the party to more combative positions. When he insinuated that former Republican senator Chuck Hagel, a Silver Star–winning veteran and President Obama's nominee for secretary of defense, might have been in the pay of Iran or North Korea, he provoked comparisons from the mainstream media to Red-baiting Senator Joseph McCarthy: "needlessly combative . . . and tone-deaf," a "swaggering piece of work," and "sweaty with ambition, devoid of charm."

Lambasted by colleagues and news media for his smears and deceptive edits of Hagel's speeches, Cruz turned the criticisms into proof he was right about Hagel: "The flurry of attacks on me has had their intended effect, which was to shift the conversation away from Chuck Hagel . . . and toward the direct, nasty, personal attacks leveled at me."

With that, the new senator went from "Ted Cruz, nuisance, to Ted Cruz, menace."[53] The fact that he had taken down the Texas establishment during his Senate run was enough to have his colleagues walking on eggshells. Suddenly, Cornyn—already one of the chamber's most conservative senators—was acting as if the junior senator was "the tail . . . wagging the dog."[54]

Cruz was setting a new, extreme standard for conservatives. James Henson, director of the Texas Politics Project at the University of Texas at Austin, saw the effect he had on other politicians: "You have a lot of incumbents who've spent their careers thinking they had impeccable conservative credentials now being called into question."[55]

While Newt Gingrich urged Republicans to find a way to replace Obamacare and Paul Ryan preached prudence to House Republicans, Cruz orchestrated loud, public fights that allowed him to show Tea Party voters where he stood. Sarah Palin, the doyenne of the Tea Party herself, praised him as a conservative so tough that he "chews barbed wire and spits out rust."[56]

Cruz followed a unique strategy of "winning by losing," hogging the spotlight as the person going the farthest and accepting nothing less than total victory. Compromises were unnecessary, always the result of cowardice or weak commitment. Such an all-or-nothing approach earned him the pre-primary support of conservative groups like the Club for Growth and the Heritage Foundation, and of billionaires like PayPal founder Peter Thiel.[57]

Senator Lindsey Graham saw "unlimited potential" in Cruz. Cruz proved he could throw a punch, and if he could "do a deal," he would earn respect. But doing deals would mean making compromises. That might make him a great senator, but Cruz wanted to be president, and compromises would be hard to sell to a Republican electorate that distrusted its leaders.[58] Cruz turned "divide and conquer" on its head, using the tactics *within* his own party, and turning every attempt by others to preserve the party's overall standing into an opportunity for self-promotion at the expense of both his colleagues and the party itself.

Before Cruz arrived in Washington, Senate Majority Leader Harry Reid and Minority Leader Mitch McConnell made a rare bipartisan deal, approved by the Senate, to make it harder for Cruz to grandstand with a filibuster on essential legislation. The agreement blocked a filibuster if both party leaders and seven members of each party opposed it.[59]

The rules change made it more difficult for Ted Cruz to prevent legislation from coming to a vote, but it couldn't stop him from going after his party colleagues. He used senatorial courtesy and parliamentary rules to force fellow Republicans to choose between following his lead or looking weak and timid by Tea Party standards. Instead of going along with compromises that protected the party's majority status (and the re-election chances of his colleagues), he introduced amendments solely to keep the culture wars alive and promote himself as the bravest of them all. And like Michelle Bachman in the previous presidential cycle, his extreme statements of popular positions forced other senators to go along.

His first move to divide Republicans for personal benefit came less than two months after he was sworn in. He offered an amendment to a bill funding the United Nations that would have prohibited US funding if any UN member state had a forced-abortion policy, and then called for a roll call vote on the amendment. It was nothing short of grandstanding: the UN has no control over the domestic policies of its member states, and Cruz's motion would have shut down the UN's peacekeeping efforts in the Golan Heights, the Congo, and Darfur, as well as the International Atomic Energy Agency.[60]

But that was irrelevant; Cruz's aim was to put senators in the position of voting for the amendment or facing attacks for supporting China's forced-abortion policy. The demagogic amendment failed, but Rubio, Rand Paul, and thirty-six other Republican senators voted for it rather than risk the sort of disingenuous, ginned-up attack usually only used against opponents in the other party.[61]

These moves won Cruz no friends on either side of the Senate aisle. "If you killed Ted Cruz on the floor of the Senate, and the trial was in the Senate, nobody would convict you," said Graham. Former Democratic senator Al Franken later joked, "I like Ted Cruz more than most of my other colleagues like Ted Cruz. And I hate Ted Cruz."[62]

But the antipathy for Cruz from the "mainstream media" and politicians from both sides of the aisles was valuable proof that Cruz was on the side of his Tea Party supporters. After seven months in the Senate, he was already organizing in Iowa, whipping a crowd of a thousand evangelical pastors and activists into a frenzy at an event. "If you're willing to help tell the story about how freedom works, how it produces opportunity," he told them, "I ask you to text the word 'growth' to 33733." The crowd "dutifully sent the text," linking them to his "uprising." Soon they all started receiving messages from his PAC.[63]

Cruz worked full-time to take advantage of those who believed the Tea Party's approach was realistic. On gun control, he said, "You don't get rid of the bad guys by getting rid of our guns. You get rid of the bad guys by using our guns." He called for a "flat tax" so that the IRS could be abolished, claimed that data showed "zero recorded [global] warming," and that climate change was a scam perpetrated by "power-greedy politicians" to impose restrictions on Americans.

Steve Deace, the most influential conservative talk show host in Iowa, frequently welcomed Cruz and his father as guests, then became an informal advisor to the senator. Like Cruz, Deace ignored the nuances of governance and despised the cowardly "girly men" of the GOP establishment.[64]

Cruz became a rock star, drawing big crowds to Republican dinners in Iowa, South Carolina, and New Hampshire. Clarity and purity on Tea Party concerns mattered more to him than any partial results. "When I'm with ya, I'm really, really, really with ya," he'd tell audiences time and again. "It ain't halfway, it ain't a little bit, it's all the way."[65]

The Gang of Eight

Democratic and Republican leaders were both eager to tackle immigration reform, which was only possible if the parties found a way to share the costs and benefits. Rubio became the key player in trying to develop a compromise; Cruz became his key opponent.

Shortly after the 2012 election, a group of senators tried to create a bipartisan immigration bill. When Rubio agreed to become the eighth member—giving the "Gang of Eight" its name—Senator Chuck Schumer (D-NY) "knew it was a big deal." Rubio became the key: the Republican who could sell reform to Tea Party activists and talk-radio stars.[66]

Rubio's best chance to be a national leader was to take an active role in breaking the immigration stalemate, even as his top advisors unsuccessfully tried to hold him back from taking on the issue. The rewards for success were immense, but the odds were low.

The most ideologically charged aspect of immigration is what to do with the 11 million Hispanics already in the United States without legal status. Many of them had children born in the United States, or children who had been born elsewhere but raised and educated in the country. Others had worked and owned businesses in the United States for over a decade; many had entered the country legally and then overstayed visas. Every year, about 300,000 children were born in the US to undocumented parents, automatically becoming citizens. By 2012, there were 4.5 million citizens under eighteen living with undocumented parents. Additionally, there were millions of voting-age citizens with undocumented family members living in the US.[67]

Regardless of party, any senator actually trying to solve the problem believed there was no realistic way forward without allowing most of the 11 million to remain in the US, either as citizens or legal residents—with or without future prospects of citizenship. Business and labor groups managed to agree on how many low-wage agricultural workers could enter depending upon the unemployment rate in the US, and nearly every senator in both parties concurred there was an urgent need for more visas for highly skilled engineers and other experts to contribute to the American economy. Even Mitt Romney in 2012, when he was attacking Rick Perry for giving in-state tuition to undocumented Texas residents, declared, "I'd staple a green card to the diploma of anybody who's got a—a degree of math, science—a master's degree, Ph.D. We want those brains in our country."[68]

The hot button issue that dominated the debate was whether those 11 million people were "undocumented," "unauthorized," or "illegal." The choice of words reflected the diversity of feelings. Even more explosive for any plan that dared use it was the word "amnesty," which amplified the fear of conservatives that it would give millions of people rights to health, education, and welfare entitlements they didn't deserve.

Any solution on immigration reform required bipartisan support—which meant, by definition, compromise. Cruz could only block compromise if the party leaders lacked the institutional power to rein him in—and the massive amounts of money now outside the party had so weakened the institutional structure, Robert Costa told Ezra Klein, that Cruz's strategy was plausible, because "leaders were at the mercy of intense minorities." Many members of Congress "live in the conservative world of talk radio and Tea Party conventions and Fox News invitations," thinking "they can achieve things in divided government that most objective observers would believe is impossible."[69]

Indeed, the week of Obama's second inauguration, Rubio had a private, unpublicized meeting with Fox News's CEO Rupert Murdoch and its president, Roger Ailes. Murdoch, an advocate of immigration reform, agreed to give Rubio's legislation a fighting chance by holding back his on-air personalities—as long as Rubio also made the case for reform with Rush Limbaugh.[70]

While talk radio had pilloried other pro-immigration politicians—like Rick Perry and Jeb Bush—Rubio was treated with kid gloves, even though he used virtually the same language about immigrants as the two governors.

Limbaugh reassured a worried caller that "Marco Rubio is not out to hurt this country or change it the way the liberals are." Hosts like Limbaugh or Mark Levin may have disagreed with the bipartisan proposal the Gang of Eight had drafted, but none of them insulted him or mocked the effort. Whether or not they wanted immigrants under any circumstances, they clearly recognized the importance of having at least one popular, young Latino senator in the party.[71]

The amnesty question even overshadowed strengthening border control. Rubio's defense against anti-immigrant hardliners was that the current system was "de facto amnesty and a barrier to accomplishing important government reforms in other areas. It is no way to run a nation of immigrants."[72]

Ted Cruz, meanwhile, dodged supporting amnesty while managing to avoid ever saying the word "deport." "I don't think the answer to our immigration problems is amnesty," he said while campaigning for the Senate. Once in Washington, his easy, absolute-seeming statement was "It's 'legal' good, 'illegal' bad."[73]

Although he diverged from Rubio in ideology and approach, Cruz was also treated delicately (albeit grudgingly) by colleagues within the party. Seldom, if ever, has a first-year senator had so much impact. If the unlikeable Cruz could rally enough voters to knock off a popular lieutenant governor in the primary of his first election, who knew what lay ahead? He had pulled off his upset while denouncing any and all legislative compromises as corrupt and unnecessary. If that message continued to resonate with voters, any politician who recognized that legislating was a serious endeavor was susceptible to defeat at the hands of Cruz, who viewed legislating as a blood sport.

Even powerful senior senators, like Cornyn—who would be up for reelection in 2014—treated Cruz with caution. For years, Texas's senior senator had advocated a "comprehensive overhaul" of immigration legislation, but he backed off rather than risk going against Cruz.[74]

Cornyn wasn't the only senator under fire. Candidates were lining up in South Carolina to go after Lindsey Graham for supporting immigration reform. The local Tea Party had taken to calling him a "community organizer for the Muslim Brotherhood." In a move timed to fuel further attacks on Graham, his former South Carolina Senate colleague Jim DeMint released a Heritage Foundation report that claimed immigration reform would cost the country $6 trillion.[75]

Despite DeMint's opposition and dubious arguments, Graham was a strong proponent of the bipartisan bill; South Carolina was benefitting from growing international and national investment in manufacturing, and Graham wanted to sustain the changes. He received cover from Ailes and Murdoch, both of whom supported immigration reform. "God bless Fox," Graham said. "Eighty percent of people [voting] in my primary get their news from Fox."

On the other side of the intraparty debate, Alabama senator Jefferson Beauregard Sessions III, named after the president of the Confederacy and the general who started the Civil War, said the Gang of Eight bill was "a kick in the teeth to decent Americans."[76]

The dispute over whether immigration reform would improve or degrade local, social, and economic life addressed what it meant to be "truly American." Sessions's remark may have sounded as archaic as his given name in much of the country, but it had support in the former Confederate states. In national surveys, 57 percent of white evangelicals felt their religion was very important to being truly American—twice the proportion for any other religious group.[77]

Closing the Window

While outside groups like Heritage Action were raising money to fight on against Obama, many conservative commentators and many of the largest donors wanted to move fast on immigration. The shock of Romney's defeat had given hope to the leaders inside and outside the party who wanted to end the impasse. Rubio and the Gang of Eight wanted to find a workable compromise and ram it through before the window of opportunity closed.

After the election, Sean Hannity told his Fox audience that immigrants were here to stay, and that once the border was controlled, a pathway to legalization was necessary: "You don't say you've got to go home." Bill O'Reilly began to follow a similar line, saying Hispanics had to be courted "to some extent" and "showing compassion towards other Hispanics is a good way to do that."[78]

Ralph Reed joined in, telling evangelicals that immigration reform was a moral issue, not solely an economic and political one. He praised Rubio's approach and reminded his audiences that "both David's palace and Solomon's temple were built with skilled artisans from Lebanon and elsewhere."[79]

Yet a successful compromise on an issue as important as immigration would make Marco Rubio a star. And that would end Cruz's shot at the nomination.

Cruz's unconventional path was to exploit the split within the party, make his colleagues look impotent, and still appear capable of delivering real change. With the full backing of DeMint, Cruz started working to block immigration reform and keep alive the battle to repeal Obamacare—with a government shutdown, if necessary.

As the eight senators crafted a plan that would be acceptable to Democrats and still attract enough Republicans to pass the Senate and have a chance in the House, Cruz teamed with Senators Jeff Sessions, Charles Grassley, and Mike Lee to mobilize opposition to any amnesty or citizenship for the 11 million undocumented persons living in the US.

Lee and Cruz were both supportive of more H1-B visas for the types of educated immigrants that high-tech industries needed and most major donors approved of. Yet they hewed close to the Tea Party by opposing any path to citizenship. Sessions went beyond opposition to amnesty, pushing for less *legal* immigration, too; he simply did not accept that immigration reform was "in harmony with the nation as a whole."[80]

The Gang of Eight knew they could not ever get bipartisan support for a bill without some citizenship, for some people, at some time. They also knew that they had to satisfy a large number of struggling white conservatives fueled by resentment for non-English-speaking immigrants who were, in their eyes, getting special help.

The final bill did have a pathway to citizenship—but not a particularly welcoming, easy, or accessible one. First there had to be major increases in border security, then applicants would have to be proficient in English, pay $2,000 in fines, and go back to the end of the line—a process that would take thirteen years.[81]

When the bill was introduced, Cruz began offering a string of amendments. One expanded the number of H1-B visas and another expanded legal immigration. At the same time, he had two amendments to show he was true to Tea Party demands: one denied access to any means-tested welfare, and the other eliminated any path to citizenship. Not one of Cruz's amendments made it onto the bill, which passed the Senate, 68 to 32, with support from 14 Republican senators.[82]

With less than a third of Republican senators willing to back the Gang of Eight bill, Cruz was earning national exposure with the anti-immigration

Tea Party supporters and setting up future attacks on Rubio for accepting eventual citizenship for some of the 11 million undocumented. The Reid-McConnell agreement prevented him from filibustering the bill, but no one could stop him from distorting it or denying that there was any need for amnesty or citizenship. At that point, the House was simply too divided and overloaded to take up any legislation as large and complicated as the Senate's Gang of Eight Bill. The representatives knew that the DeMint-led Heritage Foundation and Cruz would ensure there would be a long, bitter fight, and many of them were still reeling in the aftermath of the futile, Cruz-fomented shutdown.

Defunding Obamacare

Cruz was not finished. With Rubio downgraded from potential savior, Cruz was ready to capitalize on his praise from right-wing radio commentators. He would speak at conservative banquets, religious gatherings, and state fairs. Then he would go after Obamacare.

Cruz visited Iowa to mobilize socially conservative religious leaders; in a closed-door meeting, he lashed out at the immigration bill, quoting scripture while preaching small government. When he finished, the assembled pastors laid hands on Cruz in prayer for him—and the party. Later, over a picnic of lemonade and pork sandwiches, he talked of his pride in so upsetting John McCain that the Arizona senator called him a "wacko bird."[83]

Cruz then set off on an August "caravan" with DeMint, rallying grassroots conservatives to demand that their senators and representatives defund Obamacare or shut down the government. The Senate Conservative Fund, run by DeMint's former staffers, sent letters to voters in six states attacking senators who did not pledge to shut down the government to end Obamacare. Then, with Cruz as the main attraction, DeMint launched a nine-city tour promoting a shutdown.

As Republican senators and representatives went home for town halls during the August recess, they were hit with frenzied demands for implausible, magical outcomes. Mitch McConnell was forced to fight back, telling Kentuckians: "I'm for stopping Obamacare, but shutting down the government will not stop Obamacare."[84]

The *coup de grace* came when Cruz persuaded the House of Representatives' Freedom Caucus—forty representatives allied with the Tea Party—to refuse any increase in the federal debt limit unless President Obama delayed the Affordable Care Act for a year. Cruz assured them the Senate would support the move, and that the president would have to acquiesce to their demands rather than let the government default on its debt and trigger a financial crisis.[85]

There was never a chance that the Democratic-led Senate would actually support the House, nor that the president would accept their demands. Not even Cruz's Senate aides believed it would work. Cruz had misled members of Congress for his own advantage, and Heritage had supported him because the caravan and the shutdown were the kind of high-stakes drama that was "good for business." The minute the Republican-controlled House passed a bill defunding Obamacare, but otherwise keeping the government running for three months during negotiations, Cruz issued a press release praising the House Republicans while lamenting the Senate's lack of support.[86]

To maximize his exposure to the voters who believed a shutdown could work, Cruz staged a marathon, 21-hour faux-filibuster on the Senate floor, arguing that the Senate should defund Obamacare. It was a complete charade; Democratic Senate Majority Leader Harry Reid had already scheduled the vote and gave Cruz time for his stunt beforehand.

It was a publicity triumph for Cruz, and a massive setback for the party's national standing—as well as for efforts to dismantle Obamacare piece by piece. "The only thing more obsessive and doomed to failure in Washington than Cruz's crusade to defund Obamacare," wrote Jonathan Tilove, "is what appears to be most of the rest of Washington's campaign to demean, debunk, and destroy Ted Cruz. (Which began with Democrats, but is now especially a phenomenon among Republicans.)."[87]

Some of the senators who had supported Cruz realized that he had no endgame, no plan for what to do when Obama refused to sign legislation ending his most important accomplishment. Other senators went public with their anger at the damaging stunt. Richard Burr called Cruz's shutdown the "dumbest idea I've ever heard." Representative Charlie Dent was furious about the way Cruz risked the careers of others for his own advantage: "The problem with the tactics employed by Senator Cruz was they essentially united Democrats and divided Republicans."[88]

Burr's and Dent's criticisms were music to Cruz's ears. He was never interested in passing legislation, because 2016 was going to be a year for an outsider. Cruz couldn't be more "un-Washington" than someone outside government, Tilove wrote, "but, given that, being the most reviled man on Capitol Hill is pretty good."[89]

When Cruz met with his colleagues, it was more like a "lynch mob" than the usual session. Cruz had put Republicans from battleground states in grave danger. A former GOP national chairman, Ed Gillespie, criticized him and the Freedom Caucus for only talking about what they were against, what they wanted to block or defund. Cruz bragged about the attacks; they were proof he was doing more than anyone else to obstruct the corrupt insiders, that he was the most dangerous enemy of any form of compromise.[90]

Cruz: Mission Accomplished

Rubio lost one-third of his support in national primary polls for the presidency by backing immigration reform. Among regular primary voters, the danger signs were even more stark: by a margin of three to one, they thought the party needed to be *more* conservative on immigration, not less.[91] Although party leadership had initially sided with immigration reform, their base opposed citizenship. Cruz's line about "undocumented Democrats," borrowed from the unabashedly vocal nativist Representative Steve King, hit home.[92]

Within four months, Rubio started backing off on immigration reform, urging other senators to offer amendments to strengthen the legislation—a signal to conservatives that he wasn't 100 percent behind his signature legislative effort and that they should feel free to criticize it. He got credit from many for trying to win over the party, but his charm offensive never persuaded talk radio to go against their own audiences.[93]

Cruz emerged looking better than ever to Tea Party Republicans—his favorability numbers rose from 47 percent to 74 percent. Among non–Tea Party Republicans, his *unfavorable* ratings doubled, from 16 percent to 31 percent, while his favorable rating dropped one point, from 26 percent to 25 percent.[94]

The party establishment was so weak and unpopular with voters that Cruz actually was considered the party leader by a plurality of Republicans. A poll conducted by the left-of-center Public Policy Polling found that, after the shutdown, 21 percent of Republican voters considered Cruz the top Republican, with New Jersey governor Chris Christie at 17 percent, Boehner at 15 percent, and McConnell at 4 percent.[95]

But if voters were convinced, the money people weren't. A policy expert who ran a major Republican organization told Molly Ball that most GOP donors considered Cruz a phony:

> He knows his tactics are bound to fail, but pursues them to debase his Republican colleagues under false pretenses and endear himself to the base as the only authentic conservative. He is incapable of delivering anything but theater.[96]

In a bizarre and ominous sign for the party, a children's coloring book, *U.S. Senator "Ted" Cruz to the Future*, became a major success for its publisher, Really Big Coloring Books. It was, in fact, the company's biggest seller since its 2009 Obama book, *Yes I Did*, which sold by the truckload. For twenty weeks, Cruz's coloring book was the most popular children's coloring book at Amazon, selling 40,000 copies in the first week alone. After the government shutdown, the company added an eight-page supplement titled *Ted Saves America*.

In just one year as a senator, Cruz—the politician most responsible for the party's failure to pass any legislation, reach consensus on any issue, or expand its electoral base—had achieved the incongruous distinctions of simultaneously being the most reviled man in Washington and a role model that conservative parents held up for their children. This unlikely combination illustrated the depths of the party's crisis; an uncompromising, intolerant absolutist had persuaded many voters that his positions were, for anyone with moral courage, the obvious way forward. The bereft, defeated Republican Party of November 2012 now found itself charting a radically different course—conservative, uncompromising, and divided.

Whether the book's sales figures were "ironic or iconic," Tilove noted, they showed that the senator most prone to coloring outside the lines was now speaking to more of the Republican base than anyone else—for better or worse.[97]

4

The Great Wall of Mexico

The drive for undiluted conservatism was stifling the Republican Party and preventing any incremental progress toward conservative goals. House and Senate leaders had little ability to punish or protect colleagues funded—or attacked—by outside groups. The combination of weakened leaders and massive amounts of outside money split Republicans into permanent warfare over whose "must-pass" legislation took precedence: preventing a debt ceiling default, or somehow forcing Obama to repeal the ACA with a government shutdown that would damage the Republican brand.

The Koch network had enough clout to move congressional and Senate campaigns further to the right, block action on climate change, and thwart compromises that "diluted" their anti-government conservatism. Yet for all their money and effort, they'd failed to pass immigration reform or weaken the power of religious conservatives whose demands might repel fiscally conservative voters. Groups like the Club for Growth and Heritage Action raised money by demanding immediate, dramatic action, while sophisticated conservatives like the Kochs and their allies wanted tangible results, not just showboating that raised money without any legislative payoff.

The Koch network was ready to take the next step. Their associated organizations were planning to spend $889 million in the 2015–16 election cycle. They had expanded their organization and were poised to move from blocking legislation they opposed to passing legislation they supported. As the 2015 pre-primary jockeying began, they had built a private political army more than triple the combined size of the Republican National Committee, the Republican Senate Campaign Committee, and the Republican Congressional Campaign Committee. The network had 1,200 full-time, year-round employees in 107 field offices, and an advanced data gathering system they deployed for political candidates they favored.[1]

In the end, neither the establishment nor the Koch network exerted meaningful influence over the presidential primary; no candidate who was pro-immigration reform, for smaller government, and willing to slash entitlements would even come close to winning the nomination.

Cruz: High-Minded on the Low Road

To most Republican strategists and the wealthiest donors, the winning road to the White House was via repealing regulations and cutting taxes and spending, while minimizing the cultural issues driving away so many professional women, middle-class minorities, and younger voters. The winning road to the *nomination*, however, was through socially conservative states, and six candidates—Ted Cruz, Marco Rubio, Mike Huckabee, Bobby Jindal, former Hewlett-Packard CEO Carly Fiorina, and neurosurgeon Dr. Ben Carson—intended to keep cultural issues alive.[2]

Cruz was the first senator with the hubris, drive, and talents to take advantage of the possibilities for self-promotion opened by the changes in campaign finance and the election of an African American president. His Senate campaign endorsements came from opponents of the GOP leaders, and his core support was built on small-town and rural conservatives fearful that Obamacare was redistributing their benefits to less-deserving minorities. If he could unite the voters who supported the Tea Party insurgency in 2010 with the evangelicals who opposed abortion and gay marriage, he could win the 2016 presidential nomination.

Cruz's shutdown highlighted the erosion of Republican leadership and showed that his plan was on track. His absolutism made it easy to see where he stood. "If conservative theorists could build a cyborg in a lab vacuum-sealed against the slightest contamination by heterodox ideas," wrote David Von Drehle in a *Time* profile, "the result would be Rafael Edward Cruz."[3]

A clue to Cruz's appeal was emblazoned on the cover of *Cruz to the Future*, the bestselling 2013 coloring book, on which the senator appears next to a tree. The trunk is labeled "U.S. Constitution" and the largest bough reads, "Ten Commandments." Cruz was aiming this double-barreled message at evangelical, socially conservative primary voters—people who felt marginalized by the increasing acceptance of gay rights, changing ideas about theology and science, and surging nonwhite immigration; in other words, the exact same people who made up at least half of the voters in eleven of the first twenty primary states.[4]

In 2013–14, Cruz had supported Mississippi talk radio host Chris McDaniel in his primary challenge of the incumbent senator, Thad Cochran. McDaniel appalled many with his appeals to racism, but he also expressed the angst of certain rural, older, conservative Americans: "An older America

passes away, a new America rises to take its place.... We recoil from that culture. It's foreign to us. It's offensive to us."[5]

Cultural concerns stimulated white fright as much or more than economic
concerns did. On immigration, wrote Stan Greenberg and James Carville,
"Republicans speak literally and in graphic terms of being invaded, and the
failure to speak English makes them pretty crazy."[6] As one evangelical man in
Roanoke, Virginia, expressed in a focus group: "Don't come here and make
me speak your language. Don't fly your flag. You're on American soil. You're
American."[7]

Talk of a "Christian America" struck a chord with Tea Party supporters,
even the half of them who seldom, if ever, attended services and had weak
commitments to any denomination.[8] But Cruz's pairing of the Bible and the
Constitution particularly resonated with those who espoused an emerging
Christian nationalism. During the Clinton presidency, evangelical ministers in the Southern Baptist Convention actively promoted the belief that the
Bible should guide all public policy. This reflected a growing opposition to
the separation of church and state that journalist Michelle Goldberg also saw
among Republican representatives and senators during the George W. Bush
presidency. The idea that "biblical injunctions are more binding than secular law" was gaining support in the Republican Party and appearing in state
party platforms.[9]

By 2015, the beliefs that religious freedom was threatened, that Christians
were being discriminated against, and that racial and ethnic diversity threatened America, were motivating the political activism of a majority of evangelical ministers and was "baked into" their Republican partisanship and
ideology. Opposition to government and science—even treating food stamps
as contrary to the biblical model—reflected the merger of anti-government
movements and Christian nationalism. Now they wanted to reverse Supreme
Court rulings that conflicted with their interpretations of the Bible and tear
down the wall between *their* church and the state.[10]

"The Constitution is the secular equivalent of God," Drake University professor Dennis Goldford pointed out. "When [Cruz] talks about defending the
Constitution, it symbolically resonates with them as someone who is going
to defend the word of the Bible ... Cruz can plug in God and the Constitution
almost interchangeably. And he does." Jamie Johnson, an Iowa pastor and
state GOP central committee member, praised Cruz as "the hottest thing
right now with that 'teavangelical' nexus of Tea Party and evangelicals, limited government and the moral message."[11]

Cruz was adept at fusing conservative stances on social issues with his strict reading of constitutional law. On the campaign trail, he railed against the "judicial activism" of federal court judges who "impose[d] their policy preferences on the words of the Constitution" when deciding cases related to same-sex marriage and LGBTQ rights.[12]

Cruz leveraged his past Supreme Court engagements—including briefs he had filed to defend California children's right to say "under God" in the Pledge of Allegiance, and to block the removal of a Ten Commandments monument at the Texas State Capitol—to paint himself as a fierce defender of both the Constitution and the primacy of Christian values in the United States. A Cruz ad that ran in Iowa before the state's caucus claimed that the candidate "stood up for the Pledge of Allegiance" and the Ten Commandments. At a January 2016 debate between Republican presidential candidates, Cruz flexed his Supreme Court credentials before noting that the other candidates were "nowhere to be found" in the fight to defend the Second Amendment and, more generally, the Constitution.[13]

"Jesus loves you, but I'm his favorite"

Secular journalists, libertarians, and some Christian conservatives had a field day mocking Cruz for his rigid religious orthodoxy and for his belief that "God Wants It" was a legitimate justification for policy. The competition for the evangelical vote was turning into a bidding war between claims of what God wanted; Libertarian writer Steve Chapman predicted that Cruz's slogan would become "Jesus loves you, but I'm his favorite."[14]

In fact, Cruz didn't need to say it; his father did that for him. Once a mathematician and chemical engineer, Rafael Cruz had reinvented himself as a full-time, dynamic Dominionist who preached that the Book of Genesis mandated that "men of faith" seize power and govern by biblical principles. Before the first primary votes were cast in 2016, the elder Cruz had spoken at more than one hundred pastor meetings, many in the key states of Iowa and South Carolina. He sermonized that the Devil had "overplayed his hand" in Supreme Court decisions on LGBTQ rights and same-sex marriage. Voting "according to the word of God," he claimed, meant voting for his son: "The alternative could be the destruction of America."[15]

Cruz was well-organized and could raise the big money needed to compete in a fifty-state primary marathon. Walter Dellinger, an acting solicitor general during Bill Clinton's administration, considered Cruz "a rare talent" who could fuse "erudite constitutional analysis with politically appealing slogans."[16]

Other GOP candidates could quote the Bible and support evangelical policies, but Cruz also had an impressive string of Supreme Court victories, including a large role in overturning a District of Columbia handgun ban, and expanding interpretations of the Second Amendment to ensure the right to have a gun for self-defense. That earned him a resolution from the National Rifle Association and a lot of cash; several of the billionaires who gave him $10 million or more did so on the basis of his successes as solicitor general.[17]

In case any conservatives had missed his accomplishments for gun rights, Cruz released a video on YouTube demonstrating that he could make "machine-gun bacon" with the heat generated on the barrel of an AR-15 by firing off a long burst. Not surprisingly, he also connected the right to bear arms to the Bible. Gun ownership was not about hunting and target shooting, he said, but "about the fundamental, God-given right each and every one of us has to defend our lives, to defend our homes, to defend our children."[18]

Cruz ignored no possible convention delegate and was as creative as he was prolific in raising money. For $11,000 a person, wealthy Jews could spend the eight days of the 2014 Passover at a resort featuring internationally renowned rabbis, professional athletes, and Senator Ted Cruz. Afterward, he spent time with orthodox rabbis in New York and New Jersey, baking matzo while wearing a yarmulke embossed with his own campaign logo.[19]

Everything that threatened the nationally oriented, multiculturally inclusive goals of Republican Party elites was good for Cruz. If he could persuade voters that he could deliver limited government, restore the primacy of religious liberty over "sexual liberty," and preserve the "God-given" right to protect one's family, he had a good chance to be unstoppable with the Tea Party and evangelical parts of the base. At that point, whatever tottering, barely-alive establishment candidate remained—probably Jeb Bush—would be the last obstacle on the way to the nomination.

Fighting "Purity for Profit"

While Mitch McConnell and John Boehner worked to improve the party brand before the 2014 midterm and the 2016 presidential election, Cruz's allies at the Senate Conservative Fund, FreedomWorks, and the Club for Growth proved to be major obstacles. Like Cruz, they cared more about obstruction—mostly through blocking programs and funding primary challenges to insufficiently conservative incumbents—than they did about the party.

The financial reforms continued to widen the divides within the party. Debates that used to take place inside the party now involved moneyed groups quietly working with factions from the party, "often without the public ever knowing that the debate had even occurred."[20]

Members who disagreed with the group's demands for futile shutdowns and quixotic legislation certain to be vetoed were careful to keep their opinions to themselves. Only when Cruz's shutdown turned out to be nothing but a publicity stunt did the House and Senate leaders learn they had enough support to confront the groups.

When McConnell ignored Tea Party demands to keep Cruz's shutdown going, he expected to be attacked by colleagues and activists who thought, or claimed to believe, that Obama could be pressured into repealing his signature accomplishment. Instead, when McConnell went to a meeting of the National Republican Senatorial Committee, he got "applause and shouts of appreciation." They believed his decision was an important step toward majority status in the 2014 midterm election; ending the shutdown swung the focus back onto Obama's broken promise that everyone could keep their current insurance.[21]

Emboldened, McConnell declared war on FreedomWorks and the Senate Conservative Fund, blasting them as "traitors" seeking purity for profit. In response, the United Kentucky Tea Party derided McConnell's "Progressive Liberal voting record" and "willingness to roll over and cede power to President Obama," and withdrew their endorsement of him. But it was all talk and no action; they did not even support a candidate against him in the primary. Anyone they could find, they admitted, would be "at best another Todd Akin"—the former Missouri congressman whose controversial campaign-trail comments about "legitimate rape" had led to his defeat.[22]

Boehner, the embattled Speaker of the House, learned that he too had the support of the majority of his colleagues only at the end of the shutdown. When he told the Republican caucus he would hold a vote to reopen the government, he got a standing ovation. A month earlier, they had booed him for the same proposal. The turnaround left him thinking, "This place is irrational."[23]

After years of serving as the policy and information wing of the Republican caucus, Heritage Action staffers were alienating supporters by pushing policies that benefited Heritage fundraising and damaged the party. As a conservative aide told journalist Tim Alberta, "We can't score touchdowns on every play; our job is to put points on the board. But all they want us to do is throw Hail Marys." Dramatic headlines, win or lose, raised more money than incremental progress.[24]

Conservative members of Congress told Alberta that they "were tired of feeling threatened by an outside group that existed as a parasite living off the Republican members of Congress." The denunciations came after Heritage double-crossed their congressional supporters with a bait-and-switch move on a farm bill. Afterward, members of the Republican Study Committee (RSC) began organizing a public attack on Heritage. To quell the budding insurrection, Steve Scalise, the RSC chair, permanently kicked Heritage staff out of RSC meetings.[25]

Freedom Caucus Rises as Tea Party Organizations Fade

Once Republicans controlled Congress and opposed any and all Obama policies, it was hard for Tea Party groups to explain how they differed from the other conservative Republicans already in Congress. The Kentucky Tea Party's inability to challenge McConnell in 2014 was a dying gasp of a fading organization. Former congressman Dick Armey had been ousted at FreedomWorks, and no deep-pocketed donors were interested in working with groups that kept running candidates likely to lose winnable races while causing collateral damage to candidates in other states. The widespread grass-roots sentiments that fueled them remained, but, one by one, local Tea Party organizations closed, unable to raise money or field viable candidates.[26]

The efforts by conservative strategists like Karl Rove and the farther-right groups in the Koch network to win the Senate paid off in 2014. Well-prepared, well-financed candidates soundly defeated candidates recruited by the fringe groups, none of whom won Senate primaries. The GOP gained nine Senate seats.

Still, the end of the disorganized Tea Party groups did little to strengthen party leadership or produce positive results for the party in Washington. There was no way to stop Trojan horse colleagues from opening the gate for the obstructionists. The voters who distrusted Obama, resented programs to help minorities, and opposed immigration reform were still there for Cruz and other presidential candidates to woo. There were enough senators willing to support raising the debt ceiling to prevent another shutdown, but they couldn't stop Cruz from forcing roll-call votes designed to make him look purer and bolder than the other senators.

And Cruz now had a more formidable group to ally with in the House. As Congress reconvened in 2015, with Republicans now in control of both the House and Senate, nine of the most conservative representatives organized the Freedom Caucus. The Republican Leadership Caucus, with over 180 members, had been too big and diverse to hold together on many votes, even with Jim Jordan secretly leaking the names of waverers to outside groups who could threaten them with primary challengers.[27]

Jordan and North Carolina congressman Mark Meadows organized a smaller, far more coherent group, one big enough to block moderate legislation yet small enough to remain unified. The Republicans had a 29-seat majority in the House, but the 30–40-member Freedom Caucus was big enough to deny the party a true majority. United, they could block any bill they opposed.[28]

Money flowed into the group's House Freedom Fund. Soon, they had a major social media operation, a polished fundraising apparatus, and a press office. The more articulate among them became regulars on the major conservative networks and radio programs.[29]

Cruz was so popular with Freedom Caucus members that Democrats started calling him "Speaker Cruz." The flameout of the Tea Party as an organization did not give Boehner or McConnell more power inside their caucuses. Boehner could kick Heritage staffers out of lunches and meetings, and McConnell could denounce "purity for profit" groups, but there was little that either leader could do to control colleagues like Jordan or Cruz.[30]

Boehner Resigns to Thwart the Freedom Caucus

This far-right faction, historian Geoffrey Kabaservice observed, was "an unusual and indeed unprecedented development in the history of the party." In the 150 years since the American Civil War, there had never been a bloc concerned more about defeating moderate Republicans and blocking bipartisan compromises than developing positions that could capture the White House.

The Freedom Caucus had strict rules, and they agreed to vote as a united bloc anytime there was 80 percent agreement within the group. In the past, party leaders could threaten to withhold funds from obstructionists. Now, after McCain-Feingold and the proliferation of outside spending groups, the obstructionists had access to enough money to defend themselves from primary attacks if party leaders withheld funds.[31]

The intraparty fights between Boehner and Freedom Caucus leaders like Jordan—whom Boehner termed a "legislative terrorist"—were crippling to the House as an institution. Boehner could never deliver the votes he promised in negotiations with Obama or Pelosi. Every time he found a workable solution, obstructionists attacked him, while their allies—including the Club for Growth, Heritage's Senate Conservatives Fund, and groups in the Koch network—ran ads against the legislators who supported the compromise. "It's hard to negotiate," Boehner told Tim Alberta, "when you're standing there naked."[32]

The obstructionism was so mindless and lacking in legislative alternatives, that Nancy Pelosi privately agreed to execute a parliamentary maneuver to protect the legislative process. In 2015, Mark Meadows filed a "motion to vacate," which would depose Boehner as Speaker if the obstructionists sided with the Democrats to deny Boehner a majority. Pelosi agreed to have Democrats vote "present" so that Boehner would only need a majority of his party to quell the insurrection. "He knew I had—not his back, but the institution's back," Pelosi said. Even though his motion failed, Meadows succeeded in terms of self-promotion, earning more media coverage than any second-term representative in recent memory.[33]

The Freedom Caucus members were so determined to make waves and score a victory that they were willing to fight a battle—allegedly in the name of stopping abortion—that anti-abortion leaders begged them not to fight. In July 2015, an anti-abortion activist, David Daleiden, released a series of "sting" videos he'd secretly filmed at Planned Parenthood centers around the country that purported to show the organization selling body parts from aborted fetuses for profit.

The doctored videos could not be shown in Congress; by law, no videos can be shown in court or congressional hearings unless the complete footage is made available. Nevertheless, the Freedom Caucus wanted to use the videos as a pretext to shut down the government in order to defund Planned Parenthood (an organization that, in addition to providing women with contraception and abortion, supplies healthcare services to women who cannot afford to pay for them themselves).

A government shutdown over Planned Parenthood would have been a debacle. Karl Rove warned Republicans it was a stunt designed solely for the self-promotion of the Freedom Caucus. Carol Tobias, president of the National Right to Life Committee, considered Planned Parenthood to be "a vile organization," and she urged Congress not to hold a hearing that would help it.[34]

Congressman Mick Mulvaney knew the videos were doctored, yet he organized his fellow Freedom Caucus members to challenge Boehner to "do something" about Planned Parenthood. They told Boehner that they would not support any budget that funded even its non-abortion health services.

Boehner had one card left to play: he announced he would retire at the end of the term. That meant he could submit a bill to the floor that would pass with Democratic help, without fear of retribution from the Freedom Caucus. That defused their threat and kept the government open.[35]

The rebel representatives could still hold hearings about the videos—despite the pleas of ardent right-to-life activists—but they couldn't invite Daleiden to testify because they knew Democrats would use his appearance to highlight the missing, doctored videos. They had not even prepared well for the hearings. Rich Lowry, the senior editor of the *National Review* and a committed opponent of abortion, wrote after the hearings that

> the only thing more painful than watching Republicans not do anything about Planned Parenthood is watching them try to do something about Planned Parenthood. They gave every sign of being underprepared and overmatched.[36]

Spiritual Warfare against the Donor Class and the "Rainbow Jihad"

In politics, it is often said, if you don't have a seat at the table, you are on the menu. The religious right's issues were losing support nationally, and their political activists were determined to find a candidate that would support them inside the party.

Cruz was well placed to capitalize on their determination—they were looking for a candidate who was not only with them in the pulpit, but also capable of raising money and running a successful national campaign.

During 2015, religious activists introduced eighty-seven bills defending "religious freedom"–based exemptions from certain laws in twenty-eight state legislatures, and no candidate could offer better guidance or make better arguments for the bills than Cruz.[37]

When the GOP had first begun wooing evangelical voters, religious leaders had been the shepherds, gathering their flocks to hear Republican candidates, endorsing them from the pulpit, and earning places on party committees and presidential commissions. Their positions on abortion and gay marriage were held by a majority nationally and easy to defend. Now, in many states, social conservatives were alienating as many voters as they were attracting.

Even worse (from their standpoint), it was no longer clear that Republicans needed to support all evangelical positions to win. Cory Gardner's 2014 Senate victory in Colorado showed that a Republican candidate could move from conservative to moderate positions on abortion, gay marriage, and immigration, and still hold religious and fiscal conservatives.[38] Over half of young Republicans supported same-sex marriage, and half of all evangelicals either supported same-sex marriage (25 percent) or thought it was too late to fight the issue (25 percent).[39]

For evangelical leaders, it was now or never. They regrouped to reverse the "distortion of the political views" of the party caused by a donor class with the decadent views of "Manhattan and California zip codes."[40]

Leading opponents of gay rights were arguing that laws defending LGBTQ people from discrimination were, as Ken Blackwell of the Family Research Council wrote, "another route for suing Christians." Pastor and former Arkansas governor Mike Huckabee, preparing to run again in 2016, told pastors, "We are moving rapidly towards the criminalization of Christianity." Radio host Steve Deace, called LGBTQ activists the "Rainbow Jihad," and insisted every Republican candidate who appeared on his radio show answer two questions: whether "the sexual revolution trumps the American Revolution" and whether "someone's erotic liberty trumps your religious liberty."[41]

Tony Perkins, head of the Family Research Council and the Center for National Policy, called for spiritual warfare to save civilization. LGBTQ rights and same-sex marriage would "inevitably lead to human extinction," Perkins claimed. On another occasion, he asked, "Are re-education camps next? When are they going to start rolling out the boxcars to start hauling off Christians?"

Cruz had been courting Perkins since the 1990s, when Cruz clerked for Chief Justice William Rehnquist. Tim Alberta interviewed a dozen attendees at the meeting where Perkins's endorsement was decided. Six Republicans gave presentations: Cruz, Fiorina, Huckabee, Jindal, Rick Perry, and Rubio. Cruz won the coveted endorsement not with ideological purity, but by showing a realistic plan for winning the primary:

> The big takeaway was that he actually knew what the ask was. The others were just on autopilot giving their stump speech. . . . Cruz came in recognizing that they want to unite around one candidate, then pivoted to the argument that he was the candidate they should unite around."[42]

Confederate Flags or Factory Jobs?

In 2015, a white supremacist murdered nine African American parishioners in a Charleston, South Carolina, church, sparking movements—and counter-movements—over flying Confederate flags. The National Park Service stopped selling the flags, while groups throughout the region called on state governments to remove them from state buildings and parks.

Most Southern governors and senators supported removing the flags in order to continue attracting businesses that found the symbol repellant. As Alabama governor Robert Bentley put it, "A flag is not worth a job."[43] That may have been true for the governors, but supporting the flag was more important to the voters Cruz was targeting—most of whom were from the South or conservative rural areas elsewhere—than bringing factories to their states.

The controversy was but the latest and most dramatic example of the growing salience of racial animus. The Freedom Caucus had no qualms about taking positions that repulsed the same corporations that Republican governors were wooing to their states; three weeks after the church murders in South Carolina, they refused to support funding the National Park Service until the parks were again allowed to work with vendors that sold Confederate flags.[44]

Cruz was targeting the voters who supported the Freedom Caucus, while trying not to alienate voters outside the South. He talked about states' rights, leaving the red meat to his state campaign chairs, one of whom said the Charleston victims "waited their turn to be shot," and another who compared removing the flag to a "Stalinist purge," warning his fellow state senators that "the devil is taking control of this land." [45]

Ben Howe, a conservative blogger on the prominent RedState website, was candid about the painful changes in the party: "This isn't the most artful way to say it, but it's like, where do you go when the only people who seem to agree with you on taxes hate black people?"[46] He could have added that many of the people who had no sympathy or concern for Blacks disliked the federal government for its role in regulating business and gun control, and could avoid openly racist comments most of the time.

Systemic mistreatment of African Americans had become an ongoing flashpoint between the political parties ever since the 2012 killing of Trayvon Martin, an unarmed Black teenager, by a neighborhood watch volunteer. Protests grew after the police murder of another Black teenager, Michael Brown, in Ferguson, Missouri, in 2014. In 2015, after the Charleston church shootings, President Obama, who had long been cautious on race-related matters, condemned the ongoing murders. Conservatives accused him of race-baiting or conducting an "apology tour." Former senator Jim DeMint said that Obama "made everything a race issue" and "lit the fires" of racial discord. Tim Alberta observed that many Republicans viewed Obama's comments in support of the Black Lives Matter movement as "inflammatory if not subversive."

Racial inequity was becoming a clear stumbling block for those seeking to unify the party. Even GOP leaders like Paul Ryan and Reince Priebus, who believed that the party could not triumph in 2016 without appealing to Black and Hispanic voters, hesitated to speak openly about racial injustice, anxious that too much focus on racial inequality would detract from an overall message of American unity. Prominent Black Republicans voiced disappointment with the party's refusal to take a firm stand for racial justice; former Oklahoma congressman J. C. Watts asserted that "Republicans who ignore Ferguson . . . and Black Lives Matter are refusing to hear the depths of what people are experiencing," while ex-RNC chair Michael Steele (the first African American to hold the position) spoke of encountering, "time and again, basic ignorance among his white Republican friends about the black experience."[47]

Cruz the Unstoppable

Cruz had big money lined up and a detailed plan. In the first three months of his campaign, wealthy supporters, all billionaires, put $38 million into four

Cruz-aligned super PACs, and donors—most of whom gave small-dollar amounts—contributed $14 million directly to his campaign.

One of the super PACs released a PowerPoint about Cruz's campaign, titled "Can He Win?" The sophisticated presentation laid out his target states in the primaries, his wedge issues, and his rivals. Slides titled "The Calendar leans SOUTH" and "The Calendar leans RIGHT" signaled hard-core social conservatism and a strong anti-government approach.[48] In a presidential primary certain to have at least fifteen candidates, his combination of anti-government rhetoric and theology was a plausible strategy.

On racial animus, as on religion, Cruz was using enmity by association to show sympathy for the primary voters who most resented the racial changes under Obama. While his father preached hell and damnation for persons trampling religious liberty, Cruz allied himself with Senators Jeff Sessions and the late Jesse Helms to let local audiences know his stance. He was actively wooing Sessions, the most racially conservative senator, with whom he cosponsored a bill targeting "sanctuary cities" that did not order local police to identify undocumented residents. When Cruz talked about border security, particularly in Alabama, one of his applause lines was: "For anyone who wonders, 'Can we really secure the border?' I've got three words for you: Secretary Jeff Sessions!"[49]

In South Carolina, he went even further. Invited to participate in the Jesse Helms lecture series at the Heritage Foundation, he told a sold-out audience, "We need 100 more like Jesse Helms in the U.S. Senate." That one sentence—celebrating a man who had called the Civil Rights Act of 1964 "the single most dangerous piece of legislation ever introduced in the Congress" and claimed that every case of AIDS in America could be "traced in origin to sodomy"—was more like a loud cannon than a dog whistle.[50]

The Koch network and large American corporations wanted to stay away from the declining side in the culture wars. That meant Cruz had an advantage over Koch-backed candidates on immigration and religion, and could play to the cultural resentment of Tea Party supporters and evangelicals toward tolerance they considered anti-Christian.

The Koch brothers were sometimes described as if they were puppet masters whose machinations always succeeded. To be sure, they had major success in stopping Republican support for solar power, their climate pledge ended GOP support for addressing climate change, and they made bipartisanship a four-letter word. They'd even managed to recruit more electable candidates than the Tea Party could muster. But grass-roots opposition to immigration was too visceral for most anti-government, anti-tax legislators to follow the Koch line, and their frequent attempts to persuade activists otherwise made little or no progress.

At their Defending the American Dream Summit in 2015, the Kochs pushed hard for opening up to minorities, immigrants, and youth. The audience listened politely and clapped dutifully for the speakers, then went wild when Cruz promised that he would abolish the IRS and put its 90,000 employees on the border.[51]

In January 2015, when the Supreme Court announced it would rule on the constitutionality of same-sex marriage, many Republican governors, donors, and strategists were privately elated: an affirmative ruling would provide the party with cover to say the divisive issue was settled. As Cruz's PowerPoint noted, though, the primary calendar leaned both right and to the South.

In late March, Indiana governor Mike Pence signed a bill intended to be the crowning glory of his planned presidential run. The Indiana Religious Freedom Restoration Act allowed merchants to refuse service to gays and lesbians on religious grounds. "Tonight," he crowed, "there are 49 other governors across this country who wish they could be me!"[52]

Soon Pence was eating crow. The resulting national firestorm destroyed any chance Pence had of running for president and started a fight between evangelical leaders and national corporations. Within days, ten national conventions said they were ready to pull out of Indianapolis, the NCAA discussed moving their headquarters to another state, and NASCAR—hardly a liberal or progressive organization—announced their disagreement with the law.[53]

Cruz denounced the corporate opposition to conservative theology and praised Pence as a martyr: "The Fortune 500 is running shamelessly to endorse the radical gay marriage agenda over religious liberty, to say: 'We will persecute a Christian pastor, a Catholic priest, a Jewish rabbi.'"[54]

Cruz had launched his campaign three days before Pence signed the law, and the timing could not have been better from his perspective. Religious freedom and states' rights were front and center, and he was ensuring that evangelicals knew that he was one of them. It worked: before the year was over, he had won most of the major evangelical endorsements.[55]

Cruz had the key endorsements in Iowa: radio firebrand Steve Deace and Steve King, the most extreme of the conservative congressmen. He had been connecting with local preachers for three years, with his father working the state in his absence. The Wall Street Journal called him an "opportunistic charlatan," which probably only helped him with his targeted audience. It was actually possible that Ted Cruz was on the road to the White House. And then he hit the wall.[56]

Donald Trump, Candidate

The week after Mitt Romney's 2012 defeat, Donald Trump trademarked the phrase "Make America Great Again." He'd flirted with the idea of running for president multiple times, always backing off in the end. But he was once again preparing a run—just in case things looked right for him in 2015.[57]

Never had there been such an obvious opening for an outsider. The massive sums of money outside the party's control moved the GOP to positions that drove its favorability rating even lower than it was after the 2008 economic crisis. Mainstream Republican candidates had trouble finding an audience, and Cruz prevented party leaders from raising their standing with voters. The junior Texas senator made a national name for himself by opposing both amnesty and citizenship for undocumented immigrants, taking the luster off Rubio in the process. He had the depth and knowledge of issues Rand Paul lacked, and the eloquence and passion that Mike Lee lacked. And he used both to lead a government shutdown to burnish his name at the expense of his colleagues. The resulting intraparty paralysis allowed Trump— an actual outsider, not just a loathed and despised insider— to bulldoze the other candidates and overpower the party.

Had Trump not toyed with running so many times before, his actions after Romney's loss *might* have been taken more seriously. But few eyebrows were raised by what appeared to be another publicity stunt by the man dubbed a "sideshow" by NBC's Chuck Todd and a "serial presidential campaign explorer" by CBS News. Before he made the now-famous descent on the Trump Tower escalator to enter the race, he offered Maggie Haberman of the *New York Times* an exclusive pre-announcement story. Haberman declined; she had been part of the media circus surrounding his possible candidacy in 2011 and didn't want to be burned again.[58]

Trump's seemingly crazy antics had developed a brand name that held wide popular appeal. In 2011, Trump began a massive "birther" blitz, loudly suggesting that Obama wouldn't produce his birth certificate because he was not born in America. To those who were uncomfortable with an African American president, Trump demonstrated that he shared their unease without apology or embarrassment. He even criticized the birther label as unfair to people who didn't believe Obama was born in the country.[59] He deployed Twitter as his weapon of choice, growing his account from 300,000 followers in 2011 to 4.3 million by the time he announced his candidacy.[60]

His willingness to openly break the taboo and question Obama's legitimacy resonated with the Republican base, even if it didn't play well elsewhere. Late-night TV show hosts ridiculed him, Republican strategists and critical columnists tried to muffle him, Bill O'Reilly told him that Fox had investigated the issue and there was nothing there, and Karl Rove predicted it would marginalize him to "the nutty right."[61]

Nutty or not, the conservative fringe became Trump's private army. Trump had spent years developing an online following among disaffected, alienated right-wing conservatives, and they savaged anyone who dared criticize him. McKay Coppins learned firsthand how rabid they were in 2014, when his Buzzfeed article treated Trump's political ambitions as a publicity stunt. Trump denounced Coppins as "True Garbage," and barred him from his events in Iowa. Right-wing bloggers started to threaten and harass him, and Breitbart articles attacked the journalist, a devout Mormon, with titles like "Trump: 'Scumbag' BuzzFeed blogger ogled women while he ate bison at my resort." [62]

While his birther talk embarrassed mainstream Republicans, it didn't bother Roger Ailes enough to keep him off Fox News; one of the most popular segments on the "Fox and Friends" morning show was "Monday Mornings with Trump." It was just another example of Trump's talent for, in David Freelander's words, "jumping to the front of the parade and acting like it is where he has been all along." One of his long-time advisor Roger Stone's favorite rules, cribbed from Richard Nixon, was "The only thing worse in politics than being wrong is being boring."[63]

Political insiders thought of Trump as a self-promoting huckster or con man. His bestseller, *The Art of the Deal*, a reviewer noted, was like an inspiring and entertaining fairy tale. Former New York City deputy mayor Alair Townsend, who tangled with Trump whenever she turned down his demands for tax abatements, quipped, "I wouldn't believe Donald Trump if his tongue were notarized." But Trump's style of "truthful hyperbole" was effective with those unfamiliar with the intricacies of policy and politics. At the peak of his challenge to Obama's right to be president, 17 percent of Republican voters supported him for the party's 2012 nomination, tying him for second place with former governor Mike Huckabee, and putting him only four percentage points behind Mitt Romney.[64]

Trump later bragged about his exploitation of the fears about whether Obama was "really" American. Asked whether he had pushed the issue too far, he told ABC's Jonathan Karl, "I don't think I went overboard. Actually, I think it made me very popular . . . I do think I know what I'm doing."[65]

Trump eventually backed off from running in 2012 when he sensed that Paul Ryan's budget was politically indefensible. He correctly predicted that a popular upstate New York legislator, Jane Corwin, would lose a special congressional election because of her support for the budget, and he warned the party about cutting Medicare:

> I'm concerned about doing anything that's going to tinker too much with Medicare. I protect the senior citizens. Senior citizens are protected. They are lifeblood, as far as I'm concerned. I think Paul Ryan is too far out front with the issue. He ought to sit back and relax.[66]

Out of the race that he had never formally entered, Trump—and his endorsement—became a major prize for Romney. The conservative columnist George F. Will was incredulous that Romney could benefit from an endorsement by a "bloviating ignoramus." What voter, he asked, "is going to vote for him because he's seen with Donald Trump?"[67]

Sophisticated, principled elite conservatives like Will did not grasp how much standing the party had lost with struggling voters. His antagonism of an African American president, not to mention his television show *The Apprentice* and his famous get-rich books, gave Trump street credibility with working-class voters. Romney needed his—and their—support, and eventually beat out Newt Gingrich, Rick Perry, and several others to win the coveted endorsement. Though Romney dared not endorse or denounce the birther claims, Trump was, realistically, Romney's least-bad option for connecting with alienated, less-educated, blue-collar voters that he could not draw on his own.[68]

The Romney campaign also gave Trump a chance to meet and bond with evangelist Jerry Falwell Jr., who'd succeeded his father as chancellor of Liberty University, the largest Christian college in the country. Trump gave a convocation address at Liberty in the Fall of 2012, where Falwell publicly applauded his birther blitz. This great businessman, he told students, "handles pressure by keeping things in perspective, always reminding himself what is most important — family and God."[69]

By 2015, Trump had become an active candidate, albeit one so unconventional that his preparations were barely noticed. He kept in touch with Falwell, talked with right-wing talk radio hosts, invited conservative stars to visit him at Mar-A-Lago, and quietly started planning his move.

Trump Tower had been a regular stop on the fundraising rounds for Reince Priebus when he headed the RNC. In 2015, he noticed a change in Trump: he'd started asking pointed questions that dug into the intricacies of caucuses, delegate selection, and straw polls. After the visit, Priebus told Karen Tumulty, "I started wondering whether he was actually getting very serious about running."[70]

Trump was behaving more like a serious candidate than in any of his past trial balloons with the party, visiting Iowa and New Hampshire, paying close attention to conservative talk radio, and speaking at CPAC conferences. He accepted an invitation to speak at the 2013 Family Leadership Summit in Iowa, an important stop for any Republican presidential candidate aiming to win the caucuses in which 40 percent of attendees were Christian conservatives.[71]

Ted Cruz also attended the summit, giving Trump a chance to size up his rival. After Cruz's father covered a dizzying array of topics (including God's fury, radical Islam, Common Core educational standards, the law of the sea, and same-sex marriage), he raised the rhetoric to an even higher pitch. Gay rights was part of a plot to eliminate religion and prepare the way for socialism, Pastor Cruz preached, and "Obamacare is going to destroy the elderly by denying care, by even perhaps denying treatment to people who are in catastrophic circumstances." Ted Cruz gave a speech as passionate as his father's, calling for Christians to take the country back and end gay marriage.[72]

Afterward, Trump gave a well-received forty-minute speech. He warned Republicans about immigration reform, saying the legislation under debate in the Senate "could be a death wish" for the party. "You have to form a very, very strong barrier from people just flowing in like candy," he told the crowd. "We either have a country, or we don't have a country."[73]

Noticing how Cruz soared with the crowd, Trump recognized his opponent's potential. In his coy, indirect way, he began to insinuate that Cruz might not be eligible to serve as president. "I heard somebody told me he was born in Canada," he said. "That's really his thing."[74]

Back in New York, Trump carefully separated himself from Cruz's extreme anti-government fervor. On Fox's "On the Record with Greta Van Susteren," he again called attacks on Medicare and Social Security a fatal mistake for Republicans: "Frankly, what the Republican Party should be talking about is success and making this country successful so that they can afford certain programs that are good programs, basically. You get rid of the fraud and abuse."[75]

After his Trump Tower meeting with Priebus, Trump realized there would be a very large field of candidates. Having seen Cruz in action, he decided that he, too, would run a scorched-earth campaign. "If I were totally presidential," he told journalist Gabe Sherman, "I'd be one of the many people who are already out of the race."[76]

Roger Stone introduced Trump to Sam Nunberg, who had listened to thousands of hours of talk radio in 2014 and summarized the themes for Trump. While learning the language and rhythms of right-wing radio, Trump also delved into the growing world of conspiracy theorists. He bonded with Chris Ruddy, a Palm Beach resident and Mar-A-Lago member who founded Newsmax, a prominent far-right media corporation credited with spawning "a cottage industry of conspiracy buffs" with its lurid claims that the death of President Clinton's aide Vince Foster wasn't a suicide, but instead a murder that had been covered up.[77]

Stone's favorite line, also from Nixon, was "Politics is not about uniting people. It's about dividing people. And getting your fifty-one percent." In the art of division, few people topped Roy Cohn, the cutthroat lawyer who was the "legal hit man for red-baiting Sen. Joe McCarthy." Cohn taught Trump his "say-anything, win-at-all-costs style," and showed him "how to exploit power and instill fear through a simple formula: attack, counterattack and never apologize." Cohn had a far better student in Trump than the alcoholic McCarthy; "Donald pisses ice water," he told friends.[78]

In December 2014, Trump quietly hired Corey Lewandowski to run his campaign. Lewandowski had no national campaign experience but had been a director of voter registration for Americans for Prosperity. Just as important, he was willing to attack the party establishment, and he was ruthless.[79]

The Pied Piper versus Dog Whistles

In a primary field of competent, experienced senators and governors, how could a bullshit artist whose boasts and bluffs are beyond the usual bounds of moon-promising become a finalist in a race to determine the leader of the most powerful nation in the world? How did the person that Deborah Friedell labeled the "Tycooniest" man in the world—a cross between Hugh Hefner and Daddy Warbucks—whip a field of prominent Republicans?[80]

The answer is that Trump used his credibility as the common man's billionaire, his talent for phrasemaking, and his skill at manipulating media to promote policies that were already being advanced by conservative outlets like Breitbart News and media figures like Laura Ingraham and Ann Coulter. His savage attacks on the "corrupt" party elite and his treatment of African Americans and immigrants as "others" made it clear who he was for. And his willingness to publicly state *and endorse* the implicit goals of the voters made it easy for him to outbid the other candidates.

For years, the Republican Party had been losing ground on social issues like abortion and gay marriage. Rather than revising their policy stances to have a better shot at winning the White House—which would overtly threaten the groups to whom Republicans were beholden—they were increasingly relying on dog whistles and vilifying their opponents.

In contrast, Trump said loudly and clearly what was left implicit in the guarded and carefully evasive language of so many others. "Why use a dog whistle when you can be the Pied Piper?" said James Henson, director of the Texas Politics Project at the University of Texas. "It's clearly Donald Trump who is calling the tunes."[81]

Trump's candidacy announcement in June 2015 was well timed. He scheduled it for the day after Jeb Bush kicked off his campaign, knowing his dramatic splash would bury whatever Jeb—for whom he had a long history of animosity and contempt—would say.

There were no dog whistles in his brazen, unusual announcement speech, which was as flamboyant as it was controversial and divisive. In an astonishing "festival of narcissism," he referred to himself once every ten seconds for forty-five minutes. Trump used lines that he had been testing and refining for decades. Obamacare would be replaced with "something much better for everybody . . . much better and much less expensive." Politicians were too beholden to big donors to bring back jobs from the countries taking advantage of us—particularly China and Mexico—because "they're controlled fully by the lobbyists, by the donors, and by the special interests, fully." Other Republicans "don't talk jobs and they don't talk China. When was the last time you heard China is killing us?"[82]

The comments that resonated the loudest and longest were about immigration: "When Mexico sends its people. . . . They're sending people that have lots of problems. . . . They're bringing drugs. They're bringing crime. They're rapists. And some, I assume, are good people." The single biggest line, the one that would inspire chants at his massive and raucous rallies, was "I will build a great, great wall on our southern border. And I will have Mexico pay for that wall."[83]

After that speech, his campaign lifted off. When he announced his candidacy, Trump's favorable rating among Republicans was at 23 percent versus 65 percent unfavorable. By July, it had flipped to 57 percent favorable and 40 percent unfavorable. The Peoria project at George Washington University partnered with Zignal Labs to track all online mentions of candidates in the social media universe, including Twitter, Facebook, and millions of blogs. In the month after Trump announced, one-third of all the mentions of any candidate in either party were about him. Among only Republican candidates, he was the subject of 47 percent of social media conversations.[84]

The voters who flocked to Trump were more likely to be concerned about illegal immigration, immigrants committing crime, and the negative effect of immigrants on the economy. Michael Tesler's analysis of YouGov surveys done for the *Economist* showed that Trump was not persuading people to *adopt* these attitudes; he was persuading whites who felt victimized that he alone would do what they *already wanted*. His claim that "you wouldn't be talking about illegal immigration if it wasn't for me" was justified. After his talk of rapists and murderers, the number of mentions of the border in presidential conversations on social media doubled, from 205,000 a day to 443,000.[85]

Even with his extremely limited knowledge (or outright ignorance) of details and policy positions, Trump sucked the oxygen out of the field by connecting dots the other candidates were unable to see. He knew far less than any of them, but saw one big thing that mattered: large parts of the party's base were hurting economically, and extremely negative about Obama, but they were not against all government programs. They were most virulently against government spending when the money went to people they viewed as lazy and undeserving—which is how they viewed minorities.

He also parted with the party on raising taxes on the wealthy. "The middle class built this country, not the hedge fund guys," Trump said, "but I know people in hedge funds that pay almost nothing and it's ridiculous, OK?" It was a well-chosen target; Cruz, Rubio, and Bush had major backers on Wall Street. Bush had raised $114 million. Ted Cruz was the beneficiary of four super PACs totaling over $31 million—three of which were funded by the family of the Wall Street billionaire Robert Mercer—and his wife worked for Goldman Sachs.[86]

No other Republican dared to talk about raising taxes for entitlements. Jeb Bush's website acknowledged the last eight years had not been good for anyone but the top earners, but he talked about phasing out the current system and reforming entitlements, not strengthening the supports. Rubio championed Paul Ryan's plan to subsidize premiums. Cruz's proposals were all ways to save money: partial privatization, lowering the cost of living adjustments, raising the retirement age, and repealing the ACA.[87]

Cruz's campaign was the first to understand that Trump would be formidable. Jeff Roe, Cruz's campaign manager, realized Trump had a very high floor: while only 30 percent of the Republican primary voters had a favorable opinion of Trump, nearly all of those with favorable opinions said they would consider voting for him—an unusual result that signaled staying power. In every segment of the Republican electorate—the "liberal-to-moderates," the "somewhat conservatives," and the "very conservative"—25 to 30 percent were ready within days to consider him as their choice for president. All Cruz could do was stay close to Trump in hopes of picking up his voters if Trump crashed.[88]

Smokescreens and Flash Grenades

Trump relied on bravado, bluster, and insults to deflect attention from his inability to explain his policies. There was a method to his seeming madness. Whenever a story he disliked was leading the news cycle, he made an outrageous statement and the original story was buried.

When Senator John McCain critiqued a particularly angry and raucous Trump rally in which Trump had appeared alongside controversial Sheriff Joe Arpaio in McCain's home state of Arizona, Trump didn't back down—he doubled down. "[McCain's] not a war hero," Trump told the Family Leadership Summit in Iowa. "He was a war hero because he was captured. I like people who weren't captured." Trump apparently did not know—or care—that McCain had tried to hang himself in prison rather than shame his country by breaking to torture and making anti-American comments.[89]

After the first debate, annoyed by moderator Megyn Kelly's questions about his misogynist comments, Trump suggested she was menstruating that evening. "You could see there was blood coming out of her eyes," he told CNN, "blood coming out of her wherever." The rest of his debate performance—and those of the other candidates—were largely forgotten in the press.[90]

Slamming Kelly appealed to the latent misogyny of the party base, which already viewed Hillary Clinton as "the world's most horrible ballbuster." In fact, the line wasn't a poorly phrased, off-the-cuff remark; a close associate of Trump later confided to Maureen Dowd that Trump had practiced that line before the CNN interview.[91]

After Trump's attack on Kelly, the prominent conservative newsletter publisher Erick Erickson rescinded Trump's invitation to speak at RedState Gathering, his well-attended yearly summer convention. Erickson had given major assists to Rubio and Cruz in their first campaigns, and had no problem attacking the NRA when they were compromising instead of holding a hard line. When he criticized Trump, who he considered "out of his depth," Trump replied that Erickson was "a major sleaze and buffoon."

Laura Ingraham, Breitbart News, and the Drudge Report all piled on, while Ann Coulter noted that Erickson had once called Supreme Court Justice David Souter a "goat-[expletive] child molester." Erickson lost 30,000 subscribers the next week. In Coulter's eyes, Trump's crudeness was his fitness: "Only someone who brags about his airline's seatbelt buckles being made of solid gold would have the balls to do what Trump is doing."[92]

The week after the debate, Phyllis Schlafly threw her weight behind Trump. One of the most prominent conservatives of the past century, Schlafly, at ninety-one years of age, had lost none of the fire she displayed in 1964 when she wrote "A Choice Not an Echo," promoting Senator Barry Goldwater and lambasting the "kingmakers" from Madison Avenue and Wall Street who had pushed aside Senator Robert Taft for General Dwight Eisenhower in 1952. The woman who had single-handedly turned the tide on what appeared to be certain passage of the Equal Rights Amendment, and then led attacks on Hillary Clinton in 1992, was telling her national audience that Trump's ideas about immigration were "constitutionally sound." As she praised Trump for driving the debate with blunt talk, saying, "A nation without borders is not a nation," she dismissed Marco Rubio out of hand for making a statement in Spanish on Univision. "Why," she asked, "should we have to get somebody to translate his remarks into English?"[93]

Revealing Not Hardening

When the *New York Times* headlined a Jonathan Martin story titled "Republicans Fear Donald Trump Is Hardening Party's Tone on Race," *Wonkette* editor Ana Marie Cox tweeted, "I didn't know 'revealing' was spelled h-a-r-d-e-n-i-n-g." With his genius for using the press, honed over years of daily fussing and feuding with New York tabloids, Trump was merely recycling the positions of other Republicans—particularly Cruz—with catchier slogans and the credibility of "the people's billionaire."[94]

Trump simply reflected the growing racial animus in the country since Obama's election. White Americans tended to see race as a zero-sum game, and now believed anti-white bias was a bigger problem than anti-Black bias. Jeff Sessions echoed this when he said, "Empathy for one party is always prejudice against another."[95]

On immigration, Trump articulated the unavoidable bottom line of the Republican Party's immigration stand. After opposing any legislation that included amnesty for undocumented immigrants since 2005, no other candidate could discredit Trump's appealing (but likely unworkable) deportation policy without *de facto* supporting some form of amnesty.

Cruz's policy of no citizenship and no legal status for the 11 million undocumented immigrants meant that his policy *had* to include deportation. But Cruz believed saying so would mean death in the general election; he was determined to win the primaries without sacrificing the ability to talk later about a real solution.[96]

The problem was, he wasn't very good at not talking about it. During an interview on Fox News, he squirmed and twisted and avoided giving any real answers. Megyn Kelly asked whether a President Cruz would deport the American citizen children of two undocumented immigrants—a question Trump had explicitly answered. Cruz merely dodged: "Megyn, I get that that's the question you want to ask. . . . That's also the question every mainstream media liberal journalist wants to ask."[97]

Trump wasn't drawing great crowds because he had new positions on immigration, Muslims, Iran, Russia, or mainstream media. His core positions on all these issues had been advanced by other candidates. Trump, however, was an outsider untarnished by more than six years of unfulfilled promises to end Obamacare. He differed with all the other candidates on how far he promised to go for social conservatives, and he was the only candidate pledging to strengthen Social Security and Medicare even if it meant raising taxes. Trump calling immigrants rapists and murderers echoed the very lines Arizona governor Jan Brewer used when she and others said undocumented immigrants were a source of beheadings, kidnappings, and police killings. When he called for troops on the border, he was following the lines of Cruz and Rick Perry, both of whom had called for the right to let governors use the National Guard on the border.[98]

When Trump proposed a ban on all Muslims entering the United States, he was widely condemned. But three months earlier, Cruz had said that Muslims fleeing persecution "should be resettled in the Middle East in majority Muslim countries," while the US should provide safe haven for Christians "targeted for genocide."[99]

When Trump called Obama's agreement with Iran "the worst deal I've ever seen negotiated," and promised that the deal would be broken "unless they behave better than they've ever behaved in their lives," he was following the path of forty-seven Republican senators who had signed an open letter to Iranian leaders, designed to undermine Obama. Drafted by Senator Tom Cotton of Arkansas, who had only been in the Senate for two months, the letter told Iranian leaders that the next president could redo the deal. Donald Trump, in other words, was no more lacking in subtlety and nuance and respect for the president than these senators.[100]

Trump wasn't even the first to call the media dishonest. Before "Fake News" became a ubiquitous part of the political language, Cruz attacked the *New York Times* as the "'Hollywood gossips of the Washington press corps," and called PolitiFact's fact-checking a "particularly pernicious bit of yellow journalism."[101]

Praise of Vladimir Putin had also become a common refrain among Republicans long before Trump. Obama's tolerance and gradual acceptance of LGBTQ rights was explained as a sign of the spiritual decline of the West. In contrast to the "weak" Obama, Republicans viewed the Russian leader as a real man, willing to defend the biblical family. In letters to his followers in 2014 and 2015, Billy Graham's son, Franklin, wrote, "Isn't it sad, though, that America's own morality has fallen so far, that on . . . protecting children from any homosexual agenda or propaganda—Russia's standard is higher than our own?"[102]

Even building a wall had already been proposed. At the same Koch summit where Cruz suggested putting 90,000 IRS agents on the border, Louisiana governor Bobby Jindal promised he would build a wall in his first six months, proclaiming, "Immigration without assimilation is invasion!"[103]

Trump did more than use his credibility and media instincts to sell coarser and clearer versions of old policies. He was as loud, passionate, and direct on the issues he believed his niche cared about the most—immigration, race, and guns.

But while the other candidates competed over who would fight harder and go the furthest for social conservatives—condemning gays and Planned Parenthood—Trump was comparatively tolerant. He opposed abortion, and agreed there should be no federal funding for organizations offering abortion, but he called Planned Parenthood "a valuable women's health care organization." The other candidates were condemning an organization that had, according to polls, a more positive image than either political party, the Supreme Court, or the National Rifle Association.[104]

On gay rights, the Log Cabin Society spoke of Trump as the most positive, pro-gay candidate the GOP had ever had. While he did not support gay marriage, he had contributed to AIDS research, made his swanky Palm Beach Mar-a-Lago resort open and welcoming to gays, and approved of gay civil unions. "If two people dig each other," he'd once said, "they dig each other."[105]

Cruz the Pariah

Trump's showmanship and ability to control the campaign overwhelmed Cruz's ability to command the spotlight and dominate his rivals. Sensing that Trump wouldn't burn out, Cruz made a bold, desperate move to reclaim his self-proclaimed mantle as the bravest and toughest conservative. He twice tried to force government shutdowns, once over government funding for Planned Parenthood, and once over keeping sanctions on Iran until that nation recognized Israel.

One of the bills he tried to block, the Highway Bill, was so important and complex that there had already been bipartisan agreement that no amendments would be accepted. When Cruz tried to amend the bill with Iran sanctions—an act that would cause havoc with the futures of many senators who knew Obama would veto any bill with that amendment—his move was ruled out of order by McConnell. At that moment Cruz unleashed a tirade the likes of which are seldom if ever uttered in the US Senate:

"What we just saw today was an absolute demonstration that not only what [McConnell] told every Republican senator, but what he told the press over and over and over again, was a simple lie. . . . Like Saint Peter, he repeated it three times."[106]

A number of senators wanted to force Iran to recognize Israel, and many wanted to defund Planned Parenthood, but no senator would verify that McConnell had broken his word. It hardly mattered: Rush Limbaugh and Mark Levin both lavished praise on Cruz. Limbaugh labeled the attack "Mr. Smith Goes to Washington-type stuff," while Levin tweeted, "Let's see how many others in the Senate have a backbone & call out McConnell."

If Cruz was considered Kryptonite by many senators after his 2013 shutdown, now he was a pariah. Senators finally had grounds to take down a colleague who had been backstabbing and undermining the others since he arrived.[107] When a senator requests a roll call on a vote rather than a voice vote, Senate rules require that one-fifth of the senators accede to the request. Normally this is pro forma; maybe it gets turned down once every four or five years. Cruz was turned down twice in the next few weeks. Senators told reporters that McConnell didn't even have to ask senators to help, so eager were they to stand up to Cruz.[108]

The Crowds that Roared—and Voted

Trump never faded after his dramatic entrance and myriad insults and outrages. His poll position was almost exactly where the Cruz analytic group had predicted as 2015 ended. In all the pre-primary polls during 2015, Trump had been favored by 3 percent of all primary voters in the first half of the year. In the second half of the year, he averaged 28.5 percent, double that of his closest rival, Ben Carson. Jeb, Cruz, and Rubio were all averaging between 9 and 10 percent.[109]

As the year ended and the candidates focused on the first critical states, Trump was flying high. Anti-spending groups like the Club for Growth were trying to take him down as a big spender with a record of flip-flops, and the Kochs were dismayed by his protectionism. But Wisconsin governor Scott Walker, the only outsider who had excited big-money donors like the Kochs, had self-destructed with alarming speed, becoming the first candidate to drop out.

The last hope of the establishment, Jeb Bush, had made no headway anywhere. Only four months after he entered the race, the *National Review* declared in a headline that "Jeb Bush is Toast." Journalist Lawrence Brinton noted that while Bush had $109 million from big donors in his campaign and super PACs, he had "a near-complete lack of support from the GOP's rank-and-file donors." Based on big and small donors, the candidate in the best shape was Cruz; he was second to Bush in big campaign donations and had the most money from donors giving less than $200 dollars. Of the candidates who had been raising money, Rubio also had an outside chance, Brinton wrote, but he was careful to emphasize that Donald Trump would probably be at or near the top if he were fundraising actively.[110]

Trump didn't have to fundraise in the primary, though, because he was ratings gold for every network from Fox to CNN to MSNBC. Early in the 2016 primaries, after just two states had voted, he had received nearly two billion dollars' worth of free media coverage—more than double the total of all the other Republican candidates, and almost double that of Democratic candidates Bernie Sanders and Hillary Clinton.[111]

After three months, the Republican establishment was "thinking the un-thinkable": Donald Trump could actually win and become the standard bearer. He had changed the agenda in ways neither the establishment donors nor the Koch network had expected. Before he entered the race, the Pew Research Center reported that Republican primary voters preferred a can-didate with experience and a proven record over someone with new ideas, 57 percent to 35 percent; after Trump, they preferred new ideas over experi-ence by two to one.[112]

In state after state, Trump's crowds were bigger and louder than anyone else's. No other candidate was willing to talk about spending money on jobs and rebuilding infrastructure, or break the taboo on raising any taxes to strengthen—not privatize or limit—Social Security or Medicare, and even replace Obamacare with "something better." His direct approach to ending the immigration stalemate, support for Social Security, and attacks on glob-alization resonated with millions who had been disillusioned by Republican impotence. His vision of America turned each rally, in the words of two psychologists of leadership, into "an identity festival that embodied a politics of hope."[113]

Most conservative criticisms of Trump were for his racial attacks, his implicit support for white nationalists, his profanity, and his ignorance of government. More revealing was how *rarely* he was attacked for vowing to strengthen Medicare and Social Security, or to replace Obamacare with "something better." One of the early acknowledgements of this fact was by *National Review* editors Rich Lowry and Ranesh Ponnuru:

> A Republican party that promised fewer tax cuts for the rich and less cheap labor would have less to offer some of its top donors, but it would have a stronger connection to its voters.[114]

In New Hampshire, a key state for Jeb Bush if the establishment candidate ever were to have any chance, one of Trump's rallies outdrew Jeb Bush's neighboring rally by a factor of ten.[115]

In Iowa, Trump told a crowd, "I could stand in the middle of Fifth Avenue and shoot somebody and I wouldn't lose any voters." While the mainstream media was distracted by that bombastic smokescreen, he made his appeal to small-town social conservative voters in Sioux Center, Iowa, a town with nineteen churches and 7,500 people: "Christianity is under tremendous siege, whether we want to talk about it or we don't want to talk about it," said the man who had just bragged about his ability to murder someone without consequences. "You're going to have plenty of power, you don't need anybody else. You're going to have somebody representing you very, very well. Remember that."[116]

A week later, Trump arrived at the State Fair in his big helicopter, where a crowd of thousands had been lining up for hours to greet him and hear his speech. As the Iowa caucus grew nearer, vendors were selling so many Trump hats, buttons, T-shirts, and memorabilia that they stopped carrying other candidates' paraphernalia.[117]

In Alabama, Cruz had chairpersons in every county and an elaborate booth at the Alabama-Auburn football game, Alabama's biggest sporting event. But Trump drew the biggest crowd for a candidate in decades: thirty thousand people came to hear him speak. After Trump thrilled the crowd by flying low over the stadium in his private jet, they heard Senator Jeff Sessions, wearing a Make America Great Again hat, praise Trump for his stand on immigration.[118]

In the last two weeks before the Iowa caucuses, Trump's relationship with Falwell yielded fruit. Trump wasn't "a puppet on a string like many other candidates who have wealthy donors as their puppet masters," Falwell told his students. "Donald Trump lives a life of loving and helping others, as Jesus taught in the New Testament." The next week, he gave Trump his endorsement.[119]

Russell Moore, a theologian who headed the Ethics and Religious Liberty Commission of the Southern Baptist Convention, was incensed by Falwell's praise of Trump. "Evangelicals can love a golden calf, as long as Aaron promises to make Mexico pay for it," Moore tweeted, leaving little doubt that he believed Falwell was endorsing Trump for self-advancement, not for religion or morality.[120]

Even so, Cruz's three years of campaigning in Iowa, harvesting phone numbers from pastors, and the visits from his father carried him to a narrow victory over Trump, 27.6 percent to 24.3 percent, in the Iowa caucus. Trump then lapped the field in New Hampshire, winning 35.7 percent of the vote, to John Kasich's 15.7 percent and Cruz's 11.6 percent.

South Carolina was once again ground zero for the Republican nomination. Cruz's campaign was now relying on the religious right to do for him what they had done sixteen years earlier for George W. Bush. Cruz had reason to be optimistic. The NBC-*Wall Street Journal* national poll four days before the primary had Cruz ahead of Trump (though within the margin of error) for the first time, 28 percent to 26 percent—a dramatic swing from one month earlier, when Trump had led Cruz 33–20.[121]

Rubio and Cruz were vying to become the last alternative to Trump in the primary. When Republican primary voters were asked how they would vote if the only candidates were Cruz and Trump, Cruz would win 56–40. Marco Rubio was behind both Trump and Cruz nationally, but in a two-man race, he would also beat Trump, by nearly identical numbers. That forced Cruz to spend almost as much time fighting Rubio as going after Trump.[122]

Most of the national figures in the Republican Party thought Trump was a dangerous candidate who would set the party back many years. But at least 30 percent of all Republican voters thought Trump was the breath of fresh air and passion the party needed. Anyone who went after Trump, therefore, risked alienating his supporters, without whom they couldn't win either. It may have been time for all good men to come to the aid of their party, but without a way to compel unified action by all the Trump rivals, everyone was reluctant to sacrifice their chance to become president for the sake of the party by going first. In the eight months from the day Trump entered the campaign until the South Carolina primary, only 4 percent of the $215 million super PACs spent on ads, mailings, and calls was aimed at Trump.[123]

The night before the primary, Cruz received a rousing reception at a convention hosted by radio commentator Mark Levin's *Conservative Review*. Levin introduced Cruz with a video in which Levin hailed him as "the most conservative candidate in the race," and Rush Limbaugh was shown calling him the "person most opposed to liberalism." The next day, Trump won the South Carolina primary with 32.5 percent of the vote. Rubio beat Cruz by ninety-one votes, 22.5 percent to 22.3 percent.[124]

Cruz had counted on an evangelical hierarchy with the capacity to persuade their congregations that he could roll back the clock on issues many of them were no longer willing to fight. He'd opened his formal campaign at Falwell's Liberty University, and he and his father had courted Falwell for three years. Now, after the South Carolina primary, Pat Robertson endorsed Trump on his national television network, telling Trump before his national audience, "You inspire us all." It was a painful irony for Cruz. He had won the endorsement of many top evangelicals by advancing himself at the expense of his Republican colleagues; now those same evangelical leaders, with large businesses to protect, were advancing themselves at the expense of the collective religious good—and Cruz's campaign.

As the primary continued, Cruz won eleven states, enough to become the only plausible alternative to Trump. But it wouldn't be enough to catch up with the candidate who'd adopted Cruz's own scorched-earth strategy, and then proceeded to turn up the flames. In the choice between Cruz and Trump, it came down to politicians' fear of the consequences for supporting the former over the latter. While they hated Cruz, Senator Lindsey Graham explained, "They're afraid of Trump's voters. . . . If I can swallow my pride, they can, too."[125]

5

Strongmen Don't Pivot

As the primary season was ending, Donald Trump was irritated: why wasn't the Republican Party treating him as a hero? In his mind, his greatness was obviously without equal. He had rescued the GOP, drawing record numbers of voters to the polls and setting ratings records for the debates in which he appeared. With his marvelous slogans and catchy nicknames, he'd re-energized a party "too obsessed with ideology" to be interesting.[1]

Trump's victory was, by any standard, unprecedented. That was one of the very few things state and national party leaders, billionaire donors, legislators, and Trump himself could all agree on. Relying on free media and a very small campaign organization, the self-proclaimed "stable genius" had walked over the best and the brightest of the Republican Party. Now, he expected party leaders to fall in line behind him.

But they weren't. For the Republican leadership, elected officials, and major donors, the number and volume of the alarms he set off were also un-precedented. Trump attacked party leaders as corrupt, stupid, and weak. He used racially charged language to draw clear lines between his supporters and "the blacks" and "the Mexicans," implying that whatever their citizenship status, they didn't belong in the same way as whites did.

Most "Never Trump" Republicans—a small but steadfast contingent of conservatives who were too appalled by Trump's behavior and words to hold their noses and support him—were starting to sound like Russian nobility exiled to Paris after the Russian Revolution, working as doormen until they could reclaim their estates. In their eyes, Trump was a momentary blip, and their old ways would soon be restored. They didn't understand that his supporters had abandoned them even before Trump emerged to champion their concerns. By 2016, it was too late for a discredited establishment to roll back the clock.

For Karl Rove, the signs had been unmistakable back when Sarah Palin was chosen as John McCain's nominee for vice president:

"Everyone began to realize this woman is vacuous. . . . We went from wanting people who were experienced and qualified to wanting people who would throw bombs and blow things up. The ultimate expression of that was Donald Trump, but Sarah Palin was the early warning bell."[2]

Now that Trump was the nominee, he wanted to display his dominance over the party. He had no interest in public bargaining and compromises; his version of unity was allowing Republican politicians and party officials a chance to accept his terms. No matter what mainstream media thought of him, there was a whole online system of nativists and nationalists occupying the ideological space to the right of Fox News who were more than happy to promote Trump, unfiltered. Why compromise with the elite he had vilified and discredited before his roaring crowds?

Former GOP congressman Tom Davis attributed the party's denial of Trump's appeal to elitism and disdain for its base. The attitude of the party leaders was "we're smart, and they're stupid, and we'll just feed them abortion and guns." The *New York Times*'s Nick Confessore reached a similar conclusion: The Republican Party elite "abandoned its most faithful voters, blue-collar white Americans, who faced economic pain and uncertainty over the past decade as the party's donors, lawmakers and lobbyists prospered."[3]

Leading figures across the party had to decide how to deal with Trump. Should they ignore, defend, or criticize their nominee for president? How far did they need to go to protect the current Republican office holders, keep their donors, and remain a viable national party? They had to balance the short-term costs and benefits of offending wrathful Trump loyalists versus alienating anti-Trump voters. They also had to appraise the potential future damage to their political ambitions, and that depended upon whether he would win or lose in the general election.

A Trump presidency was inconceivable to many because nothing about him fit any images of a president; he refused to employ even the most basic platitudes that many candidates had used over time to cover up their ignorance. How could they take seriously the possibility of an event that was seemingly impossible?

And how could they take seriously the idea of a President Trump when they still did not understand his appeal to "their" voters in the first place? Haley Barbour, a former head of the RNC, viewed Trump as the voters' way of giving the party a middle finger motivated by years of overpromising. But that diagnosis ignored all the goals Trump promoted that had *never* been promised by the party.[4]

No one in either party knew how much Trump's attacks on political correctness or mobilizing of racial resentment would matter. Tom Edsall did, though; even before the voting started, the journalist pointedly pushed his readers to think the unthinkable:

How many Democratic and independent voters share Trump's implicit racial antipathy to the Black Lives Matter movement? How many worry that the police have backed off law enforcement in response to the so-called Ferguson effect, with a resulting increase in crime? And how many are offended by the concessions of university administrators to demands for speech codes, trigger warnings, "safe spaces" and even resignations?[5]

Jeff Sessions of Alabama, the one senator who wholeheartedly backed Trump, was, in the words of Philip Rucker and Robert Costa, the "intellectual godfather" of Trump's nativist populism. Thirty years earlier, in 1986, Sessions was denied a federal judgeship appointment on the basis of past racially charged statements: calling a white civil rights lawyer "a disgrace to his race," and referring to the National Council of Churches, the NAACP, and the ACLU as "communist-inspired and un-American." Now the backbencher was at the center of a presidential campaign.[6]

Racial resentment and opposition to immigration were merely the tip of the Trump iceberg. Sessions had a visceral aversion to "soulless globalism," the far right's shorthand for free trade, international alliances, and nonwhite immigration. He condemned the GOP's "Growth and Opportunity Project," with its call for diversity, tolerance, and immigration reform, as "a kick in the teeth of decent Republicans."

Sessions and Trump had bonded in 2005 when Trump testified before the Senate, ridiculing the UN's cost estimate for renovations and displaying the same disdain for the organization as Sessions. It was, the senator said, "the most impressive congressional testimony I've ever heard." Now he and his aide, Stephen Miller, were working closely with Trump and reporters from Breitbart News, fleshing out the nationalist agenda.[7]

Trump had been attacking international trade arrangements and alliances since 1987. Lest anyone think this was merely a campaign tactic, on the day after he clinched the nomination, he proclaimed that "you can throw free trade out the window." His supporters agreed with his approach; two-thirds of them thought free trade agreements were bad for the country, and 60 percent said the agreements had been bad for them personally.[8]

A Conqueror, Not a Leader

When Trump was close to securing enough delegates to become the presumptive nominee, party leaders whispered about trying to stop him short of a majority and rally behind someone more widely acceptable at the convention. Trump issued a blunt warning to them:

> I think you'd have riots. I'm representing a tremendous, many, many millions of people. . . . If you disenfranchise those people and you say, well I'm sorry but you're 100 votes short . . . I think you would have problems like you've never seen before. I think bad things would happen, I really do.[9]

At that critical juncture, Paul Manafort, a longtime Republican operative just back from Ukraine, volunteered to join Trump's campaign to manage the critical delegate selection process that Trump had overlooked.[10]

To quell the incipient uprisings before they had a remote chance of succeeding, Manafort told party leaders that Trump was simply "projecting an image" for voters and would make the customary pivot when he clinched the nomination. "The part that he's been playing is now evolving into the part that you've been expecting," Manafort assured them. "The negatives will come down, the image is going to change, but 'Crooked Hillary' is still going to be 'Crooked Hillary.' "[11]

A few days after Manafort's public reassurance, Manafort warned Trump that releasing an incendiary statement would be an unhelpful distraction. "Don't tell me how to [expletive] do P.R.," Trump fumed. Manafort quickly changed his tune. "You don't change Donald Trump," he said. "You don't 'manage' him."[12]

When the primaries ended, Trump's behavior intensified concerns inside the party. They'd ended up with an outsider who won by attacking them; now they fancifully hoped that somehow, some way, he would compromise with them and offer an olive branch.[13]

Most other primary winners move to unify the party and build bridges to opposing factions. But why ally with an establishment that had not won a national campaign since 2004? John McCain had accepted establishment demands on economic and social issues after the primaries, but still couldn't draw as many votes as George W. Bush—even with Sarah Palin on the ticket to whip up voters concerned about race, religion, and the Second Amendment. Mitt Romney couldn't win against a weak incumbent after he was forced to denounce his own Massachusetts healthcare plan, and his running mate Paul Ryan had to run away from a budget the establishment had cheered.

Trump wasn't interested in forming alliances with people who had challenged or criticized him. He wanted dominance, not a coalition. He subjected every rival or critic to public ridicule when they conceded and endorsed him. He wanted the supporters of his defeated challengers to *see* their submission. When Chris Christie endorsed him and joined his campaign, Trump joked publicly that Christie was so fat that he was forbidden from eating any of Trump's always-present Oreos.[14]

And for those within his party who *didn't* ultimately endorse him, the attacks continued. He threatened to oppose the re-election bid of the Hispanic Republican governor of New Mexico, Susana Martinez, or get someone to challenge her.[15]

Trump followed that by claiming a Hispanic federal judge was unfit to try the suits against Trump University, solely on the basis of his ethnicity—because Trump wanted to build a wall to curb illegal immigration. Arnold Schwarzenegger was so infuriated he tweeted that the judge, Justice Gonzalo Curiel, was "an American hero." Curiel had, in fact, lived under armed guard on a military base for a year while a Mexican drug lord being prosecuted in his court tried to have him assassinated.[16] The widespread condemnation Trump's remarks inspired from within his own party led many commentators, both liberal and conservative, to speculate that the Curiel episode was a turning point in Trump's candidacy—even, perhaps, the downfall of his campaign.[17]

When Trump doubled down and the public outrage increased, he ordered his surrogates to call the reporters racists. Then he added on CBS that it was possible a Muslim judge couldn't treat him fairly either because of his proposed ban on Muslim immigration. Completing the trifecta, he questioned the loyalty and patriotism of the parents of a Muslim-American soldier killed in Iraq.[18]

The week after Trump's attacks on Curiel, Mitt Romney hosted his yearly "E2 Summit" of "Experts and Enthusiasts." The meeting turned into an angry argument between Trump opponents and the few guests who supported him. Meg Whitman, the CEO of Hewlett-Packard, compared Trump to Hitler and Mussolini; former CNN anchor and E2 attendee Campbell Brown confronted Ryan, asking the uncomfortable Speaker of the House how he would explain his endorsement of Trump to a young child.[19]

Republican National Committee chair Reince Priebus brought two of Romney's top 2012 fundraisers, financier Anthony Scaramucci and restaurant executive Andy Puzder, who tried to persuade the group to support Trump for the sake of party unity. "If Joseph Stalin and Franklin Roosevelt could get together to defeat Adolf Hitler, we can end the schism in our party," Scaramucci said.[20]

For many at the Romney gathering, the issue was putting country ahead of party, and few were swayed. Roosevelt and Stalin had agreed that Hitler was their countries' biggest threat, but many E2 attendees did not agree that Hillary Clinton was a greater threat to their country or personal futures than Donald Trump.

The reaction of party leaders around the country was similar to those at the E2 Conference; not only did most expect Trump to lose, but "win or lose . . . they fear[ed] that Trump's overheated and racialized rhetoric could irreparably poison the GOP brand among the fastest-growing demographic groups in America."[21] But the future of the party was up to Donald Trump, and he saw no reason to modify his approach toward a group so reviled by his followers. "People want people to represent them who are going to stick up for what they believe in," he said.[22]

Strength and Anger

Everything Trump had said for thirty years contradicted the idea that he would change his ways and compromise with party leaders. Indeed, Trump considered his anger a winning asset. Looking back at the primary, he told Robert Draper, "A normal, very nice, very likable Republican would be hard pressed to win."

The need for strength was his constant refrain as far back as 1990, when he criticized President George H. W. Bush for talking of a "kinder, gentler" America:

I think if this country gets any kinder or gentler, it's literally going to cease to exist. I think if we had people from the business community—the Carl

Icahns, the Ross Perots—negotiating some of our foreign policy, we'd have respect around the world.[23]

Trump had a single, clear solution for international relations, foreign trade, and domestic politics: tougher leaders. When Jeb Bush said undocumented immigrants came to the United States for their families as "an act of love," Trump ran an ad with that quote alongside the mug shots of three undocumented immigrants who had killed white Americans. "Forget Love," the tagline read. "It's Time to Get Tough!"[24] The anti-Trump contingent's message of "love," as exemplified by the $5 "Love Trumps Hate" bumper stickers advertised at the top of Hillary Clinton's campaign website, seemed to Trump—and many of his voters—to be a mealy-mouthed, meaningless concession to national weakness and decline.[25]

No one who had spent months and years following Trump, writing books about him or coauthoring his own books, supported him or believed he could be a decent president. But they all took him seriously as a possible winner. Wayne Barrett, one of his biographers, said that "he was born with bullshit capabilities beyond what you and I could possibly imagine." Marie Brenner called him "the Music Man of real estate" for his ability to walk the fuzzy line between con men and entrepreneurs. Gwenda Blair noted his "shrewd" skill for "figuring out how to make his preservation in the interest of whoever might be standing in his way." Being a survivor, Tim O'Brien saw, was an "overriding strength" that meshed with Trump's view of the world as "eat or be eaten," populated by only two kinds of people: winners and losers.[26]

The elite's disdain for Trump made some voters like him even more. "I've never been this emotionally invested in a political leader in my life," one voter told the *New Yorker*'s Peter Hessler. "The more they hate him, the more I want him to succeed. Because what they hate about him is what they hate about me."[27]

Trump's emotional connection with his voters meant little to professional politicians and CEOs. They wanted a president who would help them with their legislation; Trump was not only thoroughly ignorant about policy, procedures, or economics, he'd also shown no interest in learning anything during the campaign. He told Joshua Green that when he made his dramatic entrance to launch his campaign, he had not even heard of the "Gang of Eight" and their bipartisan attempt to end the immigration deadlock. He boasted in one debate that he could renegotiate Medicare's drug payments and save $300 billion—only to be told that the entire program cost $78 billion.[28]

For most Republicans with heavily conservative constituencies, Trump's appeal to white voters who resented the attention Democrats paid to women and minorities was positive, whether he won or not. To representatives in swing districts and many governors and senators in battleground states, Trump was a nightmare. They had to deal with his misogyny, protectionism, immigration policies, and macho talk about trade wars. Many were clearly unsure whether they would be better off if he won or lost.

Anyone who expected Trump to "blow himself up in a Hindenburg of gaffes or hate speech" was overlooking his history. Paul Solotaroff traveled with Trump for a *Rolling Stone* profile and observed:

> In all the hysteria, however, what's often missed are the qualities that brought Trump here. You don't do a fraction of what he's done in life— dominate New York real estate for decades, build the next grand Xanadus for the super-rich on the far shores of Dubai and Istanbul, run the prime-time ratings table for more than 10 years and earn a third (or sixth) fortune at it—without being immensely cunning and deft, a top-of-the-food-chain killer.[29]

Big Money's Distrust and Contempt

Throughout the primaries, Trump did nothing to attract big donors, and much that repelled them. Neither his business record, his crowds, nor his bold promises persuaded them he had what it takes to be president. They were concerned about his ignorance and offended by his ad hoc populism, attacks on minorities, disdain for the party, and diatribes against the wealthy. Jonathan Martin and Alex Burns interviewed over fifty of the biggest Republican donors and found "a measure of contempt and distrust toward their own party's nominee that is unheard of in modern presidential politics."[30] The kind of billionaires and multimillionaires who wouldn't pay $50 million for a compromise weren't about to invest millions in a candidate so volatile, untrustworthy, and unlikely to win.

Before the voting started in 2016, fifty-seven persons had donated at least one million dollars to a super PAC for one of the Republican candidates. Twenty-three gave a million or more to Jeb Bush; nine to Marco Rubio; six to Ted Cruz; five to John Kasich; four to Chris Christie; three each to Scott

Walker and Rand Paul; two to Carly Fiorina; and one each to Bobby Jindal and Donald Trump. The only person who had donated a million to Trump was Phil Ruffin, co-owner of the Trump Hotel in Las Vegas.[31]

Trump had promised to self-fund his campaign, but that claim was typical of his "moral larceny." He had only loaned the money to his campaign. Moreover, his companies and hotels were charging his campaign exorbitant prices for their use.[32] Lawyers for some mega-donors announced that until Trump forgave the loans he had already made, no one else would donate big money. Finally, Trump relented, agreeing to forgive the loans and throw in $50 million more. (He also quintupled the rent he was charging the campaign and funneled money into Trump-branded products and services, from bottled water to travel on his plane.)[33]

The Kochs and their network had prepared to spend $889 million in the election, but the brothers would not invite Trump to address their network, freezing him out of all their events throughout the primaries. Trump filled out their detailed questionnaire and unsuccessfully applied for speaking slots at one of their grass-roots summits for activists and their annual gathering of mega-donors. Even his campaign's request for access to i360, the network's sophisticated data and analytics system, was denied.[34]

The Kochs' rejection of Trump was, they argued, necessary to preserve their credibility. Giving money to someone who opposed free trade and immigration, and had never supported smaller, more limited government, would make it hard to turn down any other Republicans. Instead, they decided to protect their brand name by focusing on state and local elections.[35]

Their chief strategist, Marc Short, considered Trump "an existential threat to conservatism," and desperately tried to persuade the Kochs to pour tens of millions into stopping Trump in the primaries. But Koch-controlled companies did more than mine and drill; they manufactured a variety of consumer goods, and some were already facing protests and calls for boycotts from environmental and consumer groups from the left. The men in charge of their consumer companies scarcely wanted to court outrage from the right as well. Short promptly resigned, signed on with Marco Rubio's campaign and, when that failed, returned to his pre-Koch job with Indiana governor Mike Pence.[36]

If Trump wasn't going to get money from the Kochs, he at least expected to get major help from casino magnate Sheldon Adelson. During the primaries, Trump vehemently and repeatedly denounced President Obama's deal with Iran, which Adelson had spent millions of dollars attacking; Adelson rewarded him with an endorsement op-ed in the *Washington Post*.[37]

Adelson publicly pledged to spend $100 million on the presidential campaign, but—his own endorsement aside—he was worried about Trump's competence and character. In the two weeks after Adelson's op-ed, Trump had been excoriating defeated rivals, party leaders, and anyone who criticized his race-based attacks. The two had several private dinners, but Adelson still held back, giving $65 million to various Senate and congressional campaign funds and races. Only in late September did he finally relent and spend $25 million on Trump.[38]

Eventually, Trump's campaign and super PACs received a meager $40 million from a dozen individuals or the corporations they owned and donated through. Many others discreetly gave their money to the RNC or funneled dark money to nonprofits, which could accept unlimited money without disclosing donors' names. That anonymity was particularly important in 2016 because, one fundraiser confided to a reporter, "It's embarrassing to support Trump." These donors could tolerate Trump's racism and religious bigotry as long as they weren't stigmatized for supporting him.

Billionaire mega-donors were not the only ones concerned about the personal taint of being associated with Trump. Nineteen CEOs of the Fortune 100 biggest American corporations contributed to a Republican candidate during the primaries; not one of the 100 CEOs made a personal donation to Trump in the primaries or the general election. (In 2012, thirty-two donated to Romney.)[39]

As Trump continued to flirt with white nationalists, Klansmen, and groups not seen around presidential candidates for a century, corporations began to back out of sponsoring the Republican National Convention. Within two weeks of his attack on Judge Curiel, Apple, Coca-Cola, Microsoft, Wells Fargo, UPS, Motorola, JPMorgan Chase, Ford, H&R Block, and Walgreens withdrew their support for the event at which Trump would be officially nominated.[40]

Strongman, Weak Grasp

Shut out by the Kochs and unable to impress most of the big donors, Trump asked hotelier Steve Wynn to arrange a meeting with Karl Rove. Despite Rove's public criticism of his behavior and positions, Trump knew, at least, that Rove wanted him to win.

Later, Rove told associates that he was "'stunned' by Trump's poor grasp of campaign basics," and that Trump was both "confused and scared." He had been traveling from state to state for almost a year, yet he had not thought about efficient scheduling and how a fifty-state campaign was different from fifty state primaries spread over four months.[41]

Despite his swagger and braggadocio, Trump absorbed much of what Rove patiently explained, like the importance of focusing on battleground states (and not just the states with the biggest or friendliest crowds) and the value of a running mate with Midwestern appeal. Trump began to realize that Corey Lewandowski, his campaign manager, was a tactician who did not understand campaign strategy. Three weeks later, he fired Lewandowski and put Manafort in charge of his campaign.[42]

Trump still didn't know how to make a deal with politicians who had their own brands and agendas. He expected to have full support by virtue of winning the nomination; instead, they gave limited support to the extent his positions were consistent with their agendas.

Shortly after the meeting with Rove, Chris Christie arranged a meeting with Republican governors, at which Trump was as confused as he was when he met with Rove. He didn't know how to keep up his "strongman" image while asking for help. He couldn't talk about any issue positions that required details, and talking about compromises or common interests lowered him to their level—and he never had been willing to do that. Instead, he rambled on about his poll numbers (which the governors almost certainly knew already), asked them to talk about their states, and then said goodbye—without ever asking the governors for their support.[43]

Courting Evangelical Leaders

Trump might not have been able to win over governors with his bold, implausible promises, but he found he could make bold, *plausible* promises to religious leaders. That was something else Trump had learned from Rove— the most important lesson, perhaps: the importance of the Supreme Court to evangelicals.

The growing national support for gay marriage, attacks on the efficacy and morality of gay conversion therapy, revelations of sexual abuse—and subsequent cover-ups—by members of the clergy, and the more moderate views of younger evangelicals were all threatening the power of conservative religious leaders. They may have been skeptical of a nominee with no apparent moral or religious compass, but the moral turf on which the cultures wars were fought—something they'd owned since Ronald Reagan's administration— was slipping away from them fast.

Evangelical leaders endorsed Ted Cruz for the nomination, expecting that his eloquent defense of their positions and the prominence he gained in Washington would finally give them a candidate who could win the nomination and restore their standing. Instead, Trump had carried the strongest evangelical state, South Carolina. and clinched the nomination in Indiana, where 60 percent of the Republican primary voters identified as evangelical or born-again.

Three prominent evangelical figures—Pat Robertson, Franklin Graham, and Jerry Falwell Jr.—had endorsed Trump, and were now serving as "insiders," recruiting religious leaders who would mobilize their congregations to vote for the very antithesis of a moral exemplar. All three— Robertson with a major television network, Graham with revival meetings and support for beleaguered Christians around the world, and Falwell as the head of a university with a massive online degree program—were market-driven and secure in the control of their organizations. Whether Trump won or lost, they could benefit from ratings and publicity. Those invited by the three "insiders" to meet Trump, on the other hand, *did* have to worry about losing their legitimacy. They needed to inspire and motivate their parishioners to vote for Trump or risk losing their following.[44]

Trump's opening remarks didn't help his—or their—cause. He told them he "owed so much to [religion]"—not for his personal salvation, but for the votes he'd received; he wouldn't have won the nomination otherwise. Graham reminded the crowd that God had used flawed men like King David, but instead of persuading people to support Trump, it made them queasy.[45]

At a second, larger session that day, Trump went beyond the morning's self-serving platitudes. He remembered what they wanted and offered them a deal they couldn't refuse. Without hedging or caution, he became the first presidential candidate to flat-out promise "pro-life" judges. No candidate had ever been willing to go beyond dog whistles and coded language, but Trump had no qualms about violating taboos about judicial independence. When he followed that promise with an attack on a fifty-year-old law limiting tax-exempt churches from speaking out on social issues, Family Research Council president Tony Perkins was sold:

Evangelicals had been used over and over by Republicans. And there was something different about his interaction with us. . . . You could describe it as transactional. He wanted our votes, and he made promises that most Christian candidates would never, ever make.[46]

Trump didn't stop there. He released a list of judges who had been handpicked by the leaders of the conservative Federalist Society. Now they had a cause to fire up their followers and fight the good fight. Before long, the evangelical argument for Trump was "It's the Supreme Court, Stupid."[47]

Reince Priebus and the RNC

No one was in a more difficult spot than Reince Priebus, the chair of the RNC. He had spent the previous year trying to paper over the intraparty rifts on immigration, trade, and Donald Trump. Everything about Trump's rhetoric and policies contradicted Priebus' goals for the party, yet he had to squelch open criticism from major donors and party elders.

Priebus had commissioned the Barbour Report after the Romney-Ryan ticket's defeat in 2012. He had worked hard to attract Hispanics and be less off-putting to young voters and women. Now he was trying to satisfy Trump's demands while at the same time dealing with a bombardment by "Never Trumpers," who were insisting that he disavow the nominee.

Every time Trump lashed out in his tweets, Priebus had to come up with a way to relate the party's positions to those of Trump. He had to avoid details because Trump changed positions so often without rhyme or reason, and without ever bothering to tell Priebus or any other elected officials. Michael Gerson, a head speechwriter in the George W. Bush White House, called Trump the "quantum candidate"—you could know the date or you could know Trump's position, but not both at once.[48]

Priebus could always find common ground with most Republicans by criticizing Hillary Clinton, a reliable target of the party since her husband entered the Democratic primary in 1991. Priebus warned reporters and fellow Republicans that her campaign would be a "race to the bottom"— never mind, as Mark Leibovich pointed out, that Trump had already "accused President Bill Clinton of rape, Obama of treason, Hillary Clinton of murdering Vince Foster, Cruz's dad of associating with assassins, [and] Romney of not being a 'real' Mormon."[49]

Trump expected Priebus to devote all RNC resources to the presidential campaign at the expense of governors, senators, and members of Congress. In particular, he wanted control of party fundraising committees, without personally helping the committees raise money.

Finally, Trump agreed to make twenty-four calls to top donors. He stopped after three. When he talked with donors, he did not have a good enough grasp of the issues to do questions and answers. To these important donors, it looked like he was running out the clock with his monologues, using them "to avoid answering questions."[50]

Priebus became everyone's whipping boy. He couldn't satisfy leaders who wanted to dump Trump. He couldn't get Trump to soften his language or stop attacking immigrants for the sake of governors and senators who needed Hispanic votes. And he couldn't turn over all his money and staff to Trump.

Still, thanks to years of hard work by Priebus, the RNC and the party organization were substantial assets. The Republican Party had revamped its fundraising operations and data capabilities over the previous four years. It had recovered from the setbacks after McCain-Feingold stripped them of big corporate donations, and the RNC was close to the DNC in fundraising, with $343 million to the DNC's $372 million. It also had a data system that was close or equal to that of the Democrats.[51]

Priebus had failed to promote immigration reform or bring back disenchanted Latino voters to widen the appeal of the party, but there was a strategy in place to evade the pressure to broaden the Republican electorate: decrease the Democratic electorate through voter suppression. Between 2012 and 2016, seventeen states—all with Republican governors at the time—passed legislation restricting access to voting. Twelve states required a government-issued photo ID, and five also required proof of citizenship. These restrictions had an effect of lowering Democratic turnout by about 2.5 percent, a major impact.[52]

Mitch McConnell and the Senate

Senate Majority Leader Mitch McConnell, notorious for his shrewd marshaling of Senate opposition to President Obama's signature legislative efforts, had never been a Trump supporter. His main concern was maintaining majority status in the Senate and using that position to advance the Republican coalition. As the party lost support among young voters and college-educated women, the role of social conservatives within the party's organizations grew. The Koch brothers and many of the party's biggest donors were either libertarians or less socially conservative than the evangelical communities within the party. But as with virtually every right-wing party across the world, there was a growing willingness of groups interested in cutting regulation, taxes, and entitlements to support groups whose leaders cared more about enforcing conservative moral values on issues like stopping gay marriage and abortion. This is because growing inequality was raising the demand on the left for entitlements and the costs of these redistributive policies for affluent taxpayers. This raised the attractiveness for economic conservatives of inexpensive "values-based" appeals to voters.[53]

When McConnell blocked Senate hearings on the nomination of Merrick Garland to replace the late Justice Antonin Scalia during the Republican primaries, he all but guaranteed that Supreme Court appointments would raise the stakes for social conservatives; no other group, as the philosopher and theologian Adam Kotsko observed, depended more upon the Court to impose their standards on others. Much more so than majority opinion, court rulings on the basis of the Constitution "[fit] perfectly with their refusal to recognize the legitimacy of the choices and values of anyone outside the evangelical community [whose] choices and values represent only ignorance and sin."[54]

As Trump clinched the nomination, McConnell used a book tour to reassure Republicans. Trump was "a different kind of guy for a different kind of year," he acknowledged, but the procedures and norms of the White House would be adequate to help him understand the limits of his authority:

He'll have a White House counsel. There will be others who point out there's certain things you can do and you can't do. And it's not quite like, you know, making a speech before a big audience and entertaining people. And I think he's a smart guy, and I think he's going to figure that out.[55]

Within weeks, Trump's ongoing diatribes and attacks on immigrants, Muslims, critics, and other targets were exhausting senators. "What it does is suck all the oxygen out of the chamber," Susan Collins said. "I'm trying to do my job as a senator, which does not end because we have a contentious and bizarre presidential candidate."[56]

McConnell unsuccessfully tried to tamp down Trump's hostile rhetoric. His last straw was Trump's suggestion that President Obama was sympathetic to Islamic terrorists. "I'm not going to be commenting on the presidential candidates today," he told reporters. From then on, he said as little as possible. The number two Republican senator, John Cornyn, went even further, announcing he would not talk about the nominee until after the election. "Wish me luck," he added.[57]

As senators began to complain about having to disavow or defend him after each and every one of his bombastic statements, Trump trained his sights on them: "Our leaders have to get tougher. . . . This is too tough to do it alone. But you know what? I think I'm gonna be forced to. I think I'm going to be forced to."[58]

Paul Ryan and the House

While McConnell was able to put aside any qualms with Trump's rhetoric for the sake of maintaining his majority, embattled Speaker of the House Paul Ryan—whose long-standing efforts to pass tax reform, repeal the Affordable Care Act, and promote conservative legislation had been mostly unsuccessful—faced a more difficult struggle.

Paul Ryan and Donald Trump were natural enemies, and Ryan was no better than Trump at concealing his contempt. Ryan believed in ending crony capitalism, expanding free trade, and an immigration policy without regard for religion or race. Now he was confronted by a divisive nativist who expected Ryan to defend him while he savaged all that Ryan held dear.

The shocking, unexpected loss by the Romney-Ryan ticket in 2012 prompted Ryan to rethink his language and tactics. While Romney had been attacked for splitting Americans into "makers" and "takers," it was Ryan who'd coined that way of dividing society in talks at the Heritage Foundation. Now he repeatedly expressed regret: "'Takers' wasn't how to refer to a single mom stuck in a poverty trap, just trying to take care of her family. Most people don't want to be dependent."[59]

Ryan had also turned against groups raising money with "Hail Mary," go-for-broke tactics that had soured voters on the GOP establishment. "When voices in the conservative movement demand things that they know we can't achieve with a Democrat in the White House," he said, "all that does is depress our base and in turn help Democrats stay in the White House. We can't do that anymore."[60]

As Speaker, he was faced with the same problem that had limited his predecessors, Dennis Hastert and John Boehner: moving the money outside the party had weakened the leaders and fractured the party. And now their candidate was not even a Republican. Ryan's credo was that Republicans "win when we have an ideas contest [and] lose when we have a personality contest." And Trump was nothing if not a cult of personality whose rallies separated his followers from other, less-American persons.

Early in the primaries, party elders had tried to get Ryan to jump into the race or agree to be nominated at the convention if no candidate had a majority. He refused to join the long-shot anti-Trump movement, and instead gave a speech criticizing divisive rhetoric.

When Trump clinched the nomination, Ryan said he was waiting to see if Trump unified the party before endorsing him.[61] Predictably, Trump turned on Ryan, tweeting "So many great endorsements yesterday, except for Paul Ryan!" Soon Trump was telling viewers on Breitbart News that "many people" said he would be better off without Ryan. He was particularly incensed that Ryan said Trump had *inherited* "the party of Lincoln, of Reagan, of Jack Kemp," and that conservatives were waiting to hear him embrace the principles of the party. Ninety minutes later, Trump responded: "Paul Ryan said that I inherited something very special, the Republican Party. Wrong, I didn't inherit it, I won it with millions of voters!"[62]

Priebus, Ryan's good friend, tried and failed to get them to shake hands and smile for the press. Ryan came in with a PowerPoint presentation trying show Trump the importance of his ideas on tax reform and cutting entitlements. It only confirmed Trump's view that Ryan was dull and patronizing— "a fucking Boy Scout."[63]

The session with Trump also showed that Ryan was going to stick with impractical ideas that he personally was devoted to, not Trump's equally impractical ideas. Ryan and the party elite wanted to increase immigration and cut entitlements to the bone. Trump had promised to reduce immigration and had warned against cutting Medicare for years, positions that had far more support among Republican voters than Ryan's. Half of low-income Republicans and a third of middle-income Republicans believed it was the government's responsibility to ensure everyone had coverage. Among Trump's hard-core base of non-college-educated Republicans, over 40 percent agreed.

After a month of Trump's tweets and barbs, Ryan endorsed Trump as quietly as possible, in his hometown Janesville, Wisconsin, *Gazette*. He didn't back off, though, in distancing himself from Trump's outrages, and when Trump attacked Judge Curiel, Ryan called his comments "the textbook definition" of racism. But neither did he want to engage fully with the nominee; he only acquiesced to an interview for the Father's Day issue of *People Magazine* when they agreed there would be no questions about Trump.[64]

No matter what Ryan said, he caught flak from some parts of his party. When he defended conservative principles against Trump's reversals, representatives from the most conservative districts went after him. Mick Mulvaney, always willing to shut down the government or attack the leadership, asked reporters, "Isn't it a principle that the GOP speaker would support the GOP nominee?"[65]

The Revealing Silence about Putin

Whether they criticized it, explained it away, or avoided comment on it, no Republican legislator doubted Trump's misogyny or nativism. When it came to his comments on strongmen and dictators, however, they were confused, uncertain, and worried.

Whenever he was asked about Vladimir Putin, for example, Trump unfailingly praised the Russian president. When asked about Putin's murder of journalists and dissidents, he consistently downplayed them or cast doubt on the evidence. Frequently, he would add "at least he's a leader," and follow up with strong claims of moral equivalence between Putin and the United States. When Joe Scarborough, a former Republican congressman and MSNBC host, asked how a candidate for president could condone Putin's killings, Trump asserted the US was no better: "I think our country does plenty of killing also, Joe."[66]

Was his praise of Putin indicative of an authoritarian, anti-democratic preference for strongmen? A strategy to sell more apartments to money-laundering Russian oligarchs? Or did Putin have damaging information about Trump's connections to Russian mobsters and oligarchs in the former Soviet Union? All three explanations were plausible.

Trump was the second New York real estate developer who was willing to sell apartments anonymously to overseas buyers through limited liability companies, a corporate structure that kept the owners' names secret. LLCs are often used to transfer criminal profits into clean assets. Obviously, not all of Trump's LLC sales were to criminals or oligarchs, but their influence was critical.

Kenneth McCallion, who investigated the ties between organized crime and Trump's developments during the Reagan administration, told Craig Unger that Eastern European organized crime networks had "saved his bacon." The *Financial Times* of London's investigation found "multiple ties" between Trump Soho and "an alleged international money-laundering network." They also connected the purchase of three condos in the building to an energy minister from Kazakhstan being sued for looting hundreds of millions of dollars. At the very least, as an executive who had worked with his organization said, Trump was engaging in "willful obliviousness."[67]

Foreign policy hadn't been a major focus in the Republican primaries. Save for Republican officials concerned with defense and foreign policy, Trump's discomforting and unusual affection for dictators, especially Putin, might have stayed a minor issue among Republicans—if not for Russian hacking.

On June 14, the DNC announced that, a year earlier, Russian government hackers had penetrated their computers and uploaded the party's opposition research on Donald Trump. The DNC hired CrowdStrike, a prominent California security firm, to analyze the breach; by studying the hackers' tactics and coding, the firm identified two Russian groups, acting independently. "Fancy Bear" was linked to Russia's military intelligence; "Cozy Bear" was connected to the security agency once run by Putin.[68]

The next day happened to be the day that the newly elected prime minister of Ukraine, Volodymyr Groysman, visited Congress in hopes of securing economic and military aid against Russian subversion of the country and seizure of more Ukrainian territory. Both Paul Ryan, as Speaker of the House, and Kevin McCarthy, as House Majority Leader, had private meetings with him.

Republican leaders met later that day. The meeting included Ryan, McCarthy, Majority Whip Steve Scalise, Scalise's Chief Deputy Whip, Patrick McHenry, and the party's Conference Chair, Cathy McMorris Rodgers.

A secret recording of the meeting, which was leaked a year later to the *Washington Post*, showed that everyone present was deeply anxious about the possible implications of Trump's praise of Putin and the justifications for military actions in countries bordering Russia and assassinations of critics at home and abroad. They were so troubled by the possible explanations that they couldn't even discuss the topic, fearful that someone would leak the discussion to the press—or Trump.

McCarthy and Ryan compared notes on their meetings with Groysman, and talked at length about Putin's daily shelling of Ukraine and his manipulations of their energy supply—all of which threatened to compromise the new Ukrainian government's legislation to curb corruption, create an independent judiciary, and improve the economy.

Rodgers, who had visited Ukraine a year before, reminded the others, "They're on the front lines. They're fighting for their freedom . . . their independence." The big takeaway from her trip was how "very sophisticated" the Russian propaganda operation in Europe was, likening it to "a messaging war." Ryan called the Russian actions "maniacal" and pointed out that only the US was standing up against it. Rodgers contradicted him: "We're not. We're not."

It was then that McCarthy shared the news about the DNC hack. Ryan had not heard the news, and worked to get his head around what he had just heard. "The Russians hacked the DNC."

McHenry finished the sentence for him: "To get Oppo."

"And delivered it to who?" Ryan asked.

McCarthy shared his worries about Putin. "There's . . . there's two people I think, Putin pays," he blurted out. "[Congressman Dana] Rohrabacher and Trump."

Nervous laughter broke out in the room. McCarthy emphasized he wasn't joking, telling them, "Swear to god."

Ryan immediately cut off the discussion. "This is an off the record," he began, only to be interrupted by further nervous laughter. He raised his voice: "NO LEAKS!"

Then Ryan raised the stakes further, issuing a veiled threat. "This is how we know we're a real family here."

Scalise doubled down. "That's how you know that we're tight."

"What's said in the family stays in the family," Ryan finished. His point was clear: the topic was too dangerous to discuss, and anyone who leaked it would be expelled from "the family."[69]

As damning as what was spoken during the meeting was, the silences were even more revealing about the depth of their anxieties about Trump. When McCarthy compared their presidential nominee to Rohrabacher, Putin's most important defender in Congress, no one objected or even suggested that the comparison was excessive.

When the *Washington Post*'s Adam Entous asked Ryan and McCarthy about the meeting, both denied the discussion ever took place. When told the *Post* had a recording, McCarthy's spokesman said the House Majority Leader's comments were an attempt at humor.[70]

In the minds of the GOP congressional leaders, they were stuck with Trump and would just have to hope for the best outcome. But it was becoming less clear by the day whether the best outcome was Trump or Clinton.

Running Mate Wanted—Brawling Required

As the focus moved to selecting a running mate, Trump found himself with a shrinking field of candidates. Strong potential options for vice president began withdrawing their names from contention, as few Republicans considered proximity to Trump to be to their benefit. As a former Republican presidential campaign manager put it, "Hillary has some baggage, but Trump is crazy and you can't fix crazy." Mike Murphy, a former top adviser to Jeb Bush, was even more blunt: "Everybody says, 'Look, he's so civilized, he eats with a knife and fork.' And then an hour later, he takes the fork and stabs somebody in the eye with it."[71]

Rove had emphasized the importance of the Midwest for Trump's campaign, so outreach began to a few early contenders. Donald Trump Jr. contacted an advisor to John Kasich, asking if the Ohio governor would like to be the most powerful vice president in history. Asked to explain, Trump's son said that the vice president would be in charge of domestic policy and foreign policy. What, the clearly puzzled advisor asked, would the president do? The president, the son explained, would be in charge of "making America great again."[72]

Kasich later told Jake Tapper on CNN that he never considered the offer because he had too many opinions to be a vice president. But Kasich's antipathy toward Trump was apparent; even though the Republican nominating convention was being held in Ohio, Kasich had already decided he would not attend.

New Mexico governor Susana Martinez was also contacted—before Trump attacked her for not endorsing him—and she didn't return the call. Iowa senator Joni Ernst politely declined.

Bob Corker of Tennessee, head of the Senate Foreign Relations Committee, met with Trump several times to discuss foreign policy. When Trump gave a high-profile foreign policy speech in New Hampshire, Corker was "discouraged by the results. . . . It wasn't the type [of address] that one would expect a person who is wanting to lead the greatest nation in the world to make."

After a Muslim American killed fifty people in a terrorist attack in Orlando, Trump called for banning all Muslims from any country with a history of terrorism from entering the US. The next day, Corker informed members of Trump's inner circle that he wasn't cut out to be Trump's "brawling mate."[73]

The final list came down to Chris Christie, Newt Gingrich, and Indiana governor Mike Pence, all of whom had no other options after their recent failures. Trump personally was inclined toward Christie or Gingrich, but his children persuaded him that Gingrich had no support from former colleagues, and Christie—who had once jailed Trump's son-in-law Jared Kushner's father—had fallen badly in the polls in New Jersey after his feeble presidential campaign.[74]

Trump finally named Pence as his running mate. It is indicative of the divides within the GOP that one of the most vehemently pro-life, anti-gay governors in the party, whose social policies alienated big corporations and were opposed by a majority of young Republicans, was thought to be the best available option to reassure Republicans about their erratic nominee. Social conservatives were ecstatic, but economic conservatives were dismayed.

Twenty-Five Years of Anti-Hillary Crusades

Pence won over Trump and his family during a breakfast at the Indiana Governor's Mansion. The mild-mannered governor delivered an impassioned critique of Bill and Hillary Clinton's corruption. One of the most ardent born-again evangelicals in government, he was immersed in twenty-five years of vilification of her policies—dating back to fierce opposition from Phyllis Schlafly, one of the most powerful advocates of conservative social policies—and few Republican politicians had better credentials for attacking her positions.[75]

Clinton was a deeply religious Methodist who read scriptures daily, but that didn't matter; for evangelicals, a "deep aversion" to Clinton was always in the air. Her name was roundly booed at Christian conferences. In some communities, women were forbidden to call any woman a "bitch"— except Hillary Clinton, for whom a special exception was made. At the 2004 Republican National Convention, a spokesman for the Family Research Council passed out fortune cookies with the message "#1 reason to ban human cloning: Hillary Clinton." Before the 2008 primaries began, Jerry Falwell Sr. hoped she would run because "not even Lucifer" would energize his followers more than her.[76]

The Republican Congress joined in the Clinton bashing with gusto. In 2012, Islamic militants attacked the US diplomatic compound in Benghazi, Libya, killing Ambassador J. Christopher Stevens and three others. Over the next three years, there were six investigations of the tragedy with the official goal of determining why no military or CIA rescue mission had reached the compound in time to save them.

The *unofficial* goal was to provide cover for attacking Secretary Clinton, as Kevin McCarthy made clear during an interview with Sean Hannity:

> Everybody thought Hillary Clinton was unbeatable, right? But we put together a Benghazi special committee, a select committee. What are her numbers today? Her numbers are dropping. Why? Because she's untrustable. But no one would have known any of that had happened had we not fought and made that happen."[77]

The Benghazi hearings never proved that Clinton bore any personal responsibility for the tragedy. In fact, Trump and many other Republicans were so furious after the last special committee on Benghazi concluded without finding fault that they lashed out at Chair Trey Gowdy for failing to blame her. The hearings had been ruthless, but the GOP representatives looked overmatched and poorly prepared. The most aggressive representative, Mike Pompeo, later apologized in his district for a performance so rough that he said even his wife gave him an "F."[78]

The Benghazi scandal was loud and empty, but it led to an FBI investigation that revealed Clinton had used a private e-mail server for all her official and personal e-mails. Other officials in both parties had done the same in past administrations, but that was irrelevant in the polarized atmosphere of 2015. The server and e-mail stories took their toll on the rest of her campaign; by the end of that year, her "honesty and trustworthiness" ratings dropped to nearly the same level as Trump's, 36 percent to his 35 percent.[79]

Looking back on the campaign, Jill Abramson, the former *New York Times* managing editor, acknowledged that Clinton received an unfair level of scrutiny. Clinton's lawyerly responses, sometimes convoluted and other times defensive, fed right into the growing right-wing media world of 2016.

After four years of high-stakes diplomacy and three years giving speeches—many behind closed doors, for several hundred thousand dollars—she was far removed from the immediate concerns and awareness of most voters.[80]

Trump's Unconventional Assets

Trump won the primaries despite the highest recorded unfavorable ratings of any nominee since World War II. Fortunately for him, Hillary Clinton finished the primaries with the second-worst ratings.[81]

Trump's highly visible moral, ethical, and political failings were so offensive to many observers that they failed to recognize the brilliance of his tactics. Most newspapers and mainstream media commentators condemned his ugly, politically incorrect remarks, but they were the kind of blunt, straight talk that blue-collar men viewed as evidence of manly courage.

Jeff Roe, Ted Cruz's campaign manager, was impressed with how brand-consistent Trump was. "His brand was being politically incorrect," Roe said. "He's saying everything that you've always wanted to say."[82] Above all else, he was good for ratings, and as media expert Martin Kaplan put it, "ratings swing a bigger bat than civics."[83]

People who knew Trump from reading mainstream newspapers or magazines were unaware of the star power he developed through reality TV and tabloids like the *National Enquirer*. Trump stories had been so good for *Enquirer* sales over the years that his special arrangement with the publisher, David Pecker, had the most prominent tabloid throwing mud at Rubio and Cruz when they threatened him in the primaries, and buying and burying stories from women who alleged Trump had slept with them.[84]

Between 2012 and 2016, Trump moved into the online world of nativism and white nationalism on and around Breitbart News, accruing a massive following of anti-immigration nationalists and conspiracy theorists outside of normal political media channels. He was closer to the angry, populist mood of struggling Americans—in rhetoric—than Clinton had ever been able to articulate.

Trump stories traveled farther around the Internet than Clinton stories. Researchers at Harvard University's Berkman Klein Center for Internet and Society found that, among the one hundred campaign stories most often linked in articles, posts, tweets, and blogs, there were seven Trump-focused stories for every Clinton-focused story.[85]

Trump tweeted more Breitbart stories than any other source during the primary, and he talked regularly with its executive chairman, Steve Bannon. His other retweets in the primaries featured links to Newsmax, Gateway Pundit, and Conservative Treehouse—websites where no previous presidential candidates had mobilized voters.[86]

Trump's press coverage focused on his issues, praising or attacking his stances on immigration, race, trade, and other topics. Even when his views were attacked, the online public was likely to know what they were and who agreed or disagreed with him. Clinton's coverage focused on her scandals, ranging from Benghazi, to her private e-mail server, to her very lucrative speeches behind closed doors, to the allegations of corruption involving Clinton Foundation donors.[87]

After Romney's defeat in 2012, Bannon wanted to grow the audience for his anti-immigration nationalism. Most of the online far-right figures were zealots, indulging outlandish conspiracy theories palatable only to true believers. Bannon concluded that he needed a new approach. He persuaded Robert Mercer, the billionaire investor who funded Breitbart, to bankroll a research operation that could produce a legitimate, forensic analysis of fundraising by the Clinton Foundation, and investigate all the rumors about a uranium mine sold to a Russian who donated millions to the Clinton Foundation—a sale that received government approval while Hillary Clinton was secretary of state.

For two years, Peter Schweizer and a research team worked at the Global Accountability Institute, a nonprofit financed by the Mercers, to produce *Clinton Cash*. The book was a major success. There were no smoking guns or unambiguous evidence of any quid pro quos—or even any evidence that Hillary Clinton had anything to do with the approval for the sale of the uranium mine—but there were plenty of unseemly elements to the transaction.

No matter how meaningful the work of the Clinton Foundation might be, many of its big donors had checkered pasts and were gaining access to inner circles of governments through the former president. More than $39 million in donations to the Clinton Foundation came from investors in the Uranium One transaction, and Bill Clinton was paid $500,000 for a speech in Russia. It was all legal, but "legal" was not the same as "ethical" or "admirable," and it cast further doubt on the integrity and character of the Clintons.[88] A month after the *Times* story, *Clinton Cash* was number two on the *New York Times* nonfiction bestseller list, opening the door to the mainstream media attention Bannon sought.

Clinton Cash was not the only story that raised questions about the Clintons' ethics and sensitivities. In the three years after she left the state department, Hillary Clinton earned $21.7 million for ninety-two speeches at an average of $235,000 per speech, many of them to Wall Street investment banks, including Goldman Sachs, UBS, and Morgan Stanley. Since he had left office in 2001, her husband had earned $132 million for 637 speeches.[89]

Clinton had never been comfortable articulating a rationale for her campaigns, and her inner circle was out of touch enough with the changing mood in the country that they thought high-paid speeches on Wall Street would not be a problem if she ran for president. Six months after Iowa, she had still not figured out how to deal with voters' anger.[90]

Now, thanks to the questionable sources of some Clinton Foundation funds revealed in *Clinton Cash*, and her refusal to disclose her Wall Street speeches, it was plausible for Republican voters to say that her actions and character were no cleaner than Trump's. He concocted bogus excuses for not revealing his tax returns; she made lame excuses for keeping her speeches private and using a private e-mail server. She attacked his character relentlessly for his insulting, callous treatment of women, but it was no game changer to an electorate that knew all that about Trump from day one, and who remembered that she'd defended her husband against comparable charges about affairs.[91]

Clinton led in virtually every poll from every reputable pollster, but Trump was seldom out of striking distance. He also had several strengths that went unnoticed in most press stories on the horse race. From the time he clinched the nomination, he ran ahead of Mitt Romney among non-college-educated white men, and Clinton ran behind Obama among Black voters.[92]

Now that there were more accurate polls, voter registration data, and the census report on the 2012 election, the initial conclusion that Obama had won because of a surge of nonwhite voters was shown to be wrong. Obama had more white support than the exit polls indicated, and would have won with no more minority voters than there were in 2004. In other words, Trump could beat Clinton simply by bringing back white voters who had abandoned the GOP after 2004.[93]

Exit, Voice, and Loyalty

From the time he clinched the nomination until the July 18 opening of the GOP convention, Trump generally trailed Clinton by two to four points in the Real Clear Politics daily average of recent polls. The big exception was near the end of June, when new damaging stories about Trump University emerged, and he trailed by over six points for a week. In a normal race, the early gap of two to four points, sometimes even less than two points, would not have been cause for panic for Republicans, but there was nothing ordinary or predictable about Donald Trump.[94]

Before the Republican convention, any hope of GOP unity was dead. Party leaders were telling down-ballot candidates to do what was necessary to save their own seats. Ed Rogers, a longtime strategist, found that "among Trump's sincere supporters, very few argue the merits of a Trump candidacy or presidency. There are very few zealous Trump missionaries (as opposed to anti-Clinton crusaders) remaining in the party."[95]

The first major defectors comprised nearly the entire universe of prominent Republican foreign and defense policy experts, including former directors of National Intelligence, the National Security Agency, and the CIA —people who could not support a presidential candidate who was so casual about treaties, alliances, or the dangers of intemperate foreign policy statements and praise of dictators. They were all aware that an impulsive president could trigger war.

That wave of defections was followed by at-risk senators in battleground states and a long list of former legislators. Between the Republican convention and the election, many senators, governors, and representatives refused to endorse Trump. Some reversed their stands; some did so twice.

In late June, Bloomberg News contacted Republican senators, governors, and representatives to see where they stood on Trump. At that point, over half of all Republican senators would only say they would support their party's nominee, without mentioning the nominee's name.[96]

John McCain illustrated the dilemma of senators on the ballot that year. Until he had won his primary election against a Trump supporter, he dared not criticize or dissociate himself from Trump. The minute he won the primary, he campaigned as a senator who expected Clinton to win, promising to "act as a check—not a rubber stamp—for the White House."[97]

Even attending the convention became a difficult calculation. "I'm sure it will be fun, I'm sure it will be entertaining. . . . I can watch it on TV," Lindsey

Graham said. McCain said he was staying home because "I'm in a very tough re-election campaign." Half of the senators running in battleground states also made excuses, minimizing the importance of conventions or maximizing the need to stay at home. At least nine Republican governors followed suit.

In Ohio, the location of Trump's coronation, Senator Rob Portman and Governor John Kasich both stayed away. "Nobody listens, nobody covers it," Portman claimed. Neither Ohioan gave any organizational support to Trump.[98]

Before the convention began, Trump had already lost endorsements from more senators and governors than any presidential nominee in either party since World War II, and there was unusually low attendance of candidates up for re-election. The director of the Republican Senatorial Committee told a private meeting of donors and lobbyists that candidates should "feel free" to skip the convention, offering as a reason that "conventions were a distracting spectacle."[99]

Eleven GOP senators attended the convention; they came on the stage after Mitch McConnell's speech as a show of party unity. Only one of the eleven, Joni Ernst, was from a state that Obama carried in 2012. Republican senators from blue states generally avoided the nominee as much as possible.

Neither Ryan nor McConnell had much to say about their party's nominee and standard bearer; their praise was not for Trump's virtues or ideas, but for his signature. They emphasized the value of a president who would sign *their* bills, and the importance of stopping Hillary Clinton. In his 1,400-word speech, Ryan mentioned Trump twice, reminding the audience their agenda depended upon having a Republican president. McConnell mentioned Trump four times and Clinton twenty, highlighting her character flaws and dishonesty:

> "She lied about her emails. She lied about her server. She lied about Benghazi. She lied about sniper fire. She even lied about why her parents named her Hillary."[100]

Trump's acceptance speech made it clear that he had no interest in civil liberties, the rule of law, or tolerance, and it did nothing to reassure worried politicians about a Trump presidency. "Beginning on January 20th of 2017, safety will be restored," he announced, promising an end to open borders and murderous immigrants who threatened "our very way of life."

Politicians and officials from present and past administrations were alarmed by his anti-democratic, authoritarian vows. Michael Gerson, a speechwriter for George W. Bush, saw his speech as "summoning primal forces," while noting the lack of any "moral guardrails." Stuart Stevens, Mitt Romney's strategist in 2012, called him a dark, disturbed man who "sees in the country what he sees in the mirror." But when Trump proclaimed, "Nobody knows the system better than me, which is why I alone can fix it," many voters saw it only as a sign of determination.[101]

Even at the convention, the bewildering praise of Putin's Russia became part of the coverage. Trump's disorganized campaign staff had paid no attention to the party platform, save for a single plank: a reference to offering "lethal aid" to Ukraine to help them resist Russian aggression was diluted to "appropriate aid."[102]

This highly unusual platform change might have faded from the news if documents hadn't emerged in Ukraine showing secret payments of $12.5 million to Paul Manafort from a pro-Russian politician, which only added to Ukrainian anxieties about Trump. Ukrainian television commentators tried endlessly to make sense of Trump's incoherent statements and explain why Republicans were suddenly abandoning them.[103]

Trump was not upset about the revelation of Manafort's secret payments. Shortly thereafter, however, came stories about a family "intervention" at which Manafort said he wanted to tame Trump's personality for the rest of the campaign. Corrupt connections to pro-Russian oligarchs were fine, but stories that made Trump look bad were intolerable.[104]

Paul Manafort was out, and Steve Bannon was in. The man who'd helped orchestrate *Clinton Cash* now had a direct pipeline to the GOP presidential candidate. They set about trying to trim Clinton's support from certain key voter demographics. They kept up a drumbeat of stories about her defense of Bill Clinton's alleged sexual assaults to dim her luster with young women; they reminded younger, less-engaged African American voters about her use of the racially loaded term "super-predator" to describe inner-city crime; and to persuade supporters of Bernie Sanders that the Democratic Party was crooked, they hyped WikiLeaks' hacked e-mails from the DNC that showed favoritism toward Clinton.[105]

Trump's Blue-Collar Advantage

In different ways, Trump and Sanders had won over voters with their angry determination to change the rules that had been so good for elites and not good for men without college educations. Now Trump had a double advantage over Clinton: she had no attractive alternative to his protectionist, America-first approach to jobs that spoke to white midwestern men, and she had not found a way to address their widespread economic unease in a credible manner.

After Sanders edged her out in the Michigan primary, Clinton's campaign decided that she should not target blue-collar men; her approach did more to turn them away than win them over. In fact, Clinton's problem was as much a party problem as a personal problem. Obama's ratings had slipped in the upper Midwest in his second term, thanks to his proposed Trans-Pacific Partnership trade plan. Non-college-educated white men were the only group in the country earning less in 2016 than in 1980. Trump's protectionism addressed their concerns; Clinton couldn't offer an alternative.[106]

Trump had also promised to bring back jobs in coal mining by changing environmental regulations. Coal was losing its market share because fracking had made natural gas a more economical, cleaner alternative. Clinton could not win votes in the coal mining areas of Ohio and West Virginia, however, after promising during the primaries that "we're going to put a lot of coal miners and coal companies out of business."[107]

No economists thought the jobs lost in trade would ever return, or that coal would be competitive with natural gas, but Trump's credibility as a successful deal-making billionaire was hard to overcome. Joel Benenson, Clinton's pollster, tried to dispel the mythology around Trump with ads about his string of failures and bankruptcies. But Benenson could not find any way to convince people Trump was not a success: "They know he is wealthy. He is flying around in a plane with his name on it."[108]

Clinton had no other answer to the decline this group was enduring, and never looked as committed as she looked discussing discrimination. She couldn't compete with Trump on changes that appealed to the large group of white voters she needed. The best she and her team could come up with that fit her style and beliefs was talking about what kind of a country the US would be; in other words, a country characterized by more idealism about tolerance and diversity, reinforcing doubts about who she cared about.[109] It wasn't hard for Trump to make it seem that Clinton would "rather give my job to a minority or a foreigner than fight for me to keep it."[110]

Attacking Trump for his intolerance, belligerence, and authoritarianism worked well enough for Clinton to maintain her lead through the summer. In states like Colorado, New Mexico, Arizona, and Florida, Republican senators and governors had worked hard to soften Republican policies enough to gain minority support. Senators like Cory Gardner in Colorado and Jeff Flake in Arizona feared Trump was dealing the party a fatal setback. Clinton was even winning endorsements from papers like the *Omaha World-Record* and the *Arizona Republic,* a paper that had not endorsed a Democrat in 120 years.[111]

In September, Clinton addressed an LGBTQ gala and let loose about Trump, giving her opponent's campaign an unintended gift. Unaware that media had been allowed to attend the gala, she used the same language she used in private about the "irredeemable" voters attracted to Trump's intolerance:

> You could put half of Trump's supporters into what I call the basket of deplorables.... The racist, sexist, homophobic, xenophobic, Islamophobic— you name it. And unfortunately there are people like that.[112]

"Deplorables" instantly became a defiant note of pride among the whites she had attacked, and proof that she did not care about their economic woes. The less-educated white voters were already more fearful about the impacts of immigrants on the composition of their communities, and having to deal with strange accents, exotic foods, and alien cultures. Now they were being told they were irredeemable.

Even as Clinton struggled to appeal to working-class white voters, some commentators—both within and outside the GOP—believed that Trump's obvious misogyny might be Clinton's saving grace. From the early days of the campaign, conservative women had been much less decisive in their support for Trump than their male counterparts. A March 2016 poll, conducted soon after Trump defended campaign manager Corey Lewandowski's physical assault of a female journalist, found that 47 percent of Republican women—and 70 percent of women voters overall—could not imagine voting for Trump. GOP strategist Katie Packer, who led an anti-Trump super PAC called "Our Principles," gave voice to the worry that many Republicans harbored about Trump's blatant sexism—namely, that independent and center-right female voters would flock to Clinton because "they see [Trump] as someone who's repulsive."[113]

By late summer, Trump held only a twelve-point lead over Clinton among non-college-educated white women, compared to a forty-point lead among non-college-educated white men. In a focus group of less-educated white women in Akron, Ohio, the research firm Greenberg Quinlan Rosser found that many participants were disturbed by Trump's crude demeanor and worried about his "aggressive and macho" approach to national security. Politico's Julia Sonenshein wrote that "working-class white women appear to be jumping off the Trump train," while a Democracy Corps study confidently asserted that "it is statistically impossible for Trump to turn out enough angry working-class white men to surpass Clinton."

In October, the leak of an NBC tape of Trump talking about his sexual exploits and the fact that he could grab a woman "by the pussy" was the last straw—again. Many Republicans denounced the remark, but said nothing about their endorsement. Clinton's lead temporarily jumped to seven points, and liberal and conservative commentators alike rushed to describe the *Access Hollywood* tape as a fatal blow. Sarah Isgur-Flores, the deputy campaign manager for Carly Fiorina's presidential campaign, said of the tape's release, "The race for the White House is over. Now, it's just a question of collateral damage." [114]

Almost immediately, however, it became clear that reports of the Trump campaign's death had been greatly exaggerated. Soon after the tape's release, WikiLeaks released portions of Clinton's Wall Street speeches. As the excerpts were publicized by the RNC and Trump, her lead started to diminish; they showed notable differences with her public position on the Trans-Pacific Partnership—for it in private, against it in public—and support for a Canadian-style, single-payer healthcare system. There were also chains of e-mails worrying about Clinton Foundation connections and whether to ignore or defend them.[115]

Clinton refused to discuss the leaks on the grounds that "the Kremlin has weaponized WikiLeaks to meddle," and the campaign would not "confirm the authenticity of stolen documents released by [WikiLeaks founder] Julian Assange who has made no secret of his desire to damage Hillary Clinton." While the campaign remained silent, the RNC used them to spotlight e-mails most likely to alienate Bernie Sanders' supporters, including concerns that speaking at Goldman Sachs was a mistake. [116]

Clinton's lead continued to shrink as stories about the latest WikiLeaks took hold. Then, on October 28, FBI Director James Comey dropped a bombshell: the FBI was reopening an investigation of Clinton's e-mail server. A trove of e-mails to Huma Abedin, Clinton's aide, was discovered on the laptop of Abedin's husband, former congressman Anthony Weiner, who had resigned in a scandal involving his sending sexually explicit texts to a minor.[117]

The election had been tightening for weeks; Nate Silver at FiveThirtyEight and Nate Cohn at the *New York Times* began reporting possible paths to a Trump victory. Internal polling by the Trump analytics team noted that the recent revelations from Comey were boosting Trump.[118]

Still, it looked like too little, too late. On Election Day, Reince Priebus alerted Paul Ryan that Trump would lose. In 2012, Ryan had not been prepared for defeat, but now he was ready. He was going to emphatically divorce himself and the party from the racism, protectionism, and undemocratic ways of the nominee.[119]

For the second time, Ryan had the wrong speech prepared.

6

The Republicans Pivot

On January 20, 2017, amid periodic rain, Donald John Trump stood on the West Front of the US Capitol Building, placed his hand on a Bible, and swore an oath to uphold the Constitution of the United States. If those details had a comforting familiarity about them, what came next was neither comforting nor familiar.

His sixteen-minute inaugural address was, as Mark Z. Barabak wrote in the *Los Angeles Times*, "Trumpism distilled to its raw essence: angry, blunt-spoken and deeply aggrieved." There were no olive branches extended, no willingness to treat others as partners in a joint effort. In a break with the first forty-four presidents, the closest he came to referencing democratic ideals was using the word "right" to underline *his* right to restore order, not to emphasize the rights of citizens or the rule of law: "That all changes—starting right here, and right now," and "This American carnage stops right here and stops right now."[1]

No modern presidential nominee campaigned with so little concern for democratic ideals, nor paid such minimal lip service to the basic concepts of the Constitution. His three immediate predecessors sat nearby, listening quietly while Trump trashed the values that had guided them. "That was some weird shit," George W. Bush said as they left the inauguration.[2]

When Mitch McConnell assured worried Republicans that Trump would figure it out when he got to the White House, he was underestimating the new president, or, more likely, in denial. Wayne Barrett had written about Donald Trump for decades, and knew how resourceful he was at breaking rules and getting away with it:

> Donald was looking for the dark side. He was angling for the dark side. . . .
> He was not only too big to fail, he was too big to jail. They could have put
> him in jail at any point in time. It wasn't a question of a dollar wrong here, a
> dollar wrong there, they were totally fraudulent financials.[3]

Trump was remarkable at using his celebrity to raise the value of his properties, which made the banks both his allies and his adversaries. Take the Trump name off the building and the value of the property dropped. If the banks didn't prop him up and let him maintain his lifestyle, they lost any chance of covering their investment and loans.

This was part of a familiar pattern for Trump. During his disastrous tenure as a casino magnate, the New Jersey Casino Commission's members knew that he was breaking laws and cooking the books, but they did not revoke his license; Trump's casinos had 10,000 employees and closing him down would devastate Atlantic City's economy.[4]

Trump learned a lesson from his close calls: he could act with impunity and pay few consequences. Now virtually the entire Republican Party was in the same boat as the bankers and the state of New Jersey. He was the value added that gave them control of the White House, Senate, and House. He assembled the biggest following of any Republican candidate in years. He could legitimately claim that he was the only Republican who could have won in 2016. No presidential candidate had ever raised more money from small donors—not Reagan, not Clinton, not Sanders, not even Obama.[5]

But instead of Trump clearing the way for the party to fulfill their long-standing (and undelivered) promises, the erratic, self-centered, would-be autocrat presented the GOP with a challenge: how to fulfill their commitments while he fulfilled his private goals.

Maggie Haberman covered Trump for *Page Six*, the *New York Post*'s gossip column, before joining the *New York Times*. When Trump won, the *Times*'s Washington bureau invited her and her fellow journalist Ashley Parker to brief them about Trump. The picture they painted of the president-elect— "impulsive, unaware of the workings of government, with no real ideology," someone both smarter and less competent than expected—was received with skepticism.

"Maggie and I were like aliens describing this Martian King," said Parker, now at the *Washington Post*. Elisabeth Bumiller, the Washington bureau chief, believed that the office would change the president. "I was completely wrong and Maggie was completely right," Bumiller admitted four years later.[6]

Summarizing Trump's career, Andrew Prokop pointed out that he had always been corrupt: "Whenever Trump has been in positions of power or authority, he has demonstrated a pattern of trying to enrich himself by abusing the trust others have placed in him."[7] Trump considered presidential power a monetizable asset to convert into family fortune, foreign policy a tool for strengthening personal financial alliances with like-minded rulers, and the Republican Party the foot soldiers to execute his orders.

An Irresolute President behind the Resolute Desk

Trump's inner circle had the overconfidence typical of conquering heroes who had pulled off an extraordinary upset and thought they were ready to govern on day one.[8] Steve Bannon, now his chief strategist, believed that Trump could restore American sovereignty, restrict immigration, and rebuild the country's decaying infrastructure. This would reinvigorate the working class in an economic nationalist movement that united conservatives and populists. "If we deliver," he told Michael Wolff, "we'll govern for 50 years."[9]

Bannon and Trump wanted to disrupt business as usual in the federal government. They both focused on the big moves—the great speech, the grandiose promise, the right enemy—but neither comprehended the number of steps it took to go from the speeches and promises to action; neither knew that there were well-defined rules for changing federal regulations, or understood that successful disruption required a coordinated and organized White House.

The first big move of the transition foreshadowed just how hard it would be for the party to pass legislation with Trump and his family roaming the White House. Chris Christie had spent months of work and millions of dollars developing a thorough set of transition plans, briefings, and personnel lists for staffing the administration with people who were ideological and personal fits.[10] But Jared Kushner loathed Christie, who had indicted and jailed his father while a US Attorney, and persuaded his father-in-law to demote Christie and turn the transition over to Mike Pence. At that point, Bannon and Kushner gleefully dumped all of Christie's briefing books in the trash—a move consistent both with Bannon's disinterest in bureaucracy and procedures and with Kushner's arrogance and naiveté.[11]

It was only a week later, when Trump and Kushner visited the White House, that they realized that *all* the West Wing personnel would leave with the outgoing president. They would have to build their own team—without contacts, experience, or Christie's lists of potential hires. After one year in office, they'd still only confirmed appointees in one-third of the top six hundred positions in the administration, and had only nominated people for another quarter of them—a new low among modern presidents.[12]

Like many autocrats without established political party connections, Trump relied on family members whose fortunes were tied to his own. His daughter Ivanka and son-in-law Jared Kushner were given high-ranking advisor roles. Kushner's role alternated between princeling and shadow chief of staff. Their confidence in their readiness for governing was matched only by their cluelessness about how government works.[13]

Trump also selected many longtime loyalists and yes-men to enable his political impulses. Bannon, the former head of Breitbart News, had helped fire up his campaign and taught him about right-wing media. During the campaign, Trump bonded with General Michael Flynn, whom he named National Security Advisor, over their shared disdain for Obama—though they also had other things in common. Both wanted to work with Putin on deals, both wanted to make money from the Middle East oil sheikdoms—Trump from loans, hotels and golf courses, Flynn from selling nuclear power plants—and both wanted to close financial deals that required support from Turkish president Recep Tayyip Erdoğan.[14]

Predictably, filling his staff with family and inexperienced loyalists added to the confusion swirling around the irresolute person now behind the Resolute Desk. Trump and his staffers left his party with unclear, and at times contradictory, commands. But his team wasn't built for governance; a clear direction for the administration, one that coordinated international and domestic goals, would have conflicted with his unspoken personal goal: an organization for promoting and protecting his personal business interests.

Trump was accustomed to making lucrative business deals with autocratic leaders and their beholden oligarchs, and he acted to maintain and expand his ties with them from his first day, even excluding other US personnel from some of his conversations. He was attentive to, and unfailingly flattering of, Putin and Erdoğan. He accepted Putin's claim that he did not interfere in the 2016 election, despite the unanimous conclusion of US intelligence officials, and he twice removed US Attorneys who were investigating a Turkish bank for money laundering activities that helped Iran fund its nuclear program.[15]

The Daily Vanquish

Trump told his aides to think of each day "as an episode in a television show in which he vanquishes rivals." He wanted to dominate the media and use it to intimidate Republicans and enrage progressives. One veteran of Trump's TV show, *The Apprentice*, had predicted as much before the election. "Every critic, every detractor, will have to bow down to President Trump," Omarosa Manigault said. "It is the ultimate revenge to become the most powerful man in the universe."[16] This maxim applied not only to Trump's political foes, but also to his purported allies within the party. He held a medieval view of loyalty, demanding the unswerving allegiance of a feudal tenant to his lord. In Trump's first week in office, Chief of Staff Reince Priebus issued a directive to White House staff: "Back up whatever the president said or tweeted, regardless of its accuracy."[17]

Trump didn't speak of bipartisan legislation, compromise, or cooperation, all of which were inconsistent with being infallible. Instead, he wanted to dominate the media with breaking news and inflammatory tweets—a strategy that could only work if the orders were clear and direct, with no fine print that could muddle the dramatic headline and no danger of an in-the-know official leaking an important story. That meant surprising cabinet members and congressional leaders, not working with them. Decrees came out of the blue, like Zeus hurling thunderbolts from Olympus.

At a White House social media summit for right-wing agitators, Trump emphasized the drama of delivering big stories via tweet, offering, by way of example, how he announced that the United States would recognize Israel's sovereignty over the Golan Heights: "I go 'Watch this—boom!' I press it, and within two seconds, 'We have breaking news.'"[18]

His shamelessness gave him a tactical advantage with the media and negotiators.[19] He was willing to go further than other politicians—staging bold events for factories that were never built, holding international summits promising agreements that never bore fruit, and making countless bogus claims or toothless declarations, confident that follow-up stories exposing the actual results would receive fewer headlines and could be denounced as "fake news."

He was proud of his incendiary, fictitious tweets, and bragged to the agitators about his baseless accusation that Obama had wiretapped his phone: "Like when I said . . . somebody was spying on me? That thing was like a rocket." Within six months, departing senior advisors offered a key piece of advice to their replacements: "[Know] when to be out of town" to avoid being sent out to explain or defend slanderous tweets, policy reversals, and indefensible claims.[20]

The thunderbolt tactic produced a White House incapable of making hard policy decisions, brokering deals, or taking action that would hold up to scrutiny. In Trump's first week in office, he signed an executive order banning immigration from seven Muslim-majority countries. It caused havoc at airports around the world and created confusion due to errors and lack of clarity. The order was a "target-rich environment for litigation"; by specifically calling it a "Muslim ban," he guaranteed judges would stay the order for violating the Constitution's right to freedom of religion.[21]

While media outlets, from left to right, profited from taking all his bombshells and claims seriously, big investors and hedge funds made their profits by discounting everything he said. "From the House floor to the trading floor," James Hohmann wrote, Trump was "increasingly perceived as the boy who cries wolf." Companies also learned they could only bring simple requests to the White House; complex issues were best handled by lobbying Congress.[22]

Trump's preference for personal briefings placed extra value on physical proximity to the president. Whenever he traveled, even for golfing breaks at a Trump property, an unusually large contingent of his senior staff tagged along, lest a rival undermine a plan or legislative agreement. Since loyalty could be undermined by gossip, everybody took notes—either for protection or for their book once they left the administration.[23]

The White House had multiple, competing centers of power, and no matter what was decided, the president routinely undercut his staff by changing his mind. Katie Walsh, Priebus's deputy, was the only person in the West Wing who knew how a White House usually ran—and she was bewildered by the chaos in the new regime. In March 2017, Walsh pushed Kushner about the administration's lack of focus: "Just give me the three things the president wants to focus on," she told him. "What are the three priorities of this White House?"

"Yes," the senior advisor to the president said, five months after the election. "We should probably have that conversation."[24]

The Bully's Pulpit

Donald Trump proved to be the most innovative president regarding communications since Theodore Roosevelt developed the "Bully Pulpit." But whereas Roosevelt reserved the phrase for using the prestige and visibility of the presidency "to inspire or moralize"[25]—in 1901, "bully" meant splendid, as in "bully for you"—Trump used his visibility and prestige to create a bully pulpit in the contemporary sense of the word: attacking and demoralizing the vulnerable, using nonfactual media to intimidate and expose opponents, and advancing a divisive agenda.[26]

Trump actively engaged and mobilized the online sources that were creating alternative worldviews. In 2015, he appeared on InfoWars with Alex Jones, a conspiracy theorist whose radio audience, *Rolling Stone* reported, was bigger than Glenn Beck's and Rush Limbaugh's combined; his website had nearly as many visitors as National Public Radio. Jones's targets included Limbaugh (a "whore"), the Gates Foundation (a eugenics movement), Obama and Hillary Clinton (demons who smelled of sulfur), and a New World Order trying to destroy freedom.[27] Trump often sounded, wrote Jonathan Tilove, as if Jones was "the voice in Donald Trump's head." Three days after his victory, the president-elect called Jones, showering him with praise and telling him he was call number 61, just after the King of Saudi Arabia and the Queen of England.[28]

Fox News gave Trump the equivalent of a state-controlled network, particularly through the commentators who fed their audiences his claims and promises without fact-checking or skepticism. Rupert Murdoch had favored Ted Cruz or Marco Rubio for the nomination, and his most popular commentators had been skeptical of Trump—until they saw where their audiences were going and rushed back to the front of the parade. Before he was fired for sexual harassment, former Fox CEO Roger Ailes warned Murdoch not to get too close to Trump: "Trump gets great ratings, but if you're not careful, he is going to end up totally controlling Fox News." Murdoch decided to stay close to Trump, despite his obvious flaws.[29]

But Trump's power went beyond traditional media outlets; he used Twitter to taint any charges against him, taunt reporters and politicians who contradicted him, and trigger online attacks on anyone who stood in his way. Conspiracy theories, personal insults, and patently false claims were part of his stock in trade. James Baker, the FBI general counsel, was one of several FBI agents and officials subjected to attack tweets when they followed the law instead of bending to the president. "It's just a very disorienting, strange experience for a person like me, who doesn't have much of a public profile," he said. "It's frightening. . . . You feel very exposed."[30]

Even relatively innocuous comments about Trump were treated as acts of war. Answering questions from supporters at a Rotary Club meeting, Mitch McConnell defended the party when asked about Trump's promises of fast results. "Our new president, of course, has not been in this line of work before," McConnell said. "And I think he had excessive expectations about how quickly things happen in the democratic process."

"Senator Mitch McConnell said I had 'excessive expectations,' but I don't think so," Trump tweeted in response. "After 7 years of hearing Repeal & Replace, why not done?"[31]

When Paul Ryan disinvited Trump to his district after the *Access Hollywood* tape aired during the campaign, conservative media and online activists drove Ryan's favorability ratings down and members of the Freedom Caucus talked of deposing him as Speaker on the first day of the new Congress.[32]

The innovative (and ultimately self-immolative) tactics Ted Cruz had used against a divided, unpopular Republican establishment in 2013 were reaching their apotheosis with Trump. But whereas Cruz had tried to paint himself as the most ideologically pure at the expense of his colleagues, Trump was using the full force of the presidency—and his rabid following—to humiliate or outright destroy his opponents. His longtime associates Louise Sunshine and Barbara Res described Trump as a "street fighter" who "fights very, very, very dirty."[33]

Ryan learned his lesson, and became so subservient he would not acknowledge a valid basis for any critique of Trump. Regarding Steve Bannon's appointment as White House strategist, he replied "I have no concerns. I trust Donald's judgment." What about the president's claim that there were millions of illegal votes for Hillary Clinton? "I don't know. I'm not really focused on these things." Any worries about Trump's conflicts of interest? He can handle his business interests "however he wants to." When Trump threatened to revoke security clearances for any CIA or NSA director who criticized him, Ryan claimed Trump was only "trolling people."[34]

By wielding his media influence and populist appeal as cudgels against his naysayers, Trump was able to compel grudging compliance—or silence— from an already fractious Republican establishment. Cruz's goal had been the White House; Trump's goal—which would only emerge slowly from leaks and investigations as he maneuvered to control the Republican Party and the federal government—was what he could accomplish for himself while *inside* the White House.

Family Business Is Government Business

As president, Trump possessed new powers and privileges, and more opportunities to pass off his self-interested interactions with foreign leaders as stagecraft.[35] Instead of separating government business from family business, the latter steered his foreign policy aims as much as or more than the former.

Six days after the election, the president-elect talked with Argentina's President Mauricio Macri about continued cooperation with the US on intelligence sharing and drug trafficking. With his daughter Ivanka on the line, he mentioned that the permits for a Trump-licensed building in Buenos Aires had not been approved. Within 24 hours, the permits were issued.[36]

Trump wanted to eliminate the Foreign Corrupt Practices Act, a law that made bribery of foreign government officials a crime and made it easy to investigate deals involving money plundered from the country's government. He told Rex Tillerson to "get rid of that law," but his then–secretary of state informed him only Congress could do that. Unwilling to accept any limit on his power, Trump then told senior advisor Stephen Miller to draft an executive order.[37] He ultimately failed to eliminate the law, but when the US later imposed sanctions on various Iranian firms, the list conspicuously excluded the company that built a Trump-branded hotel in Azerbaijan.[38]

Trump also made moves to exert control over the federal agencies that could get in his way, most notably in his interactions with FBI director James Comey and federal prosecutor Preet Bharara. His attempts to extract a pledge of unwavering loyalty from Comey (who was overseeing the probe into Russian interference in the 2016 election) and Bharara (whose investigations of Russian and Turkish nationals were already threatening Trump's business ties with Putin and Erdoğan) echoed the approach of Trump's mentor and fixer Roy Cohn, who liked to say, "I don't care what the law is, tell me who the judge is."[39] Trump's demand for political fealty, regardless of morality or veracity, resulted in Bharara's firing after Trump initially stated he would retain the US Attorney.[40]

The intersection of lucrative business deals and questionable governance was most glaringly obvious in Trump's dealings with Russia. On the campaign trail, Trump had long been a creative and prolific apologist for Putin's assassinations or assaults on his citizens or his country's allies. In April 2016, after Trump had won twenty-six primaries, the Russian government began to approve his applications for ten-year trademark extensions; he received six extensions during the campaign and an additional four on November 8—Election Day. And while it didn't go public until after the election, on the day of the third Republican primary debate, Trump signed a letter of intent for a 100-story tower in Moscow, with its $50 million penthouse intended for Putin.[41] In Trump's first week in office, State Department staff were ordered to draft plans to unilaterally rescind sanctions on Russia. When Senators John McCain and Chuck Schumer learned of the secret plans, they blocked them.[42]

The president's daughter and son-in-law, meanwhile, engaged in a level of self-interested international wheeling and dealing that rivaled that of the president. On the day of the first meeting between President Trump and Chinese Communist Party Secretary Xi Jinping, the Chinese government awarded Ivanka three new trademarks for her company.[43] Meanwhile, US intelligence agencies documented discussions by officials in four countries looking for ways they could take advantage of Kushner's well-known financial woes: the United Arab Emirates, China, Israel, and Mexico.[44]

Before the inauguration, Kushner met secretly with a Russian banker close to Putin who was under American sanctions. Kushner tried to conceal three meetings with the Russian ambassador; at one meeting, he and General Michael Flynn asked the ambassador to arrange a secret communications channel to Moscow. Despite all the warning signs, Trump invoked his presidential authority to grant Kushner and his daughter top-secret clearances so they could access the Presidential Daily Briefing the CIA had wanted to keep from Kushner.[45] Trump's then–chief of staff John Kelly and White House Counsel Donald McGahn knew that Kushner's clearance was being held up for a "high-level law-enforcement problem," and they both wrote memos for their files to protect themselves should a major criminal case or national security breach be involved. Given that Kushner would continue to attempt to leverage his status to get foreign investors from China and Qatar to bail out his family firm, it was a wise defensive move.

Crony Capitalism

From the start of his administration, Trump attempted to engage in crony capitalism, dispensing regulatory favors to companies in exchange for political favors. The Administrative Procedures Act of 1946, a key (but hardly known) aspect of the modern US government, became a principal component of the conflicts between cronyism and the checks and balances of the federal system. The law requires hearings and scientific evidence before any regulation can be changed by cabinet members and officials. This makes it hard for a president or his appointees to do a favor—say, changing an environmental standard or a safety requirement—for the sake of one company. It is "a core protection against arbitrary governance."[46]

Normally, administrations seeking to change or roll back regulations are successful in getting the rules changed 70 percent of the time. In its first two years, the Trump administration was successful less than 7 percent of the time; in 28 of the first 30 rules they altered, the changes were overturned.[47]

Successful or not, Trump's attempts advertised his favoritism while eroding the integrity of regulatory agencies. Lamenting the lack of effective accountability in Trump's White House, journalist Patrick Radden Keefe asked, "Whom can you call when the authorities are the ones breaking the rules?"[48]

Trump had more success with payoffs involving decisions by appointees to regulatory agencies. The FCC quickly approved the sale of Fox's entertainment division to Disney, blocked a merger that would have created a rival to Fox, and stalled a merger of Time Warner and AT&T for two years—rulings worth billions of dollars to Rupert Murdoch and his family. The regulatory moves weren't just "highly unusual," former FCC chair Reed Hundt said—they were also "pro-Fox, pro-Fox, and pro-Fox."[49]

On the legislative side, Trump's budget called for reducing funding to programs for sheltering and housing the poor, with the notable exception of a housing subsidy that paid the president's company over $5 million a year.[50]

Ryan's "Deal with the Devil"

Amid the chaos and cronyism, Mitch McConnell and Paul Ryan had to figure out how to pass as much of their legislation as possible while managing both their divided caucuses and a president who expected to call all the shots and counted on them to deliver.

Ryan only consented to take the Speakership after John Boehner's resignation if his fellow Republicans would agree to be "a proposition party, offering an agenda." The party conference had spent much of the previous year developing the "Better Way" program, which focused primarily on tax reform and omitted the more divisive issues of foreign trade and immigration policy.[51]

With Trump's support, Ryan believed his agenda could create a "virtuous cycle" that reversed the country's decline and regenerated prosperity for all. For Ryan, that meant cutting taxes far enough to end entitlements. His good friends called working with Trump "Paul's deal with the Devil."[52]

Slowly but surely, Ryan realized that the president equated honor codes with disloyalty. When Trump first called him a "fucking Boy Scout," the former altar boy thought it was a compliment, the expletive notwithstanding. But after Ryan successfully passed some bills early in Trump's administration, an approving Trump said he would stop using that nickname. Then Ryan realized it was an insult; to the president, he told Tim Alberta, "Boy Scouts are stupid because they don't cut corners, they're not lethal, they're not killers."[53]

Unlike Ryan, McConnell had no idealistic concerns or illusions about the president. He had three goals for the administration: tax reform, repealing Obamacare, and confirming judges—starting with the Supreme Court seat he had kept open for a Republican president. He wasn't worried about Trump's business deals, as Elaine Chao, his wife and Trump's secretary of transportation, was using her position to advance the interests of her family's shipping company, one of the largest in Asia.[54]

As Senate Majority Leader, McConnell controlled all judicial appointments and confirmations of major cabinet and government agency leaders, and he wielded his power efficiently. His tactics since he became majority leader in 2015 stalled Obama and provided Trump with eighty-eight district court and seventeen court of appeals appointments to fill—in addition to the Supreme Court vacancy. McConnell's mantra was "leave no vacancy behind." He sped up the confirmation process by cutting the debate time allowed for district court judges from thirty hours to two hours. Working directly with Donald McGahn, the White House counsel, he shepherded record numbers of federal judges through confirmation, all selected for their conservative legal credentials.[55] The days of bipartisan cooperation on judges was gone.

Obamacare

On matters of governance and legislation, the administration's disorganization and lack of planning yielded a great deal of sound and fury, ultimately signifying nothing.

Trump's first act as president was an executive order instructing federal agencies to take all feasible measures to roll back the Affordable Care Act. But repeal required complex legislation, and despite seven years of promises and scores of attempts, Republicans had never done the work necessary to deliver on their vows for repealing—or replacing—Obamacare. They needed a bill they could defend, not just a bill President Obama would have vetoed. Their most visible, long-standing promise became a most uncivil war within the party.

In March of 2017, Republicans reintroduced the American Health Care Act (AHCA), a bill first introduced in 2015, which would essentially scrap most of Obamacare without any replacement. The bill split the party. The Freedom Caucus opposed it because the partial repeal left in place a structure that could be expanded later. The Club for Growth and Heritage Action also called for total repeal, and the Koch brothers announced a multimillion-dollar program of ads, field staff, and mailings—open only to members of Congress who voted no on the partial repeal.[56]

When debates over the AHCA were at a critical point, Trump met with the Freedom Caucus to emphasize how important the repeal was to his agenda and eventual re-election. One by one, the members patiently explained their policy objections to the bill's critical details—mandates, benefits, price controls, subsidies, etc.—until the president cut off the discussion. "Forget about the little shit," he said. "Let's focus on the big picture here."[57]

None of the representatives changed their votes after the meeting. The president, they realized, didn't know what was in the bill, and didn't understand—or care—why the details would matter to them and their futures. The Freedom Caucus members all knew he was bluffing when he told them this was the final bill. He didn't control the agenda; *they* decided what legislation to send to *him*. All he could do was sign or veto it, and they knew he was desperate to sign anything that he could claim was a "repeal and replace."[58]

Ryan raced unsuccessfully to pass the bill before the Congressional Budget Office announced its analysis of the bill's impact. As Ryan expected, the report, when it came, was brutal: twenty-four million people would lose their healthcare. As press coverage of the repeal increased, Obamacare looked far better to voters than any of the Republican alternatives.[59] Many legislators, including some of the most conservative among them, realized that rolling back the coverage gains under Obamacare would be a political disaster. At what point, conservative columnist Jim Geraghty wondered, "is it fair to conclude their self-assurance was evidence they had no idea what they were talking about?"[60]

Republican voters did not support the new plans, moderate and Democratic voters were wildly opposed, many Republican governors were threatened, and it wouldn't even fulfill Trump's promise to cut healthcare costs for working-class Americans. Ryan pulled the legislation off the floor, admitting defeat: "Obamacare is the law of the land. It's gonna remain the law of the land."[61]

When Congress mounted a second effort to repeal Obamacare, Republican governors, some from states with Republican senators, began to go on the warpath, warning that the repeal would devastate their re-election chances. In both parties, alarms went off over the damage to their constituents, as well as state budgets and insurance companies. The non-partisan National Governors Association, a cautious organization that seldom took stands on sensitive issues, issued a letter asking the Senate not to vote on the measure.[62] The stunning failure of the GOP's longtime fore-most legislative goal was indicative not only of the Trump White House's inability to broker deals, but also of the disarray and division within the party itself.

Willing Accomplices and Useful Idiots

In both houses of Congress, Republicans forsook the rule of law in favor of the rule of public opinion. Congressman Jason Chaffetz, chair of the House Oversight Committee—the committee charged with recognizing and stopping such flagrant examples of corruption—was more than willing to ignore the president's use of his office for personal gain. "[Trump's] already rich," Chaffetz said. "I don't think that he ran for this office to line his pockets even more." Asked about Kushner's attempts to get a $400 million loan with a Chinese company while serving as a presidential advisor, Chaffetz replied, "I don't see how that affects the average American and their taxpayer dollars. Just the fact that a staff person's family is making money? It's not enough."[63]

Chaffetz's defense of overlooking—instead of overseeing—the impropri-eties of the president and his family foreshadowed a steep decline in ethical standards. Until the profiteering and cronyism of the presidential family started to bother the average voter, they could be ignored.[64]

While corruption could be overlooked, Putin was another story. Trump's consistent praise of the Russian president worried his top military and intelligence brass. Nothing had ever been as unnerving as a president who simply, time and again, disavowed their findings with a three-word explanation: "Putin told me."[65] Andrew McCabe, then the acting director of the FBI, articulated the disbelief felt by intelligence operatives: "How do you effectively convey intelligence to the American president who chooses to believe the Russians over his own intelligence services? And then tells them that to their faces?"[66]

Republicans did everything they could to insulate the party from collateral damage. House leaders had been so worried about Trump's relations with Russia before the election that Ryan had declared the topic taboo for public discussion. When Republicans learned that Attorney General Jeff Sessions did not divulge his two meetings with the Russian ambassador at his confirmation hearings, GOP senators, Ryan, Majority Leader Kevin McCarthy, and even Chaffetz took rare public stands and pressed him at once to recuse himself from the Russia investigation. With that much smoke, the Republicans wanted fire insurance.[67]

Trump, meanwhile, wanted fealty. When he asked FBI director James Comey for a pledge of personal loyalty before the inauguration, Comey answered he "would always be honest" but not "reliable in the conventional political sense." Trump wanted more—"I need loyalty. I expect loyalty"—but didn't get it. [68]

Trump fired Comey in May, when investigations of Russian interference in the election and possible perjury by Michael Flynn were heating up. The president claimed he fired Comey on the basis of a memo by the deputy attorney general, Rod Rosenstein. Realizing he had been set up to take the rap for an egregious power play—and suddenly in command because of Sessions' recusal—Rosenstein appointed Robert Mueller as special prosecutor to investigate the Comey firing.[69] As with the president's efforts to get closer to Putin, GOP leaders would play a crucial role in insulating the party from the Mueller investigation's fallout.

When Trump fired Comey, senators and representatives rushed to protect the FBI's autonomy by insisting on an independent director. John Cornyn, the Senate's number two Republican, and Representative Trey Gowdy, a former FBI agent, were floated for the role of FBI director, but both declined to consider the job.[70] Lindsey Graham, who had also coauthored a bipartisan bill to protect Mueller from being removed as independent counsel, told reporters Comey's termination "made it tough" for any member of the Senate or House to take the job; many, but not all, senators and some representatives wanted insurance should Trump cross the line. The problem they faced, however, was that the so-called line was a rapidly shifting boundary. Trump regularly raged at Sessions for recusing himself and refusing to "unrecuse" so he could fire Mueller. McConnell, in turn, defended Sessions and warned Trump that he would create a major crisis if he fired his attorney general.[71]

Meanwhile, a small band of say-anything, attack-anyone representatives become an integral part of Trump's defense, working with him to discredit the investigations. Congressman Devin Nunes of California, an erstwhile "go-along-and-get-along" backbencher who had warmed to Trump's populist politics, became a valuable ally. Nunes was the incoming chair of the House Permanent Select Committee on Intelligence, and Flynn and Trump saw during the campaign that he was the kind of easy-going, shallow *bon vivant* that fit right in with their personal business plans. Trump put Nunes on the executive committee for his transition and flattered him by announcing he was being considered for Director of National Intelligence, an idea as wildly implausible as anything else floated during the transition.[72]

Nunes possessed a startling combination of ambition and intellectual laziness. Journalist Jason Zengerle learned that Nunes read the fewest documents of any committee member and attended the fewest secure briefings at the intelligence agencies. He didn't even do his homework before the quarterly visits by the CIA director.[73] Nunes became one of the president's most valuable House assets, a perfect ally: no strong convictions, no attention to details, negligent about his responsibilities, and easy to get along with. With no House findings of wrongdoing to cloud the picture, Nunes cleared the way for other representatives to discredit revelations and attack witnesses for bias.

Along with Nunes, two members of the House Freedom Caucus, Jim Jordan and Matt Gaetz, became valuable members of Trump's cheerleading squad-cum-defense team. Jordan excelled at aggressive confrontations with witnesses and bullying recalcitrant representatives. Gaetz, to round out the group's repertoire, was a master at stunts that cheered the right and infuriated the left. "Stagecraft Is Statecraft" was his motto, and he believed that keeping people's attention was how a politician kept power. At the 2018 State of the Union address, he brought a right-wing Holocaust skeptic. At a hearing with parents of schoolchildren killed by a gunman, he told the parents that Trump's border wall would save more lives than gun control—and tried to have them ejected from the hearing when they disagreed.[74]

Jordan and Gaetz even introduced articles of impeachment against Rosenstein, claiming he was withholding documents from Congress. Rosenstein took care of the threat by telling Nunes, "If you really did prosecute me for contempt, I would call you and your staffers as defense witnesses to prove that I am operating in good faith, so I request that you preserve relevant text messages and emails."[75]

Confusion and dysfunction of the type stirred up by Nunes and his allies were as integral a part of Trump's plans as the president's own thunderbolt headlines and smokescreen tweets. A guest at a Republican fundraiser taped Nunes explaining the importance of House disrupters like him, Gaetz, and Jordan. "The left controls the universities in this country, Hollywood, and the mainstream media," Nunes had said in comments to a Fox News host. On the recording, he continued, "If Sessions won't unrecuse and Mueller won't clear the president, we're the only ones."[76]

While Nunes protected the president from investigations by the House Intelligence Committee, its Senate counterpart treated the Russian interference as a genuine problem, subpoenaing documents from Flynn and the Treasury Department.

Furious that McConnell refused to do more to protect him from the Senate's investigation, Trump pressured Senators Richard Burr and Thom Tillis to end the investigation. Burr, the chair of the Senate Intelligence Committee, pushed back and said he was going to see the investigation through, and maintained a bipartisan, professional investigation. Tillis introduced a bipartisan bill to protect Mueller from the president . McConnell, however, would not allow hearings on the bill. Every time the issue arose, he argued protection wasn't necessary because Trump wouldn't fire Mueller, siding with the senators who thought it better not to "[poke] the bear."[77]

Trump's threats did not persuade senators to stop investigating his campaign's relations with Putin. There were too many ominous warning signs. Mueller had already indicted the president's former campaign manager, Paul Manafort, and there was a steady stream of stories about secret meetings and contacts with other Russians connected to Putin.[78]

Trump Changes the Money Game

A populist president comfortable with conspiracy theories and racism—a fact made even more clear by Trump's cringe-worthy "very fine people on both sides" response to a white nationalist rally in Charlottesville, Virginia—Trump dominated the world of extreme challengers to moderate Republicans.

This changed the game for "purity for profit" groups like the Koch network. Trump's endorsement was now more valuable than their monetary contributions. The Club for Growth and the Senate Conservative Fund learned that they couldn't rely on stirring anger and fear against Trump to raise money; instead, their fundraising appeals emphasized supporting endangered Republican incumbents.[79]

The Koch network also had to adapt and put some of their plans on hold. Their donors were enjoying bonuses from a Trump presidency without the onus of supporting him; they all benefited from a tax cut that favored the billionaire class, and most gained as well from the administration's attempts at deregulation and an anti-climate change agenda. But it was harder to advance their limited-government policies as support for Obamacare increased and Republican attempts to repeal it came to an unceremonious end.

Chastened by the inglorious end to the Tea Party movement, the Koch network backed away from supporting conspiratorial and eccentric grassroots protests. When the Koch network met late in 2017, their anger was directed at senators unwilling to slash all entitlements in the fight for tax cuts. They were disenchanted with Republicans who didn't stay fully committed to their views. At the same time, they were changing their own standards of fiscal responsibility; they told supporters and surrogates to downplay the deficit, which had been their main argument against the Obama stimulus package.[80]

When Republicans passed their tax reform bill in December 2017, Charles Koch contributed $500,000 to Paul Ryan's Leadership PAC. Ryan endured and overcame the inevitable Freedom Caucus power plays, demanding the right to vote on each provision of the tax bill individually and not as a package. Ryan dropped one tax the Kochs opposed, and the Freedom Caucus, who had no plans other than obstruction, finally went along with the party.[81]

The final tax bill was both deliberately and inadvertently a major gift to the wealthiest Americans. It was a bill, wrote Thomas Edsall, "you cannot be too cynical about," rushed through without hearings and filled with rule changes that benefited wealthy taxpayers. The president told his supporters he got nothing from the bill, yet a surreptitious, last-minute provision gave real-estate investors a multimillion-dollar windfall. Despite Trump's promises about manufacturing jobs coming home with the tax reform, changes to taxes on corporate investments *increased* the inducements to replace factory workers with robots. The incentives to bring overseas profits home were also supposed to create more factory jobs, but the repatriated profits were almost exclusively used to buy back stock.[82]

The Koch network was strong enough to publicly challenge Trump, who had favored a more protectionist approach, because they weren't interested in making money from online fundraising; rather, they were spending their own money to create government policies that were profitable for their donors, and to block the tariffs advocated by some members of the administration.

By 2018, as the parties prepared for the midterms, Trump raged against the Kochs after their network announced they were willing to support free-trade Democratic incumbents against protectionist Republican challengers. "The globalist Koch Brothers, who have become a total joke in real Republican circles, are against Strong Borders and Powerful Trade," Trump tweeted. He charged that their goal was to "protect their companies outside the U.S. from being taxed."[83]

Pelosi and Schumer Outmaneuver Ryan and McConnell

By late summer 2017, Republicans needed to pass a bill that would raise the debt ceiling and avoid government default. Without a decisive president to set priorities, a beleaguered Ryan could not round up enough votes to send a debt ceiling bill to the Senate. The two Democratic minority leaders, Representative Nancy Pelosi and Senator Chuck Schumer, took advantage of the Freedom Caucus's power plays and Trump's frustration and inexperience to pull off two maneuvers that set Democrats up for the midterm.

The Freedom Caucus was no more reasonable or party-oriented now than when they had faced Obama, and they still utilized the same kind of faction-oriented obstructions. They advanced no cause but publicity for themselves, making Ryan's life so miserable he compared being Speaker to running a day-care center. Instead of putting a proposal on the table and having a vote between a Freedom Caucus plan and a Ryan plan, they used their thirty votes to make demands on Ryan, one at a time. Whenever Ryan agreed to their "final demand," another emerged.[84]

Pelosi and Schumer offered the Republicans the votes they needed to pass a three-month extension of the debt ceiling in exchange for more money for programs the Democrats wanted to protect. Ryan called it a "ridiculous idea" and insisted on an eighteen-month extension, which would carry them past the midterms.

When Pelosi and Schumer met with Trump, Pelosi interrupted a monologue by Treasury Secretary Steven Mnuchin and reminded the president that the "currency of the realm" was votes. Pelosi had the votes and Ryan didn't; centrist Republicans balked at the Freedom Caucus's kamikaze tactics, refusing to vote for extreme provisions that would die in the Senate.[85] It was a "no-lose situation" for the Democrats.

Trump agreed to the Democrats' proposals on the spot, happy to get something accomplished without more fighting with Ryan and McConnell. In private, the president even praised Pelosi and Schumer for their deal's telegenic optics, noting that McConnell and Ryan "[weren't] doing as well by comparison." In exchange for funding of domestic programs, Pelosi and Schumer agreed to support the debt ceiling increase and the emergency relief needed for Hurricane Harvey, which had devastated large parts of Louisiana and Texas. "They're the only two people who came to the meeting with a deal to be made," a White House aide explained. Democrats were very careful not to gloat or crow about their deal, while Republicans were stunned.[86]

The next February, with the three-month bill near its end and another default looming, Pelosi and Schumer did even better. Ryan couldn't pass a budget without help from the White House, and Democrats couldn't make a deal with Republicans until the president made a decision and stuck to it. Trump's indecision and vacillation, Schumer complained, "[had] reduced the Republicans to shambles," while Ryan urged the president to "come to the table." Alex Conant, a GOP strategist, explained that an indecisive president "emboldens all parties to take positions that they won't compromise."

Trump's anxious wavering and Pelosi and Schumer's doggedness paid off for the Democrats; Trump ultimately was less concerned about details than about a headline-grabbing deal he could spin. Instead of the major cuts in domestic spending Republicans wanted, Democrats won ten years of funding for the Children's Health Insurance Program (CHIP), two years of community health center funding, and more than $100 billion for disaster relief, infrastructure repairs, and opioid and mental health treatment. The Republicans, meanwhile, got the increase in defense spending they wanted.[87]

Midterm Warning: Nice Party, GOP, Be a Shame If Something Happened to It

A year into his presidency, Trump's only legislative victory was a tax cut tilted heavily toward the wealthiest Americans. Balanced against that success were rampant warning signs of a discontented electorate. Roy Cohn had taught Trump to always have an "other"—a group of unwanted, "lesser" outsiders. Predictably, the "others" noticed—and resisted—from the start.

Throughout Trump's administration, Republicans faced bad polls, frequent protests, and crowded town halls.[88] On the day after Trump's inauguration, the Women's March yielded at least 653 protests in cities and towns across the country, nine of them topping 100,000 people. It was the largest single day of mobilization in US history, larger than the Vietnam Moratoriums in 1969 and 1970. The marchers totaled between 3.3 and 5.2 million, and at least 721,000 marched in states that Trump won. His embrace of nativism and social conservatism had mobilized suburbanites and many blue-collar women.[89]

Stan Greenberg and Page Gardner conducted focus groups in battleground states three months later, and reported that female, blue-collar Trump supporters were wavering. In 2016, Trump carried non-college white women by 21 points. Spending billions on a wall—a "vanity project"—while cutting Meals on Wheels and medical research suggested he was out of touch with their struggles.[90]

In November 2017, the Virginia gubernatorial election provided a bellwether for the midterms. Ed Gillespie ran as a Trump Republican in Virginia, embracing the president's messages on immigration, crime, and support for the Confederate flag. Democrat Ralph Northam won with the biggest margin of any Virginia Democrat in thirty-two years. Other Republican governors were rattled. "When Republicans lose white married women, that's a strong message," Tennessee governor Bill Haslam said. Governors Larry Hogan and Scott Walker met with Vice President Pence and candidly asked him to persuade the president to stay away during the midterm campaigns unless the candidate invited him.[91]

Democratic fundraising stunned Republicans, too. A year before the midterms, 162 Democrats had raised over $100,000 each for races against 82 incumbent Republicans. There was so much opposition to the GOP direction under Trump that two or sometimes even three Democratic candidates *in the same primary race* had raised that much money.[92]

Trump's moves to secure quasi-autocratic control of government powers had resulted in a hamstrung Republican Party, emboldened Democrats, and an ever-growing cloud of controversy around the Oval Office. As 2017 ended and the midterm elections approached, two of the president's hard-nosed campaign associates, Corey Lewandowski and David Bossie, reiterated the threat Trump made to Republican Party leaders after the *Access Hollywood* tape: the president expected loyalty and was ready to "take down the GOP if it resists."[93]

In March 2018, a young Democrat and military veteran, Conor Lamb, won a special congressional election in a Pennsylvania district Trump had won by 20 points. Republicans were in denial, arguing that Lamb had run as a Republican—that he'd even praised Trump. In fact, Lamb had campaigned against the Trump tax cuts and against new restrictions on abortion, and his most frequent attacks were against Ryan's proposed cuts to Social Security.[94]

Ryan saw what was ahead—ugly intraparty stalemates and a looming Democratic wave in the 2018 midterm election—and had no interest in trying to overcome the Freedom Caucus's self-promotional stunts. A month after Lamb's victory, he announced he would retire in April. For all his talk of leading a "proposition party," Paul Ryan had failed. Despite being esteemed as a "policy wonk," he had never turned his ideas into viable legislation. Ryan only got his reputation as a "big thinker," Barney Frank once wryly observed, "because he is being graded on a curve."[95]

Predictably, Jim Jordan blamed Ryan for the deficit spending, ignoring the ways that his caucus's refusal to support passable budget reductions gave the Democrats leverage to win *increases* in spending for safety-net programs. Twice, a majority of Republican representatives had preferred a compromise with Democrats over a pyrrhic Freedom Caucus win.[96]

Trade Wars: Easy to Start, Not So Easy to Win

The specter of China's explosive economic growth over the previous couple of decades had made that country a prime target of Trump's speeches during his campaign. Its share of world manufacturing grew from 4 percent in 1991 to 24 percent in 2012. This was a massive, one-time "China Shock" that was highly unlikely to ever be reversed, and Nobel Prize–winning economist Paul Krugman warned that "major disruptions now would be more likely to come from an attempt to reverse globalization than from leaving the current trade regime in place."[97] American and Chinese companies were part of essential worldwide supply chains upon which most exports from advanced industrial countries depended, and trade wars are always disruptive—unless you believed, as Trump did, that "trade wars are good and easy to win."

In March 2018, without alerting Ryan or McConnell, Trump announced he was imposing a 25 percent tariff on imported steel and a 10 percent tariff on imported aluminum. He could act unilaterally because Commerce Secretary Wilbur Ross produced a dubious ruling that steel and aluminum imports threatened American national security.[98]

The tariffs were opposed by Ryan, McConnell, the Chamber of Commerce, the Koch network, virtually every senator, and roughly half of congressional representatives, but Trump dismissed this opposition. His trade advisor, Peter Navarro, assured interviewers that no country "is going to retaliate [against] the most lucrative and biggest market in the world."[99]

But retaliation was inevitable, and Ryan and McConnell knew it. McConnell sent farm-state senators to talk to Trump, while 107 members of the House signed a letter asking the president to reconsider. When Trump held firm, McConnell dutifully blocked a vote on Bob Corker's bill requiring Senate approval for the national security justification for tariffs. Private arguments with Trump were McConnell's limit; the potential fallout of openly antagonizing Trump bothered him more than the economic damage to manufacturing and agriculture that would be caused by the tariffs.[100]

Japan, Canada, and the European Union met to coordinate their response to the tariffs. Meanwhile, Chinese president Xi Jinping told European diplomats that Trump's bullying was like a "no-rules freestyle boxing match"—an accurate description, since the president had no specific demands or strategy. China's retaliation, in contrast, put direct electoral pressure on the president, with tariffs aimed at agricultural products from pro-Trump states. Hog futures dropped 29 percent, soybean futures 18 percent, and corn 12 percent.[101]

By August, the Department of Agriculture was preparing to spend up to $12 billion to compensate farmers for the "unjustified tariff retaliation." Farm debt reached the highest level since 1980. Farm bankruptcies, despite the government assistance, were the highest since the Great Recession of 2008; in Indiana, Wisconsin, and Illinois, bankruptcies in 2018 doubled those of 2008. Nationally, nearly 40 percent of all farm income, Paul Krugman calculated, was from the government, trade assistance, disaster assistance, the farm bill, and insurance indemnities.[102]

After two years of tariff wars, the value of American steel producers had dropped—some as much as 36 percent—while wreaking havoc on companies with a combined two million employees that relied on imported specialty steels not produced in the US.[103] The trade war championed by Trump and Navarro had become a setback for American agriculture and industry. The benefits of import protection were minor compared to the losses from tariffs on manufacturing inputs and retaliatory tariffs on exports.[104] The Republican leadership had predicted it, and, through their inaction, ensured it.

While McConnell was unwilling to challenge Trump, governors were desperate to stem the losses to agriculture and manufacturing. Kentucky's Republican governor, Matt Bevin, hosted a meeting of the National Governors Association's "U.S.-China Governors Collaboration Summit," which featured a meeting with four hundred Chinese business and political leaders. The Republican governors were trying to limit the damage from the trade war and bring back Chinese investment without angering Trump. Over the previous year, Chinese investment in the US had dropped 83 percent, while it rose 80 percent in Canada.[105]

Forced Separation

In April 2018, Jeff Sessions enacted the "zero-tolerance" immigration procedures the president had been loudly demanding: every person entering the US illegally would be prosecuted. What few understood, even in the White House or the Department of Homeland Security, was that the government was *legally* required to separate children from parents who were being prosecuted. The zero-tolerance that Trump wanted thus guaranteed that young children and babies brought into the country illegally would be held in facilities apart from their parents. Sessions and other top immigration officials supported the policy, believing that it would deter future illegal immigration.[106]

Even callously anti-immigration legislators were shocked by the public reaction. ProPublica obtained videos of anguished, sobbing children crying out for their parents from behind bars or barbed wire fences. There was no preparation, inadequate personnel, and no directions.[107]

At the White House, Stephen Miller was pleased by the photos of desolate, poorly-cared-for children. He believed that the outrage was "a feature, not a bug," and that it helped his cause by emphasizing that the US-Mexico border was open; he believed the "closed border" side would always win. He was right when it came to Trump supporters—but wrong about the rest of the country.

The photos of detained immigrant children soon became a PR nightmare for the administration. Border Patrol agents and guards tried to block any more photos of the children, but stories of their overcrowded, unsanitary conditions kept popping up. Even worse were the stories when the government tried to explain why they did not have records of who the children's parents were or where they were being held.[108]

Suddenly, zero-tolerance was equated with zero decency. Evangelist Franklin Graham called the family separation "disgraceful" on the Christian Broadcasting Network. Soon, the president announced that families would be reunited, but added that he still would enforce zero-tolerance. That the two vows were incompatible did not faze him.[109]

Trump and the RNC fell back on "white fright," emphasizing fear of migrants and violent gangs. Republican-aligned PACs ran 280,000 commercials highlighting violent Latin American gangs like MS-13 and targeting sanctuary cities. The clincher, in Trump's eyes, was a caravan of 3,000 to 5,000 migrants—mostly composed of groups of one or two parents with young children—trudging slowly through Central America to seek asylum at the Tijuana border crossing. Trump was determined to stop the caravan, threatening to cut off aid to Guatemala, Honduras, El Salvador, and ultimately Mexico if they didn't stop it.

Ted Cruz, in danger of losing his Senate seat to Democratic challenger Beto O'Rourke, dropped his dog whistle approach to deportation and one-upped the president about the border with a joking open letter to the caravan:

Dear Members of the Caravan: Please be advised, we have identified homes for you that are willing to take you in. These homes have volunteered to give you a place to stay, to give you food, to give you health care. You don't have to work for any of it. Each of these homes has helpfully self-identified by placing a small black and white Beto sign in the front yard. And when you get there, just kick the door down. They don't believe in walls, Let yourself in. Make yourself at home."[110]

Fox News's daily coverage of the caravan drew higher ratings than the last month of the 2016 presidential campaign. To emphasize the "threat" to America, Trump suggested the caravan might include Muslim terrorists and violent killers, and ordered the Pentagon to send 5,200 soldiers to defend the border. It was pure theater, but with no completed wall, no trade victories, and no major successes, white fright about an open border with Mexico gave Trump an issue to mobilize supporters.[111]

The Party of Trump

Trump urged voters to treat the midterm election as a referendum on him, telling his audiences, "I want you to vote. Pretend I'm on the ballot." He hardly needed to say it. At a conference in Michigan, former Speaker John Boehner told the audience, "There is no Republican Party. There is a Trump Party. . . . The Republican Party is taking a nap somewhere." Senator Bob Corker was more candid, calling the party "a cult-like situation."[112]

Boehner and Corker were right. In ten NBC/*Wall Street Journal* polls during 2018, 56 percent of Republicans said they were more a supporter of Trump versus 38 percent who said they were more a supporter of the party. No president since World War II had so dominated American politics, never had so many Americans said their vote would be shaped by who should control Congress, and never had the two parties' ratings of the president been so divergent.[113]

Midterm results affirmed how powerful Trump's appeal was at motivating Republicans. Republican congressional candidates received 50.9 million votes, a 14 percent increase from 44.8 million in the 2010 Tea Party wave. But Trump motivated Democrats and independents, too. Democratic candidates received 60.6 million votes, close to the 63 million votes Trump received in 2016. Democrats in ninety-nine districts received more votes in 2018 than Hillary Clinton had received in the same districts in 2016, while thirty-five Republicans received more votes than Trump.[114] In addition to picking up a whopping 41 seats in the House, Democrats also gained seven governors, who would supervise elections in 2020 and have veto power over reapportionment after the 2020 census. The one positive result for the GOP was that they gained two Senate seats in a very GOP-friendly Senate election, leaving McConnell in charge of confirmations and defending Trump.

Republicans had expected a far better performance from Trump than they received, but the party was just as much to blame. "The initial ecstasy over Trump 'signing their stuff,'" Rich Lowry wrote, "has given way to the reality that they don't have stuff to send him."[115] Every time the Freedom Caucus refused to compromise, the Democrats gained.

With the Democrats back in the majority in the House, Nancy Pelosi retook the Speaker's gavel. Her election night speech left no doubt as to what the Democrats planned to do: "Today is about more than Democrats and Republicans. . . . It is about restoring the Constitution's checks and balances to the Trump administration."

Pelosi was not intimidated by Trump. Her father had been a congressman and the mayor of Baltimore, and she was accustomed to the way tough guys treated women. She told Fareed Zakaria that she had called women friends in New York who knew Trump: "First, he will flatter," they told her. "Then he will bully, and then he will sue."

Steve Bannon observed her at a meeting with Trump in 2017. When Trump claimed he won the popular vote, Pelosi replied, "Well, Mr. President, that's not true. . . . There's no evidence to support what you just said, and if we're going to work together, we have to stipulate to a certain set of facts." Bannon whispered to colleagues, "She's an assassin."[116]

Bannon was right; Pelosi saw through Trump. Unless a spending bill was passed by December 22, the government would be required to shut down. Trump demanded $5.7 billion for his wall or he would refuse to sign; contrary to all evidence, he was certain that immigration and a secure border was a winning issue.

It all came to a head during a televised meeting between Trump and the Democratic leadership. Trump belittled the Speaker-elect, saying she couldn't talk now without endangering her Speakership. Pelosi's retort went viral: "Mr. President, please don't characterize the strength that I bring to this meeting as the leader of the House Democrats, who just won a big victory." Schumer finished off the job, reminding Trump that he had threatened a shutdown if he didn't get his wall funded.

Trump took the bait: "I am proud to shut down the government for border security. . . . So I will take the mantle. I will be the one to shut it down. I'm not going to blame you for it." With that, the president gave the Democrats reason to hold out for more concessions, and boosted Pelosi's popularity for good measure.[117]

Without a Republican-controlled House to protect him, Trump was flailing. Three days after he agreed to accept blame for a government shutdown, he made another impulsive decision: at the urging of President Erdoğan of Turkey, Trump agreed to withdraw troops from Syria, abandoning American allies who had done much of the fighting with Americans, and effectively setting the Kurds up for slaughter, as if they were the undocumented workers his hotels would casually discard at the end of a season.

Appalled, Secretary of Defense James Mattis resigned. "You're going to have to get the next Secretary of Defense to lose to ISIS," he told Trump. "I'm not going to do it."[118] Republican senators were distressed by Mattis's resignation, opposed to letting Putin have Syria, and unwilling to stand back while Erdoğan destroyed the Kurdish military. McConnell said he was "particularly distressed" by Mattis's resignation, and Lindsey Graham warned that a precipitous pullout from Syria would pave the way for another 9/11.[119] Then six senators penned a joint letter urging Trump to reconsider his decision. Senator Pat Toomey called Trump's views "very, very distinct from the vast majority of Republicans and probably Democrats, elected and unelected."[120]

The Dow Jones average dropped to its lowest level of the year as the president pushed the government toward a shutdown and created a foreign policy crisis.[121] When the longest government shutdown in US history ended on January 25, he still didn't have funding for his wall.

To Impeach or Not to Impeach

Nancy Pelosi's biggest management issue was holding back her base's clamor for impeachment. Activists and volunteers had been ready to impeach Trump after his Muslim ban during his first week in office. The fervor grew as he reversed Obama's policies, began to roll back clean air and water standards, and attacked the social safety net.

Trump had keen instincts for inflaming the left and delighting his base. His misogyny, boosterism for coal and oil, talk of "shithole" countries and rapists at the border and "very fine people on both sides," and his constant trolling of mainstream media as "fake news"—even when he was the confidential source of the stories he attacked—raised ratings and kept enough

Democrats eager to impeach Trump to make any realistic calculus on impeachment look like moral cowardice to many.

Pelosi focused on the long game. Her main goal was putting a Democrat in the White House, and she was determined to hold the caucus together and deliver the 2020 Democratic nominee legislation to campaign on. To accomplish that, Pelosi needed to wait until the rest of the country caught up with activists, fundraisers, and partisan media. She carefully built a case against Trump, while the party also passed common-sense (and doomed) legislation that showed voters that McConnell and the GOP, no matter what they promised, would not vote for their reasonable bills.

It was similar to what she'd done in 2007 as Speaker of the House under a Republican president. She kept the focus on legislation that showed her party was ready to govern, daring Republicans to vote "no" on popular bills like raising the minimum wage, which they had buried in committees for six years. The bill passed easily; now that they could not hide their votes, all but four Republican senators voted for the raise.[122]

Pelosi's task now was more difficult than in 2007. It was a pipe dream to believe Mueller's report would be so damning that Republican senators would turn on the president. Trump also had two very competent enablers supporting him: McConnell and Attorney General William Barr, who replaced Jeff Sessions after the midterm.

McConnell blocked bipartisan legislation to protect Mueller's investigation. He considered Trump unfit and unwilling to learn, but he understood that impeaching him could destroy the party. The minute the Democrats captured the House, he began studying impeachment procedure and educating his colleagues about the traps to avoid.[123] With the three senators who had consistently stood up to Trump gone (John McCain had died, and Bob Corker and Jeff Flake had retired), GOP senators and representatives fell in line, attacking Mueller's motivations and credibility in advance. Lindsey Graham didn't even try to hide his political expedience: "If you don't want to get re-elected, you're in the wrong business."[124]

Representatives Jim Jordan, Mark Meadows, and Matt Gaetz continued to make names for themselves by obstructing the machinery of government, browbeating recalcitrant Republicans, bullying witnesses, and disrupting Democrats. Their tactics earned them regular spots on Fox News, and they had few qualms about pushing the boundaries of credibility or reason. Jordan was now the senior Republican on the Oversight Committee, and when Democrats requested documents from someone, Jordan wrote to them urging them not to comply with Democrats' requests. Whether or not they complied with his letter, they could be certain that the Freedom Caucus and president were singling them out for attention.[125]

Once Mueller's report was released, Barr took over. Many Republicans thought Barr would be an establishment lawyer; instead, he proved to be a zealot defending his vision of near-absolute presidential powers and traditional Catholic faith against modern tolerance and moral relativism. Donald Ayer, who worked under Barr as deputy attorney general for George H. W. Bush, believed Barr was a danger to the country. The only reason Ayer could imagine for Barr to accept a position with Trump was the chance "to advance his extraordinary lifetime project of assigning unchecked power to the president."

Barr was not going to defend the president based on the facts of the case; rather, he was challenging the law. The president "*is* the Executive branch," he wrote to the Department of Justice (DOJ) in 2018, "the sole repository of all Executive powers conferred by the Constitution." Trump was the third president (after both Bushes) for whom Barr had made this same argument publicly; tellingly, when Bill Clinton made similar arguments during his impeachment investigation, Barr had called his claims "preposterous."[126]

After Mueller submitted his report, Barr issued his own brief, exculpatory four-page summary, which Jeffrey Toobin called "an obvious act of sabotage against Mueller and an extraordinary gift to the President." Mueller complained in writing about the distorted summary but otherwise remained silent, while Trump declared victory and lobbed attacks at his "treasonous" enemies. Mueller, who had gained a reputation as a person of exceptional character, did not believe an attorney general would distort his report. For Trump and Barr, such integrity and honor were a "weakness they could exploit."[127]

When Barr released the actual (if redacted) Mueller report twenty-five days later, over a thousand former federal prosecutors from both parties protested Barr's initial interpretation of the report. There was more than enough evidence to indict Trump, the report pointed out, except for the DOJ opinion preventing federal criminal prosecution of a sitting president.[128]

The professional and ethical criticism did not faze Barr's advocacy for the president. In the months that followed, Barr slammed an investigation of the Trump campaign that had been authorized by federal judges as "spying," and publicly rejected the DOJ Inspector General's report that the Russia probe was properly initiated and overseen without bias.[129] Barr also helped Trump fulfill a personal favor for President Erdoğan by ending the prosecution of a Turkish bank for its role in Iranian money laundering—a case which implicated Erdoğan's finance minister and, potentially, Erdoğan's own family.[130]

Pelosi under Fire

Democrats pressed Pelosi in May to initiate an impeachment inquiry. For representatives on the committees that conduct an inquiry, it was the chance to flex their muscle in the center ring. For representatives in safely liberal districts, it was a chance to satisfy voters itching to remove Trump.

Pelosi was still not ready; there was no straightforward way to explain "What was the obstruction of justice about?"[131] She batted aside the alternative of merely censuring Trump. "If you're going to go, you've got to go," she said. "In other words, if the goods are there, you must impeach."[132]

The "goods" soon arrived. A whistleblower filed a formal complaint about the president's improper manipulation of military aid for personal political gain, stemming from an April 21 phone call with newly elected Ukrainian president Volodymyr Zelensky. The transcript of the call forcefully suggested that Trump had withheld critical, congressionally approved aid pending Zelensky's announcement of an investigation into Joe Biden—one of the front-runners to oppose Trump in the upcoming election—and his son.

The Inspector General forwarded the whistleblower complaint to Barr, who buried it. The whistleblower then alerted Adam Schiff, the Democratic Intelligence Committee chair. In August, the movement to impeach took off.

On September 24, Congress opened the formal inquiry. It would, of course, have a much easier pathway in the Democrat-controlled House than the GOP-led Senate. Pelosi understood the dynamics at play: Trump would say "'The Democrats impeached me but the Senate'—he wouldn't say Republicans—'exonerated me.'" They moved ahead, and the House approved two articles of impeachment—for abuse of power and obstruction of Congress—on December 18.[133]

McConnell was determined to make the Senate trial as short as possible, and Trump, with Barr's help, ordered everyone in the administration not to testify. "Participating in this inquiry under the current unconstitutional posture would inflict lasting institutional harm," White House Counsel Pat Cipollone wrote.[134]

Trump's threats did not deter all career officials. Two former ambassadors to Ukraine, Marie Yovanovitch and William B. Taylor Jr., and two members of the NSC, Lieutenant Colonel Alexander Vindman and Dr. Fiona Hill, made a case that is likely to stand the test of time—even though it did not persuade many Republicans.

Ted Cruz became the poster boy for John Boehner's conclusion that the GOP was now the party of Trump. Before the testimony began, Cruz claimed that there was "considerable evidence" that Ukraine interfered in the 2016 election—a Russia-backed conspiracy theory for which a Senate Select Intelligence Committee investigation had found no evidence—and that the charge that Trump offered President Zelensky a quid pro quo was hearsay. Once quid pro quo had been established by several witnesses, Cruz changed his tune, saying it "doesn't matter."[135]

The trial lasted all of three weeks. McConnell was gambling that Trump would maintain the GOP's grip on the White House, and that they could repair the damage after the election. One Republican senator, Mitt Romney, joined Democrats in voting "yes" for one of the charges. Senator Lamar Alexander, about to retire, voted to acquit Trump without declaring him innocent. If the Senate removed Trump from office, Alexander said, "it would just pour gasoline on cultural fires that are burning out there."[136]

Eager to put the episode behind them, endangered Republican senators said that Trump would change. "I believe he will be much more cautious in the future," Susan Collins said, "[because impeachment] is a pretty big lesson."[137]

Instead, Trump wasted no time in returning to his standard operating procedure—revenge. Government officials who testified against him were demoted, recalled, or fired. He replaced the director of national intelligence, Richard Maguire, for briefing senators on Russia's preference for him in 2016. He also admitted that he had sent attorney Rudy Giuliani to Ukraine after denying it during his trial.[138]

Wealth versus Health: The War on Government Backfires

Trump never worried about the long term in his business planning, and he was no different in government. When told his tax cuts would eventually spike the national debt, he retorted, "Yeah, but I won't be here." That same attitude pervaded all his planning. Happy to cut government in general—and his predecessor's policies in particular—he reversed Obama's decision to station employees from the Centers for Disease Control and Prevention (CDC) throughout China, where they worked with Chinese scientists on pandemics and new viruses. Trump's national security advisor, John Bolton, also disbanded his council's global health security unit.[139]

By January 7, 2020, scientists at the National Institute of Health and the CDC knew something was happening in China involving a new coronavirus. By mid-January it was known that it spread from person to person, not only from animals, and that it was airborne and deadly. By the end of the month, Robert O'Brien, the director of the National Security Council, warned the president that the virus would be "the biggest national security threat you face in your presidency."[140] A week after O'Brien's warning, Trump had a telephone conversation with President Xi Jinping of China about the dangers from an airborne coronavirus. As he would tell Bob Woodward two months later, however, "I still like playing it down."[141]

Nancy Messonnier, director of the CDC's Immunization and Respiratory Diseases Center, briefed reporters on February 25 that community spread of the novel coronavirus was inevitable; the only questions were "when this will happen, and how many people in this country will have severe illnesses." She advised people to start planning for disruption. The day before her warning, the news that COVID-19 was spreading in Europe and Asia caused the Dow Jones Industrial Average to drop 1,030 points. It shed another 900 points after her warning, the largest two-day drop in over two years.[142]

Trump didn't ask for a briefing, or even attempt to verify if the warning was accurate. Instead, he phoned Health and Human Services Secretary Alex Azar, shouting at him for allowing the alarming warning. "It's going to disappear," the president predicted soon after. "One day, it's like a miracle. It will disappear." On that day, there were only fifteen confirmed cases in the US.[143]

Despite that seemingly small number, the intelligence community, infectious disease experts, immunologists, and members of the president's staff knew a major crisis was unfolding. That week, several White House economic advisors spoke at a board meeting of the Hoover Institution, a conservative think tank. Unprompted, they repeatedly referred to the uncertain effects the virus would have on the economy, signaling to the investors in the room that the situation was far more serious than these same economists had said publicly.[144]

Republican senators who had received the intelligence briefings also saw the looming crisis. Faced, on one hand, with a vindictive president who wanted no bad news, and the possibility, on the other hand, of a lethal pandemic, they stayed quiet in public.

After the February 27 briefing, Senator Richard Burr, who had worked in epidemic planning for years, warned donors that this virus would be more like the catastrophic 1918 Spanish influenza pandemic than any epidemic since then. But he didn't challenge the president—instead, he sold his stocks in vulnerable companies.[145]

The senators' failure to challenge the president that day will go down as the beginning of further political decline in the US. If they had been executives of a private corporation, and had buried information about a product as potentially lethal as COVID-19, they would surely face prosecution. Instead, the country with the most advanced medical scientists and doctors in the world would end up with one of the highest rates of mortality, and the least effective leadership.

The president spent the next two months engaging in what Gabriel Sherman called "magical thinking." It was intentional deceit that placed the health of the stock market above the health of American citizens. Trump believed it was necessary to his political survival to act as if the virus was weak; if the country locked down, the economy would slump, and he would lose the election. When there were fourteen Americans with COVID-19 quarantined on the Diamond Princess cruise ship, he wanted the ship kept offshore, because "I like the numbers being where they are."[146]

When the situation became critical—a rising number of cases and deaths, and a movement by governors to lock down their states—Trump instituted daily press briefings by scientists, then hijacked them. He spent much of the time lavishing praise on himself, and he resented Dr. Anthony Fauci when the infectious disease expert became the trusted voice of reason.

Trump and the senior White House staff all knew how easily the virus spread. When someone sneezed during an Oval Office briefing on April 13, everyone in the room, including the president, "bailed out," Trump told Woodward later that day. That same evening, he made Fauci walk back comments he made on CNN that earlier mitigation "could have saved lives."[147]

Trump railed to friends about "alarmist" doctors and Nancy Pelosi for "using [the pandemic] against me" when they urged him to act. Mitch McConnell falsely accused the Obama administration of leaving no pandemic "game plan" for the new administration. He apologized after *Politico* revealed there was a detailed, presumably unread, sixty-nine-page playbook covering everything from contact tracing to mortuaries.[148]

When Americans needed presidential leadership, and all eyes were on him, Donald Trump could only blame others. "I don't take responsibility at all," he said on March 13.

Shop till You Drop?

There was no public plan for how to reopen the economy, no contingency plans, no testing plans, and no decision about what a recovery would look like.[149] Undaunted, Trump began talking about reopening the economy in full by Easter Sunday—ignoring all evidence from the top scientists at the CDC.

The CDC developed a comprehensive plan in April and passed it to the president's staff in the White House. Their guidelines were never released; the White House suppressed them. Instead, a secret group (comprising Trump's chief of staff Mark Meadows, Jared Kushner, economic advisor Kevin Hassett, and one scientist, Dr. Deborah Birx) was assembled to find a way to "justify declaring victory in the fight against the virus."

They developed a plan called "state authority handoff," designed to pass the buck to governors and let them take the heat instead of the president. But the handoff required more testing, and the president was not willing to let the number of confirmed cases go up. Instead, he questioned the value of testing and downplayed its significance.

Hassett, who had never done any work with epidemic data or similar models, was delegated to create an econometric model to guide the response. Dr. Birx, who had worked with epidemiological models for years, also had a model developed in England. In April, both models showed signs of progress that the secret group used to justify opening the economy. Unlike the assumptions generated by Birx and Hassett, however, Fauci and many outside experts warned that the outcome depended on how people changed their behavior when restrictions were loosened.[150]

In isolation from government agencies and medical experts, Kushner's group worked around the clock to develop a national testing plan, which they realized was necessary to control the virus. The plan included protocols for the daunting tasks of handling the surging demand for supplies, creating expanded testing capacity, developing surveillance systems to identify hot spots quickly, and easing legal and contractual roadblocks. But then, according to a member of Kushner's group, the plan "just went poof into thin air."[151]

A political decision was made that it was better for the president's re-election prospects to leave the crisis to governors. At that time, the most severely affected states had Democratic governors; the White House "could blame those governors, and that would be an effective political strategy," a member of Kushner's group told Katherine Eban. Although the task force members did not know who made that cold-blooded calculation, there were only three people in the White House likely to have been involved: Trump, Mark Meadows, and Mick Mulvaney, the director of the Office of Management and Budget, and acting White House Chief of Staff until Meadows took over. All three were ruthless enough to push for the strategy, and all three were reckless enough to make the decision without talking to scientists before doing so.[152]

Increasingly anxious about the stock markets in the face of state-wide shutdowns, Trump began calling on people to "liberate" their states from social distancing and quarantines. In Michigan, one of his must-win states, he attacked the Democratic governor, Gretchen Whitmer, for criticizing the federal response and lack of testing. His dutiful protestors, wearing Make America Great Again hats, crowded together around the statehouse, dusting off the shopworn chant of "Lock Her Up."[153]

Even as Fox News commentators did their shows safely from home, they urged viewers to put "freedom before fear" and praised Alex Jones for denouncing COVID as a "made-up" virus. Earlier, Texas lieutenant governor Dan Patrick told Tucker Carlson that Patrick's "fellow seniors should risk their health for the sake of the economy."[154]

In May, Pence went to Iowa, talking about reopening the economy and resuming in-person church services. The day of his visit, Iowa had more cases among its three million residents than South Korea had among its population of fifty-one million. Farmers were euthanizing livestock and going bankrupt, while Pence was cheerily saying, "I hope the people of Iowa have a sense of just how fortunate you are," citing Trump's support for a $764 billion small-business loan program. Iowa senator Joni Ernst was furious; under normal circumstances her re-election would be safe, but thanks to the mismanagement of the crisis, to say nothing of the trade wars' damage to her state's farmers, her seat was a toss-up.[155]

The Republican governors of Florida, Arizona, and Texas supported Trump's approach to politicize concerns about the virus. In May, Florida governor Ron DeSantis, formerly one of Trump's most partisan defenders in the House, declared victory over the virus and proclaimed anything else was a "typical partisan narrative." When North Carolina said that it would enforce testing, mask-wearing, and social distancing at the Republican convention, the RNC announced they would move it to Florida. Three weeks later, DeSantis had to walk back from his victory and order bars closed immediately. Similar retreats were imposed in Arizona and Texas, two states with major urban outbreaks and overwhelmed medical systems. The fate of the Republican convention was uncertain; Florida now wanted masks and testing as well.[156]

In late June, the government announced it was ending its support for testing sites, raising a furor around the country. Trump believed that the rising number of cases was solely the result of more testing, and told a paltry rally crowd in Tulsa that he'd ordered the government to "slow the testing down, please." The next week, he stated he was ending support for drive-through testing as well.

Senators from states where the governors followed Trump's lead—no shutdowns, masks optional—were in trouble. The Republican Senate majority suddenly seemed endangered. Texas senators Ted Cruz and John Cornyn, the latter up for re-election, wrote a formal letter urging the government to reconsider the testing reduction.[157]

Republican governors were once again paying the price for the White House's happy talk and inaction. They began holding group calls, trying to coordinate their policies as they began urging or even requiring the use of masks. Arkansas governor Asa Hutchinson went on ABC's *This Week* and called on national leaders to set an example. A number of the governors arranged a group call with Pence, pushing the vice president to get Trump to become less complacent. Pence guaranteed mask-wearing would be a consistent message, but it was almost a month before the president wore a mask or urged others to do so.[158]

With Trump trailing Joe Biden by double-digits in most national polls—and the Senate majority hanging in the balance—most Republican senators still held back on public criticism of Trump. Privately, they were also unnerved by his heightened racial animus in the wake of George Floyd's killing by Minneapolis police and increasing public support of the Black Lives Matter (BLM) movement. While southern governors removed

Confederate symbols from their state flags and statues of Confederate generals, Trump defended them as a key part of American culture, while calling BLM anti-American.[159]

For weeks, Republican senators were quiet while the president tried to stir up his base with attacks on radical leftists. Mitch McConnell returned to Kentucky to tend to his voters, lest his own seat become threatened. Stating scientifically correct positions, McConnell stressed the importance of mask wearing, praised Dr. Fauci, and urged everyone to follow the CDC guidelines. Republican House and Senate leaders nudged Trump to encourage masks, but he resisted. By fall, all but five of the twenty-six Republican governors were urging everyone to wear masks, with eleven of them issuing mandates. [160]

Speaking to a private group, Paul Ryan was bleak; Biden was winning key suburban voters, and that would make Michigan, Wisconsin, and Pennsylvania unwinnable for the president. Arizona was moving away from the GOP too. Privately, Republicans were debating when senators should break from Trump. A strategist close to McConnell said that if Trump hadn't recovered by Labor Day, he would be "on his own."[161] Openly breaking with the president, however, was still a vote-loser in most states. There were few votes likely to shift after Labor Day, and the loss of the president's strongest supporters outweighed likely gains. As a result, only a few senators up for election in Democratic states were openly critical of the president—and only after surviving their primaries.

When Labor Day arrived, Republicans were too divided to agree on a second relief budget to deal with the economic effects of the virus, let alone the devastating forest fires across the western US and the hurricanes and near-Biblical floods along the Gulf Coast. The revelations in Woodward's book compounded Trump's problems with the coronavirus; while half the country believed "the worst is yet to come," 61 percent believed the president had "given up fighting coronavirus"— and 23 percent of his 2016 voters believed he wanted what was best for himself, not what was best for the country.[162]

Support for masks and fears about the virus, however, did not solve the problems of those who owned or worked for small businesses, or the millions of parents who could not afford to stay home and take care of children when schools were closed. Widespread testing was not available in the US because the president believed it would hurt the economy and make him look bad. Without massive testing, there was no way to allay widespread concerns about shopping, travel, or interactions with strangers. By the end of October, the death toll was nearing 250,000, the number of US cases was about to reach nine million, and any vaccine would be months away. Nevertheless, many persons believed taking a chance on the coronavirus was a less dangerous gamble than giving up work, losing their small business, or having their children out of school for a year.

Republican senators worked to hold on to disaffected Republican voters without alienating hard-core Trump supporters or the independent voters they needed to survive. Their future depended on whether there was enough distrust of the Democratic Party, emboldened after the midterms, to shield them from the expected Biden victory against Trump.

7

Conclusion

What Can Be Done?

At the beginning of this book, I noted that political parties have been, and always will be, made up of a diverse coalition of groups. From a voter's point of view, a party's brand depends upon the benefits it delivers on the issues they care most about—which, in heterogeneous parties, means delivering benefits on many issues.

But there's more to successful parties than simply what they do for you; there's also what the other party *won't* do. As the authors of *Voting* so eloquently wrote after the 1948 election,

> What unifies a great heterogeneous party is this: On those matters which are important or relevant or salient to particular voters in the same party, they are uniformly against the opposition. . . . Party members need not agree on specific issues; their unity is at a different level. Their unity lies in the fact that on something important to each, they share a common position of disagreement with the opposition . . . they have, for one reason or another, the same opposition.[1]

No matter how strongly supporters of a party oppose the other party, however, all coalitions eventually fracture. Crackups are an inevitable part of the American federal system and can endure for many election cycles. They occur when factions within a party battle over irreconcilable policies and nonnegotiable demands. At some point, one group's standard positions will lose support and become unacceptable to other groups in the party. Politicians or major donors within a party will feel threatened by the way an opposition-party president, an economic change, a Supreme Court ruling, or a demographic shift disrupts their relationship with the party. Once this occurs, the heterogeneous groups within the party will no longer be able to maintain their truce. When these groups are only held together by animus and distrust of the opposition, there is a limit to how long they can endure before the opposition wins some of the party's voters and they are no longer competitive at the national level.

Donald Trump won in 2016 with promises that brought back disaffected Republicans who had sat out the 2008 and 2012 elections, but the party could not deliver on those promises. The Republicans had major successes on tax cuts for wealthy Americans, filling the federal courts with conservative judges, and reducing corporate regulations. But they could not replace Obamacare with something better, restore manufacturing jobs that moved to other countries, or lower the trade deficit with China.

Parties have a hard time adapting—both to their own failures and the successes of the other party. Controlling the House, Senate, and White House makes it even harder for a party to paper over its internal splits, as it cannot blame the other side for its failure to deliver on its own promises or its inability to reverse the other side's accomplishments.

As we have seen in earlier chapters, the Affordable Care Act, which Congress passed without a single Republican vote, turned out to be an insurmountable problem for the GOP—and a key factor in its current crackup. The party's leaders could neither repeal it entirely nor walk away from their attempts to repeal it, even as Republican governors (like Mike Pence in Indiana) quietly accepted the Medicaid expansion, millions of voters with preexisting conditions received affordable insurance, and no Republican replacement plan polled well.

After three years of living with Obamacare, even most Republicans opposed cutbacks in Medicaid and supported subsidies for low- and middle-income Americans. The fear that a Black president's program helped the poorest at the expense of "hard-working Americans" dwindled. Generating opposition to such a complicated bill had been easy; keeping the popular parts and eliminating all the unpopular elements was undoable.[2] Yet that did not stop Republicans from further attempts to repeal Obamacare, even as millions were losing their insurance in the midst of a global pandemic.[3]

Donald Trump is no longer president, but Trumpism will remain the animating force of the Republican Party for the time being. It won't end with his defeat because it didn't begin with him. Trump merely gilded his outsider status with cleverer, more bombastic versions of pledges other candidates had already made. "When people say all this started with Trump," journalist Talia Levin noted, "what they're saying is, 'I became aware of it when I started paying attention.'"

There was no reason for anyone who knew Trump's history to believe that he would leave Washington quietly." What have you seen of him," Maggie Haberman reminds, "that ever makes you think he's just going to go away?"[4]

Although Joe Biden won decisively, making Trump only the fifth American president in the last 108 years to lose their reelection bid, Republican senators, representatives, and governors fared much better than pollsters predicted. The Democrats' House delegation dropped from 232 to 222. Vulnerable Republican senators in Maine, Iowa, and North Carolina won handily, and only stunning, unprecedented victories in two runoff elections in Georgia gave Democrats the 50 seats they needed to gain effective Senate control (the vice president casts a vote when there is a tie).

Unified government means Democrats can confirm judges and presidential appointments in a timely fashion. However, dreams of bold actions on climate, courts, taxation, and rebuilding the government depend upon support from all fifty senators with no more than four naysayers in the House.

Trump's election defeat became a source of new turmoil and division within the Republican Party—with very real consequences for the balance of power in the new Congress, as well as for the 2024 presidential primary.

McConnell's status as majority leader depended on the Georgia runoff elections in January 2021—and those, in turn, hinged on Trump's quixotic legal crusade to reverse his election defeat in the six closely-contested states that accounted for Biden's path past 270 electoral votes. More than 100 judges, many appointed by his own administration, ruled against Trump's factually deficient and increasingly desperate lawsuits. Instead of conceding, Trump doubled down, calling on Republicans to reject the results in those states, and Flynn floated the idea of declaring martial law at one point.[5]

With time running out before Congress ratified Biden's electoral college victory, Trump placed a call to Georgia secretary of state Brad Raffensperger, literally begging him to "just find" 11,780 votes so the president wouldn't have to "play this game with the courts" —and then insinuating Raffensperger committed criminal offenses by refusing to do so.[6]

Trump's incessant attacks on Raffensperger and Republican Georgia governor Bryan Kemp forced the state's incumbent senators, Kelly Loeffler and David Perdue, to tiptoe an awkward line: should they attack or defend Republican state officials, and what should they say about all the federal and state judges who found no merit to the president's claims?

McConnell called on Republican senators to accept the results and avoid a split in the party that could give the Democrats two wins in Georgia, and a Senate majority. Paul Ryan found it "difficult to conceive of a more anti-democratic and anti-conservative act." But McConnell could not prevent Missouri Senator Josh Hawley from taking advantage of the ritual certification of the election to defy the Senate Majority Leader, engineer a constitutional crisis, and support Trump.[7]

As Hawley disputed Pennsylvania's results, Ted Cruz jumped in to support a broader legal challenge, justifying his unprecedented assault on each state's right to run their elections because "allegations of fraud and irregularities in the 2020 election exceed any in our lifetimes." This blithely ignored that the courts rejected the loser's allegations, that Republicans controlled the legislatures in five of the six states in question, and that the president had fired the head of the Cyberstructure and Infrastructure Security Agency for stating the election had been one of the safest in history—a finding confirmed by Attorney General Barr.

Both Hawley's and Cruz's resolutions were certain to fail but toying with the Constitution allowed them to monetize their faux outrage and raise cash for 2024.[8]

There was no clear answer to who, if anyone, could hold Trump's voters—and if they would still vote. At every level, the party was still split between acceptance and fighting to hold on to power—even among evangelical leaders. Family Research Council head Tony Perkins signed a letter stating that "President Donald J. Trump is the lawful winner of the presidential election." Meanwhile, Pat Robertson, the most influential televangelist, stated on air that it was time for Trump to move on: "the president still lives in an alternate reality."[9]

Throughout the drama and Trumpian pipe dreams, the party establishment was attempting to paper over the racial and nativist basis for Trump's appeal to white voters—particularly blue-collar men—who responded to his blend of racial resentment, anti-immigration sentiments, and support for Christian nationalism. Democratic pollster Stanley Greenberg credited Trump's "race war" attacks on Black Lives Matter and his warnings about multiracial America with a dramatic surge in support for Trump in the last month before the election. Republicans planning to run in the 2024 presidential primary appeared to agree that those voters were necessary for victory. They were supporting Trump for their political future, not his.[10]

McConnell spoke to the other Republican senators before Congress met to accept each state's results and confirm the outcome, a ritual that emphasized the importance of the peaceful transition of power. Given the president's conduct, he told colleagues that he had voted to declare war twice, and once voted to impeach a president, but this vote had become the most important vote of his career. He was not the only one worried about Trump's behavior; all ten living former secretaries of defense signed a joint column in the *Washington Post* reminding current officials and generals of their solemn duty to stay out of politics and protect the Constitution.[11]

On January 6, Cruz addressed the Senate, arguing that 39 percent of the country believed the election "was rigged," so the Senate had an obligation to deal with that "threat to legitimacy" by investigating the charges. As he was finishing, he slyly added, "I am not arguing for setting aside the result of this election."[12]

Hawley, a graduate of Yale Law, and Cruz, an alum of Harvard Law, both were clerks for Chief Justices of the Supreme Court. They knew that Trump's claims were too specious and factually challenged to pass muster in court; they were counting on equally unprincipled senators and representatives to certify the election, while they promoted themselves as heirs to the outgoing president's followers.[13]

While Cruz was playing devil's advocate, Trump, his sons, and Rudy Giuliani were firing up a large, angry gathering of supporters. "Let's have trial by combat," Giuliani said, while Trump urged them to head to the Capitol and "make your voices heard." "You will never take back our country with weakness," he continued.[14]

As the debate unfolded inside the Capitol, the inconceivable happened: a mob of Trump supporters broke into the building, occupied the offices, and began a day of violent confrontations; one woman was killed by a gunshot.

For six months Pentagon officials had been tracking violent protests around the country, worried that the president would invoke the Insurrection Act to deploy US military forces to quell a local protest. Now it was the president himself inciting an insurrection; that was the word used by news organizations like NPR and Republican senators Tom Cotton and Mitt Romney. The *Kansas City Star* minced no words in their editorial, titled "Sen. Josh Hawley has blood on his hands in Capitol coup attempt."[15]

For hours, Trump remained silent, even as Biden gave a speech attacking the protests and calling on the President to call off his horde and defend the Constitution. Trump finally posted a short video in which he talked more about the election having been stolen from him than about the violence. He ended his talk with:

There's never been a time like this where such a thing happened where they could take it away from all of us—from me, from you, from our country. This was a fraudulent election, but we can't play into the hands of these people. We have to have peace. So go home. We love you. You're very special. You've seen what happens. You see the way others are treated that are so bad and so evil.

I know how you feel, but go home, and go home in peace.[16]

Eventually, order was restored, the senators and representatives returned to the floor of the Capitol, and they certified the election for Joe Biden. Lindsey Graham ridiculed Cruz's and Hawley's cynicism when he addressed their alleged concern for those who felt the election was rigged. How, he asked, would people who believed in a conspiracy be dissuaded by a commission appointed by Nancy Pelosi, Mitch McConnell, and Chief Justice John Roberts?

It Takes a Candidate to Rebuild a Party

Both parties have experienced serious crackups in the past, but they were not insurmountable. The three brief case studies below show how party rifts were overcome long enough for a president to win two terms and alter the course of the party.

Historically, it takes a candidate for president to change a party's direction by building a new coalition within the party *before* their election. American parties have no CEO and no permanent controlling establishment or group. This leaves parties with no straightforward way to persuade legislative leaders or activists to accept a new program or demand less for the sake of victory, and no way to cut off outside funding for troublemakers and consensus breakers.

Moreover, voters shift positions faster than party elites. A politician's standing is associated with the issues and constituencies they represent, such as gun owners, teachers, or ethnic or religious groups. Changing their public stance without losing their position within the party is a slow and arduous process.

Stuart Stevens, one of the most articulate and clear-headed critics of the Republican Party and Trump, wrote that "only fear will motivate the party to change—the cold fear only defeat can bring."[17] Historically, though, defeat is not enough. Those whose survive usually hold the safest seats in the most partisan districts, and they have the least incentive to change the party's direction.

Ending a crackup requires a candidate to build a supporting bloc within the party, one organized to develop new approaches and defend each other. Together, they can overcome the party's resistance *without* alienating the leaders of the group.

If presidential candidates are crucial to changing a party's direction, though, they're also easy targets for scapegoating if the change turns out to be a ruinous one. Time and again, party leaders will rationalize the defeat of their party's candidate for president by saying either that the candidate was not liberal or conservative enough, that the candidate was personally weak and unappealing, or that the defeat was a one-time event due to the unusual appeal of the other party's candidate.

But skepticism is important in the face of such claims. Blaming the presidential candidate often means ignoring what the rest of the party was doing. Mitt Romney, for example, could only win the primaries and receive extensive financial support from the Koch network in the general election by veering to the right and repudiating his initial positions on healthcare, climate change, and social policies.[18]

Whenever you hear politicians say an election loss was not about the party but about a candidate's failings, you can be sure it *was* about the party, too. It is safer to blame the candidate than to deal with disparate intraparty demands that put the candidate in untenable positions. When candidates are at a disadvantage because of the actions or inactions of party legislators, it means there was a taboo that no one dared violate—a topic that, if raised, would create a split between critical groups in the party.

Three times since World War II, presidential election defeats were accompanied by major setbacks for the party, which created divides between politicians defending the current orthodoxy and those trying to shift direction. Yet Dwight Eisenhower, Richard Nixon, and Bill Clinton all managed to get to the White House (and win re-election) despite the logjams created by party factions who were unwilling to make the adjustments necessary to win a presidential election.

In each case, their party's senators or congressional representatives defended policies that benefited their own standing but could not be successfully defended in a national presidential campaign. With a new, disruptive synthesis of the interests of party voting blocs, each of the three men evaded the obstructive party leaders' demands without alienating those leaders' supporters. None of the syntheses eliminated the fault lines within the candidate's party, but they successfully healed them long enough for the party to compete at every level and win two White House terms.

Each of the three was cheered wildly within their party for finally winning the White House, then criticized later for being insufficiently progressive or conservative by the then-current standards. All this is to say that winning programs are always compromises, not ideal solutions—and that no consensus is permanent.

These cases are the background for questions both parties will face, post-Trump: What form of political party organization in the House and Senate are *realistic* given Supreme Court rulings on political contributions to candidates and super PACs? How can parties build government institutions capable of handling pandemics and all the challenges of a modern economy in a global system? What kind of party organization is still possible? What lessons from past party changes are still applicable?

In other words: Without fairy dust, what can be done?

From Dewey to Eisenhower

Ahead of the midterm elections in 1946, America faced post–World War II chaos: there were shortages of bread and meat caused by mismanaged price controls, and housing shortages had been worsened by troubles converting from wartime production. Soldiers demanding faster returns to the US were rioting on bases overseas. If that weren't enough, there were several corruption cases involving President Truman's friends and assistants.[19] The Republican midterm campaign slogan was all of two words: "Had Enough?"[20] The electorate answered affirmatively, and the GOP took control of the House and Senate for the first time since 1928.

With the 1948 presidential election approaching, one of the GOP candidates, Senate Majority Leader Robert Taft—hailed as "Mr. Republican" for his revival of the party after the Great Depression—mounted a campaign to repeal Franklin Delano Roosevelt's New Deal. He began a scorched-earth campaign to remove every protection for unions, eliminate every assistance program, and reduce the federal government to its prewar size.

His opponent, New York governor Thomas Dewey, easily beat Taft in the 1948 primaries, with the support of most Republican governors and party moderates from the industrial states. The party platform, crafted by Dewey and his allies, accepted parts of the New Deal, endorsed rent controls in the postwar housing crisis, and was open to postwar defense alliances and international organizations—all of which were anathema to Taft and his fellow conservatives.

Then, in a stunning tactical move, Truman called a special session of Congress and asked conservative Republicans to pass Dewey's moderate platform without waiting. It was a calculated gamble: Taft had to decide whether to support Dewey's program—effectively ending his own future presidential prospects—or undermine Dewey's credibility by showing his program would not succeed. With constitutional claims and sleight of hand, Taft chose the latter.[21] In the 1948 election, Truman kept the White House and Republicans lost seventy-five House seats and twelve Senate seats.

Republicans quickly turned the whodunit into a "hedunit," blaming Dewey for a bland, uninspiring campaign, and ignoring that they had destroyed his chances in the special session. This gave the surviving representatives and senators cover from accepting any blame, and allowed Taft to run again for president in 1952. With Dewey out of the way, he expected a clear path to the nomination, which he believed would finally offer the country a chance to elect a true conservative instead of rejecting a moderate.

After his loss, Dewey paid a visit to Dwight D. Eisenhower, who was then the president of Columbia University, to persuade him to run for president. No one else, Dewey believed, could save the Republican Party from Taft and his ilk, who were determined to repeal all of the New Deal and restore American isolationism. "If they believe they are going to stop farm price supports, pensions, unemployment insurance, and social advances," Dewey told a friend via letter, "they are crazy and they are likely to lose our freedom for us . . . by leading the country into a [Democratic] one-party system."[22]

Eisenhower was an ideal presidential candidate for either party after World War II. He had a sterling personal reputation on war and peace—the top issue of the day—and in contrast to generals like Douglas MacArthur, Eisenhower's demeanor and character didn't alarm the public. As an outsider, he could also bridge the divides in the Republican Party without taking stands that would alienate regular voters.

The party had lost the farmer vote in 1948 over its opposition to price supports and the collapse of grain prices. Whereas Taft had staked out absolutist positions, Eisenhower had never needed to take a stand on any of the specific policies. Taft and his allies were also vehemently opposed to stationing American troops in Korea and Europe. Given how much respect and trust he commanded, Eisenhower's support of NATO and the UN would reassure many skeptical citizens.

Eisenhower demurred from giving an answer to Dewey; instead, he left Columbia to become the first commander of NATO in 1951, though he cautiously watched both Taft and the growing network of Republican officials and influentials building support for a "Draft Eisenhower" movement.

Ironically, it was Taft, not Dewey, who finally persuaded Eisenhower to run. Fearing the damage an Eisenhower candidacy would wreak on his own presidential aspirations, Taft visited the general at NATO headquarters in Europe to discourage him from running. He explained his positions on international security and mutual cooperation, which only served to convince Eisenhower that Dewey was right and Taft had to be stopped.[23]

Dewey's team of advisors formed the core of Eisenhower's campaign (and, later, his administration). Eisenhower's press secretary, James Hagerty, his secretary of state, John Foster Dulles, and his campaign manager and attorney general, Herbert Brownell, had all worked with Dewey during his years of opposition to the old GOP orthodoxy.

The ensuing primary battle between Eisenhower and Taft was as bitter as anything in recent elections, both for its attempts to suppress or impede voting and for its racial, religious, and nativist fearmongering.

In many states, Taft supporters used every trick in their books to disenfranchise Eisenhower voters. In Texas, for example, many Taft supporters agreed with the Texas Republican Party chairman, who proclaimed, "I'd rather lose with Bob Taft than win with Eisenhower." [24] The Texas primary turnout was the biggest in state history; tens of thousands of independents and Democrats flocked to support Eisenhower. All primary voters signed a pledge to vote for the Republican nominee, whether it was Taft or Eisenhower, but the state party convention, party activists, and elected officials loyal to Taft nevertheless tossed out 510 of the 519 Eisenhower delegates to the national convention. Brownell, who was in charge of the delegate hunt and finally got the delegates seated, recounted the fight:

> "They just didn't count the vote. They changed caucuses to houses across the street. . . . It was a crude, rough deal. They'd been doing it since the Civil War. Taft's father did it before him. . . . The idea that the public should be allowed in a Republican caucus was unheard of in places like Texas, Mississippi, or Alabama."[25]

At the national convention in Chicago, Taft backers passed out flyers warning of "Ike the Kike, financed by Phooey Dewey's international bankers." Taft supporters and delegates marched through the streets of Chicago and into the convention singing "Onward, Christian Soldiers" while loudspeakers outside played "Poor Blind Ike." After days of negotiations and threats, Eisenhower's winning delegates from Texas and other Southern states were seated, and Taft's twelve-year attempt to reverse the entire New Deal and return the federal government to its prewar stature was over.[26] Eisenhower moved the Republican Party from one dominated by anti-government isolationists into one that no longer tried to roll back all New Deal safety net programs. During his 1952 campaign, Eisenhower hailed the social gains of the New Deal as the "floor that covers the pit of disaster." "Should any political party attempt to abolish Social Security, unemployment insurance, and eliminate labor laws and farm programs," he later wrote to his staunchly conservative brother, Edgar, "you would not hear of that party again in our political history."[27]

Eisenhower worked with Senator Lyndon Johnson and other Democrats on domestic legislation, and Democrats supported his basic anti-Communist foreign policy. Despite his party's resistance to most federal programs, he succeeded in developing NATO and supporting the United Nations. From the isolationism of Taft, Eisenhower had turned the GOP into a party able to build alliances and defend the US against Communist aggression, a major concern from 1945 until the 1970s.

Richard Nixon: Renewing the GOP after 1964

The more vehement isolationist and anti-government groups no longer dominated the national party after the Eisenhower years, but they remained active, particularly in the Western and Southern states. These groups accused Eisenhower of being a tool of the "Eastern Establishment," a phrase Phyllis Schlafly coined for the twin enemies of "freedom"—Wall Street and Madison Avenue.[28]

Spurred by President Lyndon Johnson's passage of the Civil Rights Act of 1964 and major anti-poverty programs, and by the use of federal marshals and the FBI to protect civil rights workers, conservative activists persuaded Arizona senator Barry Goldwater to enter the 1964 primaries. The Goldwater campaign vilified and humiliated his primary opponents, the moderate Republican governors William Scranton of Pennsylvania and Nelson Rockefeller of New York. The combination of Goldwater's extreme positions and incivility cost him valuable newspaper endorsements. From 1940 through 1960, an average of 77 percent of the top 100 American newspapers had endorsed the Republican candidate; in 1964, only 45 percent endorsed Goldwater.[29]

Despite a landslide victory for Johnson in the general election, conservatives considered the election a major breakthrough. Goldwater carried only six states—his home state plus the five "cotton belt" Southern states where white Democrats rebelled against forced integration—but activists believed that the 26 million votes cast for a true conservative advocate of "states' rights" showed the future was theirs. Few newspapers covered their cause, so they had campaigned mainly through books. In 1964, over 18 million copies of Schläfly's *A Choice Not an Echo*, John A. Stormer's *None Dare Call It Treason*, and J. Evetts Haley's *A Texan Looks at Lyndon* were distributed to bookstores and supermarkets. Add in the sales of Goldwater's own *The Conscience of a Conservative*, and the number of books sold about the cause was greater than the number of votes cast for Goldwater.[30]

No one expected former vice president Nixon to return to the national stage after he lost to John F. Kennedy in 1960 (followed by a humiliating loss for the California governorship in 1962). But Nixon managed to bridge the party divides that reopened after 1964 between the moderate governors of New York, Pennsylvania, and other states, and the pro–states' rights Southerners opposed to integration.

Nixon stayed on good terms with the Goldwater campaign, endorsing the candidate while still opposing Goldwater's most extreme-sounding policies, including making Social Security voluntary, selling the Tennessee Valley Authority, letting states enforce civil rights law themselves, and passing a national right-to-work law. He also avoided attacking or defending Goldwater's arguments for eliminating all welfare.

Nixon cleverly maneuvered to have a mini-summit with Goldwater, Rockefeller, and Scranton, at which Goldwater revised his statements about extremism and nuclear weapons, and all three shook hands with Goldwater. That photographed détente guaranteed that Nixon could not be criticized later by Rockefeller or Scranton for endorsing Goldwater after Goldwater lost.[31] He was now a loyal Republican who voted for his party, like other moderates. No one could attack him for being "too close" to Goldwater from the left, or accuse him of abandoning Goldwater from the right.

Nixon changed the debate on segregation from "now or never" into "fast versus slow." He questioned forced integration without ever defending segregation. He did not want to alienate either the moderate and liberal Republicans in the Northeast or Goldwater's forces in the West and South. In a 1964 speech in Cincinnati, Nixon attempted to walk that thin line:

> We oppose segregation in our schools either by law or in fact. But this problem must be dealt with in an orderly transition. We believe it is detrimental to both Negro and white children to uproot them from their communities and to haul them from one school to another in order to force integration in an artificial and unworkable manner.[32]

In his 1968 campaign, Nixon evaded the press, never divulging his secret plan for Vietnam or explaining how he would quell antiwar and civil rights protests. But he didn't have to: those two dominant issues were answered by his strong personal track record on foreign policy and the overwhelming perception of the Republican Party as the party of law and order, standing firm against both antiwar protests and riots in minority areas of cities around the country.

In office, President Nixon's "Southern Strategy" began the evolution of the once solidly Democratic South into a Republican bastion, and the conversion of urban white ethnic communities in the Midwest and Northeast (such as Jewish and Italian Americans) into GOP voters. The Nixon Justice Department gave tacit support to de facto segregation in schools and suburbs by slowing enforcement of forced integration. At the same time, they were quick to enforce African American voting rights in the South. Republican defense of white enclaves and growing numbers of minorities in the Democratic Party gave whites who resisted integration a home in the Republican Party.[33]

Nixon broke the elite logjam separating moderates like George Romney (Mitt Romney's father and the then-governor of Michigan), Nelson Rockefeller, and William Scranton from Western and Southern conservatives. His firm Cold War anti-Communism was conservative enough for Republicans and moderate Democrats repelled by the "anti-Americanism" and "cultural liberalism" they associated with the New Left. And unlike George Wallace or the Goldwater supporters, Nixon managed to side with voters resistant to integration without alienating the middle-class Republicans who *wanted* to be for integration—as long as it didn't inconvenience them or their neighborhoods. As Ross Douthat wrote, "Nixon knew

how to channel an angry, 'who's looking out for me?' populism without letting himself be imprisoned by its excesses."[34]

Bill Clinton and the Democratic Leadership Council

It took the Democratic Party twenty-four years to recover from the 1968
crisis, when violent attacks on protestors at the Chicago convention split the
party between liberals (who pushed for more national programs to combat
poverty and segregation, and support for the emerging feminist and environmental movements) and middle-class voters (who were more concerned
about inflation and rising taxes).

During that period, former Georgia governor Jimmy Carter was the only
Democrat to win the White House, in large part because he was a moderate
and a Southerner. The majority of Democratic representatives and many
of the senators, following the policy demands of Senator Edward Kennedy,
pushed to extend the Great Society programs of Johnson. But neither the
economy nor the public mood were in favor of more redistributive programs,
and Carter only broke away from Kennedy after a long, bitter primary fight
in New Hampshire.

Amid the disgrace of the Watergate scandal and Nixon's resignation during
his second term, Carter was able to win a close election against incumbent
Gerald Ford in 1976, but he could not bridge his party's divides. When the
rise of OPEC sent oil prices and inflation soaring, congressional Democrats
still insisted on increased spending on their programs, while Carter wanted
to control inflation.

When Carter called for less spending, Senator Ernest Hollings (D-SC),
chair of the Senate Budget Committee, denounced the president as a "hyp-
ocrite" who wanted a "campaign budget" to win re-election. Kennedy acknowledged the unpopularity of liberal spending programs, but argued
that "a party must sail against the wind."[35] Carter, of course, wanted a presidential campaign budget, while Hollings and Kennedy wanted to protect
the programs—and pork—that held the congressional majority coalition
together. Carter's national favorability ratings were dependent upon the
economy as well as government programs, while a majority of the legislators
believed their re-election depended solely upon the government programs
and projects most valuable to their states or districts.

Ronald Reagan beat Carter decisively in 1980, winning forty-four states and 489 electoral votes. Four years later, against Carter's vice president, Walter Mondale, Reagan's victory was even more lopsided; he took forty-nine states and 525 electoral votes. Mondale claimed only thirteen electoral votes from his home state of Minnesota and the District of Columbia.

Mondale had won the nomination by defending unions, the Great Society programs of Lyndon Johnson, and the New Deal policies of Franklin Delano Roosevelt. His defeat was one of the rare instances where party leaders could not blame the messenger for the resounding repudiation of the message. Instead, Democratic activists tried to write off the loss as due to the special talents of President Reagan. My analysis of the election in the *Washington Post* argued that Democrats were in trouble because they could not justify their racial and economic policies publicly, and "public silence . . . does not combat the private mutterings of racists." Roger Wilkins, a prominent civil rights leader and editorial writer, condemned me as a "poll-taking professor from San Diego" who wanted Democrats to turn their back on Blacks. "It is hard to believe," Wilkins wrote, "that the next Republican candidate will be nearly as formidable as Ronald Reagan."[36] Indeed, the next Republican candidate, George H. W. Bush, was not as formidable. He won anyway.

By the mid-1980s, the most at-risk incumbents in the Democratic Party were governors and legislators from the moderate or conservative states in the South and West. Under the leadership of Al From, the former executive director of the House Democratic Caucus, elected officials such as Governors Bill Clinton (Arkansas), Bruce Babbitt (Arizona), and Chuck Robb (Virginia); Senators Al Gore (Tennessee), Joe Biden (Delaware), and Sam Nunn (Georgia); and Congressman Richard Gephardt (Missouri) formed the Democratic Leadership Council (DLC).[37]

After Bush came from 17 points behind to easily defeat Michael Dukakis in 1988, Democratic party activists continued to argue that no fundamental changes were needed to regain the White House. They still controlled Congress, after all, and they contended that a candidate to the left of Dukakis would mobilize nonvoters. Writing for the DLC, William Galston and Elaine Kamarck confronted these denials and called for new approaches to enlarge the party's appeal. Democrats' favorability ratings were dropping; blue-collar, low-income voters weren't just staying home, they were leaving the party. Post-election polls showed that even if low-income citizens had voted, Dukakis still would have lost.[38]

None of the established groups inside the Democratic Party welcomed the DLC or their call for policies that would broaden the party's appeal. Union leaders attacked them for being pro-trade; civil rights activists disparaged them as "the Rhett Butler Brigade" (so named for the Confederate character from *Gone with the Wind*) because so many were from border states or the former Confederacy; liberal activists denigrated them as the "southern white boys caucus"; and Jesse Jackson claimed DLC stood for "Democrats for the Leisure Class."[39]

Despite fierce objections from groups within the party, the DLC pushed forward in its attempts to shape a strengthened and unified Democratic Party. When Bill Clinton stepped down as head of the DLC to run for president in 1992, he was no lone wolf defying interest groups and activists within the party. His campaign announcement was composed mainly of chunks of speeches he had been making for years while flying around the country for the DLC.

Clinton had conceived his campaign while talking with all the major groups within the party, developing themes that could bridge the divide between the core interest groups and the wider public. When he made the very same points about work, welfare, jobs, and crime to both whites and Blacks during the campaign, he used arguments he had been using for years that other members of the DLC supported. Although Clinton was staunchly pro-choice, he could still win votes from anti-abortion voters because his statement that "abortion should be legal, safe, and rare" acknowledged their misgivings. The statement outraged many pro-choice activists when Hillary Clinton used it, but the two of them nevertheless managed to win over pro-choice Democrats without backing down.[40] Clinton had the DLC experience to shape his campaign, and supportive public officials who shared his vision were ready to support his policies and help bridge the divides within the Democratic Party in 1992.

In 1984 and 1988, Walter Mondale and Michael Dukakis had tiptoed around the racial friction between whites concerned about crime and welfare dependency, and Blacks concerned about police violence and employers reluctant to hire them for anything but entry-level jobs. Like Nixon, Clinton found a way to reach disaffected voters without alienating the rest of his party. He could support welfare without looking like a "tax and spend" liberal because he considered welfare "a second chance and not a way of life," believed a job was the best social program, and stood up to Jesse Jackson's demands for the same redistribution and entitlement commitments that Jackson had extracted from Mondale and Dukakis. Clinton could go around Jackson because he had governors and senators on the same page to sound his themes, as well as widespread support from other Black leaders who saw how Clinton had governed and approved of what he was saying to both white and Black audiences.

At a national convocation of Jackson's Rainbow Coalition, Clinton ended a standard speech with a direct reference to an honored guest at the head table, recording artist Sister Souljah. In an interview following the 1992 LA riots, Souljah had said "If black people kill black people every day, why not have a week and kill white people?" Clinton's riposte—aimed to gain national attention—was that her remarks were "filled with a kind of hatred you do not honor." "If you took the words 'white' and 'black' and reversed them," he said, "you might think David Duke was giving [her] speech."[41]

While that confrontation continues to rankle some Black activists, Clinton's words persuaded many whites who might not otherwise trust him to deal with crime that he was serious. Instead of trying to protect comity among liberal elites, he gambled—successfully—that he could talk about the issue without breaking the coalition. It was credible, not cheap campaign talk, because he made the statement in front of Jackson on Jackson's home ground.[42]

This Time Is Different

The rules and norms of democracies have evolved over the centuries to control the competition for power. If they couldn't change human nature, at least they constrained the drive for personal power and treasure. In the cases of Eisenhower, Nixon, and Clinton, these very norms and rules allowed candidates to forge coalitions between warring groups and lead their parties to two-term executive victories.

Although they occurred in markedly different chronological and political contexts, these crackup case studies share a number of key features. All three candidates had widespread support from party members, elected politicians, and experienced professionals. They belonged to parties with leaders who could work together; none had many party members supporting primary challengers to their colleagues. No outside group had a larger organization than the party, or financed legislators to function as a separate, uncompromising party within the party.

Despite the rampant anti-partyism saturating our public discussions—that is, the idea that parties are a necessary evil—it is precisely the ability of parties to work within their diverse interests and find common ground for legislation that is essential to the future of the United States. Parties are, in fact, a necessary virtue.

This time, the crackup is different from the ones that came before. The institutions that evolved over the last two centuries for controlling the power of those in charge of the national government are no longer adequate to the challenge. In no country is the decay more obvious than the first democracy of the modern age; the nation with the most advanced scientists and doctors was brought down by a virus that other European and Asian countries handled with a small fraction of the disruption and deaths suffered by Americans.

What makes this time so different? Campaign finance reforms weakened Republican leaders in the House and Senate, and torrents of outside money funded candidates who pushed the party ever more to the right, forcing it into unwinnable battles for the sake of the donors and without regard for the future of the party. The never-ending drive to repeal Obamacare and the complete disavowal of any evidence of climate change are just two examples of the ways that campaign finance reforms have made it harder for the party to legislate and compromise.

Three consecutive Republican Speakers of the House—Dennis Hastert, John Boehner, and Paul Ryan—all recognized the problems caused by moving big money outside the party. Hastert, who served as Speaker from 1999 (before the McCain-Feingold legislation) until 2007 (five years after its passage), saw the divisive effects of the change. Hastert saw "kind of a homogenizing effect" when big donations had gone directly to the parties; "People didn't come out of there too far to the right or too far to the left." With big money outside the party, things changed: "It used to be they're looking over their shoulders to see who their general [election] opponent is. Now they're looking over their [shoulders] to see who their primary opponent is."[43] Republican politicians could now find financial support for more extreme policies and more aggressive tactics than the party consensus would have considered before the change.

When Republicans retook control of the House in 2011, Boehner wanted to avoid battles that would hurt the party, but he could not control the gung-ho "Tea Party" freshmen class or stop his colleagues from self-promotion at the expense of their chances of defeating Obama in 2012. Boehner tried repeatedly to make incremental progress on taxes and entitlements by dealing directly with Vice President Joe Biden, but no deal was ever good enough to satisfy the most aggressive new members of Congress, whose resistance to compromise was rewarded with media coverage and financial support.

When Boehner compared his plight to negotiating while "standing there naked," the Freedom Caucus's power plays had paralyzed the party. The ultimate irony of the Freedom Caucus's obstructionism was that a group opposed to bipartisan legislation ultimately tried to overthrow their party's leader with a tactic that depended upon bipartisanship to succeed. Forcing a vote on whether Boehner should remain speaker would only depose Boehner if the Democrats joined the Freedom Caucus in voting to overthrow him. Once Pelosi said she would have Democrats vote present (i.e. neither supporting nor opposing his removal), the threat was foiled; Boehner could keep his position solely with votes from the other Republicans.[44]

Boehner's successor fared no better. As speaker, Paul Ryan tried to navigate the party to a position where a conservative Republican could win in 2016, and then unsuccessfully attempted to deliver on the party's commitments when Trump won. Ryan confided to Alberta that the party's fractures made legislating impossible: "We basically run a coalition government without the efficiency of a parliamentary system."[45]

Unlike Ryan and Boehner, Mitch McConnell was less worried about the party's path forward as long he was still Senate Majority Leader. Taking a strictly transactional approach, he accepted the Kochs' anti-climate-change stance when they helped deliver a Senate majority in 2014. Then, after Trump won, McConnell was quick to take an opportunistic tack: "I thought to myself, 'These opportunities don't come along very often. Let's see how we can maximize it.' "[46]

In 2009, John David Dyche, a columnist and commentator for the *Louisville Courier-Journal*, wrote an admiring book about McConnell's understanding of Senate rules and procedures and his legislative mastery. But after watching McConnell use his tactical skills to exonerate a "hideous . . . utterly unfit" President Trump in the impeachment trial, Dyche concluded that McConnell had "no ideology except his own political power."[47]

That isn't to say there aren't voices of reason within the GOP. In their 2008 book *Grand New Party*, Ross Douthat and Reihan Salam laid out a plan to win back the working class via conservative approaches to many of the problems bedeviling families and minorities. They took government seriously and were willing to spend money to solve problems with programs like job training.[48] The flood of money from wealthy donors determined to stop government bailouts and reverse Obamacare never gave them a chance.

Meanwhile, in Congress, Marco Rubio had party support in states where the growing Hispanic presence made winning votes from the middle class and small business owners important. Rubio became the lead senator during the coronavirus bailouts in working to help small businesses, and could still become more than the "sombrero on the elephant."

Senator Cory Gardner—who renounced his past vote for fetal "personhood" and endorsed the "morning after" pill—was a model of the way Republicans could hold evangelical voters and win over suburban moderates and blue-collar families. He showed that a moderate religious program was acceptable to evangelical voters—if not their leaders—and he attacked Obamacare without threatening other entitlements like Medicare and Social Security. He supported citizenship for undocumented immigrants who served in the armed forces—a position Trump opposed—and announced that the Senate would not vote to seat Roy Moore, if the controversial former chief justice of the Alabama Supreme Court won his Senate election. He also refused to allow a single judge to be confirmed until the Trump administration allowed states to legalize marijuana sales.[49]

His fellow senators saw his importance and put him in charge of the Republican Senate Campaign Committee after 2016. If Gardner had survived his re-election bid in 2020, he and Rubio—conservative politicians who take government seriously enough to solve problems for constituents who are neither wealthy nor intolerant of other religions and ethnic groups—would have been both allies in making the party attractive and rivals for the 2024 presidential nomination. Once Trump went all out to please evangelical leaders with his pro-life and anti-gay promises—and all out against immigration reform—Gardner had no chance in Colorado.

Now, in this new, post-McCain-Feingold and *Citizens United* era, it is an open question whether Rubio or anyone else will be able to create a new synthesis in the manner of Eisenhower, Nixon, or Clinton.

Litmus Tests versus Legislative Coalitions

Anyone who believes that someone like Donald Trump is solely a Republican problem should think twice. That the GOP was the first party to suffer a crackup in the post-McCain-Feingold/*Citizens United* era does not mean their opposition is exempt. Make no mistake: these changes will prove just as problematic for Democrats as for Republicans.

In the 2016 and 2020 presidential primaries, Vermont senator Bernie Sanders developed a rabid following with his passionate defense of absolutist positions like "Medicare for All" and full-bore attacks on wealth and the establishment. "Medicare for All" became a rallying cry for progressive Democrats, soon to be joined with demands for a "Green New Deal" to fight climate change.

Both issues gained enough legitimacy to widen the window of goals that could be discussed without being ridiculed by reporters—a major accomplishment. But as litmus tests, both are untenable for a political party; they illustrate the very big distinction between activists' demands and widespread political support for viable legislation.

"Medicare for All" is both a great bumper sticker and—because of its costs—a policy unlikely to be implemented in the US. Sanders never paid attention to details; he could not explain why Vermont's four-year effort to create a single-payer plan failed, and why the calculated cost to families was triple the initial estimate. Governor Peter Shumlin called the failure of Vermont's single-payer plan "the greatest disappointment of my political life," but the problems—even in a state where preexisting conditions were already protected before Obamacare—were insurmountable.[50]

The last four Democratic economists to chair the Council of Economic Advisors, all of whom believed in the need to provide healthcare for everyone, wrote Sanders early in the primaries with their concern about weak premises and inadequate calculations. The one economist who backed Sanders's plan, they pointed out, assumed an economic growth rate even higher than the "most grandiose" Republican predictions. Sanders's claims, they argued, undermined the Democrats' brand as a party that wanted government to work and used "responsible arithmetic." From budget analysts to Social Security economists, experts thought his plan would cost almost as much as the national budget.[51]

Great bumper stickers can be a boon for fundraising, but they do not always lead to great policies—and often shackle political parties. Sanders's Medicare for All plan would be a litmus test every bit as binding and dangerous as Grover Norquist's anti-tax pledge or the Koch brothers' anti-climate-change pledge. Economist Paul Krugman pointed out that the three countries with the highest-rated healthcare systems in the world (the

Netherlands, Australia, and Britain) have three radically different systems. Britain has socialized medicine; Australia has a single-payer system; and the Netherlands—the highest-rated system—uses highly regulated, subsidized private insurance.[52] Deciding which plan would be best prior to comparisons of costs, time to implement each plan, and levels of support and resistance for the policy is perilous no matter how worthy the goal.

As far-fetched as his proposals were, Sanders's vocal support of left-wing causes helped to shift attention to the progressive wing of the Democratic Party. In the 2018 midterm, the major gains for the Democratic Party came in the suburbs, where college-educated voters rejected Republican incumbents. The headlines and energy, however, came from progressive primary victories against prominent Democrats. A twenty-eight-year-old former bartender in Queens and former Sanders campaign organizer, Alexandria Ocasio-Cortez, triumphed over Representative Joe Crowley, once considered a likely future Speaker of the House; it was the biggest shocker since Dave Brat beat the number three Republican, Eric Cantor, in a 2014 primary.

A former resident of Queens himself, Trump noticed Ocasio-Cortez on a cable channel early in the primary campaign. Star-struck by her talent, he instructed his people to tell Crowley "he's got himself a problem . . . [and better] start campaigning."[53] AOC, as she quickly became known, soon had one of the biggest Twitter followings in politics—another metric that Trump was bound to appreciate. When she arrived in Washington, he said "She's got a good sense—an 'it' factor, which is pretty good, but she knows nothing. She knows nothing. But with time, she has real potential."[54]

While Ocasio-Cortez was smarter and better educated than the president's comment suggested, she was new to the ways of Congress, and there is no way in Washington to tell new representatives to wait until they learn more. While established politicians always think experience is the best guide, newcomers think everyone should help them fulfill their promises to their constituents.

Because of her immense media savvy and multimillion-member social media following, activists and progressive writers treated AOC as a powerhouse who was already "setting the agenda." Smitten by the idea of a Joan of Arc wielding a sharp mind and a sharper Twitter finger, author Antonio Garcia Martinez called her a "a harbinger of a new American political reality." But despite her initial absolutism about Medicare for All and the Green New Deal, claims about Ocasio-Cortez "seizing power" and "wielding control" were premature; her fellow Democratic representatives did not fall in line.[55]

Ocasio-Cortez's first move in Washington was to stage a sit-in at Speaker Pelosi's office, demanding action on climate change. Demonstrating the predictable overreach of first-term activists with idealistic goals, she wanted a new committee to write a Green New Deal, without input from the rest of the party and its related committees. This was the same failed approach Hillary Clinton used when she tried to write and pass a healthcare bill without input from the relevant committees. Instead, Pelosi set up a committee to refer legislation to the appropriate people, without giving the new committee subpoena power; she was not about to let the party make dramatic headlines that didn't lead to legislation.[56]

The Justice Democrats, a political action committee formed by veterans of Bernie Sanders' presidential campaigns, attempted to reframe all issues as stark, moral choices. It was the same logic employed by Sanders, Ted Cruz, and Donald Trump, and it left no room for details or other ways of examining the problems. In this vision, the real enemy of progress was "radical conservatives in the Democratic Party."

But as evidenced by a fight over funds that included money to aid the plight of children separated from their parents at the border, there are practical limits to clear, absolute, and moral choices. The funds to care for the children actually perpetuated the family separation policy, and Saikat Chakrabarti, one of the Justice Democrats and AOC's then-chief of staff, tweeted that anyone who supported the funding was enabling a racist system.

Black representatives were furious at being compared to racist southern representatives in the 1940s; they already distrusted Justice Democrats like AOC because they believed her main support in Queens came not from persons of color, but from "privileged gentrifiers" who didn't appreciate what it took to gain political power. Democrats from border districts also believed caring for the children was too important to hold up funding; El Paso representative Veronica Escobar said, "We have to meet our obligations as human beings and fund the needs for the care of these children."[57]

Tensions continued to simmer between establishment Democrats like Pelosi and the progressive freshman "Squad" led by AOC. "All these people have their public whatever and their Twitter world. But they didn't have any following," Pelosi told Maureen Dowd. "They're four people and that's how many votes they got." Ocasio-Cortez fired back to her 4.7 million followers: "That public 'whatever' is called public sentiment. And wielding the power to shift it is how we actually achieve meaningful change in this country."[58]

The interaction underscored the dissonance between Twitter followers and congressional votes. A year after she arrived in Congress, AOC had more Twitter power, measured by retweets and likes, than any political figure except Donald Trump, and more than the combined totals of the *Washington Post, New York Times,* CNN, NBC, MSNBC, and ABC. She raised money and endorsed candidates for open seats while refusing to fund any primary opponents of members of the Congressional Black Caucus. She showed her star power and work ethic in hearings with well-prepared, penetrating questions and interviews. But as Pelosi once told Trump, votes are "the currency of the realm," and AOC had not yet enlarged her coalition by working with others and finding common ground.[59]

She insisted that Joe Biden won the 2020 presidential primary because corporate lobbyists preferred him, ignoring the fact that African American voters had trusted Biden and not Bernie Sanders, her preferred candidate. When questioned about what role she would play in a Biden administration, she groaned. "In any other country, Joe Biden and I would not be in the same party," she said. "But in America, we are."

Her absolutism, like that of Sanders, missed the point; whether she was in a parliamentary system or the cumbersome, divided-powers system of the US, she would still have to build coalitions with people who only partly agreed with her. Abigail Spanberger, a former CIA intelligence officer and fellow freshman representative, was blunt: "There are some people who don't really seem to understand the math of the majority making."[60]

Ocasio-Cortez and many other Democrats were struggling with the reality of coalition parties. Decades ago, George Reedy made the point that "true ideological discussion never takes place at the political party level," but rather "in other organizations which are not constrained by the necessity of holding together coalescing forces."[61]

American parties *do* have to hold together coalescing forces. This emphasizes a further point: not every interest or group will be represented by a party. It is not even unusual for popular positions to be ruled out of bounds by both parties. When Lyndon Johnson was sworn in as president after the assassination of John F. Kennedy, he overcame resistance from fellow Southerners to pass the Civil Rights Act of 1964 with the support of more than two-thirds of the House and Senate. This bill established the party's firm commitment to civil rights, starting with voting rights. There was no way the party could talk about racism without making their political problem worse.

When the Civil Rights Act passed, George Wallace's opposition to integration—"I say segregation now, segregation tomorrow, segregation forever"—made him a national figure. In the 1964 Democratic primaries, he won over 30 percent of the vote in Wisconsin, Indiana, and Maryland.

Democratic senator Hubert H. Humphrey downplayed the consequences of these results. The other candidates, after all, had received two-thirds of the vote, and in each state party leaders blamed Wallace's success on local protests over the governor's policies. In other words, political leaders explained away a racist candidate's success by saying it stemmed from local issues, not race.[62]

A party can only ignore the supporters of the other side of a hot-button issue as long as they are doing "enough" to win over the advocates with less ugly, divisive approaches to the issue—or win without them. It is no easier for either party on gun control, women's rights, or any issue where the party has a firmly established commitment.

There is nothing inherently noble or virtuous about the inescapable fact that some issues are rendered taboo by a party. For decades, Democrats were only able to pass New Deal programs like Social Security by excluding farm laborers from coverage; that was how they won support from Southern Democrats unwilling to cover Black agricultural laborers.

Breaking these types of taboos is never painless for a party. In 1948, while running for the Senate, Humphrey delivered a historic speech against states' rights (as conceptualized by Southern states, at least) and for a stronger civil rights plank at the Democratic National Convention. In so doing, Humphrey mobilized the growing support after WWII for desegregation. A convention majority agreed with him, shattering a truce between liberal and Southern delegates. In the aftermath, the "Dixiecrats"—a breakaway states' rights party—carried four southern states for (then) Democratic senator Strom Thurmond.[63]

As different as Donald Trump and Bernie Sanders are, they both argue that top-down solutions can be easily accomplished with the right person in charge. (For Trump, the key issues were restricting immigration, repealing Obamacare, protecting entitlements, and bringing back manufacturing jobs; for Sanders, they were universal Medicare, redistribution of wealth, free tuition, restructuring banks, and fighting inequality.) Trump, based on his four years in office, did not prove the strength of this argument. He did much better for his family than for his party or followers, for whom he delivered on none of his promises regarding immigration, infrastructure, manufacturing jobs, or strengthening Medicare and Social Security.

Trump and Sanders also, not coincidentally, received very little support from legislators in their parties. In 2016, Sanders had superdelegate endorsements from two senators and seven representatives at the Democratic National Convention, while Hillary Clinton had superdelegate endorsements from 20 governors, 45 senators, and 177 representatives. During the 2016 Republican primary, only one senator, Jeff Sessions, endorsed Trump, joined by twelve representatives and three governors. It emphasizes how far downhill party politics have gone in America that Sanders and Trump could do so well with so little support from working legislators.

What would Alexandria Ocasio-Cortez have done if there had been thirty representatives willing to block the border funding bill that funded humane conditions for the children imprisoned without adequate beds, food, medicine or trained staff? Most of her fellow Democrats believed it was better to provide funding for decent childcare, rather than shut down the government to end child separation—a grand but futile gesture that would hurt the party without helping the children. Would she have tried to shut down all border control at the cost of leaving the children in heart-wrenching conditions?

I do not ask these questions as an underhanded critique of AOC. She has the brains, energy, and media talent to be a future party leader—but which kind of party leader? She could be the next Barney Frank, who helped draft and pass some of the most important legislation of the last thirty years, while bedeviling conservatives with his one-liners. Or she could be the next Bernie Sanders, who served in the House and Senate over thirty-five years, and yet, as Frank pointed out, campaigned "free of responsibility for anything that happened during his tenure [and] vigorous in his insistence that nothing that was done while he was there had any value."[64]

Frank's words from fifteen years ago, when he was a congressman, bear repeating now. Attacking the notion that pragmatism and idealism are opposed, he said, "The more you care about your values, the more you are morally obligated to get them implemented . . . to reconcile your ideals and the real world."[65] The Democratic Party's ability to avoid a catastrophic crackup in the post-McCain-Feingold world will hinge upon its members' aptitude in following this advice.

There are some signs that Ocasio-Cortez understands coalition-building and the limits of absolutist litmus tests. She leveraged her millions of online followers to help Senator Ed Markey become the first Massachusetts politician to defeat a Kennedy. Markey, who cosponsored the Green New Deal, overcame a primary challenge from Representative Joseph P. Kennedy III, thanks in part to the enthusiasm and energy of environmental activists, who—like AOC—were willing to overlook Markey's earlier votes for currently incendiary issues like the 1994 crime bill and the Patriot Act, as well as his opposition to busing.[66] Overlooking past votes that were now toxic when a legislator supported her highest priority was a small step; would she now overlook the same transgressions from legislators who did not support her highest priority?

A future Democratic crackup could occur over any number of issues. On climate change, there could be splits over the role of nuclear power and the transition to renewable energy. On any form of universal healthcare, there will be battles over reorganizing hospitals, doctors, and nurses—as well as the already present fight for the medical rights and needs of minorities, undocumented persons, women, and the elderly. Immigration reforms such as the 2013 "Gang of Eight" proposal—allowing a path to citizenship that takes thirteen years—would be denounced today as "too little, too late." There could also be fights over whether documented immigration should be prioritized for foreign-born students who attend college here, family members of current citizens, or for people who could take unfilled jobs.

On each of these issues, there are politicians with stark, absolutist positions, and many voters who will oppose the personal, shorter-term consequences of the shift. Add in a few billionaires outside the party, and no consensus will be possible. Republicans and Democrats mistrust each other's leaders more than in the past, and even trust their own side less than they once did.[67] This means that any party with a bold, ambitious agenda is asking voters to invest in a project being undertaken by a group they are not certain they can trust.

And these are only the most obvious current possibilities. There will always be unexpected culture shifts, economic changes, and fights over priorities. Cracks were already emerging in the immediate aftermath of the disappointing 2020 House results. After the Democrats lost a net of twelve seats, they held the slimmest majority for either party in eighteen years. Moderates vented their rage at progressives, whose calls for defunding the police or talk of socialism fueled attack ads used against the moderates. Representative Abigail Spanberger of Virginia, who won re-election by less than 2 percent, was furious. With that type of language, she told the caucus, "we will get fucking torn apart in 2022." Representative Conor Lamb of Pennsylvania concurred: "We pay the price for these unprofessional and unrealistic comments. . . . These issues are too serious for the people we represent to tolerate them being talked about so casually."

Representative Rashida Tlaib of Michigan, a member of the "Squad," side-stepped the problems with language. "It's unrealistic and unprofessional to be okay with people dying because air pollution is causing cancer in their communities," she said. "It's unrealistic and unprofessional to look away while Black folks get gunned down in the streets by police." Ocasio-Cortez argued that the representatives who lost their seats were "sitting ducks" who had antiquated messaging and did not devote enough resources to social media outreach.[68]

A month later, Ocasio-Cortez lost her all-out bid for the seat on the House Energy and Commerce Committee allocated to New York by the party. Kathleen Rice, a moderate, beat AOC in the steering committee vote, forty-six to thirteen. The vote was payback from angry moderates and established representatives who resented her for attacking them in primaries. "I'm taking into account who works against other members in primaries and who doesn't," said Representative Henry Cuellar, who narrowly defeated a primary opponent endorsed by Ocasio-Cortez.[69]

Democratic control of Congress depends on whether moderates and progressives develop approaches defensible to both types of districts. What neither Tlaib, Ocasio-Cortez, or Lamb mentioned is that Republican presidential candidates usually win in more than half of all congressional districts. While it takes 218 congressional victories to win a House majority, Barack Obama carried only 209 in 2012, Hillary Clinton carried only 205 in 2016, and Joe Biden will end up carrying about 224 districts in 2020. With 222 seats, Democrats have barely enough for control, and likely not enough to pass bold legislation or maintain majority status for more than two years.

We're starting to witness a progressive, leftist rerun of the language problems Republicans endured when Tea Party candidates talked about "legitimate rape" and used other inflammatory phrases in defending pro-life positions. As David Axelrod stated then, such extreme versions of party positions were inconvenient but not inconsistent. They cost the Republicans four Senate elections and the same problems could easily cost the Democrats their House majority in 2022.[70]

There will also be passionate arguments over America's role in the world economy. When President Biden starts dealing with foreign trade and tariffs, the fights will be as divisive for Democrats as they have been for Republicans. Donald Trump demonstrated that "America First" means "America Alone," but that still does not settle the issue of how a national government can handle global supply chains, or the role of American corporations whose executives worry as much about other countries as their own communities.

While he hadn't predicted someone as authoritarian as Trump, Professor Samuel Huntington foreshadowed the backlash in 2004 when he coined the term "Davos Men" for the new global elite that meet yearly in Davos, Switzerland. The coming divide in America, Huntington predicted, would pit cosmopolitans (who cared about the world in general more than about America in particular) against nationalists. Many academics regarded the concept of patriotism as outdated or morally dangerous, but for most Americans, Huntington pointed out, societal security was about language, culture, religion, and national identity—not a world without boundaries or national identities.[71] The backlash against the "Davos Men" could prove as conducive to a Democratic crackup as it has been in the Republican implosion.

The Emperor's New Clothes

In Hans Christian Andersen's children's story "The Emperor's New Clothes," swindlers convince the emperor that they can make him a suit of clothes "so fine and pure . . . that it could only be seen by the best and most discriminating people." When the emperor parades through the town naked, no one dares says a word until a child speaks up: "But he has nothing on at all."

The story is often cited as a tale about aristocratic vanity and the ability of "a brave, insightful individual to set things right."[72] But Andersen's fable was not a tale extolling the power of one person speaking truth to power, but rather a critique of fawning, incompetent ministers who inherited their positions. He wrote it when the limited press freedoms in Denmark were under attack and it was dangerous to criticize the monarch or his ministers. The growing middle class was chafing under incompetent hereditary ministers like those in his tale, who chose self-preservation over the risk of being betrayed by a minister who perpetuated the false belief there was cloth to be seen.[73]

Each of the ministers was *responsive* to the needs and beliefs of the leader and the ways their behavior affected their personal future. Had there only been a way for them to act collectively, they could have acted *responsibly* and prevented the spectacle.

In late June 2020, with no end to the COVID pandemic in sight and a president unable to formulate a national strategy (or even wear a mask every day), former Reagan speechwriter Peggy Noonan captured the national sense of the president: "He hasn't been equal to the crises. He never makes anything better. And everyone kind of knows."[74] It hardly mattered to any Republicans in a position to stop him or force any changes. They had known for years, but they were unable to act together and force any changes.

Over seventy years ago, Charles Adrian observed that "there is no collective responsibility in a nonpartisan body." Political parties, however, have "a past to honor and a future to protect."[75] But honoring the past and protecting the future only works when party leaders can develop and defend a consensus.

Without collective responsibility, legislatures can't create comprehensive programs because the coordination necessary for ongoing adjustments and bargaining doesn't exist. Instead, every decision is an ad-hoc coalition for one vote. This makes it easy for individual politicians to pass the buck and tell their constituents it was votes from other legislators that caused an unfavorable outcome.

The American federal system—where we vote for hundreds of legislators and administrators at the city, county, state, and national levels—makes the problem of "accountability" particularly difficult for voters. As Margit Tavits has shown, "If lines of responsibility are not clear, the ability of voters to evaluate and punish politicians—as well as to create incentives for performance—declines."[76]

Responsible political parties are not necessary for politicians to do well, but they are necessary for the government to do well for the country. Ted Cruz, Devin Nunes, Matt Gaetz, and Mark Meadows are prime examples of politicians doing well for themselves while stymying their colleagues' plans to solve very contentious problems and legislate. The more vote-swapping and horse-trading individual politicians can do without party constraints, the more opportunities there are for cronyism, graft, and side payments—and the fewer opportunities there are for voters to connect any group of legislators with specific outcomes they support or oppose.[77]

Although campaign finance reforms have set the current political landscape apart, the breakdown in unity exemplified by Cruz, Meadows, and Nunes has historical parallels. From 1910 to 1952, California had state legislative elections that were very close to the nonpartisan elections Adrian studied. Candidates could run in each party's primary, and their party affiliation was unlisted. "Reelection was virtually guaranteed, and few people were watching over their shoulders," observed Seth Masket. The result was a combination of endless bickering in the legislature, and legislators doing well for themselves, if not for their state.[78]

What Can Be Done?

The problem of collective responsibility is at the heart of the problems facing both political parties going forward. There are three interrelated issues that brought us to this point: campaign finance reforms, the evolution of presidential primaries, and the diminished power of legislative leaders to control their caucuses.

Holes in campaign finance regulation allow purity-for-profit groups to play shell games, moving money around and hiding the names of persons who fund "grass roots" movements. Political parties have allowed the admirable goal of democratization to turn presidential primaries into a way for candidates to become better known, instead of a way to decide which person is best qualified to be president. And legislative leaders cannot honor their party's past or protect its future if they are overpowered by outside spending from persons and groups willing to sacrifice the party's future for their short-term gains. Because these issues are all connected, any solutions must find some way to make parties more effective so that they can be collectively responsible, and not just a collection of individual politicians all responsive to their individual voter bases.

Idealists argue that greater participation among voters is a solution for the complex problems of legislation. This ignores the value of tradeoffs that are part of any legislation. Direct participation can motivate and mobilize citizens, but the slogans and signs that reverberate so deeply have never been sufficient. As political philosopher David Plotke has written, "democracy means compromises of principle because it is a way to make decisions where resources are limited and preferences are strong."[79]

Utopian ideals about increased citizen participation on issues are unreasonable. In the real world, the concerns of voters ebb and flow. Passionate engagement with an issue can be sporadic, prompted by an unexpected, catastrophic event; it can also be short-lived, lasting only while that catastrophic event continues to generate headlines.

During periods of intense citizen focus, responsive politicians scramble to solve problems and then shift to the next hot-button issue that arises. Responding to immediate demands can win points for politicians, but it also produces periods where they pass up the opportunity to spend time and money on prevention. The old folk saying that an ounce of prevention is worth a pound of cure is, from an electoral standpoint, wrong. Neil Malhotra has shown that, politically speaking, a single ounce of mitigation is worth a pound of prevention. For every dollar spent dealing with the devastation of Hurricane Katrina, for example, politicians earned as many votes as sixteen dollars spent on preventing storm damage.[80]

In politics, any explanation for a problem contains an implicit solution. Regrettably, it is also generally the case that if the solution were easy, the problem would already be solved. There are, however, important steps that can restore some (if not all) of both parties' ability to legislate before it is too late.

Campaign Finance Reform

The first step is addressing the changes to campaign finance laws that have eroded the last remaining guardrails in the federal system. For the foreseeable future, it is safe to assume that there will be more money in the hands of outside groups than in the hands of party leaders and candidates. There are still important ways to moderate the influence of super PACs and the hit-and-run groups that launch attacks and disappear before anyone can learn who they really were. The most significant of these is increased transparency.

In the rulings that opened the door for unlimited spending by corporations or individuals, the Supreme Court stressed the importance of transparency and assumed that "with the advent of the Internet . . . prompt disclosure of expenditures can provide shareholders and citizens with the information needed to hold corporations and elected officials accountable."[81] Instead, moving the money outside the political parties has made it easier for activists to hide their donors and obscure the biases and motives of their funding sources.

Transparency is essential to fight corruption, prevent illegal contributions, and inform voters. The laws against corruption and illegal contributions can punish wrongdoing even when the information emerges after the election.

But after the election is too late; campaigns can only respond, and voters can only consider motives and sources, if the information is available in time.

Source credibility is one of the most important ways for citizens to evaluate information. Having high regard for Jesse Jackson or Rush Limbaugh, for example, does not mean that you assume they are a reliable source for information about a decision. A substantial amount of research shows that people follow an endorser's "advice when they perceive the endorser both to be knowledgeable and to share their interests."[82]

The biggest problems today with bots, rumors, deceptive stories, and conspiracy theories come when the actual source of a story is not available. People reading a standard "old-school" newspaper or magazine can take into account whether the story is credible and whether the source shares their interests. When people receive stories in e-mails, or from online sites not associated with a specific news source or network (e.g., Facebook), they are far more vulnerable to deception. Evaluating stories only on tone, mood, and common opinions is unreliable.[83]

Dark money is all about providing donors with ways to influence people without their names and motives being exposed. It makes it far easier to run attacks on candidates and referenda while avoiding any of the usual consequences to personal or corporate reputations. When corporations must take their consumers' reactions into account, they spend far less money on super PACs than wealthy individuals—or corporations whose names are not on consumer products. No corporate CEO donated to Trump's campaign, and many corporate sponsors pulled out of the GOP convention to avoid offending their young, affluent consumers.

The risk of revealing campaign contributions has become more important in recent years, as public opinion has shifted on social issues. Chick-Fil-A became a right-wing cause célèbre by donating to charities with a strong anti-LGBTQ stance. In 2019, however, as the company expanded throughout the country—and their need for an expanded customer base followed—the company announced a new "focused giving" approach, concentrating on education, homelessness, and hunger, rather than anti-LGBTQ causes.[84]

Dark money also allows legislators to escape accountability by voters. If a senator or representative suddenly changes sides on an issue when there is a flood of dark money from benefactors, voters would presumably find that information relevant, no matter which side of the issue they supported.

However, this information is often difficult or impossible to come by for the average voter. The prompt disclosure of expenditures the Supreme Court envisioned is neither timely or complete. The Internet makes it easier for groups like the Koch network to create complex networks of nonprofit entities to move money without anyone learning about the donors until well after the political campaign has ended—if ever.

Ironically, the Supreme Court's *Citizens United* ruling attributed the same game-changing virtues to the Internet as the activists who believed that Twitter and Facebook would make the world more democratic. This is only true if the rules governing nonprofits and political communications are strengthened and enforced, which must be done in order to increase transparency and allow voters to make informed decisions about source credibility.

As things now stand, groups with very few members and big contributions get an edge over groups with many members and modest contributions, because the big money groups can conceal their donors. Through the intricate shell games that move the money around a network of advocacy groups, such groups can also take advantages of loopholes in the tax codes that allow them to qualify for tax exempt status.

When Sal Russo, founder of the Tea Party Express PAC, wanted to hide the donors to attack ads on two California referenda, he engaged in a money-swapping deal with Sean Noble (then an Arizona resident), who ran many of the biggest Koch network dark money campaigns. Russo agreed to donate $25 million raised in California to Noble's PAC, and then have Noble contribute $25 million of out-of-state money to Russo's campaign, thereby enabling him to hide the California donors' names. After several years of litigation, Russo and Noble confessed, arranged plea bargains, and divulged the names of the California residents who had tried to hide their support for an anti-union measure and a temporary tax increase; $9 million came from the Fisher family that had founded The Gap, and $6 million came from Charles Schwab, the owner of the online investor firm.[85]

The Supreme Court rulings assumed there would be no corruption, in part because the sources of the money would be known. How big-money donors earned their wealth or what cause they support is typically known to strategists, and can be used to expose their motives. But the amount of dark money is growing; by 2015, it made up nearly one-third of all campaign spending.[86] This growth makes it increasingly difficult for voters to tell where candidates' funding comes from.

Some states have attempted to bring transparency and limits to political contributions. With bipartisan support, Montana enacted strict disclosure requirements on political committees spending money on local elections in 2015, and in 2019 the US Supreme Court turned down a challenge to the state's strict contribution limits.[87] California also has rigid requirements on disclosures, and it managed, after a long battle, to establish the same requirements for out-of-state money spent on California campaigns.

However, little has been done at the federal level to end the shell games that move money from one group to another and make it hard even to learn what group is behind the ads. Sophisticated networks, like Charles Koch's, use large webs of nonprofits to do the actual spending on ads, and these groups are virtually untraceable. Until their parent group files an IRS report—usually after the campaign—we only see groups with vague and uninformative names like ASME, TOHE, or RION.[88]

In 2012, Senate Democrats tried to pass a bill requiring stricter requirements on disclosure, but Mitch McConnell ensured it did not have enough Republican support to even hold a vote. Requiring public disclosure, McConnell argued, was nothing but "donor harassment and intimidation."[89]

Under the current rules, donors can set up a PAC, say they are not running any ads, then run ads and disband, leaving nothing behind that allows opponents or reporters to find out where the money came from, or even if the ads are backed by foreign donors trying to help a candidate. Foreign contributions to domestic campaigns are illegal, but these laws are even more poorly enforced than other campaign finance laws, and shell companies have been set up by foreign governments, including Russia and China, to put money into campaigns. Nonprofit groups are required to report donors confidentially to the IRS, but under President Trump, the Treasury Department proposed dropping the requirement to provide names of foreign donors, even confidentially.

The US Chamber of Commerce, for one, receives much of its money from foreign countries, and has argued that any accidental leak of donors could reduce corporate free speech. This is a common argument from major donors and fundraisers: revealing the names of persons paying for attack ads would subject them to attack ads, too.[90] But the current spotty enforcement of laws requiring disclosure of foreign donors' names has opened the door for potential international meddling in US races. Disclosures after the election can be used to prosecute violations of campaign laws after the fact, but they do little to help make the elections more transparent.[91]

This is a correctable problem. One of the ways to make campaign finance more accountable is to require groups to disclose their donors when they purchase ad time on television, radio, billboards, video games, or the Internet. There is no technical reason that donor lists and amounts cannot be compiled almost instantaneously, and donors giving more than a specific amount identified. Many of the PACs, in fact, have no more than one or two donors.

Further, instead of the secretive ways campaigns relay information to super PACs without breaking rules, it would be worthwhile to consider whether it would be better to allow coordination and require the candidate to be heard saying, "I approve this message." If this were the case, candidates could no longer deny responsibility for the ads they want run; indeed, the need to take personal responsibility for dubious attacks might dissuade some super PAC funders and change the type of ads used.

Presidential Primaries

For over two hundred years, the major political parties have held national conventions where delegates select their party's candidates for president and vice president. Each party determines how many delegates each state receives and sets its own rules for their selection. Until the 1960s, there was a mixture of delegates selected by party leaders, often big city mayors or governors, and delegates selected by voters, sometimes in primaries or caucuses or at state conventions. The big shift toward a nomination process dominated by primaries began as a response to concerns about the legitimacy of backdoor deals among politicians whom activists increasingly believed were out of touch. By 1972, voters in both parties chose most delegates in primaries.

The primary system and the growth of candidate-centered organizations has gradually taken the power to screen candidates out of the hands of the very people who depend upon the winner to enact their proposals. It has made primaries a way for candidates to become famous enough to matter, instead of a way to choose among candidates who have already displayed an ability to govern. The rapidly expanding size of the primary field—seventeen major Republican candidates in 2016, and twenty-nine major Democratic candidates in 2020—has not been helpful in either party, if judged by the effect of the process on the eventual winner.

When the major arms of each party—the Republican and Democratic national committees, congressional campaign committees, or Senate campaign committees—allocate money to specific campaigns, their collective interest in gaining or keeping majority status results in hard-nosed decisions about which candidate is most likely to win the election. Those decisions, of course, are heavily influenced by polls, but they also take into account many other types of information, including the candidate's value to their caucus, the importance of defeating a particular opponent, and so on. When it comes to presidential candidates, however, individual legislators may endorse a candidate, but the party as a whole typically stands back and lets voters decide.

But parties are not required to stand back. Thanks to federal court rulings, they have far more authority to control who is on the ballots in primaries and general elections than they currently exercise. In 1992, the Georgia Republican Party did not allow long-time neo-Nazi and Klansman David Duke to run in the presidential primary. Duke pursued the case to the 11th Circuit Court of Appeals, which upheld the right of political parties to define their membership and regulate elections—including the right to decide who could appear on the ballot. In other cases—such as when the Democratic National Committee punished Michigan and Florida for changing their 2008 presidential primary dates by counting each of their convention delegates as only half a vote—the Supreme Court has not intervened.[92]

The parties' laissez-faire attitude toward presidential candidates has gone to extremes. Both parties set the bar so low that in 2016, candidates were allowed into debates without having released their full tax returns or medical records—or even pledged to support the winner. Requiring those actions would be a minor but important step for either party; no one who hasn't planned far enough ahead to do this is ready to run for president, let alone be one.

Without changes in the requirements to appear in debates or compete in the primary, the parties will have to take active steps beyond their anyone-can-run approach. The collapse of support for the party establishment among Republicans created wide-open primaries in 2012 and 2016, with more than ten candidates competing each time. With so many candidates to choose from, good self-promoters can seem more appealing than someone who can credibly govern.

Senator Lindsey Graham, a representative when Newt Gingrich was Speaker, considered Gingrich one of the best salesmen in the party, but also too undisciplined and erratic to accomplish his goals.[93] As Speaker, Gingrich was determined to make all decisions himself, from shutting down the government in 1995 to impeaching Bill Clinton for lying about an affair (while he himself was having an affair and lying about it). GOP legislators seemed to agree with Graham's assessment: in 2012, of the eighty-one Republican representatives who had served with Gingrich, only two endorsed him in his presidential campaign.[94]

Despite Gingrich's inability to build an organization or attract small donors, he still managed to capitalize on some aspects of the diffusion of power from party organizations—namely, the support of billionaire backers. Sheldon Adelson donated $15 million to start a pro-Gingrich super PAC used to attack Mitt Romney. Gingrich understood this was going to be commonplace for billionaires; all they had to do was decide "this year, instead of buying a new yacht, I'm going to spend $70 million on a candidate."[95]

In 2019, there were fifty persons on the Forbes 400 list worth at least $10 billion, which means there are fifty individuals for whom a political investment of 1 percent of their wealth—$100 million—is enough to shake up any election in America.

HR 1, the "For the People Act" passed by the Democratic-controlled House in 2019, would close some of the gap between the influence of the most wealthy and other Americans by introducing voluntary public campaign financing that would match donations of $200 or less at the rate of six to one.[96] While that bill would seem to restore some of the balance between small donations and billionaire-led super PACs, it would also increase the flow of cash to single-issue candidates and make it easier for someone with the support of a passionate segment of the party to win with a platform that could not achieve majority support.

Over half of the candidates in recent primaries in both parties failed to win a single delegate to their party's nominating convention. These candidates simply water down the discussion among the candidates who actually have a chance to win based on their existing support and accomplishments. They also raise fringe issues with minimal support in the party or try to revive issues that the majority of the party is uninterested in or opposed to addressing. This makes it harder to settle the existing, ongoing battles on the most important issues facing the party and country.[97]

In recent primaries in both parties, there have been so many candidates that a two-level competition has emerged: one level consists of candidates with enough money and standing to make the "center ring" in debates, and the other consists of candidates with lower standing who try and use the smaller stage to elevate their profile. Instead of sorting the candidates by money and polls, why not require candidates to win active support from the legislators they would be working with in office? To be clear, I am not suggesting a return to the first years of our new democracy, where members of Congress selected their party's candidate. But requiring a candidate to win endorsements from a fixed number of senators or representatives or governors or big-city mayors would force a demonstration of the kinds of bargaining powers a president must use to work in a democratic, non-authoritarian way.

If a party's legislators lost all credibility with the electorate through their performance—as GOP legislators did—their endorsements would be worthless and an outsider with authoritarian instincts could still win. In most years, however, the process of garnering endorsements would be better preparation for the new administration, and make it more likely the party and president were ready to roll early in the new administration.

This would deprive some talented persons with admirable goals of a chance to make their name. But the point of a presidential primary, after all, is to end up with a candidate who can win and govern. Could a smart, articulate person with little national or state-level experience do any better than Donald Trump at staffing an administration? Could anyone who enters the White House govern without a solid phalanx of qualified appointees equipped to run the government? As I wrote in an earlier book, voters believe that presidents have more power than they actually have in a democracy, and candidates have to overpromise to meet expectations. Therefore, it is critical for candidates to "understand the distinction between what sells and what works. Both are necessary; knowing the difference is critical."[98]

Reviving Legislative Leadership

Both Democrats and Republicans have multiple groups associated with, but distinct from, the party apparatus: environmental groups, unions, energy and mining corporations, religious groups, and other interest groups with a large stake and a loud voice in the party's direction. But these loud voices can drown each other out, destroying the coordination required to enact legislation. Someone must allocate the time for debating a bill, someone must decide which subset of the legislature drafts the bill and what kinds of amendments are allowed, and so on.[99] In the post-McCain-Feingold era, the person who makes the final decisions can be a member of the legislature or an outsider with their own agenda, willing to destroy the long-term prospects of the party for the short-term gains they can earn from a change in the tax code, deregulating an industry, or changing a critical environmental rule.

My research on how voters reason about their votes, and how candidates develop strategies for campaigning and governing, has led me to the conclusion that there can be no return to effective modern government until party leaders in the House and Senate once again have the resources to build consensus and enforce legislative norms.

The changes in campaign finance have meant new representatives and senators no longer had to go along to get along. With so many ways for its members to maintain an identity besides "Democrat" or "Republican," a party could become an immobile, inefficient parliament, as Ryan realized when he gave up on accomplishing anything as Speaker.

The growth of billionaire PACs and "purity for profit" groups has so weakened the power of party leaders that opportunists like Ted Cruz can intimidate colleagues and crash the regular order of legislation for personal advancement. His behavior would not have been possible in the past, when Senate leaders could still enforce norms. Cruz was no out-of-control alcoholic like Senator Joseph McCarthy, maligning outsiders and Democrats as Communists and dupes; rather, he was a carefully calibrated politician taking advantage of years-in-the-making breakdowns in the power of leaders to control their caucuses.

When Cruz argued before the Supreme Court, Dahlia Lithwick saw him operate in a style that perfectly matched the court's norms of deference, ego-constraints, and brevity; he "could not lie . . . change the subject, [or] evade the facts or the law." In the Senate, however, Cruz became an over-rehearsed, hyper-competitive, "just-add-water outrage machine."[100]

Cruz was the innovator Paul Ryan credited with grasping the new reality where "you can . . . shortcut your way toward the top of the political pile because you're a better entertainer." Once Cruz made his name, Ryan reflected, "there were a million mini-me's that said, 'Well, shit, if this freshman senator from Texas can do it, I can do it.'"[101]

Strengthening party leaders means limiting the power of small groups within a party to undermine the foundations of the federal system of checks and balances, not returning to the days of autocratic committee chairs. It also means strengthening the policy capability of both chambers to evaluate their legislation.

In 2019, Democrats made changes to two House rules that limit the power of disgruntled representatives to shut down the government or humiliate the speaker when they cannot get their way inside their caucus. The existing rules, which were most beneficial to "purity for profit" groups and the Koch network, supported any group willing to block partial repeals of programs or fight to cut more spending that most of their party supported.

Under the House rules from 2011 to 2019, there were separate votes for a budget and the authorization for the increase in debt ceiling necessary to pay for that same budget. Playing politics with the latter vote was great for showboating and fundraising, but not for legislation or long-term changes in policies. If the debt ceiling is not raised, the resulting defaults—from bonds and treasury notes to military pay and social security—would be catastrophic. This is why every temporary shutdown has been resolved in time to avoid default.

Still, even though the threat of default seldom changes policy, it is very valuable for any group that claims their policy goal—whether it's shrinking government, redistributing wealth, or taking action on climate change—is more important than business as usual.

Instead of first voting to pass a budget and then voting a second time to authorize raising the debt ceiling, Democrats reverted to a rule first adopted in 1979 that deemed the debt ceiling raised when the budget was passed. The Gephardt Rule, named in honor of former Democratic Speaker Richard Gephardt, means representatives who cannot persuade a majority of their caucus to accept a spending cut can no longer use the debt ceiling vote to threaten to crash the economy if they don't get their way.[102]

The second change involved the "Motion to Vacate" rule. Under the old rule, any representative could file a motion to "vacate the chair," which, if passed, would throw out the Speaker. As we've seen with the Freedom Caucus's actions, the only purpose for that rule is grandstanding and self-promotion; when Mark Meadows first threatened to file that motion to humiliate Speaker John Boehner, he did not even have the support of the Freedom Caucus—it was a one-person publicity stunt. Now, under the current rules, a motion to vacate requires a party majority.[103]

These two changes are necessary, but not sufficient, to restore the parties' power to check and oversee the president. In response to the cumbersome pace of federalism, the use of executive powers have grown; the Brennan Center for Justice's compilations found 136 emergency powers available to the president. Only thirteen of these powers require Congress to declare an emergency; twelve others require certification from someone appointed by the president, such as an agency head or member of his cabinet.[104]

Without the inconvenience of a Senate confirmation hearing, the president can legally designate temporary appointees willing to do his bidding. The people who directed the unusual deployment of armed federal agents—whose uniforms bore no identification or insignia—to break up mostly peaceful Black Lives Matter protests in June 2020 were officials on temporary appointments to posts within Immigration, Customs, or Homeland Security.[105] Without additional legislation and rule changes, neither the House nor Senate can move quickly enough to stop a president like Trump from evading all oversight by appointing acting secretaries, acting deputy secretaries, and the like.

Troubled by Trump's liberal use of these emergency powers, Representative Katie Porter, along with several committee chairs, prepared legislation to limit the time that temporary appointments can serve without Senate confirmation, and require them to testify upon congressional request.[106] This legislation, if a president signed it, would make it harder for another president to go so far beyond what the laws intended.

It may sound mundane or trivial, but adding policy muscle to the House and Senate is necessary to legislate and keep up with the changes in technology, finance, healthcare, and climate change. Congress needs more policy backup and expertise than it currently has —and even more than it had in 1994, when newly enshrined Speaker Newt Gingrich reduced committee staffs and killed the Commission on Intergovernmental Relations (which figured out ways to coordinate the levels of government) and the Office of Technology Assessment (which provided scientific advice).[107]

Gingrich's goal was to eliminate any experts who could second-guess his grandiose plans. Since then, the GOP has moved to limit and weaken almost every governmental scientific group that gets in its way on energy policy, cutting entitlements, or buttressing the rights of gun owners. When the Congressional Budget Office (CBO) disclosed that the Republican alternative to Obamacare would deprive twenty million people of insurance and raise government spending, Mick Mulvaney and Senator Roy Blunt attacked the CBO—which was run by a Republican analyst selected by Republican leadership—as outdated and unwanted. Restoring these institutions would add muscle and efficiency to any party interested in legislation that would stand the test of time.[108]

Limiting presidential overreach or passing legislation to deal with healthcare, climate change, immigration, or the tax code are simply impossible without effective parties. Speakers and majority leaders cannot fire presidents or cabinet secretaries, but if they have adequate authority within their caucuses, the power of the purse can be mighty.

These potential changes are but a small part of restoring balance in the American federal system. Further, these ideas—like any kind of reform that promises to be the last word on an issue—should be approached with a watchful eye toward the future. There is no last move in politics. Advocates of the McCain-Feingold reforms and the justices who ruled in favor of *Citizens United* can both tell you there are always unintended consequences to any major change.

Even though I've made every effort to examine the effects of my proposed changes, it is certain they would have unintended and unexpected effects if enacted. Such is the nature of our political system. If nothing else, however, I hope that this book has explained to readers why the health of a legislature is even more important to the health of a democracy than the openness and fairness of its elections. Without collective responsibility and checks on the ability of wealthy individuals and groups to game the political system, the rule of law declines as fast as inequality rises.

Appendices

Table A.1 The 2004 John Kerry Vote would defeat John McCain in 2008

State	Electors	Kerry 04	Obama 08	McCain 08
States Where Kerry 2004 Vote would beat McCain 08 (284 Electors)				
California	55	**6,745,485**	8,274,473	5,011,781
Connecticut	7	**857,488**	997,773	629,428
D. C.	3	**202,970**	245,800	17,367
Delaware	3	**200,152**	255,459	152,374
Hawaii	4	**231,708**	325,871	120,566
Illinois	21	**2,891,550**	3,419,348	2,031,179
Iowa	7	**741,898**	828,940	682,379
Maine	4	**396,842**	421,923	295,273
Maryland	10	**1,334,493**	1,629,467	959,862
Massachusetts	12	**1,803,800**	1,904,098	1,108,854
Michigan	17	**2,479,183**	2,872,579	2,048,639
Minnesota	10	**1,445,014**	1,573,354	1,275,409
New Hampshire	4	**340,511**	384,826	316,534
New Jersey	15	**1,911,430**	2,215,422	1,613,207
New Mexico	5	**370,942**	472,422	346,832
New York	31	**4,314,280**	4,804,945	2,752,771
Ohio	20	**2,741,167**	2,940,044	2,677,820
Oregon	7	**943,163**	1,037,291	738,475
Pennsylvania	21	**2,938,095**	3,276,363	2,655,885
Rhode Island	4	**259,760**	296,571	165,391
Vermont	3	**184,067**	219,262	98,974
Washington	11	**1,510,201**	1,750,848	1,229,216
Wisconsin	10	**1,489,504**	1,677,211	1,262,393
Total	**284**			
States Won by Obama Gains (80 Electors)				
Colorado	9	1,001,725	**1,288,633**	1,073,629
Florida	27	3,583,544	**4,282,367**	4,046,219
Indiana	11	969,011	**1,374,039**	1,345,648
Nevada	5	397,190	**533,736**	412,827
North Carolina	15	1,525,849	**2,142,651**	2,128,474
Virginia	13	1,454,742	**1,959,532**	1,725,005
Total	80			

Table A.1 *continued*

State	Electors	Kerry 04	Obama 08	McCain 08
States won by McCain (174 Electors)				
Alabama	9	693,933	813,479	1,266,546
Alaska	3	111,025	123,594	193,841
Arizona	10	893,524	1,034,707	1,230,111
Arkansas	6	469,953	422,310	638,017
Georgia	15	1,366,149	1,844,123	2,048,759
Idaho	4	181,098	236,440	403,012
Kansas	6	434,993	514,765	699,655
Kentucky	8	712,733	751,985	1,048,462
Louisiana	9	820,299	782,989	1,148,275
Mississippi	6	458,094	554,662	724,597
Missouri	11	1,259,171	1,441,911	1,445,814
Montana	3	173,710	232,159	243,882
Nebraska*	5	254,328	333,319	452,979
North Dakota	3	111,052	141,403	168,887
Oklahoma	7	503,966	502,496	960,165
South Carolina	8	661,699	862,449	1,034,896
South Dakota	3	149,244	170,924	203,054
Tennessee	11	1,035,160	1,087,437	1,479,178
Texas	34	2,832,704	3,528,633	4,479,328
Utah	5	241,199	327,670	596,030
West Virginia	5	326,541	303,857	397,466
Wyoming	3	70,776	82,868	164,958
Total	174			

Notes: The "Obama" and "McCain" columns show the two candidates' popular vote in each state for the 2008 presidential election. The "Kerry" column shows Kerry's popular vote in each state received in 2004.

*Obama won one Electoral Vote in Nebraska where the winner of each the three congressional districts received an electoral vote and two go to the statewide total vote.

Table A.2 The 2004 John Kerry vote would have won the 2012 Presidential Election

State	Electors	Kerry	Obama	Romney
States where Kerry 2004 vote would defeat Romney (275 Electors)				
California	55	**6,745,485**	7,854,285	4,839,958
Connecticut	7	**857,488**	905,109	634,899
D. C.	3	**202,970**	267,070	21,381
Delaware	3	**200,152**	242,584	165,484
Hawaii	4	**231,708**	306,658	121,015
Illinois	20	**2,891,550**	3,019,512	2,135,216
Iowa	6	**741,898**	822,544	730,617
Maine	4	**396,842**	401,306	292,276
Maryland	10	**1,334,493**	1,677,844	971,869
Massachusetts	11	**1,803,800**	1,921,761	1,188,460
Michigan	16	**2,479,183**	2,564,569	2,115,256
Minnesota	10	**1,445,014**	1,546,167	1,320,225
New Hampshire	4	**340,511**	369,561	329,918
New Jersey	14	**1,911,430**	2,126,610	1,478,749
New Mexico	5	**370,942**	415,335	335,788
New York	29	**4,314,280**	4,485,877	2,490,496
Ohio	18	**2,741,167**	2,827,709	2,661,437
Oregon	7	**943,163**	970,488	754,175
Pennsylvania	20	**2,938,095**	2,990,274	2,680,434
Rhode Island	4	**259,760**	279,677	157,204
Vermont	3	**184,067**	199,239	92,698
Washington	12	**1,510,201**	1,755,396	1,290,670
Wisconsin	10	**1,489,504**	1,620,985	1,407,966
Total	**275**			
States Won by Obama Gains (57 Electors)				
Colorado	9	1,001,725	**1,323,102**	1,185,243
Florida	29	3,583,544	**4,237,756**	4,163,447
Nevada	6	397,190	**531,373**	463,567
Virginia	13	1,454,742	**1,971,820**	1,822,522
Total	57			

Table A.2 *continued*

State	Electors	Kerry	Obama	Romney
States Won by Romney (206 Electors)				
Alabama	9	693,933	795,696	**1,255,925**
Alaska	3	111,025	122,640	**164,676**
Arizona	11	893,524	1,025,232	**1,233,654**
Arkansas	6	469,953	394,409	**647,744**
Georgia	16	1,366,149	1,773,827	**2,078,688**
Idaho	4	181,098	212,787	**420,911**
Indiana	11	969,011	1,154,275	**1,422,872**
Kansas	6	434,993	439,908	**689,809**
Kentucky	8	712,733	679,370	**1,087,190**
Louisiana	8	820,299	809,141	**1,152,262**
Mississippi	6	458,094	562,949	**710,746**
Missouri	10	1,259,171	1,223,796	**1,482,440**
Montana	3	173,710	201,839	**267,928**
Nebraska	5	254,328	302,081	**475,064**
North Carolina	15	1,525,849	2,178,391	**2,270,395**
North Dakota	3	111,052	124,827	**188,163**
Oklahoma	7	503,966	443,547	**891,325**
South Carolina	9	661,699	865,941	**1,071,645**
South Dakota	3	149,244	145,039	**210,610**
Tennessee	11	1,035,160	960,709	**1,462,330**
Texas	38	2,832,704	3,308,124	**4,569,843**
Utah	6	241,199	251,813	**740,600**
West Virginia	5	326,541	238,269	**417,655**
Wyoming	3	70,776	69,286	**170,962**
Total	206			

Notes: The "Obama" and "Romney" columns show the two candidates' popular vote in each state for the 2012 presidential election. The "Kerry" column shows Kerry's popular vote in each state received in 2004.

Table A.3 Congressional Party Composition, 2000–2020

Congressional Election	Majority Party	Democrats	Republicans	Republicans from Confederacy (Proportion Within Party)
2000	Republicans	212	223	72 (32.4%)
2002	Republicans	207	228	76 (33.3%)
2004	Republicans	203	232	82 (35.3%)
2006	Democrats	234	201	76 (37.8%)
2008	Democrats	258	177	72 (40.7%)
2010	Republicans	192	243	94 (38.7%)
2012	Republicans	201	234	98 (41.9%)
2014	Republicans	188	247	101 (40.9%)
2016	Republicans	194	241	99 (41.1%)
2018	Democrats	235	200	90 (45%)
2020	Democrats	222	213	100 (46.9%)

The eleven states of the Confederacy are South Carolina, Mississippi, Florida, Alabama, Georgia, Louisiana and Texas, the first seven states to secede, plus Virginia, Arkansas, Tennessee and North Carolina, states that joined as the war started.

Notes

Introduction

1. Lepore 2014.
2. Hetherington 1998, 2015; Hetherington and Rudolph 2015.
3. Diamond 1997, 157–58.
4. Goodman 2016.
5. Craig 2016; Barrett 2011; Goodman 2016; *New York Times* 2016.
6. Gabriel 2011.
7. Gwirtzman 1975.
8. Nellis 2016.
9. Cox and Weingast 2018, 279–81.
10. Cox 2016.
11. Fiorina 1980, 26.
12. Rosenblum 2008, 1.
13. Szalai 2017 .
14. Ibid.
15. Rosenblum 2008, 307; Disch 2009, 622.
16. Plotke 1997, 32; Hetherington 1998, 2015.
17. Fishkin and Gerken 2014, 46; Gerken and Fishkin 2015.
18. Coronavirus Resource Center 2021; Veterans Administration 2020.
19. Census Bureau Household Pulse 20 2020.
20. Balz and Branigan 2003.

Chapter 1

1. *Newsweek* 2000b.
2. Martin 2015. The *Times* used "slop" as a euphemism.
3. Goldmacher 2016.
4. Taylor 2015; *Frontline* 1997.
5. Lemann 2003, 78.
6. *Newsweek* 2000.
7. Gibbs et al. 2000.
8. Gooding 2004.
9. Ibid.
10. Alexander 2001a, 2001b; Kirkpatrick 2008.

11. Alexander 2001b.
12. Green 2002; *Newsweek* 2000a; Stevenson 2001.
13. Lemann 2003, 75.
14. Ibid., 71.
15. Lee 2016, 4; Bonica and Cox 2018, 212.
16. Tokaji and Strause 2014, 97; Cassidy 2005, 44; Scherer 2004.
17. Schelling 1971, 66; Cassidy 2005.
18. Cassidy 2005; Schelling 1971.
19. Alvarez 2001; Hook 2001; Sanger 2001.
20. Popkin 2012, 38.
21. Baylor 2018, 161.
22. Rich 2001.
23. Carney 2001, Rich 2001; Weekly Standard 2001; Bruni 2001; *New York Times* 2000.
24. Bruck 2004.
25. Cusack 2007; Kaiser 2008.
26. Kirkpatrick 2008.
27. Alexander 2001b.
28. Jacobson 2003.
29. Popkin 2012, 150; Krugman 2002.
30. Bank et al. 2008, 155–56.
31. Dickerson 2004.
32. Wamhoff and Gardner 2018; Cohen 2017; Rosenthal 2016.
33. Purdum 2007, Alexander 2001a, Kirkpatrick 2008; Foer 2002; Reiff and McGahn 2014; Blumenthal 2013.
34. Kelner and La Raja 2014.
35. La Raja 2003; New York Times 2003.
36. Seib 2017.
37. Justice 2004b; Brown and Cochran 2005.
38. La Raja and Schaffner 2015; La Raja 2003.
39. Issacharoff and Karlan 1999.
40. Cigler 2006, 210.
41. Franz 2013; Greenblatt 2015.
42. Lee et al. 2016, 17; Mayer 2016.
43. Brown and Cochran, 2005; Justice 2004a.
44. Boatright 2007; Munger 2006.
45. Cigler 2006, 240.
46. Gibbs and Dickerson 2004; Barnes 2004.
47. Stevenson 2005a.
48. Tierney 2005.
49. Stevenson 2005a; Edsall and Harris 2005.
50. Pew 2005, 3.
51. Stevenson 2005b; Fund 2005.
52. CBS News/*New York Times* 2005.
53. Morris 2006.

54. Ibid.
55. Ibid.
56. Ferguson 2004; Smith and Grimaldi 2005; *Moyers on America* 2004.
57. Committee on Indian Affairs 2006, 17, 21; Stone 2006, 20.
58. Becker and Van Natta 2008.
59. Stone 2006, 2–23, 166.
60. Cigler 2006, 228.
61. Edsall 2007; Zappone 2007; Kuhnhenn 2007.
62. Nunberg 2003; Welch 2008.
63. Alberta 2019, 17–18.
64. Edsall and Weisman 2004.
65. Alberta 2019, 17.
66. ibid., 18.
67. Davis 2008.

Chapter 2

1. *The Onion* 2008.
2. Lupia 2010.
3. Grann 2008.
4. Cassidy 2005; Dickinson 2008; Baylor 2018.
5. Edsall 2008; Tesler 2013.
6. Pettigrew 2017, 109.
7. Balz and Johnson 2009; Jaffe 2018.
8. Kindy 2008; Mayer 2008; Grann 2008; Couric and Goldsmith 2018.
9. Lupia 2010; Acharya et al. 2018; Berger 2018; Bertocchi and Dimico 2014; Rogowski and Schuit 2018; Mann 2020.
10. RCP Staff 2008.
11. Tesler 2015; Stephens-Davidowitz 2014.
12. Tesler and Sears 2010, 18–28, 54.
13. Bai 2012.
14. Kelner and La Raja 2014.
15. Mayer 2016, 10.
16. Ibid., 29.
17. Ibid., 13–14.
18. Ibid., 25–28.
19. Gerken and Fishkin 2015.
20. Mayer 2016, 215–16.
21. Ibid.
22. Schor 2009.
23. Farley 2009.

24. Mayer 2016, 213–16; Stone 2011. The three senators were Susan Collins, Olympia Snowe, and Arlen Specter.
25. Maxwell and Parent 2012; Blumer 2009.
26. Blumer 2009.
27. Ames and Levine 2009; Tilove 2017.
28. Mayer 2016, 206–7.
29. Kinder and Dale-Riddle 2012; Bradberry and Jacobson 2015; Bedard 2010; Rosenthal and Trost 2012.
30. Mian and Sufi 2015.
31. Kalleberg and von Wachter 2017, 1; Dickens et al. 2017, 203–8.
32. Vogel and McCalmont 2011; Benkler et al. 2018; Mayer 2010.
33. Vogel and McCalmont 2011.
34. Mayer 2010.
35. Prior 2014, 309.
36. Tesler, Fried, and Harris 2015, 417; Waldman 2014; Martin 2012.
37. Martin 2009; Klein 2009.
38. Allen 2015; Brant-Zawadzki and Teo 2011; Beutler 2009; Pollack 2014.
39. Axelrod 2015, 378; Martin 2012; Waldman 2014.
40. Dowd 2009 .
41. Ibid.; Center for Responsive Politics 2018.
42. Dowd 2009; Finkelstein 2010.
43. Blumenthal 2013; Tokaji and Strause 2014, 93.
44. Bonica et al. 2016, 146; Bonica et al. 2013, 112–13.
45. Ryan 2013.
46. Lizza 2011, 40; Mayer 2016, 409.
47. Lizza 2011, 40; Federal News Service 2011.
48. Rothenberg 2010.
49. Disch 2012, 133–34.
50. Kamarck 2018; Kleefeld 2010; Steinhauer and Rutenberg 2010; Jacobson 2011.
51. Booth 2010; Chapin 2010.
52. Zernike 2015; Peters and Meier 2015; Hohmann 2012.
53. Martin 2012.
54. Draper 2013, xiii; Devroy 1995.
55. Lee 2003; Burkeman 2003; Chotiner 2007; Davenport and Lipton 2017.
56. Draper 2013, xiii.
57. Curry 2015, 182; Mayer 27, 2016; Bacon 2010.
58. Curry 2015, 183; Draper 2013, 72–73.
59. *Washington Post* 2010; Alberta 2018.
60. Herszenhorn and Pear 2011.
61. Tanden 2014.
62. Draper 2013, 225–26.
63. Hulse 2011; Allen 2011.
64. Lizza 2013b; Appelbaum 2011.
65. Lizza 2013a, 2013b; Fahrenthold and Kane 2011.

66. Allen and Sherman 2011.
67. Ibid.; Cogan 2011.
68. Bresnahan and Sherman, 2011.
69. Hulse and Cooper 2011; Balz 2011.
70. CBS/*New York Times* 2011.
71. Goldfarb 2011; Randall 2011.
72. Draper 2011.
73. Haberman 2012; Draper 2011; Balz 2013, 247–48.
74. Shear 2011.
75. Schwarz 2011.
76. Mayer 2010, 352–53.
77. Chait 2012; Lizza 2012, 24–27; Mayer 2010, 350–51.
78. Draper 2013, 150; Lizza 2012.
79. Draper 2013, 151, 67.
80. Amira 2011.
81. Draper 2013, 167.
82. O'Brien 2011; Epstein 2011.
83. Center for Responsive Politics 2013a, 2013b; Confessore 2003; Mayer 2010, 390; Stevens 2015.
84. Brown 2011.
85. Calmes 2015, 19.
86. Martin 2012.
87. Weisman 2011; Stolberg 2011.
88. Draper 2012; Trinko 2012; Bingham 2012; James 2012.
89. Kwon 2012; Clement and Guskin 2017; Green 2012.
90. Baylor 162.
91. Sokolove 2005; Haberman and Burns 2012.
92. Fikac 2012; Haberman and Burns 2012.
93. VandeHei and Allen 2012; Edsall 2012.
94. Simon 2012; Dunham et al. 2012.
95. Mayer 2010, 388.
96. Isenstadt 2012.
97. Nagourney 2012; Confessore 2012; Kohn 2012.
98. Kohn 2012; *New Jersey Star-Ledger* 2012.
99. Nakamura and Tumulty 2012.
100. Ibid.
101. *Washington Post* 2012.
102. Peters and Stelter 2012.
103. Sherman 2014, 382; Bruni 2012.
104. Sherman 383.
105. Orwell 2008, 209.
106. Douglas 2013.

Chapter 3

1. Edsall 2012.
2. Fallows 1994; Seelye 1994.
3. Scheiber 2012; Haberman and Schultheis 2012; Dickerson 2012; Hohmann and Palmer 2012; Taylor 2013.
4. File 2013; Lupia 2010.
5. Noonan 2012.
6. Markon and Tumulty 2012; Martin 2012a.
7. Binder 2019.
8. Barbour et al. 2013, 51 .
9. Ibid., 15, 19, 21–22.
10. Ball 2013; Mider 2015; Frum 2016; Tumulty 2012.
11. Martin and Haberman 2013.
12. Vogel 2015.
13. Vogel 2014b.
14. Mayer 2016, 393.
15. Ibid., 298–306.
16. Thrush 2013.
17. Gentilviso 2012; Wheaton 2015.
18. Friedersdorf 2012.
19. Mayer 2016, 456.
20. Ibid., 454; Vogel 2014a, 18.
21. Confessore 2014.
22. Martin 2013a.
23. Steinhauer 2013; Lizza 2013b.
24. Lizza 2013b; Hulse 2014.
25. Klein and Soltas 2013.
26. Tanenhaus 2018.
27. Klein 2013; Edsall 2013a.
28. Downes, 2012; Steinhauer 2012.
29. Tanenhaus 2014.
30. Shiller 2018.
31. Martin 2012b.
32. Martin 2013b.
33. Hohmann 2012; Associated Press 2014.
34. Mayer 2016, 457.
35. Ibid.
36. Weisman 2013a.
37. McLaughlin 2013.
38. *Time* 2013. The ten nominees were Bashar Assad, president of Syria; Jeff Bezos, Amazon founder; Ted Cruz, Texas senator; Miley Cyrus, singer; Pope Francis, leader of the Catholic Church; Barack Obama, president of the United States; Hassan

Rouhani, president of Iran; Kathleen Sebelius, secretary of health and human services; Edward Snowden, NSA leaker; and Edith Windsor, gay rights activist.

39. Von Drehle 2013.
40. Mishak 2015.
41. Peters 2015.
42. Wong 2011.
43. Blake and Weiner 2011; Parker 2012.
44. Martin 2012b; Raju 2012.
45. Horowitz 2015; Fabian 2011.
46. Martin 2013c; Allen and VandeHei 2012; Grunwald 2013; *Politico* 2013.
47. Viguerie 2012; Kane 2012; Ferguson 2015.
48. Herman 2012.
49. Johnson 2015; Tilove 2013d.
50. Herman, 2012.
51. Stewart 2015.
52. Drucker 2013; Tilove 2013e.
53. Tilove 2013e; Cassata and Weber 2013.
54. Gillman 2013.
55. Tilove 2013d; Gillman 2013.
56. Costa 2013.
57. Ibid.
58. Bruni 2013.
59. Raju and Gibson 2013; Tilove 2013a.
60. Dennis 2013.
61. Ibid.
62. Stolberg 2018; Flegenheimer 2017.
63. Jacobs 2013.
64. Deace 2015; Calmes 2015; Times 2016.
65. Alberta 2015.
66. Lizza 2013a, 48.
67. Passel and Cohn 2015; Krogstad and Passel 2015.
68. Federal News Service 2011.
69. Klein 2013.
70. Horowitz 2016; Altman 2013.
71. Altman 2013; Horowitz 2016.
72. Leary 2013.
73. Zezima and O'Keefe 2015; CBS News 2012.
74. Tilove 2013d; Gillman 2013.
75. Severson 2013; Orangeburg Times and Democrat 2013.
76. Green 2017, 108.
77. Stokes 2017, 22.
78. Weiner 2012; O'Reilly 2014.
79. Reed 2013.
80. O'Keefe 2013.

81. Finley 2016.
82. Fleischman 2013; Aguilar 2013.
83. Slater 2013.
84. Cottle 2013.
85. Draper 2013.
86. Ibid.; Coppins 2015, 166; Ball 2016.
87. Tilove 2013c; Weisman 2013b; Tumulty and Hamburger 2013; Kapur 2013.
88. Draper 2013; Tilove 2013b.
89. Tilove 2015.
90. Goldmacher 2013; Martin 2013b; Pappas 2015; Slater 2013.
91. Edsall 2013b.
92. McMorris-Santoro 2013.
93. Soltas 2013.
94. Pew Research Center 2013.
95. McCalmont 2013.
96. Ball 2016.
97. Tilove 2013a.

Chapter 4

1. Vogel 2015.
2. Draper 2016c.
3. Von Drehle 2013.
4. Sipes 2015.
5. Harwood 2015.
6. Carville 2014.
7. Greenberg and Carville 2014.
8. Braunstein and Taylor 2017, 33, 52.
9. Guth 2005; Goldberg 2006, 27.
10. Guth et al. 1997; Guth 2021; Stewart 2020.
11. Slater 2014; Lambrecht 2016.
12. Toobin 2014.
13. Lambrecht 2016.
14. Chapman 2015.
15. DuBose and Harper 2015; Hohmann 2015b; Tilove 2016b.
16. Toobin 2014, 44.
17. Kruse 2015; Lambrecht 2016.
18. Fahey and Wells 2015; Von Drehle 2013; Tilove 2018.
19. Haberman 2014; Lewak 2015; Glueck 2016.
20. Vogel 2014a.
21. Hulse and Martin 2014.
22. Alberta 2013; Lavender 2013; Feldman 2013; O'Connor 2013.

23. Alberta 2019, 179–80.
24. Alberta 2013
25. Ibid.
26. Glueck 2015c; Gardner 2012.
27. French 2015.
28. Ibid.
29. Clarke 2017a, 13.
30. Fleming and Fuller 2015.
31. Greenblatt 2015; Clarke 2017b.
32. Clarke2017a; Alberta 89, 104.
33. Alberta 2019, 235, 241.
34. Calmes 2015b; Rove 2015; Palmer and Bresnahan 2015.
35. Dickinson 2015.
36. Lowry 2015.
37. Stewart 2015.
38. Edsall 2015a.
39. Hinch 2014; Jones et al. 2014.
40. Vogel 2014b.
41. Blackwell and Shackelford 2015; Calmes 2015c, 49; Posner 2018.
42. Alberta 2015.
43. Robertson and Fausset 2015; Hohmann 2015a.
44. Ornstein 2015a, 2015b.
45. Glueck 2015b.
46. Malone 2016.
47. Fisher 2015; Alberta 2020.
48. Sipes 2015.
49. Glueck 2015a.
50. Bendery 2013.
51. Mider 2015.
52. Wren 2015.
53. Martin 2015a.
54. Edsall 2015b; Martin 2015a.
55. Draper 2016c.
56. Gehrke 2014.
57. Martosko 2015.
58. Byers 2013, 2017.
59. Falcone 2011.
60. Parker and Eder 2016; Schreckinger 2015.
61. Haberman 2011; Halperin and Heilemann 2013, 129.
62. Coppins 2014, Coppins 2015.
63. *Huffington Post* 2011; Freelander 2015; Toobin 2008.
64. Singer 1997; Malanga 2016; D'Antonio 2015, 186; Hart Research Associates and Public Opinion Strategies 2011.
65. Balz 2016.

66. O'Brien 2011; Hernandez 2011.
67. *Politico* 2012.
68. Peters 2011.
69. Trent 2012.
70. Tumulty 2017.
71. Jacobs and Noble 2013.
72. Falcone 2013; Jacobs and Noble 2013.
73. Hunt 2013.
74. Bell 2013.
75. Fox News 2013.
76. Sherman 2016.
77. Green 2017, 104–5.
78. Toobin 2008; O'Harrow and Boburg 2016; Kruse 2016.
79. Kranish and Fisher 2016, 294; Sherman 2016.
80. Friedell 2015.
81. Tilove 2016a.
82. Milbank 2015b.
83. *Washington Post* 2015.
84. Cillizza 2015; Cornfield 2015.
85. Tesler 2015; Tesler and Sides 2016; Cornfield 2015.
86. Knowles 2015.
87. Gosselin 2015; Stokols 2015; Edsall 2016.
88. Stein 2016.
89. Hayes 2015.
90. Martin and Haberman 2015.
91. Sherman 2016; Dowd 2017.
92. Draper 2016b.
93. Schlafly 2015a, 2015b. Later, before the primaries began, she defended the constitutionality of his call to ban all Muslims.
94. Martin 2015b; Scalzi 2015.
95. Valentino et al. 2018; Norton and Sommers 2011; Lithwick 2013.
96. Gass 2015.
97. Ibid.
98. Milbank 2015a; Trujillo 2014.
99. *New York Times* 2016.
100. Federal News Service 2016; Gerson 2015; Sanger 2015. Cotton's letter was self-promotion that undercut a bipartisan deal to change the policy. When the senators signed the letter, a bipartisan deal already had support from sixty-five senators, two short of a veto-proof bill, to require Senate approval of the agreement.
101. Tilove 2013, 2015; Cruz 2015, 237.
102. Graham 2014, 2015.
103. Mider 2015.
104. Hart Research Associates and Public Opinion Strategies 2015; Draper 2016a.
105. Haberman 2016.

106. DeBonis 2015.
107. Calmes 2015a.
108. Everett 2015a, 2015b.
109. Skelley 2019.
110. Brinton 2015; Zezima and Gold 2015.
111. Confessore and Yourish 2016.
112. Johnson 2015.
113. Reicher and Haslam 2017a, 2017b.
114. Lowry and Ponnuru 2015.
115. Newkirk and Arit 2015.
116. Dias 2020.
117. Gabriel 2016.
118. Schieffer and Gray 2015.
119. Schreckinger 2016; Collins 2016.
120. Hounshell 2016.
121. Hart Research Associates and Public Opinion Strategies 2016.
122. Hohmann 2016.
123. Gold and Narayanswamy 2016.
124. Hohmann 2016.
125. Martin and Flegenheimer 2016.

Chapter 5

1. Draper 2016b.
2. Alberta 2019, 24–25.
3. Seib and O'Connor 2016; Confessore 2016.
4. Barbour and Westervelt 2016.
5. Edsall 2015a.
6. Rucker and Costa 2017; Totenberg 2017.
7. Green 2016, 2017; Bazelon 2017; Rucker and Costa 2017; Palmeri 2017; Linskey 2016.
8. Garrett 2016; Smith 2016.
9. Haberman 2016b.
10. Thrush 2017.
11. Waldman 2016a; Vogel and Stokols 2016.
12. Fineman 2016; Draper 2016b; Vogel and Stokols 2016.
13. Parker 2016.
14. Leibovich 2016; LeTourneau 2016.
15. Hohmann 2016c.
16. Begley 2016; Rappeport 2016b.
17. Drew 2016; Greenfield 2016; Hewitt 2016a.
18. Cirilli, Bender, and Jacobs 2016; Werner 2016.

19. Rucker and Balz 2016.
20. Rucker 2016.
21. Goldmacher 2016a.
22. Hulse 2016.
23. Goldmacher 2016b; Draper 2016b; Plaskin 1990.
24. Edsall 2015b.
25. Samuelsohn 2016.
26. Kranish and Fisher 2016, 89; Brenner 1990; Kruse 2018; Sargent 2019.
27. Hessler 2017.
28. Green 2016.
29. Solotaroff 2015.
30. Martin and Burns 2016a.
31. *New York Times* 2016.
32. Rappeport 2016a; Barrett 2015.
33. Burns and Haberman 2016a; Allison, Keller, and Migliozzi 2016; Barrett 1979.
34. Vogel and Martel 2015; Mayer 2018.
35. Gold 2016.
36. Alberta 2019, 288–89.
37. Adelson 2016.
38. Stone 2016.
39. Ballhaus and Mullins 2016; Maguire 2018
40. Neidig 2016; Palmer 2016; Peters 2016; Martin 2016.
41. Burns and Haberman 2016b.
42. Alberta 2019, 324; Haberman, Burns, and Parker 2016.
43. Burns and Haberman 2016b.
44. Alberta 2019, 326–27 .
45. Ibid., 327.
46. Ibid., 328.
47. Homans 2019; Hewitt 2016.
48. Leibovich 2016; Gerson 2016.
49. Leibovich 2016.
50. Burns and Haberman 2016b.
51. Alberta 2019, 357.
52. Brennan Center Staff 2016.
53. Tavits and Potter 2014.
54. Kotsko 2019. There was no way McConnell could issue a unifying statement for his GOP colleagues on contentious social issues. During the primaries, the three senators running for president—Cruz, Rubio, and Paul—voted against giving same-sex couples the same VA and Social Security benefits as heterosexual couples. The six senators up for re-election from battleground states had all voted for the bill.
55. Hewitt 2016b.
56. Leibovich 2016.
57. Kim and Everett 2016.
58. McCaskill 2016.

59. Pierce 2011; Sherman 2016.
60. Waldman 2016b.
61. Reilly 2016.
62. McCaskill and Gass 2016; Reilly 2016.
63. Alberta 2019, 321.
64. Hulse 2016; Leibovich 2016.
65. Steinhauer 2016.
66. Rappeport 2015.
67. Unger 2017; Burgis 2016.
68. Nakashima 2016.
69. Entous 2017.
70. Ibid.
71. Neumann 2016; Haberman 2016a; Martin 2016.
72. Draper 2016a.
73. Kim and Everett 2016.
74. Parker, Burns, and Haberman 2016.
75. Ibid.
76. Bailey 2016; Kolbert 2005; Coppins 2018.
77. Abcarian 2015; Raju, Walsh, and Kopan 2015.
78. Glasser 2019, 54.
79. Shane and Schmidt 2015.
80. Thrush 2016.
81. Saad 2016.
82. Stein 2016.
83. Grynbaum and Abrams 2016; Williams 2016.
84. Alberta 2019, 305–7.
85. Faris et al., 86.
86. Ibid., 11; Warzel and Vo 2016.
87. Faris et al. 2017, 6.
88. Green 2017, 153; Becker and McIntire 2015; Andrews 2015.
89. Yoon 2016.
90. Allen and Parnes 2017, 53–56; Kapur 2015.
91. Von Drehle 2017.
92. Cohn 2016a.
93. Ibid.
94. Real Clear Politics 2016.
95. Rogers 2016.
96. Tartar and Breitman 2016.
97. Phillips 2016.
98. Peters 2016.
99. Brownstein 2016; Burns 2016.
100. Hohmann 2016a.
101. Hohmann 2016b; Fisher 2015.
102. Mak and Corse 2016; Marshall 2017.

103. Nemtsova 2016.

104. Costa, Delreal, and Johnson 2016; Lizza 2016.

105. Green and Issenberg 2016.

106. Enten 2016.

107. Chozick 2016.

108. Balz and Rucker 2016.

109. Ibid.

110. Allen and Parnes 2017, 178, 194.

111. Martin and Burns 2016b; Arizona Republic 2016.

112. Allen and Parnes 2017, 315.

113. Colpaert 2016.

114. Sonenshein 2016.

115. Cheney and Wheaton 2016.

116. Ibid.

117. Helderman, Zapotosky, and Horwitz 2016.

118. Green 11; Silver 2016a, 2016b, 2016c; Cohn 2016b; Brownstein 2019.

119. Alberta 2018.

Chapter 6

1. Barabak 2016; Beaver and Stanley 2017.

2. Traister 2017.

3. Shephard and Ross 2016.

4. Kruse 2019a.

5. Campaign Finance Institute 2017.

6. Smith 2020.

7. Prokop 2016.

8. Popkin 2012, 138.

9. Caldwell 2017b; Shane 2016; Wolff 2016.

10. Christie 2019, 5.

11. Ibid.

12. Bender and Lee 2016; Tenpas 2018; Hohmann 2018b. The "A Team" includes chiefs of staff and deputies for president and vice president, directors and deputy directors of the NSC and OMB, chairs of Council on Environmental Quality and National Economic Council, press secretary, etc.

13. Thrush, Haberman, and Lafraniere 2017.

14. Grimaldi, Harris, and Viswanatha 2017; Grimaldi, Nissenbaum, and Coker 2017; Rosenberg and Mazzetti 2017; Memoli 2017.

15. Bernstein 2020; Bolton 2020, 212, 301, 457; Massoglia and Evers-Hillstrom 2019; Rucker and Leonnig 2020, 280–81, 340. Trump's organizations had financial interests in twenty-six other countries.

16. Zimmerman 2016.

17. Newman 2018, 169–70.

18. Landler 2019.
19. Swisher 2020.
20. Ibid.; Colvin 2019. The conspicuous absence of Jared and Ivanka was a running joke among their detractors.
21. Landler 2019; Gerstein 2017; Almasy and Simon 2017; Wittes 2017. Wittes called the order "malevolence tempered by incompetence." The errors in the order could have been corrected with a simple clarification, but Trump characteristically insisted his order was perfect as written.
22. Milbank 2019; Thrush and Haberman 2017; Confessore 2017; Hohmann 2017b.
23. Wolff 2018, 114, 68; Baker and Karni 2019.
24. Wolff 124–25, 67–68. When Walsh, finally fed up, decided to leave later that month, Kushner—who considered her "demanding and petulant"—told reporters she was pushed out for leaking, so as to minimize the impact if she described the incompetence and infighting inside the White House.
25. Morris 2001, 319; Gamm and Smith 1998, 97; Popkin 2007. When Roosevelt began to publicly advocate for his preferred policies, party leaders called it an undignified spectacle that should be left to professionals, and the *New York Times* equated it with downgrading the role of Congress: "Congress, so far as the President is concerned, is the people, and to it his appeals of one sort and another will be addressed."
26. Safire 2008, 88; Elving 2017.
27. Zaitchik 2011; Tilove 2016b; Nguyen 2015; Beauchamp 2016.
28. Tilove 2016a.
29. Sherman 2018a.
30. Packer 2020.
31. Williams 2017; Wagner 2017.
32. Woodward 2018, 44.
33. Kruse 2019b. Louise Sunshine was his director of special projects and Barbara Res was his chief engineer and executive vice-president at the Trump Organization.
34. Frum 2017; Wagner 2018.
35. Greif 2019.
36. Frum 2018, 58, Ollstein 2016. The permit was the motive for the call, which was arranged by Eric Trump through the family's Argentine partner.
37. Rucker and Leonnig 2020, 171.
38. Kirkpatrick 2017; Davidson 2017.
39. Von Hoffman 1988.
40. Filkins 2016; Dent et al. 2017; Wattles 2017; Schmidt 2017. Bharara was prosecuting Reza Zarrab, a Turkish-Iranian, for money laundering; the case was a political headache for Erdoğan because it involved bribes of $45 million for Erdoğan's minister for the economy, and a donation of $4.6 million for a charity run by Erdoğan's wife. He was also investigating a money-laundering scheme involving Lev Leviev, a Russian tycoon known as the "king of diamonds," who was close to Putin. Bharara refused to resign so that the record would show Trump had reversed his earlier announcement.
41. Cormier and Leopold 2018a, 2018b; McIntire 2017.
42. Isikoff 2017; Schor 2017.

43. Cormier and Leopold 2018a, 2018b; Widdicombe 2016; Entous and Osnos 2018.

44. Harris et al. 2018.

45. Nakashima, Entous, and Miller 2017; Melber, Mandell, and Lablans 2017; Schmidt 2020, 298–302; Lind 2017; Rucker and Leonnig 2020, 93. Schmidt learned that Kushner's clearance was being held up over a "high-level law enforcement problem," not just incomplete paperwork.

46. McCubbins, Noll, and Weingast 1987; Sanger-Katz 2019; Rudalevige 2018, 94.

47. Sanger-Katz 2019.

48. Radden Keefe 2017.

49. Grynbaum and Lee 2019; Mayer 2020, 49. Murdoch's sale gave Disney half of American box office sales, and the Sinclair Broadcast-Tribune Media merger would have created "the next Fox." The Justice Department lost the suit to block the AT&T-CNN merger after two years of litigation, the first anti-trust suit they lost in ten years.

50. Smith 2017; Boburg 2017.

51. Tax Reform Task Force 2016.

52. Rago 2016; Alberta 2019, 399.

53. Alberta 2019, 321, 449.

54. Forsythe et al. 2019.

55. Homans 2019.

56. Schleifer 2017; Bade, Dawsey, and Haberkorn 2017; House and Dennis 2017.

57. Alberta 2017.

58. Barro 2017; Tsebelis 2017.

59. Bump 2017; Kane 2017; Shapiro and Shaw 2017; Kaplan 2017.

60. Geraghty 2017; Everett 2017.

61. Abramson 2017.

62. Burns 2017.

63. Coppins 2017.

64. Ibid.

65. Sellers and Farenthold 2017; Caldwell 2017a; Harris, Dawsey, and Leonnig 2019.

66. Bertrand 2019.

67. Demirjian, O'Keefe and Phillip 2017; Entous 2017.

68. Miller, Entous, and Nakashima 2017; Hohmann 2017a; Rosenberg and Mazzetti 2017; Kaiser 2020; Schmidt 2017; Parker, Abutaleb, and Dawsey 2018.

69. Harris and Lee 2017; Savage 2017.

70. Demirjian, Sullivan and O'Keefe 2017. Several senators even suggested Justice Merrick Garland, the Obama Supreme Court nominee who never received a hearing.

71. Ibid.; DeBonis 2017; Dennis 2018; Peterson, Nicholas, and Gurman 2018; Shin, Esteban, and Keating 2019.

72. Zengerle 2018.

73. Ibid.

74. Marshall 2018; Thrush 2019; Tracy 2020.

75. Rucker and Leonnig 2020, 188–89.

76. Stanley-Becker 2018; Hohmann 2018a.

77. Martin, Haberman, and Burns 2017; Jalonick 2018.

78. Stone and Gordon 2017; Thielman and Sneed 2017; Ioffe and Foer 2017.

79. Severns and Woellert 2018.

80. Costa and Sullivan 2018, Severns 2020, Fang and Surgey 2018.

81. Rove 2017; Fang and Surgey 2018.

82. Edsall 2017, 2018; Kamin et al. 2018; Browning and Bain 2017; Gravelle and Marples 2019.

83. Lee and Wagner 2018.

84. Wall Street Journal 2017; Alberta 263. The Wall Street Journal editorial urged the Freedom Caucus to be more like the Democrats: "Individuals run for leadership, the Members vote, and then everyone accepts the results and moves on together."

85. Bade 2017; Lizza 2017; Dovere 2017a.

86. Nicholas, Ballhaus, and Hughes 2017; Lizza 2017.

87. Parlapiano and Andrews 2018; Bouchard 2018; Davis and Haberman 2018; Binder 2019; Dovere 2017a.

88. Dowd 2019b.

89. Chenoweth and Pressman 2017. Chenoweth and Pressman used news reports and photos to estimate the number of marchers, using established methods for analyzing crowds.

90. Gardner and Greenberg 2017; Norman 2017. That same week Gallup reported that the percentage of Americans believing Trump "keeps his promises" dropped from 62 percent to 45 percent.

91. Martin and Burns 2017.

92. Schneider 2017.

93. Dovere 2017b.

94. Weigel 2018.

95. MacGillis 2012.

96. Watkins 2018.

97. Krugman 2019b; Autor et al. 2016.

98. Amiti et al. 2018. Most steel imports came from military allies and were specialty steel not produced domestically.

99. de Rugy 2019; Everett 2018.

100. Werner et al. 2018; Bender et al. 2018; Glasser 2018; Riga 2018; Bolton 2018.

101. Peker et al. 2018; Sanger and Erlanger 2018; Newman and Haddon 2018.

102. Newman and Haddon 2018; Newman and Bunge 2019; Krugman 2019a.

103. Lynch and Long 2018; Colvin 2019; Hsu 2018; Flaaen and Pierce 2019; Zhang 2020; Hofman 2019. Harley-Davidson moved production of motorcycles sold in Europe out of the US to avoid EU tariffs. General Motors warned tariffs on imported parts would cut exports and kill American jobs.

104. Hsu 2018; Flaaen and Pierce 2019; Zhang 2020.

105. Craig 2019.

106. Rucker and Leonnig 2020, 265–66. In 2017, when he'd been Trump's secretary of homeland security, John Kelly had refused to enact zero-tolerance and separate children from their parents.

107. Ibid., 267.

108. Coppins 2018; Sherman 2018b; Edwards-Levy 2018.

109. Sells 2018; Rucker and Leonnig 2020, 267–69.

110. Tilove 2018.

111. Mayer 2019, 45; Cooper et al. 2018; Laporta and DaSilva 2018.

112. Glasser 2018; Riga 2018; Bierman 2018.

113. Jacobson 2019, 13, 23; Jacobson and Liu 2020, 7.

114. Silver 2018. Professors Gary Jacobson and Seth J. Hill provided the data for the congressional district comparisons to 2016.

115. Lowry 2018.

116. Rucker and Leonnig 2020, 27, 312; Council on Foreign Relations 2019. Bannon compared Pelosi to Katharine Hepburn in *The Lion in Winter*, thinking "These men are all clowns," while she plotted her return to power.

117. Rucker and Leonnig 2020, 333–34. Later, Pelosi said debating the wall was "like a manhood thing for him. As if manhood could ever be associated with him."

118. Goldberg 2019.

119. Rucker and Leonnig 2020, 341; Caralle 2018; CNN News 2019.

120. Hohmann 2018c; Sherman, Palmer, and Lippman 2018. Pelosi pointed out that Trump's decision to grant Erdoğan open season on attacking Kurds came the day after sentencing began in the conviction of Michael Flynn, who had acted as a paid foreign agent of Turkey while advising Trump during the campaign and transition.

121. Hohmann 2018c; Rucker, Costa, and Dawsey 2018.

122. Labaton 2007; Republican Senators resisted until Democrats agreed to add a tax cut for small businesses to soften the blow.

123. Hulse, Fandos, and Cochrane 2020.

124. Leibovich 2019.

125. Cheney 2018; Haberman and Fandos 2019. Ron DeSantis was one of the president's "warriors" in 2018 but left to run for, and ultimately win, the Florida gubernatorial election.

126. Ayer 2019; Bazelon 2019b; Rohde 2020. Italics in the Barr memo.

127. Parker and Dawsey 2019; Toobin 2020, 54–55; Fallows 2020a.

128. Zapotosky 2019. When this story was written, 450 former prosecutors and DOJ officials had signed. The number grew to more than 1,000 after the letter was published. It included prosecutors involved in both the Nixon and Clinton impeachments.

129. Ayer 2019.

130. Orden and Scannell 2020.

131. Tracy 2019.

132. Wagner 2019.

133. Dowd 2019a.

134. Bazelon 2019a.

135. Harris, Dawsey, and Leonnig 2019; Senate Select Committee on Intelligence 2019; Rupar 2020; Sommer, Tani, and Kirell 2020; Barnes and Rosenberg 2019.

136. Stolberg and Hulse 2020.

137. Kim 2020; Bowden 2020.

138. Alemany 2020.
139. Suebsaeng and Markay 2018; Fallows 2020b; Garrett 2020.
140. Woodward 2020, xiii.
141. Ibid., xviii.
142. Werner et al. 2020; Associated Press 2020.
143. Abutaleb, Parker, and Dawsey 2020.
144. Kelly and Mazzetti 2020. Tomas J. Philipson and Larry Kudlow were the officials alerting the investors.
145. Mak 2020.
146. Sherman 2020a; Shear, Fink, and Weiland 2020.
147. Woodward 315; Parker 2020.
148. Sherman 2020a; Dale 2020. The playbook drew on the experiences of sixteen years in the Bush and Obama administrations dealing with SARS, H1N1, and Ebola.
149. Parker et al. 2020.
150. Shear et al. 2020; Shear 2020.
151. Eban 2020.
152. Ibid.
153. New York Times 2020.
154. Niemietz 2020; Hennesy-Fiske 2020.
155. Jacobs and Wayne 2020; Sherman 2020b.
156. Klein 2020.
157. Vazquez 2020.
158. Burns, Martin, and Haberman 2020.
159. Milbank 2020.
160. Burns, Martin, and Haberman 2020.
161. Ibid.
162. Global Strategy Group Staff 2020, 8.

Chapter 7

1. Berelson et al. 1954, 206.
2. Shapiro and Shaw 2017; Bump 2017.
3. Fadulu and Goodnough 2020.
4. Hasan 2020; Swisher 2020.
5. Hohmann, 2021a.
6. CNN 2021.
7. Hohmann 2021a.
8. Peters 2021; Will 2021; Itkowitz, and Debonis 2021.
9. Gerson, Sonmez, and Bailey.
10. Greenberg 2020.
11. Carter et al. 2021; Hohmann 2021b.
12. Cruz 2021.

13. Will 2021.
14. Blake 2021, Haberman 2021.
15. Steinhauer et al. 2021; Romo 2021; Dorman 2021; Phillips 2021; Kansas City Star 2021.
16. WBUR Newsroom, 2021,
17. Stevens 2020.
18. Popkin and Kim 2007.
19. Lee 1966; Karabell 2000, 37.
20. Lee 1970, 69; Bone 1952.
21. Popkin 2012, 151–58.
22. Smith 1982, 553.
23. Ibid., 579.
24. Ibid., 586.
25. Ibid., 587.
26. Ibid., 589, 91–92.
27. Griffith 1982, 102.
28. Blake 2016.
29. Perlstein 2001, 426–27.
30. Janson 1964a, 1964b.
31. Rovere 1964a; Stone 1964; New York Times 1964; Kabaservice 2016.
32. Hess and Broder 1967, 168–69.
33. Frymer and Skrentny 1998; Boyd 1970.
34. Douthat 2015.
35. Greenhouse 1980; Clymer 1978.
36. Popkin 1984; Wilkins 1984.
37. From and McKeon 2013.
38. Galston and Kamarck 1989.
39. From and McKeon, Kindle location 1174.
40. Sullivan 2008, 92–93. The line was developed by this writer when a San Diego legislator, Lucy Killea, was threatened with excommunication for voting for funding clinics where abortions were performed.
41. Popkin 2007, 43–45.
42. Ibid., 44–45.
43. Ryan 2013.
44. Alberta 2019 , 104, 235–41.
45. Ibid., 570.
46. Ibid., 600.
47. Mayer 2020, 57; Dyche 2009.
48. Douthat and Salam 2008.
49. Edsall 2014, 2015; Tumulty and Sullivan 2018.
50. Goodnough 2015.
51. Calmes 2016; Tabarrok 2016.
52. Krugman 2019.
53. Alberta 2019, 494–95.

54. Ibid., 576.
55. Rothschild and Allen 2019.
56. Edmondson et al. 2019.
57. Freedlander 2019; Thebault 2019; Davis 2019.
58. Davis 2019.
59. Rothschild and Allen 2019.
60. Freedlander 2020; Steinhauer 2020.
61. Reedy 1987, 130.
62. Rovere 1964b, 194–95.
63. Lawrence 1948.
64. Frank 2016.
65. Bollen 2006, xviii.
66. McGrane 2020; Berman 2020.
67. Brenan 2019.
68. Bade 2020; Bade and Werner 2020; Herndon 2020a, 2020b; Kopan 2020.
69. Ferris and Caygle 2020.
70. Stein 2012. Most readers will find one of these "inconvenient but not inconsistent" formulations acceptable and the other unacceptable. I am not suggesting they are morally equivalent.
71. Huntington 2004.
72. Robbins 2003, 660; Andersen (1837) 1959.
73. Robbins 660.
74. Noonan 2020.
75. Adrian 1952, 776.
76. Tavits 2007.
77. Adrian 776.
78. Masket 2009, 71.
79. Plotke 1997, 19, 32.
80. Healy and Malhotra 2009.
81. Weiner 2015, 2.
82. Lupia and McCubbins 1998, 2019.
83. Lupia and McCubbins 1998, 2019; Lupia 1994, 2016; Druckman and Lupia 2000.
84. Del Valle 2019.
85. Hohmann 2016; Gold and Hamburger 2013.
86. Weiner 2015, 7.
87. Dietrich 2019.
88. Barker and Meyer 2014.
89. Weisman 2012.
90. Fang 2020.
91. Massoglia 2015.
92. The David Duke case is *Duke v. Massey*, 87 F.3d 1226 (11th Cir. 1996). I am grateful to Prof. Richard Pildes with explaining the latitude granted to parties in national elections.
93. VandeHei and Allen 2012.

94. Easley 2012.
95. Gold and O'Keefe 2015.
96. 116th Congress 2019b.
97. Pildes 2019.
98. Popkin 271–72.
99. Cox 2009.
100. Lithwick 2016.
101. Alberta 2019, 594.
102. 116th Congress 2019a.
103. Ibid.
104. Brennan Center 2019.
105. Miroff and Dawsey 2020.
106. Porter 2020.
107. Cottle 2017.
108. Ibid.

References

Introduction

Balz, Dan, and Tania Branigan. (2003). "A Fresh Appetite for an Ex-President; Clinton's Aid Would Be Welcome, Candidates Say." *Washington Post*, September 14.

Barrett, Wayne. (2011). "Inside Donald Trump's Empire: Why He Didn't Run for President in 2012." *Daily Beast*, May 26. https://www.thedailybeast.com/articles/2011/05/26/inside-donald-trumps-empire-why-he-wont-run-for-president.

Census Bureau Household Pulse 20. (2020). *Household Pulse Survey: Measuring Social and Economic Impacts During the Coronavirus Pandemic*. Washington, DC: U. S. Department of Commerce.

Coronavirus Resource Center. (2021). "Cumulative Cases." January 1. https://coronavirus.jhu.edu/data/cumulative-cases.

Cox, Gary W. (2016). *Marketing Sovereign Promises: Monopoly Brokerage and the Growth of the English State*. New York: Cambridge University Press.

Cox, Gary W., and Barry R. Weingast. (2018). "Executive Constraint, Political Stability and Economic Growth." *Comparative Political Studies* 51(3): 279–303. https://ssrn.com/abstract=2618059.

Craig, Susanne. (2016). "Trump Boasts of Rapport with Wall St., but the Feeling Is Not Quite Mutual." *New York Times*, May 23. https://www.nytimes.com/2016/05/24/business/dealbook/donald-trump-relationship-bankers.html.

Diamond, Jared M. (1997). *Guns, Germs, and Steel: The Fates of Human Societies*. New York: W. W. Norton.

Disch, Lisa. (2009). "On the Side of the Angels: An Appreciation of Parties and Partisanship." *Perspectives on Politics* 7(3): 621–24.

Fiorina, Morris P. (1980). "The Decline of Collective Responsibility in American Politics." *Daedalus* 109(3): 25–45.

Fishkin, Joseph, and Heather K. Gerken. (2014). "The Two Trends That Matter for Party Politics." *NYU Law Review* 89(32):32–47.

Gabriel, Trip. (2011). "In Reversal, Bachmann's Struggles Now Include Fund-Raising." *New York Times*, September 23.

Gerken, Heather, and Joseph Fishkin. (2015). "Whose Party Is It Anyway?." *Election Law Blog*, June 16. https://electionlawblog.org/?p=73489.

Goodman, Amy. (2016). "Trump's 'Greatest Mentor' Was Red-Baiting Aide to Joseph McCarthy and Attorney for NYC Mob Families." *Democracy Now*, July 5. http://www.democracynow.org/2016/7/5/trumps_greatest_mentor_was_red_baiting.

Gwirtzman, Milton S. (1975). "The Democrats: A Choice between Old Faces and Blank Faces." *New York Times*, March 23.

Hetherington, Marc J. (1998). "The Political Relevance of Political Trust." *American Political Science Review* 92(4): 791–808.

———. (2015). "Why Polarized Trust Matters." *The Forum: A Journal of Applied Research in Contemporary Politics* 13(3): 445–58.

Hetherington, Marc J., and Thomas J. Rudolph. (2015). *Why Washington Won't Work: Polarization, Political Trust, and the Governing Crisis.* Chicago: University of Chicago Press.

Lepore, Jill. (2014). "Bad News: The Reputation of Roger Ailes." *New Yorker*, January 20, 70–74.

Nellis, Gareth. (2016). *The Fight Within: Intra-party Factionalism and Incumbency Spillovers in India.* Unpublished manuscript.

New York Times. (2016). "Transcript: Donald Trump at the G.O.P. Convention." *New York Times*, July 22.

Plotke, David. (1997). "Representation Is Democracy." *Constellations* 4(1): 19–34.

Rosenblum, Nancy L. (2008). *On the Side of the Angels: An Appreciation of Parties and Partisanship.* Princeton, NJ: Princeton University Press.

Szalai, Jennifer. (2017). "Why Is 'Politicization' So Partisan?" *New York Times Magazine*, October 17. https://www.nytimes.com/2017/10/17/magazine/why-is-politicization-so-partisan.html.

Chapter 1

Alberta, Tim. (2019). *American Carnage: On the Front Lines of the Republican Civil War and the Rise of President Tru.* New York: Harper Collins.

Alexander, Paul. (2001a). "John McCain's War on the White House." *Rolling Stone*, June 7. http://www.RollingStone.com/politics/story/18420159/john_mccains_war_on_the_white_house.

———. (2001b). "The Rolling Stone Interview: John McCain." *Rolling Stone*, September 27. http://www.RollingStone.com/politics/story/18421121/the_rolling_stone_interview_john_mccain.

Alvarez, Lisette. (2001). "A Senator's Unaccustomed Limelight." *New York Times*, April 6. https://www.nytimes.com/2001/04/06/us/a-senator-s-unaccustomed-limelight.html.

Bank, Steven A., Kirk J. Stark, and Joseph J. Thorndike. (2008). *War and Taxes.* Washington, DC: Urban Institute Press.

Barnes, Fred. (2004). "Realignment, Now More Than Ever." *Weekly Standard*, November 22. https://www.weeklystandard.com/fred-barnes/realignment-now-more-than-ever.

Baylor, Christopher. (2018). *First to the Party: The Group Origins of Party Transformation.* Philadelphia: University of Pennsylvania Press.

Becker, Jo, and Don Van Natta Jr. (2008). "McCain and Team Have Many Ties to the Gambling Industry." *New York Times*, September 28. http://www.nytimes.com/2008/09/28/us/politics/28gambling-web.html?_r=1&hp=&pagewanted=all&oref=slogin.

Blumenthal, Paul. (2013). "*Citizens United*, McCain-Feingold Fueled Congress' Shutdown Politics." *Huffington Post*, October 16.

Boatright, Robert G. (2007). "Situating the New 527 Organizations in Interest Group Theory." *The Forum* 5(2): 1–23.

Bonica, Adam, and Gary W. Cox. (2018). "Ideological Extremists in the U.S. Congress: Out of Step but Still in Office." *Quarterly Journal of Political Science* 13(2): 207–36.

Brown, Elizabeth, and Shaylyn Cochran. (2005). "Pac-Men Lobbyists." Washington, DC: Center for Public Integrity, October 3. https://www.publicintegrity.org/2005/10/03/6552/pac-men-lobbyists.

Bruck, Connie. (2004). "Hollywood Science: Should a Ballot Initiative Determine the Fate of Stem-Cell Research?" *New Yorker*, October 18.

Bruni, Frank. (2001). "Gaining, and Losing, Too." *New York Times*, February 2. https://www.nytimes.com/2001/02/02/us/gaining-and-losing-too.html.

Carney, James. (2001). "Behind the Scenes: How Bush Chose Ashcroft." *Time*, January 14. http://content.time.com/time/nation/article/0,8599,95190,00.html.

Cassidy, John. (2005). "The Ringleader: How Grover Norquist Keeps the Conservative Movement Together." *New Yorker*, August 1.

CBS News/*New York Times*. (2005). "The Social Security Debate Continues." March 2.

Cigler, Allan J. (2006). "Interest Groups and Financing the 2004 Elections." In *Financing the 2004 Election*, edited by David B. Magleby, Anthony Corrado, and Kelly D. Patterson, 208–40. Washington, DC: Brookings Institution Press.

Cohen, Patricia. (2017). "Bump in U.S. Incomes Doesn't Erase 50 Years of Pain." *New York Times*, September 16. https://www.nytimes.com/2017/09/16/business/economy/bump-in-us-incomes-doesnt-erase-50-years-of-pain.html?em_pos=small&emc=edit_up_20170918&nl=upshot&nl_art=5&nlid=7641649&ref=headline&te=1&_r=0.

Committee on Indian Affairs. (2006). " 'Gimme Five'—Investigation of Tribal Lobbying Matters." Second Session, One Hundred And Ninth Congress, 109.

Cusack, Bob. (2007). "Democrats Say McCain Nearly Abandoned GOP." *The Hill*, March 28.

Davis, Tom. (2008). "Memorandum to Republican Leadership: Where We Stand Today." Real Clear Politics, May 14. https://www.realclearpolitics.com/articles/2008/05/post_38.html.

Dickerson, John F. (2004). "Confessions of a White House Insider." *Time*, January 10.

Edsall, Thomas B. (2007). "Happy Hours." *New York Times*, January 18. https://www.nytimes.com/2007/01/18/opinion/18edsall.html.

Edsall, Thomas B., and John F. Harris. (2005). "Bush's Agenda May Undercut Demo Pillars." *Deseret News*, January 30. https://www.deseret.com/2005/1/30/19874533/bush-s-agenda-may-undercut-demo-pillars.

Edsall, Thomas B., and Jonathan Weisman. (2004). "Wall Street Firms Funnel Millions to Bush." *Washington Post*, May 24. https://www.washingtonpost.com/archive/politics/2004/05/24/wall-street-firms-funnel-millions-to-bush/a9db7c1a-0f32-48af-86b9-1a788d8c322c/.

Ferguson, Andrew. (2004). "A Lobbyist's Progress." *Weekly Standard*, December 20. https://www.weeklystandard.com/andrew-ferguson/a-lobbyists-progress

Foer, Franklin. (2002). "Petty Cash; Will McCain-Feingold Breed Democratic Fratricide?" *New Republic*, June 2.

Franz, Michael. (2013). "Interest Groups in Electoral Politics: 2012 in Context." *The Forum: A Journal of Applied Research in Contemporary Politics* 10(4): 62–79.

Frontline (1997). "Interview—Dr. Rudi Dornbusch." PBS *Frontline*, April 8. https://www.pbs.org/wgbh/pages/frontline/shows/mexico/interviews/dornbusch.html

Fund, John. (2005). "The Personal 'Lockbox.' " *Wall Street Journal*, May 9.

Gibbs, Nancy, James Carney, John F. Dickerson, and Michael Duffy. (2000). "McCain's Moment." *Time*, February 7. http://www.cnn.com/ALLPOLITICS/time/2000/02/07/mccain.html.

Gibbs, Nancy, and John F. Dickerson. (2004). "Person of the Year." *Time*, December 19.

Goldmacher, Shane. (2016). "Inside the GOP's Shadow Convention." *Politico*, July 19. https://www.politico.com/magazine/story/2016/07/rnc-2016-gop-republican-party-leaders-future-donald-trump-214065.

Gooding, Richard. (2004). "The Trashing of John McCain." *Vanity Fair*, November.

Green, Joshua. (2002). "The Other War Room: President Bush Doesn't Believe in Polling—Just Ask His Pollsters." *Washington Monthly*, April. http://www.washingtonmonthly.com/features/2001/0204.green.html.

Greenblatt,Alan.(2015)."TheWaningPowerofStatePoliticalParties."*Governing*,December. http://www.governing.com/topics/politics/gov-waning-power-state-parties.html.

Hook, Janet. (2001). "Senate Passes Budget; Bush Tax Cut Slashed." *Los Angeles Times*, April 7. http://articles.latimes.com/2001/apr/07/news/mn-48158.

Issacharoff, Sam, and Pam Karlan. (1999). "The Hydraulics of Campaign Finance Reform." *Texas Law Review* 77.

Jacobson, Gary C. (2003). "The Bush Presidency and the American Electorate." In *The George W. Bush Presidency: An Early Assessment*, edited by Fred I Greenstein. Baltimore: Johns Hopkins University Press.

Justice, Glen. (2004a). "Despite New Financing Rules, Parties Collect Record $1 Billion." *New York Times*, October 26. https://www.nytimes.com/2004/10/26/politics/campaign/despite-new-financing-rules-parties-collect-record-1.html.

——— (2004b). "New Rules on Fund-Raising Bring Lobbyists to the Fore." *New York Times*, April 20. https://www.nytimes.com/2004/04/20/us/new-rules-on-fund-raising-bring-lobbyists-to-the-fore.html

Kaiser, Robert G. (2008). "The Friend He Just Can't Shake." *Washington Post*, September 1. http://www.washingtonpost.com/wp-dyn/content/article/2008/08/31/AR2008083102142_pf.html.

Kelner, Robert, and Raymond J. La Raja. (2014). "McCain-Feingold's Devastating Legacy." *Washington Post*, April 11. https://www.washingtonpost.com/opinions/mccain-feingolds-devastating-legacy/2014/04/11/14a528e2-c18f-11e3-bcec-b71ee10e9bc3_story.html.

Kirkpatrick, David D. (2008). "After 2000, McCain Learned to Work Levers of Power." *New York Times*, July 21. https://www.nytimes.com/2008/07/21/us/politics/21mccain.html.

Krugman, Paul. (2002). "The Memory Hole." *New York Times*, August 6.

Kuhnhenn, Jim. (2007). "Senate Votes to Raise Minimum Wage to $7.25 an Hour Over 2 Years." *Seattle Times*, February 1.

La Raja, Raymond J. (2003). "Why Soft Money Has Strengthened Parties." In *Inside the Campaign Finance Battle*, edited by Anthony Corrado, Thomas E. Mann, and Trevor Potter, 69–96. Washington, DC: Brookings Institution Press.

La Raja, Raymond J., and Brian F. Schaffner. (2015). *Campaign Finance and Political Polarization: When Purists Prevail*. Ann Arbor: University of Michigan Press.

Lee, Chisun, Katherine Valde, Benjamin T. Brickner, and Douglas Keith. (2016). "Secret Spending in the States." Washington, DC: Brennan Center for Justice, June 26. https://www.brennancenter.org/our-work/research-reports/secret-spending-states.

Lee, Frances E. (2016). *Insecure Majorities: Congress and the Perpetual Campaign*. Chicago: The University of Chicago Press.

Lemann, Nicholas. (2003). "The Controller: Karl Rove Is Working to Get George Bush Reelected, but He Has Bigger Plans." *New Yorker*, May 12. https://www.newyorker.com/magazine/2003/05/12/the-controller.

Martin, Jonathan. (2015). "Republicans Like Their 2016 Options, Assuming They Avoid Chaos." *New York Times*, January 18.

Mayer, Jane (2016). *Dark Money: The Hidden History of the Billionaires Behind the Rise of the Radical Right*. New York: Doubleday.

Morris, Rachel. (2006). "Borderline Catastrophe: How the Fight over Immigration Blew up Rove's Big Tent." *Washington Monthly*, October.

Moyers on America (2004). "Capitol Crimes." PBS, September 29. https://www.pbs.org/moyers/moyersonamerica/print/capitolcrimes_transcript_print.html.

Munger, Michael. (2006). "Unintended Consequences 1, Good Intentions 0." Carmel, IN: Library of Economics and Liberty, January 9. http://www.econlib.org/library/Columns/y2006/Mungergoodintentions.html.

Newsweek. (2000a). "Face to Face Combat." *Newsweek*, November 20, 92.

———. (2000b). "Pumping Iron, Digging Gold, Pressing Flesh." *Newsweek Special Edition*, November 20. https://www.newsweek.com/pumping-iron-digging-gold-

New York Times. (2000). "Mr. Bush's Rightward Lurch." *New York Times*, December 23. https://www.nytimes.com/2000/12/23/opinion/mr-bush-s-rightward-lurch.html.

———. (2003). "The Case for McCain-Feingold." *New York Times*, September 7.

Nunberg, Geoffrey. (2003). "The Nation: Freedom vs. Liberty; More Than Just Another Word for Nothing Left to Lose." *New York Times*, March 23. http://www.nytimes.com/2003/03/23/weekinreview/nation-freedom-vs-liberty-more-than-just-another-word-for-nothing-left-lose.html.

Pew Research Center. (2005). "Bush Failing in Social Security Push." Washington, DC: Pew Research Center, March 2. https://www.pewresearch.org/politics/2005/03/02/bush-failing-in-social-security-push/.

Popkin, Samuel L. (2012). *The Candidate: What It Takes to Win—and Hold—the White House*. New York: Oxford University Press.

Purdum, Todd S. (2007). "Prisoner of Conscience." *Vanity Fair*, February.

Reiff, Neil, and Don Mcgahn. (2014). "A Decade of McCain-Feingold." *Campaigns and Elections*, April 16. http://www.campaignsandelections.com/magazine/1705/a-decade-of-mccain-feingold?section_path=%2Fmagazine.

Rich, Frank. (2001). "Journal: Give Me That Old-Time Partisanship." *New York Times*, January 6. https://www.nytimes.com/2001/01/06/opinion/journal-give-me-that-old-time-partisanship.html.

Rosenthal, Howard. (2016). "Why Do White Men Love Donald Trump So Much?" *Monkey Cage* (blog). *Washington Post*, September 8. https://www.washingtonpost.com/news/monkey-cage/wp/2016/09/08/why-do-white-men-love-donald-trump-so-much/.

Sanger, David E. (2001). "Bush Tax Plan Sent to Congress, Starting the Jostling for Position." *New York Times*, February 9. https://www.nytimes.com/2001/02/09/us/bush-tax-plan-sent-to-congress-starting-the-jostling-for-position.html.

Schelling, Thomas C. (1971). "Choosing the Right Analogy: Factory, Prison, or Battlefield." In *Cybernetics, Simulation, and Conflict Resolution: Proceedings of the Third Annual*

Symposium of the American Society for Cybernetics, edited by Douglas E. Knight, Huntington W. Curtis, and Lawrence J. Fogel, 59–67. New York, Spartan Books.

Scherer, Michael. (2004). "Grover Norquist: The Soul of the New Machine." *Mother Jones*, January–February. https://www.motherjones.com/politics/2004/01/grover-norquist-soul-new-machine/.

Seib, Gerald F. (2017). "That's the Way the Party Crumbles." *Wall Street Journal*, February 25. https://www.wsj.com/articles/thats-the-way-the-party-crumbles-1487954429.

Smith, R. Jeffery, and James V. Grimaldi. (2005). "A 3rd Delay Trip under Scrutiny: 1997 Russia Visit Reportedly Backed by Business Interests." *Washington Post*, April 6. http://www.washingtonpost.com/wp-dyn/articles/A28319-2005Apr5.html.

Stevenson, Richard W. (2001). "This, It Appears Sure, Is the Year of the Tax Cut." *New York Times*, February 1. https://www.nytimes.com/2001/02/01/us/this-it-appears-sure-is-the-year-of-the-tax-cut.html.

———. (2005a). "For Bush, a Long Embrace of Social Security Plan." *New York Times*, February 27. https://www.nytimes.com/2005/02/27/politics/for-bush-a-long-embrace-of-social-security-plan.html.

———. (2005b). "On Social Security, a Search for Rivals." *New York Times*, May 9. https://www.nytimes.com/2005/05/09/politics/on-social-security-a-search-for-rivals.html.

Stone, Peter H. (2006). *Heist: Superlobbyist Jack Abramoff, His Republican Allies, and the Buying of Washington*. New York: Farrar, Straus and Giroux.

Taylor, Timothy. (2015). "The Hemingway Law of Motion: Gradually, Then Suddenly." *Conversable Economist* (blog), January 17. https://conversableeconomist.blogspot.com/2015/01/the-hemingway-law-of-motion-gradually.html.

Tierney, John. (2005). "Can Anyone Unseat F.D.R.?" *New York Times*, January 23. https://www.nytimes.com/2005/01/23/weekinreview/can-anyone-unseat-fdr.html.

Tokaji, Daniel P., and Renata E. B. Strause. (2014). *The New Soft Money: Outside Spending in Congressional Elections*. Columbus: Ohio State University Moritz College of Law.

Veterans Administration. (2020). *America's Wars*. Office of Public Affairs.

Wamhoff, Steve, and Matthew Gardner. (2018). *Federal Tax Cuts in the Bush, Obama, and Trump Years*. Washington, DC: Institute on Taxation and Economic Policy. https://itep.org/federal-tax-cuts-in-the-bush-obama-and-trump-years/.

Weekly Standard. (2001). "How Ashcroft Won." *Weekly Standard*, January 1. http://www.weeklystandard.com/how-ashcroft-won/article/12063.

Welch, Matt. (2008). "When Coalitions Dissolve: As the GOP Breaks Apart, Some Blame the Vanishing Breed of Free Market Republicans." *Reason*, May. https://reason.com/2008/04/04/when-coalitions-dissolve/.

Zappone, Christian. (2007). "House Passes Minimum-Wage Hike Bill." *CNN Money*, January 11. https://money.cnn.com/2007/01/10/news/economy/minimum_wage/.

Chapter 2

Acharya, Avidit, Matthew Blackwell, and Maya Sen. (2018). *Deep Roots: How Slavery Still Shapes Southern Politics*. Princeton, NJ: Princeton University Press.

Alberta, Tim. (2018). "This Is a Place That Just Sucks Your Soul." *Politico*, June 15. https://politi.co/2t9ItKl.

Allen, Jonathan. (2011). "Disaster Aid under New Scrutiny." *Politico*, May 26. https://www.politico.com/story/2011/05/disaster-aid-under-new-scrutiny-055776.

Allen, Jonathan, and Jake Sherman. (2011). "With John Boehner Bailing, Eric Cantor Ascends as GOP Voice." *Politico*, July 11. http://www.politico.com/news/stories/0711/58746.html.

Allen, Mike. (2015). "Luntz to GOP: Health Reform Is Popular." *Politico*, May 5. https://www.politico.com/story/2009/05/luntz-to-gop-health-reform-is-popular-022155.

Ames, Mark, and Yasha Levine. (2009). "Exposing the Rightwing PR Machine: Is CNBC's Rick Santelli Sucking Koch?" *The Exiled*, February 27. http://exiledonline.com/exposing-the-familiar-rightwing-pr-machine-is-cnbcs-rick-santelli-sucking-koch/.

Amira, Dan. (2011). "GOP Congressmen Would Like Democrats to Please Stop Mentioning That They Voted to Kill Medicare." *New York Magazine*, May 11. https://nymag.com/intelligencer/2011/05/gop_congressmen_would_like_dem.html.

Appelbaum, Binyamin. (2011). "Debt Ceiling Date Does Not Budge." *New York Times*, July 1. https://thecaucus.blogs.nytimes.com/2011/07/01/debt-ceiling-date-does-not-budge/.

Axelrod, David. (2015). *Believer: My Forty Years in Politics*. New York: Penguin Press.

Bacon, Perry, Jr. (2010). "GOP 'Young Guns' Attack Ex-Leaders." *Washington Post*, September 4.

Bai, Matt. (2012). "How Much Has *Citizens United* Changed the Political Game?" *New York Times*, July 22.

Balz, Dan. (2011). "Debt-Ceiling Debate Shows a Republican Party at War with Itself." *Washington Post*, July 29. https://www.washingtonpost.com/politics/debt-ceiling-breakdown-puts-gop-at-risk/2011/07/29/gIQAtjE9gI_story.html?utm_term=.cd798ef21189.

Balz, Daniel J. (2013). *Collision 2012: Obama vs. Romney and the Future of Elections in America*. New York: Viking.

Balz, Daniel J., and Haynes Bonner Johnson. (2009). *The Battle for America 2008: The Story of an Extraordinary Election*. Waterville, ME: Thorndike Press.

Baylor, Christopher. (2018). *First to the Party: The Group Origins of Party Transformation*. Philadelphia: University of Pennsylvania Press.

Bedard, Paul. (2010). "Rick Santelli Gets Credit for Tea Party Movement." *US News & World Report*, January 25. https://www.usnews.com/news/blogs/washington-whispers/2010/01/25/rick-santelli-gets-credit-for-tea-party-movement.

Benkler, Yochai, Rob Faris, and Hal Roberts. (2018). *Network Propaganda: Manipulation, Disinformation, and Radicalization in American Politics*. New York: Oxford University Press.

Berger, Thor. (2018). "Places of Persistence: Slavery and the Geography of Intergenerational Mobility in the United States." *Demography* 55(4): 1547–65.

Bertocchi, Graziella, and Arcangelo Dimico. (2014). "Slavery, Education, and Inequality." *European Economic Review* 70: 197–209.

Beutler, Brian. (2009). "Americans for Prosperity Compares Health Care Reform to Holocaust, Tells Protesters to Put 'Fear of God' in Members of Congress." *Talking Points Memo*, August 7. https://talkingpointsmemo.com/dc/americans-for-prosperity-compares-health-care-reform-to-holocaust-tells-protesters-to-put-fear-of-god-in-members-of-congress.

Bingham, Amy. (2012). "Mitt Romney's Abortion Evolution." ABC News, October 12. https://abcnews.go.com/Politics/OTUS/mitt-romneys-abortion-evolution/story?id=17443452.

Blumenthal, Paul. (2013). "*Citizens United*, McCain-Feingold Fueled Congress' Shutdown Politics." *Huffington Post*, October 16. https://www.huffpost.com/entry/citizens-united-shutdown_n_4108252.

Blumer, Tom. (2009). "Rant for the Ages: CNBC's Rick Santelli Goes Off; Studio Hosts Invoke 'Mob Rule' to Downplay (Transcript)." *Newsbusters*, February 19. https://www.newsbusters.org/blogs/nb/tom-blumer/2009/02/19/rant-ages-cnbcs-rick-santelli-goes-studio-hosts-invoke-mob-rule.

Bonica, Adam, Nolan McCarty, Keith T. Poole, and Howard Rosenthal. (2013). "Why Hasn't Democracy Slowed Rising Inequality?" *Journal of Economic Perspectives* 27(3): 103–24.

———. (2016). "Campaign Finance and Polarization." In *Polarized America: The Dance of Ideology and Unequal Riches*, edited by Nolan M. McCarty, Keith T. Poole, and Howard Rosenthal, 145–70. Cambridge, MA: MIT Press.

Booth, Michael. (2010). "Tancredo's Remarks Rain on Senate Candidate Buck's Party." *Denver Post*, July 8. https://www.denverpost.com/2010/07/08/tancredos-remarks-rain-on-senate-candidate-bucks-party/.

Bradberry, Leigh A., and Gary C. Jacobson. (2015). "The Tea Party and the 2012 Presidential Election." *Electoral Studies* 40: 500–5008.

Brant-Zawadzki, Alex, and Dawn Teo. (2011). "Anatomy of the Tea Party Movement: Recessrally.com." *Huffington Post*, May 25. https://www.huffingtonpost.com/alex-brantzawadzki/anatomy-of-the-tea-party_b_380687.html.

Bresnahan, John, and Jake Sherman. (2011). "GOPers Chant 'Fire Him' at Staffer." *Politico*, July 27. https://www.politico.com/news/stories/0711/60035.html.

Brown, Carrie Budoff. (2011). "Daniels Defends Call for Truce on Social Issues." *Politico*, March 13. https://www.politico.com/blogs/politico-now/2011/03/daniels-defends-call-for-truce-on-social-issues-034165.

Bruni, Frank. (2012). "The Oracle's Debacle." *New York Times*, November 10. http://www.nytimes.com/2012/11/11/opinion/sunday/bruni-the-oracles-debacle.html.

Burkeman, Oliver. (2003). "Memo Exposes Bush's New Green Strategy." *Guardian*, March 3. http://www.theguardian.com/environment/2003/mar/04/usnews.climatechange.

Calmes, Jackie. (2015). "'They Don't Give a Damn about Governing': Conservative Media's Influence on the Republican Party." Cambridge, MA: Shorenstein Center on Media, Politics and Public Policy, July.

Cassidy, John. (2005). "The Ringleader: How Grover Norquist Keeps the Conservative Movement Together." *New Yorker*, August 1.

CBS/*New York Times*. (2011). "Amid Skepticism about Job Creation Plans, Views of Government, Congress Decline." CBS/*New York Times*, October 25.

Center for Responsive Politics. (2013a). "FEC Report: Red, White and Blue Fund (Santorum)." Washington, DC: Center for Responsive Politics, April 16. https://www.opensecrets.org/pacs/lookup2.php?strID=C00503417&cycle=2012.

———. (2013b). "FEC Data: Winning Our Future, 2012 Cycle (Gingrich)." Washington, DC: Center for Responsive Politics, September 10. https://www.opensecrets.org/pacs/lookup2.php?cycle=2012&strID=C00507525.

———. (2018). "Rep. Joe Wilson Summary." Washington, DC: Center for Responsive Politics, August 18. https://www.opensecrets.org/members-of-congress/summary?cid=N00024809&cycle=2010&type=I.

Chait, Jonathan. (2012). "The Legendary Paul Ryan." *New York Magazine*, April 29.

Chapin, Laura. (2010). "Ken Buck's Abortion Stance Cost Him a Senate Seat." *U.S. News & World Report*. November 5. https://www.usnews.com/opinion/blogs/laura-chapin/2010/11/05/ken-bucks-abortion-stance-cost-him-the-senate-seat.

Chotiner, Isaac. (2007). "The Architect of the GOP Takeover Flees Washington." *New Republic*, January 29.

Clement, Scott, and Emily Guskin. (2017). "Exit Poll Results: How Different Groups Voted in Alabama." *Washington Post*, December 13.

Cogan, Marin. (2011). "Frosh Tout Clout, Risk Being Left Out." *Politico*, July 11. https://www.politico.com/story/2011/07/frosh-tout-clout-risk-being-left-out-058744.

Confessore, Nicholas. (2003). "Welcome to the Machine." *Washington Monthly*, July/August.

Confessore, Nick. (2012). "Ryan Has Kept Close Ties to Wealthy Donors on the Right." *New York Times*, August 13.

Couric, Katie, and Brian Goldsmith. (2018). "What Sarah Palin Saw Clearly." *Atlantic*, October 8. https://www.theatlantic.com/ideas/archive/2018/10/what-sarah-palin-understood-about-politics/572389/.

Curry, James M. (2015). *Legislating in the Dark: Information and Power in the House of Representatives*. Chicago: University of Chicago Press.

Davenport, Coral, and Eric Lipton. (2017). "How G.O.P. Leaders Came to View Climate Change as Fake Science." *New York Times*, June 3.

Devroy, Ann. (1995). "House Republicans Get Talking Points." *Washington Post*, February 2.

Dickens, William T., Robert K. Triest, and Rachel B. Sederberg. (2017). "The Changing Consequences of Unemployment for Household Finances." *RSF: The Russell Sage Foundation Journal of the Social Sciences* 3(3): 202–21.

Dickinson, Tim. (2008). "Make-Believe Maverick: A Closer Look at the Life and Career of John McCain Reveals a Disturbing Record of Recklessness and Dishonesty." *Rolling Stone*, October 15. http://www.RollingStone.com/news/coverstory/make_believe_maverick_the_real_john_mccain.

Disch, Lisa. (2012). "The Tea Party: A 'White Citizenship' Movement? In *Steep: The Precipitous Rise of the Tea Party*, edited by Lawrence Rosenthal and Christine Trost, 133–151. Berkeley: University of California Press.

Douglas, William. (2013). "When Gingrich Held Power, His GOP Lieutenants Tried to Topple Him." McClatchy, May 29. http://www.mcclatchydc.com/news/politics-government/election/article24720205.html.

Dowd, Maureen. (2009). "Boy, Oh, Boy." *New York Times*, September 12.

Draper, Robert. (2011). "Building a Better Mitt Romney-Bot." *New York Times Magazine*, November 30.

———. (2012). "The Mitt Romney Who Might Have Been." *New York Times*, October 2. http://www.nytimes.com/2012/10/07/magazine/mitt-romney.html?_r=0.

———. (2013). *When the Tea Party Came to Town*. New York: Simon & Schuster.

Dunham, Will, Thomas Ferraro, David Brunnstrom, and Bill Trott. (2012). "Romney Accuses Obama of Political Motivation on Immigration." Reuters, June 17. https://www.reuters.com/article/us-usa-immigration/romney-accuses-obama-of-political-motivation-on-immigration-idUSBRE85E0VA20120617.

Edsall, Thomas B. (2008). "Dark Clouds: Obama Assassination Threats Weigh on Voters." *Huffington Post*, August 25. http://www.huffingtonpost.com/2008/08/25/dark-clouds-obama-assassi_n_121327.html.

————. (2012). "Debt Splits the Left." *New York Times*, February 5. http://campaignstops.blogs.nytimes.com/2012/02/05/debt-splits-the-left/.

Epstein, Jennifer. (2011). "Dick Cheney: 'I Worship the Ground Paul Ryan Walks On.'" *Politico*, May 26. https://www.politico.com/news/stories/0511/55749.html.

Fahrenthold, David A., and Paul Kane. (2011). "Cantor Emerges as Key Player in Debt Negotiations." *Washington Post*, July 11.

Farley, Robert. (2009). "DeMint Says Stimulus Plan Would Bar Students from Having Prayer Meetings in Dorms." PolitiFact, February 13. https://www.politifact.com/truth-o-meter/statements/2009/feb/13/jim-demint/demint-stimulus-prayer-dorms-religion/.

Federal News Service. (2011). "Republican Presidential Candidates Debate Sponsored by the Western Republican Leadership Conference (WRLC) and CNN." Federal News Service, October 8.

Fikac, Peggy. (2012). "Christian Conservatives Reach 'Strong Consensus' for Santorum." *Houston Chronicle*, January 14.

Finkelstein, Matt. (2010). "Rep. Paul Broun Compares Health Care Reform to 'the Great War of Yankee Aggression.'" *Political Correction*, March 19. http://politicalcorrection.org/blog/201003190002.

Fried, Amy, and Douglas B. Harris. (2015). "The Strategic Promotion of Distrust in Government in the Tea Party Age." *The Forum: A Journal of Applied Research in Contemporary Politics* 13(3): 417–43.

Gerken, Heather, and Joseph Fishkin. (2015). "Whose Party Is It Anyway?" *Election Law Blog*, June 16.

Goldfarb, Zachary A. (2011). "S&P Downgrades U.S. Credit Rating for First Time." *Washington Post*, August 6.

Grann, David. (2008). "The Fall: John McCain's Choices." *New Yorker*, November 17. http://www.newyorker.com/reporting/2008/11/17/081117fa_fact_grann?currentPage=all.

Green, Joshua. (2012). "The Secret Republican Guide to Talking about Gay Marriage." *Bloomberg Businessweek*, May 11. http://www.businessweek.com/printer/articles/25042-the-secret-republican-guide-to-talking-about-gay-marriage.

Haberman, Maggie. (2012). "Axelrod: Romney's Message Was at War with Itself." *Politico*, November 11. http://www.politico.com/blogs/burns-haberman/2012/11/axelrod-romneys-message-was-at-war-with-itself-149232.html.

Haberman, Maggie, and Alexander Burns. (2012). "Dobson Decried Callista Gingrich as 'Eight-Year Mistress' at Conservative Confab." *Politico*, January 17. https://www.politico.com/blogs/burns-haberman/2012/01/dobson-decried-callista-gingrich-as-eight-year-mistress-at-conservative-confab-111199.

Herszenhorn, David M., and Robert Pear. (2011). "Republicans Reject Cost Estimate of Health Law Repeal." *The New York Times*, January 6.

Hohmann, James. (2012). "Ron Paul Aides Ponder 'Frustrating' Race." *Politico*, March 8. https://www.politico.com/news/stories/0312/73746_Page2.html.

Hulse, Carl. (2011). "Budget Deal Reached to Avert Shutdown." *New York Times*, April 8.

Hulse, Carl, and Helene Cooper. (2011). "Leaders Agree on Framework of Deal to End Debt Crisis." *New York Times*, July 31. https://www.nytimes.com/2011/08/01/us/politics/01FISCAL.html.

Isenstadt, Alex. (2012). "GOP Memo: 'Don't Say Entitlement Reform.'" *Politico*, August 13. https://www.politico.com/story/2012/08/gop-memo-dont-say-entitlement-reform-079673.

Jacobson, Gary C. (2011). "The Republican Resurgence in 2010." *Political Science Quarterly* 126(1): 27–52.

Jaffe, Greg. (2018). "One Moment from McCain's 2008 Run Made Clear His Character and Foretold Trump's Rise." *Washington Post*, August 26. https://www.washingtonpost. com/politics/one-moment-from-mccains-2008-run-made-clear-his-character-and-foretold-trumps-rise/2018/08/26/f44d8268-a94e-11e8-a8d7-0f63ab8b1370_story. html.

James, Frank. (2012). "Mitt Romney: Repeal 'Obamacare' (Romneycare Was Different)." NPR, *It's All Politics*, March 7. https://www.npr.org/sections/itsallpolitics/2011/03/07/ 134329380/mitt-romney-abolish-obamacare-romneycare-was-different.

Kalleberg, Arne L., and Till M. Von Wachter. (2017). "The U.S. Labor Market during and after the Great Recession: Continuities and Transformations." *RSF: The Russell Sage Foundation Journal* 3(3): 1–19.

Kamarck, Elaine. (2018). "Actually, National Democrats Should Interfere in Primaries." *New York Times*, May 3.

Kelner, Robert, and Raymond J. La Raja. (2014). "McCain-Feingold's Devastating Legacy." *Washington Post*, April 11. https://www.washingtonpost.com/opinions/mccain-feingolds-devastating-legacy/2014/04/11/14a528e2-c18f-11e3-bcec-b71ee10e9bc3_ story.html.

Kinder, Donald R., and Allison Dale-Riddle. (2012). *The End of Race?: Obama, 2008, and Racial Politics in America.* New Haven, CT: Yale University Press.

Kindy, Kimberly. (2008). "PR Consultant Helped Palin Grab Spotlight." *Washington Post*, October 10. http://www.washingtonpost.com/wp-dyn/content/article/2008/10/09/ AR2008100903429.html?nav=hcmodule.

Kleefeld, Eric. (2010). "Sharron Angle Attacked for Alleged Scientology Ties." *Talking Points Memo*, May 27. https://talkingpointsmemo.com/dc/ sharron-angle-attacked-for-alleged-scientology-ties.

Klein, Ezra. (2009). "Is the Government Going to Euthanize Your Grandmother? An Interview with Sen. Johnny Isakson." *Washington Post*, August 10. http://voices. washingtonpost.com/ezra-klein/2009/08/is_the_government_going_to_eut.html.

Kohn, Sally. (2012). "Paul Ryan's Speech in 3 Words." Fox News, August 30. http://www. foxnews.com/opinion/2012/08/30/paul-ryans-speech-in-three-words.html.

Kwon, Lillian. (2012). "Southern Baptists Experiencing Accelerating Decline in Membership." *Christian Post*, June 13.

Lee, Jennifer. (2003). "A Call for Softer, Greener Language." *New York Times*, March 2.

Lizza, Ryan. (2011). "Romney's Dilemma: How His Greatest Achievement Has Become His Biggest Liability." *New Yorker*, June 6.

———. (2012). "Fussbudget: How Paul Ryan Captured the G.O.P." *The New Yorker*, August 6. https://www.newyorker.com/magazine/2012/08/06/fussbudget.

———. (2013a). "Eric Cantor, the Sequester, and the Death of the Grand Bargain." *New Yorker*, February 28. https://www.newyorker.com/news/daily-comment/ eric-cantor-the-sequester-and-the-death-of-the-grand-bargain.

———. (2013b). "The House of Pain: Can Eric Cantor, the Republican Majority Leader, Redeem His Party and Himself?" *New Yorker*, March 4. https://www.newyorker.com/ magazine/2013/03/04/the-house-of-pain.

Lupia, Arthur. (2010). "Did Bush Voters Cause Obama's Victory?" *PS: Political Science & Politics* 43(2): 239–41.

Mann, James. (2020). "Donald Trump Is No Dick Cheney." *New York Times*, January 12.

Martin, Jonathan. (2009). "Palin Calls Dems' Health Care Plan 'Evil,' Cites Threat to Trig." *Politico*, August 7. https://www.politico.com/blogs/ben-smith/2009/08/palin-calls-dems-health-care-plan-evil-cites-threat-to-trig-020515.

———. (2012). "The GOP's Media Cocoon." *Politico*, November 12. http://www.politico.com/news/stories/1112/83704.html?hp=t1.

Maxwell, Angie, and T. Wayne Parent. (2012). "The Obama Trigger: Presidential Approval and Tea Party Membership." *Social Science Quarterly* 93(5): 1384–401.

Mayer, Jane. (2008). "The Insiders: How John McCain Came to Pick Sarah Palin." *New Yorker*, October 27. http://www.newyorker.com/reporting/2008/10/27/081027fa_fact_mayer.

———. (2010). "Covert Operations: The Billionaire Brothers Who Are Waging a War against Obama." *New Yorker*, August 30, 44.–55.

———. (2016). *Dark Money: The Hidden History of the Billionaires Behind the Rise of the Radical Right*. New York: Doubleday.

Mian, Atif, and Amir Sufi. (2015). *House of Debt: How They (and You) Caused the Great Recession, and How We Can Prevent It from Happening Again*. Chicago: University of Chicago Press.

Nagourney, Adam. (2012). "Medicare Rises as Prime Election Issue." *New York Times*, August 13.

Nakamura, David, and Karen Tumulty. (2012). "Storm Provides Obama with a Commander-in-Chief Moment." *Washington Post*, October 30. http://www.washingtonpost.com/politics/decision2012/storm-provides-obama-with-a-commander-in-chief-moment/2012/10/30/5e645952-22c2-11e2-ac85-e669876c6a24_story_1.html.

New Jersey Star-Ledger. (2012). "Election Day Nostalgia: Best Quotes of the 2012 Campaign." *New Jersey Star Ledger*, November 6. http://connect.nj.com/staff/njoslstaff/posts.html.

O'Brien, Michael. (2011). "Paul Ryan Launches Effort to Defend Budget, GOP Presidential Field in Iowa." *The Hill*, August 9. https://thehill.com/blogs/blog-briefing-room/news/176061-paul-ryan-seeks-money-for-ads-defending-presidential-hopefuls-in-iowa.

The Onion. (2008). "Black Man Given Nation's Worst Job." *The Onion*, November 5. https://web.archive.org/web/20081111220634/http://www.theonion.com/content/news_briefs/black_man_given_nations.

Orwell, George. (2008). "In Front of Your Nose." In *Facing Unpleasant Facts: Narrative Essays*, edited by George Packer, 209–13. Orlando, FL: Harcourt.

Peters, Jeremy W., and Brian Stelter. (2012). "On Fox News, a Mistrust of Pro-Obama Numbers Lasts Late into the Night." *New York Times*, November 6.

Peters, W. Jeremy, and Barry Meier. (2015). "Rand Paul Linked to Doctors' Group That Challenges Vaccinations." *New York Times*, February 4.

Pettigrew, Thomas. (2017). "Social Psychological Perspectives on Trump Supporters." *Journal of Social and Political Psychology* (5)1: 107–16. https://jspp.psychopen.eu/article/view/750/html.

Pollack, Harold. (2014). "Let's Talk about 'Death Panels.'" *Politico*, July 6. https://www.politico.com/magazine/story/2014/07/death-panels-108553.html.

Prior, Francis B. (2014). "Quality Controlled: An Ethnographic Account of Tea Party Messaging and Action." *Sociological Forum* 29(2): 301–17.

Randall, Eric. (2011). "Rasmussen Poll Shows Gingrich Crushing Romney." *Atlantic*, December 1. https://www.theatlantic.com/politics/archive/2011/12/rasmussen-poll-shows-gingrich-crushing-romney/334855/.

RCP Staff. (2008). "Barack Obama at the Al Smith Dinner (Transcript)." Real Clear Politics, October 16. http://www.realclearpolitics.com/articles/2008/10/barack_obama_at_the_al_smith_d.html.

Rogowski, Jon C., and Sophie A. Schuit. (2018). "Electoral Institutions and Democratic Legitimacy." *Public Opinion Quarterly* 82(2): 343–65.

Rosenthal, Lawrence, and Christine Trost. (2012). *Steep: The Precipitous Rise of the Tea Party*. Berkeley: University of California Press.

Rothenberg, Stuart. (2010). "Is Jim DeMint Barack Obama's Ace in the Hole?" *Roll Call*, July 12. https://www.rollcall.com/2010/07/12/is-jim-demint-barack-obamas-ace-in-the-hole/.

Ryan, Erica (2013). "Hastert: Primary Challenges Making Congress 'Kind of Neurotic.'" NPR, *It's All Politics*, October 8. http://www.npr.org/sections/itsallpolitics/2013/10/08/230256554/hastert-primary-challenges-making-congress-kind-of-neurotic.

Schor, Elana. (2009). "The Four Republican Senators Open to Working with Obama." *Talking Points Memo*, February 5. https://talkingpointsmemo.com/dc/the-four-republican-senators-open-to-working-with-obama.

Schwarz, Gabriella. (2011). "Utah Dems Accuse Huntsman of Pandering." CNN, June 27. https://politicalticker.blogs.cnn.com/2011/06/20/utah-dems-to-huntsman-youre-pandering/.

Shear, Michael D. (2011). "Pawlenty Hopes 'I'm Sorry' Is Enough." *New York Times*, May 6.

Sherman, Gabriel. (2014). *The Loudest Voice in the Room: How the Brilliant, Bombastic Roger Ailes Built Fox News—and Divided a Country*. New York: Random House.

Simon, Roger. (2012). "Obama's Immigration Trap." *Politico*, June 18. http://www.politico.com/news/stories/0112/72268.html.

Sokolove, Michael. (2005). "The Believer." *New York Times*, May 22. https://www.nytimes.com/2005/05/22/magazine/the-believer.html.

Steinhauer, Jennifer, and Jim Rutenberg. (2010). "Rebel Republican Marching On, with Baggage." *New York Times*, September 15.

Stephens-Davidowitz, Seth. (2014). "The Cost of Racial Animus on a Black Candidate: Evidence Using Google Search Data." *Journal of Public Economics* 118: 26–40.

Stevens, Stuart. (2015). "The G.O.P.'s Crowded Stage." *New York Times*. July 31.

Stolberg, Sheryl Gay. (2011). "For Bachmann, Gay Rights Stand Reflects Mix of Issues and Faith." *New York Times*, July 16. https://www.nytimes.com/2011/07/17/us/politics/17bachmann.html.

Stone, Daniel. (2011). "The Tea Party Pork Binge." *Daily Beast*, October 31. https://www.thedailybeast.com/ex-nsa-boss-mike-rogers-i-wish-trump-had-pressed-putin-on-election-meddling-in-helsinki.

Tanden, Neera. (2014). "A Short History of Republican Attempts to Repeal Obamacare." *Politico*, January 30. https://www.politico.com/magazine/story/2014/01/house-republicans-obamacare-repeal-votes-102911.

Tesler, Michael. (2013). "The Return of Old-Fashioned Racism to White Americans' Partisan Preferences in the Early Obama Era." *Journal of Politics* 75(1): 110–23.

———. (2015). "The Conditions Ripe for Racial Spillover Effects." *Political Psychology* 36: 101–17.

Tesler, Michael, and David O. Sears. (2010). *Obama's Race: The 2008 Election and the Dream of a Post-racial America*. Chicago: University of Chicago Press.

Tilove, Jonathan. (2017). "First Reading: Brendan Steinhauser on How the Left Borrowed His Tea Party Playbook." *Austin American Statesman*, February 14.

Tokaji, Daniel P., and Renata E. B. Strause. (2014). *The New Soft Money: Outside Spending in Congressional Elections*. Columbus: The Ohio State University, Moritz College of Law.

Trinko, Katrina. (2012). "Romney and Global Warming." *National Review*, August 25. https://www.nationalreview.com/2011/08/romney-and-global-warming-katrina-trinko/.

Vandehei, Jim, and Mike Allen. (2012). "The Right Drops a Bomb on Newt." *Politico*, January 26. https://www.politico.com/story/2012/01/the-right-drops-a-bomb-on-newt-072000.

Vogel, Kenneth P., and Lucy McCalmont. (2011). "Top Radio Talkers Sell Endorsements." *Politico*, June 15.

Waldman, Paul. (2014). "Yes, Opposition to Obamacare Is Tied Up with Race." *Washington Post*, May 23.

Washington Post. (2010). "Highlights of House Republicans' 'Pledge to America.'" *Washington Post*, September 22. http://www.washingtonpost.com/wp-dyn/content/article/2010/09/22/AR2010092206096.html.

———. (2012). "Romney Prepared Victory Speech for Election, but Delivered Concession Speech Instead." *Washington Post*, November 7.

Weisman, Jonathan. (2011). "GOP Debate: The Audience Again Delivers a Message." *Wall Street Journal*, September 23.

Zernike, Kate. (2015). "Rand Paul Rode Tea Party Fervor to Washington, Then Yielded." *New York Times*, November 4.

Chapter 3

Aguilar, Julian. (2013). U.S. Senate Passes Immigration Reform Bill. *Texas Tribune*, June 27.

Alberta, Tim. (2015). "Man of the Movement: Inside the Secret Meeting Where Ted Cruz Trounced His Rivals." *National Journal Magazine*, June 6. http://www.nationaljournal.com/magazine/ted-cruz-council-national-policy-20150605.

Allen, Mike, and Jim Vandehei. (2012). *Politico*. December 4.

Altman, Alex. (2013). "Marco Rubio's Agile Courtship of Conservative Media: The Task of Pitching an Immigration-Reform Bill to the Conservative Press Has Fallen to the Republican Star." *Time*, January 30.

Associated Press. (2014). "GOP Governors Say Obamacare Is Here to Stay." *Huffington Post*, October 20. http://www.huffingtonpost.com/2014/10/20/gop-obamacare_n_6016458.html.

Ball, Molly. (2013). "The Immigration Fight Is the Battle for the Soul of the GOP." *Atlantic*, July 17.

———. (2016). "Why D.C. Hates Ted Cruz." *Atlantic*, January 25.

Barbour, Henry, Sally Bradshaw, Ari Fleischer, Zori Fonalledas, and Glenn McCal. (2013). *Growth and Opportunity Project*. Republican National Committee, March 21. https://online.wsj.com/public/resources/documents/RNCreport03182013.pdf.

Binder, Sarah. (2019). "How Did Congress Pass Humanitarian Aid for Migrant Children So Quickly? Here Are 3 Takeaways." *Washington Post*, June 29. https://www.washingtonpost.com/politics/2019/06/29/how-did-congress-pass-humanitarian-aid-migrant-children-so-quickly-here-are-takeaways/?utm_term=.6476667284c2.

Blake, Aaron, and Rachel Weiner. (2011). "How Soon Is Too Soon for Marco Rubio?" *Washington Post*, August 23. https://www.washingtonpost.com/blogs/the-fix/post/how-soon-is-too-soon-for-marco-rubio/2011/08/23/gIQA5pr6ZJ_blog.html.

Bruni, Frank. (2013). "The G.O.P.'S Nasty Newcomer." *New York Times*, February 15. https://www.nytimes.com/2013/02/17/opinion/sunday/ted-cruz-the-gops-nasty-newcomer.html.

Calmes, Jackie. (2015). "Steve Deace and the Power of Conservative Media." *New York Times*, November 8.

Cassata, Donna, and Paul Weber. (2013). "Cruz's Tactics Boil Washington, but Impress Texas." *Washington Examiner*, February 25. https://www.washingtonexaminer.com/cruzs-tactics-boil-washington-but-impress-texas.

CBS News. (2012). "Ted Cruz Sounds Off on Hispanic Vote after Historic Senate Win." *CBS News*, November 7. https://www.cbsnews.com/news/ted-cruz-sounds-off-on-hispanic-vote-after-historic-senate-win/.

Confessore, Nicholas. (2014). "A National Strategy Funds State Political Monopolies." *New York Times*, January 11.

Coppins, McKay. (2015). *The Wilderness: Deep Inside the Republican Party's Combative, Contentious, Chaotic Quest to Take Back the White House*. New York: Little, Brown.

Costa, Robert. (2013). "Cruz 2016." *National Review*, May 1.

Cottle, Michelle. (2013). "Has Jim DeMint Gone Too Far?" *Daily Beast*, August 30.

Deace, Steve. (2015). "Why I'm Endorsing Ted Cruz for President." *Washington Times*, August 19.

Dennis, Steven T. (2013). "Landrieu Angrily Confronts Cruz over Abortion Amendment." *Roll Call*, March 23.

Dickerson, John. (2012). "Why Romney Never Saw It Coming." *Slate*, November 9. http://www.slate.com/articles/news_and_politics/politics/2012/11/why_romney_was_surprised_to_lose_his_campaign_had_the_wrong_numbers_bad.html.

Downes, Lawrence. (2012). "Rick Santorum Is Afraid, Very Afraid." *Taking Note* (blog). *New York Times*, December 3.

Draper, Robert. (2013). "The War Within: Inside the Making of the Shutdown." *Politico Magazine*, November.

Drucker, David. (2013). "Cruz's Grass-Roots Role at NRSC Still Evolving." *Roll Call*, January 29.

Edsall, Thomas B. (2012). "Is Rush Limbaugh's Country Gone?" *Campaign Stops* (blog). *New York Times*, November 18.

———. (2013a). "Has the G.O.P. Gone Off the Deep End?" *Opinionator* (blog). *New York Times*, July 17.

———. (2013b). "Marco Rubio's Un-American Dream." *Opinionator* (blog). *New York Times*, August 14.

Fabian, Jordan. (2011). "Rubio Casts Doubt on Tea Party Caucus." *The Hill*, January 24. https://thehill.com/blogs/blog-briefing-room/news/139599-rubio-casts-doubt-on-senate-tea-party-caucus-.

Fallows, James. (1994). "Talent on Loan from the GOP." *Atlantic*, May 1.

Federal News Service. (2011). "Republican Presidential Candidates: Dar Constitution Hall, Washington, D.C." Federal News Service, November 22.

Ferguson, Andrew. (2015). "Washington Builds a Bugaboo: How Does Senator Ted Cruz Tick Off Liberals? Let Us Count the Ways." *Weekly Standard*, September 23.

File, Thom. (2013). *The Diversifying Electorate: Voting Rates by Race and Hispanic Origin in 2012 (and Other Recent Elections)*. Current Population Survey Reports, P20-569. Washington, DC: Economics and Statistics Administration, US Census Bureau. https://www.census.gov/prod/2013pubs/p20-568.pdf.

Finley, Allysia. (2016). "Cruz's Immigration Misfire." *Wall Street Journal*, February 24. http://www.wsj.com/articles/cruzs-immigration-misfire-1456335513.

Flegenheimer, Matt. (2017). "Ted Cruz 2.0? Senator Adjusts with Trump in Office and Houston under Water." *New York Times*, September 8. https://www.nytimes.com/2017/09/08/us/politics/ted-cruz-hurricane-harvey.html.

Fleischman, Jon. (2013). "A Wide Ranging Interview with Senator Ted Cruz (R-Texas)." *Flash Report*, June 23. http://www.flashreport.org/blog/2013/06/23/a-wide-ranging-interview-with-senator-ted-cruz-r-texas/.

Friedersdorf, Conor. (2012). "Fake History in the Making: Karen Hughes' Bad Advice for the GOP." *Atlantic*, November 12. http://www.theatlantic.com/politics/archive/2012/11/fake-history-in-the-making-karen-hughes-bad-advice-for-the-gop/265089/.

Frum, David. (2016). "The Great Republican Revolt." *Atlantic*, January/February. http://www.theatlantic.com/magazine/archive/2016/01/the-great-republican-revolt/419118/?utm_source=nl__linkcoverstories1_122215.

Gentilviso, Chris (2012). "Todd Akin on Abortion: 'Legitimate Rape' Victims Have 'Ways to Try to Shut That Whole Thing Down.'" *HuffPost*, August 19. https://www.huffingtonpost.com/2012/08/19/todd-akin-abortion-legitimate-rape_n_1807381.html.

Gillman, Todd J. (2013). "John Cornyn Appears to Move to the Right, Pulled by New Senate Partner Ted Cruz." *Dallas News*, January 31. https://www.dallasnews.com/news/local-politics/2013/01/31/john-cornyn-appears-to-move-to-the-right-pulled-by-new-senate-partner-ted-cruz.

Goldmacher, Shane. (2013). "How Jim DeMint Pulls the Strings in Washington." *National Journal Magazine*, October 3. http://www.nationaljournal.com/magazine/how-jim-demint-pulls-the-strings-in-washington-20131003?mrefid=.

Green, Joshua. (2017). *Devil's Bargain: Steve Bannon, Donald Trump, and the Storming of the Presidency*. New York: Penguin Press.

Grunwald, Michael. (2013). "Immigrant Son: Marco Rubio Wants to Sell the GOP on a Path to Citizenship for Undocumented Americans. So Why Is His Mom Calling?" *Time*, February 7.

Haberman, Maggie, and Emily Schultheis. (2012). "The Man at the Heart of Romney's Poll Questions." *Politico*, November 4. http://www.politico.com/news/stories/1112/83288.html.

Herman, Ken. (2012). "For Cruz, Winning May Have Been Easy Part." *Austin American-Statesman*, November 7.

Hohmann, James. (2012). "Republicans at a Crossroads." *Politico*, November 19. http://dyn.politico.com/printstory.cfm?uuid=514D7CB1-6CF2-4317-9C18-620FDE5E336D.

Hohmann, James, and Anna Palmer. (2012). "Romneyworld Reckoning Begins." *Politico*, November 7. http://www.politico.com/news/stories/1112/83549.html.

Horowitz, Jason. (2015). "Ted Cruz and Marco Rubio Grow Apart as Their Ambitions Expand." *New York Times*, November 1.

———. (2016). "Marco Rubio Pushed for Immigration Reform with Conservative Media." *New York Times*, February 27.

Hulse, Carl. (2014). "'Vote No, Hope Yes' Defines Dysfunction in Congress." *New York Times*, February 13.

Jacobs, Jennifer. (2013). "Ted Cruz Asks Iowa Evangelical Activists to Text Him Their Cellphone Numbers." *Des Moines Register*, August 10.

Johnson, Eliana. (2015). "The Paradox of Ted Cruz." *National Review*, August 24.

Kane, Paul. (2012). "Ted Cruz Wins Texas Senate Primary in a Victory for Tea Party." *Washington Post*, July 31.

Kapur, Sahil. (2013). "Ted Cruz Negotiated Terms of 'Filibuster' with Reid Ahead of Time." *Talking Points Memo*, September 24.

Klein, Ezra. (2013). "Why Boehner Doesn't Just Ditch the Hard Right." *Wonkblog* (blog). *Washington Post*, October 2.

Klein, Ezra, and Evan Soltas. (2013). "Newt Gingrich Explains How the GOP's Obamacare Tactics Backfired." *Washington Post*, August 20. http://www.washingtonpost.com/blogs/wonkblog/wp/2013/08/20/wonkbook-newt-gingrich-explains-how-the-gops-obamacare-tactics-backfired/?print=1.

Krogstad, Jens Manuel, and Jeffrey S. Passel. (2015). "5 Facts About Illegal Immigration in the U.S." Washington, DC: Pew Research Center, November 19.

Leary, Alex. (2013). "Sen. Marco Rubio's Role in Immigration Debate Draws Tea Party Criticism." *Tampa Bay Times*, February 1. https://www.tampabay.com/news/politics/national/sen-marco-rubios-role-in-immigration-debate-draws-tea-party-criticism/1273129/.

Lizza, Ryan. (2013a). "Getting to Maybe: Inside the Gang of Eight's Immigration Deal." *New Yorker*, June 24.

———. (2013b). "The House of Pain: Can Eric Cantor, the Republican Majority Leader, Redeem His Party and Himself?" *New Yorker*, March 4. https://www.newyorker.com/magazine/2013/03/04/the-house-of-pain.

Lupia, Arthur. (2010). "Did Bush Voters Cause Obama's Victory?" *PS: Political Science & Politics* 43(2): 239–41.

Markon, Jerry, and Karen Tumulty. (2012). "Romney: Obama's Gift Giving Led to Loss." *Washington Post*, November 14. https://www.washingtonpost.com/politics/romney-obamas-gift-giving-led-to-loss/2012/11/14/c8d7e744-2eb7-11e2-89d4-040c9330702a_story.html.

Martin, Jonathan. (2012a). "The GOP's Media Cocoon." *Politico*, November 12. http://www.politico.com/news/stories/1112/83704.html?hp=t1.

———. (2012b). "Jindal: End 'Dumbed-Down Conservatism.'" *Politico*, November 13. https://www.politico.com/story/2012/11/jindal-end-dumbed-down-conservatism-083743.

———. (2013a). "GOP Battle Plan: Pick Your Fights with Obama." *Politico*, January 28. http://www.politico.com/story/2013/01/new-gop-mantra-be-positive-and-prudent-86792.html?hp=t3_3.

———. (2013b). "G.O.P. Elders See Liabilities in Shutdown." *New York Times*, October 4.

———. (2013c). "Marco Rubio as the Anti-Mitt Romney." *Politico*, February 13. Available at http://www.politico.com/story/2013/02/marco-rubio-as-the-anti-mitt-romney-87571.html?hp=t3_3.

Martin, Jonathan, and Maggie Haberman. (2013). "CPAC Muddle Mirrors GOP Mess." *Politico*, March 13. http://www.politico.com/story/2013/03/cpac-muddle-mirrors-gop-mess-88793.html#.UUBggeLcaQM.twitter.

Mayer, Jane. (2016). *Dark Money: The Hidden History of the Billionaires Behind the Rise of the Radical Right*. New York: Doubleday.

McCalmont, Lucy. (2013). "Poll: 21% Say Cruz Is GOP Leader." *Politico*, November 1. http://dyn.politico.com/printstory.cfm?uuid=501830B4-8C9B-4C6B-8CA0-D1A4FB2911E1.

McLaughlin, Ariana. (2013). "Marco Rubio, Republican Savior." *Time*, February 7. http://time.com/3817883/marco-rubios-life-in-pictures/.

McMorris-Santoro, Evan. (2013). "Steve King: Undocumented Immigrants Are 'Undocumented Democrats.'" BuzzFeed, March 16. https://www.buzzfeednews.com/article/evanmcsan/steve-king-undocumented-immigrants-are-undocumented-democrat.

Mider, Zachary. (2015). "The Koch Brothers Have an Immigration Problem." *Bloomberg Politics*, August 27. http://www.bloomberg.com/politics/articles/2015-08-27/the-koch-brothers-have-an-immigration-problem.

Mishak, Michael J. (2015). "What Kind of Leader Is Marco Rubio? An Investigation." *National Journal*, November 5.

New York Times. (2016). "Ted Cruz: Republican United States Senator from Texas." *New York Times*. https://www.nytimes.com/interactive/2016/us/elections/ted-cruz-on-the-issues.html.

Noonan, Peggy. (2012). "Noonan: 'People Are Afraid of Change.'" *Wall Street Journal*, November 9. https://www.wsj.com/articles/SB10001424127887323894704578107460045098692.

O'Keefe, Ed. (2013). "Senate Approves Comprehensive Immigration Bill." *Washington Post*, June 27. https://www.washingtonpost.com/politics/senate-poised-to-approve-massive-immigration-bill/2013/06/27/87168096-df32-11e2-b2d4-ea6d8f477a01_story.html?utm_term=.4cf414864e08.

O'Reilly, Bill. (2014). "Bill O'Reilly: More Controversy over Illegal Aliens (Transcript)." Fox News, April 10. http://www.foxnews.com/transcript/2014/04/10/bill-oreilly-more-controversy-over-illegal-aliens/.

Orangeburg Times and Democrat. (2013). "Graham Relying on GOP Uniting on His Re-Election." *Orangeburg Times and Democrat*, May 8. https://thetandd.com/news/opinion/editorial/graham-relying-on-gop-uniting-on-his-re-election/article_b78fd9ea-b799-11e2-bba3-001a4bcf887a.html.

Pappas, Alex. (2015). "John Boehner Calls Ted Cruz a 'Jackass' at Fundraiser." *Daily Caller*, August 30.

Parker, Ashley, and Michael Barbaro. (2012). "Seeking No. 2, Romney Campaign Puts Caution over Flash." *New York Times*, July 18.

Passel, Jeffrey S., and D'vera Cohn. (2015). "Number of Babies Born in U.S. to Unauthorized Immigrants Declines." Washington, DC: Pew Research Center, September 11.

Peters, Jeremy W. (2015). "A Hillary Clinton Match-Up with Marco Rubio Is a Scary Thought for Democrats." *New York Times*, March 22.

Pew Research Center. (2013). "Tea Party's Image Turns More Negative: Ted Cruz's Popularity Soars among Tea Party Republicans." Washington, DC: Pew Research Center, October 16.

Politico. (2013). "Full Text: Rubio's GOP Response." *Politico*, February 12. https://www.politico.com/story/2013/02/gop-rebuttal-marco-rubio-response-english-spanish-full-text-087554.

Raju, Manu. (2012). "Rubio Opens GOP Soul Searching." *Politico*, November 7.

Raju, Manu, and Ginger Gibson. (2013). "Reid, McConnell Reach Filibuster Deal." *Politico*, January 24. https://www.politico.com/story/2013/01/reid-mcconnell-reach-senate-filibuster-deal-86674.html.

Reed, Ralph. (2013). "Ralph Reed: Immigration Rights and Wrongs." *USA Today*, February 12. https://www.usatoday.com/story/opinion/2013/02/12/ralph-reed-immigration-rights-and-wrongs/1914813/.

Scheiber, Noam. (2012). "Exclusive: The Internal Polls That Made Mitt Romney Think He'd Win." *New Republic*, November 30. http://www.tnr.com/blog/plank/110597/exclusive-the-polls-made-mitt-romney-think-hed-win#.

Seelye, Katharine Q. (1994). "Republicans Get a Pep Talk from Rush Limbaugh." *New York Times*, December 12.

Severson, Kim. (2013). "Challengers to South Carolina Senator Are Lining Up on the Right." *New York Times*, August 26. http://www.nytimes.com/2013/08/26/us/politics/challengers-to-south-carolina-senator-are-lining-up-on-the-right.html?hp&_r=0&pagewanted=print.

Shiller, Robert (2018). "Why Our Beliefs Don't Predict Much about the Economy." *New York Times*, October 19. https://www.nytimes.com/2018/10/12/business/why-our-beliefs-dont-predict-much-about-the-economy.html.

Slater, Wayne. (2013). "Ted Cruz's Impassioned Conservatism Has Many on Right Viewing Him as a Presidential Contender." *Dallas Morning News*, July 24.

Soltas, Evan. (2013). "Wonkbook: Can Marco Rubio Really Walk Away from Immigration Reform?" *Washington Post*, April 1.

Steinhauer, Jennifer. (2012). "Dole Appears, but G.O.P. Rejects a Disabilities Treaty." *New York Times*, December 5. https://www.nytimes.com/2012/12/05/us/despite-doles-wish-gop-rejects-disabilities-treaty.html.

———. (2013). "Divided House Passes Tax Deal in End to Latest Fiscal Standoff." *New York Times*, January 1. https://www.nytimes.com/2013/01/02/us/politics/house-takes-on-fiscal-cliff.html.

Stewart, Katherine. (2015). "Ted Cruz and the Anti-Gay Pastor." *New York Times*, November 16. http://www.nytimes.com/2015/11/16/opinion/campaign-stops/ted-cruz-and-the-anti-gay-pastor.html.

Stokes, Bruce. (2017). "What It Takes to Truly Be 'One of Us.'" Washington, DC: Pew Research Center, February 1.

Stolberg, Sheryl Gay. (2018). "Senate Odd Couple Tries to Salvage an Immigration Deal." *New York Times*, June 26. https://www.nytimes.com/2018/06/26/us/politics/ted-cruz-dianne-feinstein-immigration-deal.html.

Tanenhaus, Sam. (2014). "Can the G.O.P. Be a Party of Ideas?" *New York Times Magazine*, July 6. https://www.nytimes.com/2014/07/06/magazine/can-the-gop-be-a-party-of-ideas.html.

———. (2018). "On the Front Lines of the GOP's Civil War." *Esquire*, February. http://www.esquire.com/news-politics/a14428464/gop-never-trump/.

Taylor, Paul, and Mark Hugo Lopez. (2013). "Six Take-Aways from the Census Bureau's Voting Report." Washington, DC: Pew Research Center, May 8. https://www.pewresearch.org/fact-tank/2013/05/08/six-take-aways-from-the-census-bureaus-voting-report/.

Thrush, Glenn. (2013). "GOP's State Victories Haunt Obama." *Politico*, July 26. https://www.politico.com/story/2013/07/obamas-states-of-despair-2010-losses-still-haunt-94775.html.

Tilove, Jonathan. (2013a). "Color Me Ted, Color Me Red. Iconic or Ironic, Cruz Coloring Book in Its Third Printing in Its First Week." *Austin American-Statesman*, December 13.

———. (2013b). "Cruz: U.S. Shutdown Worth Risking to Slay Obamacare." *Austin American-Statesman*, July 31.

———. (2013c). "Forget About Abbott v. Davis. How About Cruz v. Perry?" *Austin American-Statesman*. September 25.

———. (2013d). "Is Texas Big Enough for Charismatic Cruz?" *Austin American Statesman*, August 24.

———. (2013e). "The New Rock Star." *Austin American-Statesman*, February 24.

———. (2015). "First Reading: As Senate Boos Cruz, Ted Gets Lotsa Lege Love from Texas Republicans." *Austin American-Statesman*. September 30.

Time. (2013). "The Top Ten Finalists for Person of the Year in 2013." *Time*, December 9. https://poy.time.com/2013/12/09/top-ten-finalists-for-person-of-the-year/.

Tumulty, Karen. (2012). "Latino Voters Take Center Stage in Both Presidential Campaigns." *Washington Post*, April 18.

Tumulty, Karen, and Tom Hamburger. (2013). "Key Republicans Signal Willingness to Back Down on Effort to Defund Health-Care Law." *Washington Post*, October 10. http://www.washingtonpost.com/politics/key-republicans-signal-willingness-to-back-down-on-effort-to-defund-health-care-law/2013/10/09/865b9284-30f6-11e3-89ae-16e186e117d8_print.html.

Viguerie, Richard A. (2012). "Ted Cruz's Victory Foretells Conservative Takeover of GOP." ConservativeHQ, July 31.

Vogel, Kenneth P. (2014a). *Big Money: 2.5 Billion Dollars, One Suspicious Vehicle, and a Pimp–On the Trail of the Ultra-Rich Hijacking American Politics*. New York: PublicAffairs.

Vogel, Kenneth P. (2014b). "Koch Brothers Plan $125m Spree." *Politico*, May 9. https://www.politico.com/story/2014/05/koch-brothers-americans-for-prosperity-2014-elections-106520.

———. (2015). "How the Koch Network Rivals the GOP." *Politico*, December 30. http://social.politico.com/story/2015/12/koch-brothers-network-gop-david-charles-217124.

Vogel, Kenneth P., and Lucy McCalmont. (2011). "Top Radio Talkers Sell Endorsements. *Politico*, June 15.

Von Drehle, David. (2013). "Ted Cruz, the Barn Burner." *Time*, December 11.

Weiner, Rachel. (2012). "Sean Hannity: I've 'Evolved' on Immigration." *Washington Post*, November 12. https://www.washingtonpost.com/news/post-politics/wp/2012/11/08/sean-hannity-ive-evolved-on-immigration/?utm_term=.6039dd70c1e0.

Weisman, Jonathan. (2013a). "Push to Require Online Sales Tax Divides the G.O.P." *Wall Street Journal*, April 29.

———. (2013b). "With Health Law Cemented, G.O.P. Debates Next Move." *New York Times*, December 26. http://www.nytimes.com/2013/10/02/us/politics/a-committed-group-of-conservatives-outflanks-the-house-leadership.html?_r=0.

Wheaton, Sarah. (2015). "Rape Controversies Return to Haunt GOP: The Party Still Struggles over Abortion Language." *Politico*, January 22.

Wong, Scott. (2011). "Rubio Courts Establishment GOPers." *Politico*, August 24. Available at https://www.politico.com/story/2011/08/rubio-courts-establishment-gopers-061931.

Zezima, Katie, and Ed O'Keefe. (2015). "Ted Cruz Unveils Immigration Plan—On Marco Rubio's Home Turf." *Washington Post*, November 13. https://www.washingtonpost.com/

news/post-politics/wp/2015/11/13/ted-cruz-unveils-immigration-plan-on-marco-rubios-home-turf/.

Chapter 4

Alberta, Tim. (2013). "Republican Lawmakers Retaliate against Heritage Foundation." *National Journal*, August 28. https://www.nationaljournal.com/s/71633/republican-lawmakers-retaliate-

———. (2015). "Man of the Movement: Inside the Secret Meeting Where Ted Cruz Trounced His Rivals." *National Journal Magazine*, June 6. http://www.nationaljournal.com/magazine/ted-cruz-council-national-policy-20150605.

———. (2019). *American Carnage: On the Front Lines of the Republican Civil War and the Rise of President Trump*. New York: Harper Collins.

———. (2020). "Is This the Last Stand of the 'Law and Order' Republicans?" *Politico Magazine*, June 8. https://www.politico.com/news/magazine/2020/06/08/last-stand-law-and-order-republicans-306333.

Balz, Dan. (2016). "Pushing Racial Boundaries, Trump Draws Rebuke from a Fretful GOP." *Washington* Post, June 4.

Bell, Benjamin. (2013). "Donald Trump: Sen. Ted Cruz 'Perhaps Not' Eligible for White House 'If' Born in Canada." ABC News, August 11. http://abcnews.go.com/blogs/politics/2013/08/donald-trump-sen-ted-cruz-perhaps-not-eligible-for-white-house-if-born-in-canada/.

Bendery, Jennifer. (2013). "'Ted Cruz: 'We Need 100 More Like Jesse Helms' in the Senate." *Huffington Post*, September 14. https://www.huffingtonpost.com/2013/09/11/ted-cruz-jesse-helms_n_3909610.html.

Blackwell, Ken, and Kelly Shackelford. (2015). "Same-Sex Marriage Ruling Starts New Religious Freedom War." Family Research Council, June 26. http://www.frc.org/op-eds/same-sex-marriage-ruling-starts-new-religious-freedom-war.

Braunstein, R., and M. Taylor. (2017). "Is the Tea Party a 'Religious' Movement? Religiosity in the Tea Party versus the Religious Right." *Sociology of Religion* 78(1): 33–59.

Brinton, Lawrence. (2015). "Jeb Bush Is Toast." *National Review*, October 22. https://www.nationalreview.com/2015/10/gop-primary-fundraising-jeb-bush-ted-cruz-donald-trump/.

Byers, Dylan. (2013). "Trump's Circus Is Back in Town." *Politico*, August 14. https://www.politico.com/story/2013/08/donald-trump-presidential-run-095506.

———. (2017). "Maggie Haberman: The New York Times Reporter Trump Can't Quit." *CNN Money*, April 7. https://money.cnn.com/2017/04/07/media/maggie-haberman-trump/index.html.

Calmes, Jackie. (2015a). "As the G.O.P. Base Clamors for Confrontation, Candidates Oblige." *New York Times*, July 27. https://www.nytimes.com/2015/07/28/us/politics/as-the-gop-base-clamors-for-confrontation-candidates-oblige.html.

———. (2015b). "Government Shutdown Could Harm Anti-abortion Cause, Campaigner Says." *New York Times*, September 16.

———. (2015c). "'They Don't Give a Damn about Governing': Conservative Media's Influence on the Republican Party." Cambridge, MA: Shorenstein Center on Media, Politics and Public Policy, July.

Carville, James, and Stan Greenberg. (2014). "Why the GOP Really Hates the Immigration Executive Order." Democracy Corps, November 21. https://democracycorps.com/wp-content/uploads/2014/11/dcor-rpp-immigration-exec-order-11.21.14.pdf.

Chapman, Steve. (2015). "Ted Cruz's New Campaign Slogan: 'Jesus Loves You, but I'm His Favorite.'" Reason, March 26. https://reason.com/archives/2015/03/26/ted-cruz-and-the-born-again-gop.

Cillizza, Chris. (2015). "Boy, Was I Wrong About Donald Trump. Here's Why." Washington Post, August 4. https://www.washingtonpost.com/news/the-fix/wp/2015/08/04/boy-was-i-wrong-about-donald-trump-heres-why/.

Clarke, Andrew J. (2017a). "The House Freedom Caucus: Extreme Faction Influence in the U.S. Congress."Berlin Conference on Polarization, institutional design and the future of representative democracy. www.democratic-anxieties.eu/berlin.

———. (2017b). "Trump Is Tweeting Threats at the Freedom Caucus. Good Luck with That." Washington Post, April 5. https://www.washingtonpost.com/news/monkey-cage/wp/2017/04/05/trump-is-tweeting-threats-at-the-freedom-caucus-good-luck-with-that/.

Collins, Eliza. (2016). "Christian Leaders Balk at Falwell's Trump Endorsement." Politico, January 26. http://social.politico.com/story/2016/01/jerry-falwell-jr-endorses-trump-218238.

Confessore, Nicholas, and Karen Yourish. (2016). "$2 Billion Worth of Free Media for Donald Trump." New York Times, March 15. https://www.nytimes.com/2016/03/16/upshot/measuring-donald-trumps-mammoth-advantage-in-free-media.html.

Cornfield, Michael. (2015). "The 7 Things You Need to Know about How Donald Trump Has Hogged the Presidential Campaign Conversation." Monkey Cage (blog). Washington Post, August 15. https://www.washingtonpost.com/blogs/monkey-cage/wp/2015/08/15/the-7-things-you-need-to-know-about-how-donald-trump-has-hogged-the-presidential-campaign-conversation/.

Cruz, Ted. (2015). A Time for Truth: Reigniting the Promise of America. New York: Broadside Books.

D'Antonio,Michael.(2015).NeverEnough:DonaldTrumpandthePursuitofSuccess.NewYork: Thomas Dunne.

Debonis, Mike. (2015). "Ted Cruz Calls Mitch McConnell a Liar on the Senate Floor." Washington Post, July 24. https://www.washingtonpost.com/news/post-politics/wp/2015/07/24/ted-cruz-calls-mitch-mcconnell-a-liar-on-the-senate-floor/.

Dias, Elizabeth. (2020). "'Christianity Will Have Power." New York Times, August 9. https://www.nytimes.com/2020/08/09/us/evangelicals-trump-christianity.html?action=click&module=Top%20Stories&pgtype=Homepage.

Dickinson, Tim. (2015). "Meet the Right-Wing Rebels Who Overthrew John Boehner." Rolling Stone, October 6. https://www.rollingstone.com/politics/politics-news/meet-the-right-wing-rebels-who-overthrew-john-boehner-73320/.

Dowd, Maureen. (2017). "Cruella De Trump." New York Times, July 1. https://www.nytimes.com/2017/07/01/opinion/sunday/donald-trump-cruelty-dowd.html.

Draper, Robert. (2016a). "Mr. Trump's Wild Ride." New York Times, May 18. http://www.nytimes.com/2016/05/22/magazine/donald-trump-primary-win.html.

———. (2016b). "National Revolt: How Donald Trump Set Off a Civil War within the Right-Wing Media." New York Times, October 2.

———. (2016c). "Ted Cruz's Evangelical Gamble." New York Times Magazine, January 31. https://www.nytimes.com/2016/01/31/magazine/ted-cruzs-evangelical-gamble.html.

Dubose, Lou, and Hannah Harper. (2015). "Ted Cruz's Dad Has a Very Sketchy Resume: Rafael Cruz's Credentials Are Exaggerated, at Best." *Salon*, October 19. https://www.salon.com/abtest3/2015/10/19/ted_cruzs_dad_has_a_very_sketchy_resume_rafael_cruzs_credentials_are_exaggerated_at_best/.

Edsall, Thomas B. (2015a). "Losing the Tea Party Baggage." *New York Times*, January 6. http://www.nytimes.com/2015/01/07/opinion/cory-gardner-losing-the-tea-party-baggage.html.

———. (2015b). "Will Infighting Help the Republicans in 2016?" *Opinionator* (blog). *New York Times*, April 8.

———. (2016). "What About Ted Cruz?" *New York Times*, February 9.

Everett, Burgess. (2015a). "Cruz Sternly Rebuked by GOP." *Politico*, September 29.

———. (2015b). "How McConnell Outfoxed Ted Cruz." *Politico*, September 29.

Fahey, Mark, and Nicholas Wells. (2015). "Ted Cruz Sizzles up 'Machine-Gun Bacon.'" CNBC, August 4. http://www.cnbc.com/2015/08/04/ted-cruz-sizzles-up-machine-gun-bacon.html.

Falcone, Michael. (2011). "Mulling a White House Run, Trump Releases His Birth Certificate." ABC News, March 28. https://abcnews.go.com/Politics/donald-trump-embraces-birther/story?id=13240431.

———. (2013). "Ted Cruz's Father: 'Obamacare Is Going to Destroy the Elderly.'" ABC News, August 11.

Federal News Service. (2016). "Transcript of Republican Debate in Miami." *New York Times*, March 11. https://www.nytimes.com/2016/03/11/us/politics/transcript-of-the-republican-presidential-debate-in-florida.html.

Feldman, Josh. (2013). "Glenn Beck Claims Mitch McConnell Called Tea Party Senators 'Traitors.'" *Mediaite*, October 8. https://www.mediaite.com/online/glenn-beck-claims-mitch-mcconnell-called-tea-party-senators-traitors/.

Fisher, Marc. (2015). "The GOP's Identity-Politics Crisis: Holding Race-Card Aces but Loath to Play Them." *Washington Post*, November 29. https://www.washingtonpost.com/politics/the-gops-identity-politics-crisis-a-diverse-field-but-an-aversion-to-tout-it/2015/11/29/48c6f040-8fad-11e5-ae1f-af46b7df8483_story.html.

Fleming, Matthew, and Matt Fuller. (2015). "The Return of 'Speaker Cruz.'" *Congressional Quarterly*, June 23.

Fox News (2013). "Trump: Christie Will Run for President in 2016, Should Avoid Romney's Disastrous Mistakes ('On the Air' Transcript)." Fox News, August 20.

Freelander, David. (2015). "A 1980s New York City Battle Explains Donald Trump's Candidacy." Bloomberg, September 29.

French, Lauren. (2015). "9 Republicans Launch House Freedom Caucus." *Politico*, January 26. https://www.politico.com/story/2015/01/house-freedom-caucus-conservative-legislation-114593.html.

Friedell, Deborah. (2015). "Tycooniest." *London Review of Books*, October 22.

Gabriel, Trip. (2016). "Our Man in Iowa: Polls Point to Donald Trump, as Do Odd Indicators." *New York Times*, January 31.

Gardner, Amy. (2012). "FreedomWorks Tea Party Group Nearly Falls Apart in Fight between Old and New Guard." *Washington Post*, December 25. https://www.washingtonpost.com/politics/freedomworks-tea-party-group-nearly-falls-apart-in-fight-between-old-and-new-guard/2012/12/25/dd095b68-4545-11e2-8061-253bccfc7532_story.html.

Gass, Nick. (2015). "Ted Cruz Dodges Megyn Kelly's Questions on Deportation." *Politico*, August 26. http://www.politico.com/story/2015/08/megyn-kelly-ted-cruz-immigration-question-121756.html.

Gehrke, Joel. (2014). "Ted Cruz Tries, and Fails, to Win over the WSJ." *National Review Online*, December 3. https://www.nationalreview.com/2014/12/ted-cruz-tries-and-fails-win-over-wsj-joel-gehrke/.

Gerson, Michael. (2015). "The True Scandal of the GOP Senators' Letter to Iran." *Washington Post*, March 12. https://www.washingtonpost.com/opinions/a-half-baked-missive-from-the-gop/2015/03/12/ccf10b8e-c835-11e4-b2a1-bed1aaea2816_story.html.

Glueck, Katie. (2015a). "Ted Cruz Supersizes His Campaign." *Politico*, December 20. http://www.politico.com/story/2015/12/ted-cruz-southern-spectacle-campaign-217018.

———. (2015b). "Ted Cruz's Angry Allies." *Politico*, July 15. http://www.politico.com/story/2015/07/ted-cruzs-angry-allies-119827.html.

———. (2015c). "Tea Party Reeling." *Politico*, January 19. http://www.politico.com/story/2015/01/tea-party-reeling-114375.html.

———. (2016). "Why Cruz Went to That Matzo Bakery." *Politico*, April 7.

Gold, Matea, and Anu Narayanswamy. (2016). "Super PACs Have Spent More Than $215 Million on the Presidential Race. Guess How Much against Trump?" *Wall Street Journal*, February 20.

Goldberg, Michelle. (2006). *Kingdom Coming: The Rise of Christian Nationalism*. New York: W.W. Norton & Co.

Gosselin, Peter. (2015). "Donald Trump Has Republican 'Reformicons' Worried." *Bloomberg Politics*, August 19.

Graham, Franklin. (2014). "Putin's Olympic Controversy." *Decision Magazine*, February 28. https://billygraham.org/decision-magazine/march-2014/putins-olympic-controversy/.

———. (2015). "From Franklin Graham: The Real Story of Christmas." *Decision Magazine*, November 25. https://billygraham.org/decision-magazine/december-2015/from-franklin-graham-the-real-story-of-christmas/.

Green, Joshua. (2017). *Devil's Bargain: Steve Bannon, Donald Trump, and the Storming of the Presidency*. London: Penguin Press.

Greenberg, Stanley B., and James Carville. (2014). "Inside the GOP: Report on the Republican Party Project." Democracy Corps, June 12.

Greenblatt, Alan. (2015). "The Freedom Caucus' Unprecedented Insurgency." *Politico*, October 15. http://www.politico.com/magazine/story/2015/10/the-freedom-caucus-historic-rebellion-213256.

Guth, James L., John C. Green, Corwin E Smidt, Lyman A. Kellstedt, et al. (1997). *The Bully Pulpit: The Politics of Protestant Clergy*. Lawrence, Kan.: University Press of Kansas.

Guth, James L. (2005). "Southern Baptist Clergy, the Christian Right, and Political Activism in the South." In *Politics and Religion in the White South*, ed. Glenn Feldman, Lexington: University Press of Kentucky. 187–214.

Guth, James L. (2021). "Protestant Clergy and Christian Nationalism" *Perspectives in Religious Studies* (forthcoming) 47.

Haberman, Maggie. (2011). "Giuliani: Time to Bury the Birthers." *Politico*, March 18. https://www.politico.com/story/2011/03/giuliani-time-to-bury-the-birthers-051575.

———. (2014). "Ted Cruz Is Billed as a Passover Vacation Attraction." *Politico*, December 29. http://www.politico.com/story/2014/12/ted-cruz-is-billed-as-a-passover-vacation-attraction-113870.html.

———. (2016). "Donald Trump's More Accepting Views on Gay Issues Set Him Apart in G.O.P." *New York Times*, April 22.

Halperin, Mark, and John Heilemann. (2013). *Double Down: Game Change 2012*. New York: Penguin Press.

Hart Research Associates and Public Opinion Strategies. (2011). "NBC News/Wall Street Journal Survey." April 11.

———. (2015). "NBC News/Wall Street Journal Survey." July.

———. (2016). "NBC News/Wall Street Journal Survey." February 16.

Harwood, John. (2015). "Angry Bent of Party Let Trump Rise." *New York Times*, July 31.

Hayes, Stephen F. (2015). "Trump GOP Candidacy Blows Up: Refuses to Rule Out Third Party Bid." *Weekly Standard*, July 18.

Hernandez, Raymond. (2011). "If a Seat Is Lost, Blame G.O.P. Medicare Plan, Trump Says." *New York Times*, May 11. http://thecaucus.blogs.nytimes.com/2011/05/11/if-a-seat-is-lost-blame-g-o-p-medicare-plan-trump-says/.

Hinch, Jim. (2014). "Evangelicals Are Changing Their Minds on Gay Marriage." *Politico*, July 7. http://www.politico.com/magazine/story/2014/07/evangelicals-gay-marriage-108608_full.html#.U8QKJo1dXT0.

Hohmann, James. (2015a). "The Daily 202: Marco Rubio Is Playing to Win the Sheldon Adelson Primary." *Washington Post*, June 25.

———. (2015b). "The Daily 202: Ted Cruz's Dad Embraces an Attack Dog Role." *Washington Post*, August 31. https://www.washingtonpost.com/news/powerpost/wp/2015/08/03/the-daily-202-takeaways-from-the-koch-donor-summit/.

———. (2016). "Will South Carolina Republicans Buy That Marco Rubio Is Just as Conservative as Ted Cruz?" *Washington Post*, February 19. https://www.washingtonpost.com/news/powerpost/paloma/daily-202/2016/02/19/daily-202-will-south-carolina-republicans-buy-that-marco-rubio-is-just-as-conservative-as-ted-cruz/56c694fc981b92a22d2708c7/?utm_term=.19a00a2432d5.

Hounshell, Blake. (2016). "Evangelical Leader Blasts Falwell for Hosting Trump." *Politico*, January 18.

Huffington Post. (2011). "Donald Trump Gets Fox News Segment." *Huffington Post*, April 1.

Hulse, Carl, and Johnathan Martin. (2014). "Retreat on Debt Fight Seen as G.O.P. Campaign Salvo." *New York Times*, February 17.

Hunt, Kasie. (2013). "In Iowa, Donald Trump Warns Republicans About Hillary, Immigration." NBC News, August 11.

Jacobs, Jennifer, and Jason Noble. (2013). "Attendees See Preview of 2016." *Des Moines Register*, August 11.

Johnson, Eliana. (2015). "The Establishment Thinks the Unthinkable: Trump Could Win the Nomination." *National Review*, October 19. https://www.nationalreview.com/2015/10/gop-establishment-thinks-trump-could-win/.

Jones, Robert P., Daniel Cox, and Juhem Navarro-Rivera. (2014). "A Shifting Landscape: A Decade of Change in American Attitudes about Same-Sex Marriage and LGBT Issues." Washington, DC: Public Religion Research Institute, February 26.

Knowles, David. (2015). "Donald Trump Says He Wants to Raise Taxes on Himself." *Bloomberg Politics*, August 27.

Kranish, Michael, and Marc Fisher. (2016). *Trump Revealed: An American Journey of Ambition, Ego, Money, and Power.* New York: Scribner.

Kruse, Michael (2015). How Ted Cruz Became Ted Cruz. *Politico Magazine,* January 5.

———. (2016). "'He Brutalized for You': How Joseph McCarthy Henchman Roy Cohn Became Donald Trump's Mentor." *Politico,* April 8. http://www.politico.com/magazine/story/2016/04/donald-trump-roy-cohn-mentor-joseph-mccarthy-213799.

Lambrecht, Bill. (2016). "Supreme Court Arguments Key to Cruz's Rise." *Houston Chronicle,* January 24.

Lavender, Paige. (2013). "Tea Party Group Withdraws Endorsement of Mitch McConnell." *Huffington Post,* October 9. https://www.huffpost.com/entry/tea-party-mitch-mcconnell_n_4071868.

Lewak, Doree. (2015). "At $11,000 a Head, This Is the Poshest Passover in the World." *New York Post,* April 2.

Lithwick, Dahlia. (2013). "Book Review: *My Beloved World* by Sonia Sotomayor." *Washington Post,* January 11. https://www.washingtonpost.com/opinions/book-review-my-beloved-world-by-sonia-sotomayor/2013/01/11/7a93dcd6-55cd-11e2-bf3e-76c0a789346f_story.html.

Lowry, Rich. (2015). "It's the Abortion, Stupid." *Politico,* October 1.

Lowry, Rich, and Ramesh Ponnuru. (2015). "Trump Wrongs the Right." *National Review,* October 19. http://www.nationalreview.com/article/425010/trump-wrongs-right-rich-lowry-ramesh-ponnuru.

Malanga, Steven. (2016). "My Pen Pal, Donald Trump." *City Journal,* May 12. http://www.city-journal.org/html/my-pen-pal-donald-trump-14442.html.

Malone, Clare. (2016). "The End of a Republican Party." FiveThirtyEight, July 18. http://fivethirtyeight.com/features/the-end-of-a-republican-party/.

Martin, Jonathan. (2015a). "Parties Trade Places in Culture Wars in Skirmish over Rights Measures." *New York Times,* April 4.

———. (2015b). "Republicans Fear Donald Trump Is Hardening Party's Tone on Race." *New York Times,* September 8.

Martin, Jonathan, and Matt Flegenheimer. (2016). "Cruz Is Naming Friends, but G.O.P. Brass Is Silent." *New York Times,* March 28.

Martin, Jonathan, and Maggie Haberman. (2015). Hand-Wringing in G.O.P. after Donald Trump's Remarks on Megyn Kelly. *New York Times,* August 8. http://www.nytimes.com/2016/03/28/us/politics/ted-cruz-names-friends-but-silence-from-gop-brass-deafens.html.

Martosko, David. (2015). "Trump Trademarked His Slogan 'Make America Great Again'—in 2012!" *Daily Mail,* May 15. http://www.dailymail.co.uk/news/article-3077773/Trump-trademarked-slogan-Make-America-Great-just-DAYS-2012-election-says-Ted-Cruz-agreed-not-use-Scott-Walker-booms-TWICE-speech.html.

Mider, Zachary. (2015). "The Koch Brothers Have an Immigration Problem." *Bloomberg Politics,* August 27. http://www.bloomberg.com/politics/articles/2015-08-27/the-koch-brothers-have-an-immigration-problem.

Milbank, Dana. (2015a). "Donald Trump Is the Monster the GOP Created." *Washington Post,* July 8. https://www.washingtonpost.com/opinions/donald-trump-is-the-monster-the-gop-created/2015/07/08/5b0bb834-259b-11e5-aae2-6c4f59b050aa_story.html.

———. (2015b). "Donald Trump's Festival of Narcissism." *Washington Post,* June 16. https://www.washingtonpost.com/opinions/donald-trumps-festival-of-narcissism/2015/06/16/fd006c28-1459-11e5-9ddc-e3353542100c_story.html?utm_term=.04e3f1ebf7df.

New York Times. (2016). "Ted Cruz on the Issues." *New York Times*, April 18. https://www. nytimes.com/interactive/2016/us/elections/ted-cruz-on-the-issues.html.

Newkirk, Margaret, and John Arit. (2015). "Donald Trump Bests Jeb Bush in New Hampshire Town Hall Duel." *Bloomberg Politics*, August 27.

Norton, Michael I., and Samuel R. Sommers. (2011). "Whites See Racism as a Zero-Sum Game That They Are Now Losing." *Perspectives on Psychological Science* 6(3): 215–18.

O'Brien, Michael. (2011). "Trump Blames Ryan Budget for GOP Woes in NY Special Election." *The Hill*, April 11. http://thehill.com/blogs/blog-briefing-room/news/ 160533-trump-blames-ryan-budget-for-gop-woes-in-ny-special-election.

O'Harrow, Robert, Jr., and Shawn Boburg. (2016). "The Man Who Showed Donald Trump How to Exploit Power and Instill Fear." *Washington Post*, June 17. https:// www.washingtonpost.com/investigations/former-mccarthy-aide-showed-trump-how-to-exploit-power-and-draw-attention/2016/06/16/e9f44f20-2bf3-11e6-9b37-42985f6a265c_story.html.

O'Connor, Patrick. (2013). "Kentucky Tea Party Groups Deride McConnell." *Wall Street Journal*, July 22. https://blogs.wsj.com/washwire/2013/07/22/kentucky-tea-party-groups-deride-mcconnell/.

Ornstein, Norm. (2015a). "Maybe This Time Really Is Different." *Atlantic*, August 21. http://www.theatlantic.com/politics/archive/2015/08/maybe-this-time-really-is-different/401900/.

———. (2015b). "The Republican Road Block Ahead." *Atlantic*, August 5. http://www. theatlantic.com/politics/archive/2015/08/why-the-gop-needs-to-brace-for-the-road-block-ahead/400499/.

Palmer, Anna, and John Bresnahan. (2015). "McConnell Moves Ahead with Vote to Defund Planned Parenthood." *Politico*, July 28.

Parker, Ashley, and Steve Eder. (2016). "Inside the Six Weeks Donald Trump Was a Nonstop 'Birther.'" *New York Times*, July 2.

Peters, Jeremy W. (2011). "Trump to Moderate Republican Debate." *New York Times*, December 2.

Politico. (2012). "George Will: Donald Trump 'Bloviating Ignoramus.'" *Politico*, May 29. https://www.politico.com/video/2012/05/george-will-donald-trump-bloviating-ignoramus-012196.

Posner, Sarah. (2018). "The Secret History of Bathroom Bills." *Investigative Fund*, January 22. https://www.theinvestigativefund.org/investigation/2018/01/22/secret-history-bathroom-bills/

Reicher, Stephen D., and S. Alexander Haslam. (2017a). "Donald Trump and the Politics of Hope: A Social Identity Analysis of the Leader's Appeal." *Scientific American Mind*, March/April, 42–50.

———. (2017b). "The Politics of Hope: Donald Trump as an Entrepreneur of Identity." In *Why Irrational Politics Appeals: Understanding the Allure of Trump*, edited by Mari Fitzduff, 25–40. Santa Barbara, CA: Praeger.

Robertson, Campbell, and Richard Fausset. (2015). "Straddling Old and New, a South Where 'a Flag Is Not Worth a Job.'" *New York Times*, June 28.

Rove, Karl. (2015). "Government Shutdown as Self-Promotion." *Wall Street Journal*, September 24.

Sanger, David E. (2015). "G.O.P. Is Vague on Using Power Abroad." *New York Times*, August 16. http://www.nytimes.com/2015/08/16/us/politics/hawkish-gop-offers-no-plan-for-us-action.html.

Scalzi, John. (2015). "Retweet of NYT Headline." *Twitter*, September 7.

Schieffer, Theodore, and Noah Gray. (2015). "30,000 Turn Out for Donald Trump's Alabama Pep Rally." CNN, August 21.

Schlafly, Phyllis. (2015a). "Donald Drives the Debate." *Town Hall*, August 18. https://townhall.com/columnists/phyllisschlafly/2015/08/18/donald-drives-the-debate-n2039964.

———. (2015a). "Donald Trump Channels Pat McCarran." *Town Hall*, December 15. https://townhall.com/columnists/phyllisschlafly/2015/12/15/donald-trump-channels-pat-mccarran-n2093674.

Schreckinger, Ben. (2015). "Meet the Man Who Makes Donald Trump Go Viral." *Politico*, October 1. http://www.politico.com/story/2015/09/trumps-social-media-guy-214309.

———. (2016). "Trump Calls for Christian Unity at Liberty U." *Politico*, January 18.

Sherman, Gabriel. (2016). "Inside Operation Trump, the Most Unorthodox Campaign in Political History." *New York*, April 4. http://nymag.com/daily/intelligencer/2016/04/inside-the-donald-trump-presidential-campaign.html.

Singer, Mark. (1997). "Trump Solo: No Wonder He's Got No Time for Marla." *New Yorker*, May 19, 56–71.

Sipes, Chris. (2015). "Cruz: Can He Win." *Keep the Promise*, July 18.

Skelley, Geoffrey. (2019). "How Early Primary Polls Foreshadowed Surprises Like Obama's Rise and Trump's Win." FiveThirtyEight, April 9. https://fivethirtyeight.com/features/what-more-than-40-years-of-early-primary-polls-tell-us-about-2020-part-2/.

Slater, Wayne. (2014). "Christian Conservatives Look for Candidate to Rally Around." *Dallas Morning News*, August 11. http://www.dallasnews.com/opinion/editorials/20160907-we-recommend-hillary-clinton-for-president.ece.

Stein, Sam. (2016). "Sad! These Three Campaign Gurus for Jeb Bush, Ted Cruz and Marco Rubio Have Had Some Time to Reflect on Their Loss to the Donald. And Do They Ever Have Stories to Tell." *Huffington Post Highline*, June 14. https://highline.huffingtonpost.com/articles/en/sad/.

Stewart, Katherine. (2015). "Ted Cruz and the Anti-Gay Pastor." *New York Times*, November 16. http://www.nytimes.com/2015/11/16/opinion/campaign-stops/ted-cruz-and-the-anti-gay-pastor.html.

Stewart, Katherine. (2020). "The Religious Right's Hostility to Science Is Crippling Our Coronavirus Response." *The New York Times*, March 27, https://www.nytimes.com/2020/03/27/opinion/coronavirus-trump-evangelicals.html?action=click&module=RelatedLinks&pgtype=Article.

Stokols, Eli. (2015). "Jeb Bush Defends Medicare 'Phase Out' Comment." *Politico*, July 23.

Tesler, Michael. (2015). "How Anti-Immigrant Attitudes Are Fueling Support for Donald Trump." *Monkey Cage* (blog). *Washington Post*, November 24. https://www.washingtonpost.com/news/monkey-cage/wp/2015/11/24/how-anti-immigrant-attitudes-are-fueling-support-for-donald-trump/.

Tesler, Michael, and John Sides. (2016). "How Political Science Helps Explain the Rise of Trump: The Role of White Identity and Grievances." *Washington Post*, March 3. https://www.washingtonpost.com/news/monkey-cage/wp/2016/03/03/how-political-science-helps-explain-the-rise-of-trump-the-role-of-white-identity-and-grievances/.

Tilove, Jonathan. (2013). "Thus Spake Cruz." *Austin American-Statesman*, September 25.

———. (2015). "Will God Punish America for Rejecting Ted Cruz, and If Not, What's Up with That?" *Austin American-Statesman*, May 9. http://politics.blog.mystatesman.

com/2016/05/09/will-god-punish-america-for-rejecting-ted-cruz-and-if-not-whats-up-with-that/.

———. (2016a). "Cruz, Trump Vie for Top Outsider." *Austin American-Statesman*, March 13.

———. (2016b). "The Passion of the Cruz. Or How Ted Overcame His Martyr Complex." *Austin American-Statesman*, September 26. http://politics.blog.mystatesman.com/2016/09/26/the-passion-of-the-cruz/.

———. (2018). "Trump-West 2020: Why Trump Will Dump Draggin' Energy Mike for Dragon Energy Kanye on the Ticket." *Austin American-Statesman*, May 7. http://politics.blog.mystatesman.com/2018/05/07/trump-west-2020-why-trump-will-dump-draggin-energy-mike-for-dragon-energy-kanye-on-the-ticket/.

Toobin, Jeffrey. (2008). "The Dirty Trickster: Campaign Tips from the Man Who Has Done It All." *New Yorker*, June 2, 54–63.

———. (2014). "The Absolutist: Ted Cruz Is an Unyielding Debater—and the Far Right's Most Formidable Advocate." *New Yorker*, June 30, 34–45.

Trent, Amy. (2012). "Trump Talks Tough at Liberty University." *Lynchburg News Advance*, September 24. https://www.newsadvance.com/news/local/trump-talks-tough-at-liberty-university/article_43b796a0-4416-593d-bfc2-a942732c3722.html.

Trujillo, Mario. (2014). "Cruz Introduces 'Stop Amnesty' Bill." *The Hill*, July 14. https://thehill.com/blogs/floor-action/212600-cruz-introduces-proposal-to-defund-immigration-program.

Tumulty, Karen. (2017). "Priebus Faces Daunting Task Bringing Order to White House That Will Feed Off Chaos." *Washington Post*, January 1. https://www.washingtonpost.com/politics/priebus-faces-daunting-task-bringing-order-to-white-house-that-will-feed-off-chaos/2017/01/01/5a2ba9e4-cd31-11e6-a87f-b917067331bb_story.html.

Valentino, Nicholas A., Fabian G. Neuner, and L. Matthew Vandenbroek. (2018). "The Changing Norms of Racial Political Rhetoric and the End of Racial Priming." *Journal of Politics* 80(3): 757–71.

Vogel, Kenneth P. (2014a). *Big Money: 2.5 Billion Dollars, One Suspicious Vehicle, and a Pimp–On the Trail of the Ultra-Rich Hijacking American Politics*. New York: PublicAffairs.

———. (2014b). "Social Conservatives' Money Plans." *Politico*, January 2. https://www.politico.com/story/2014/01/social-conservatives-fundraising-101666.

———. (2015). "How the Koch Network Rivals the GOP." *Politico*, December 30. http://social.politico.com/story/2015/12/koch-brothers-network-gop-david-charles-217124.

Von Drehle, David. (2013). "Ted Cruz, the Barn Burner." *Time*, December 11.

Washington Post. (2015). "Donald Trump Announces a Presidential Bid." *Washington Post*, June 16. https://www.washingtonpost.com/news/post-politics/wp/2015/06/16/full-text-donald-trump-announces-a-presidential-bid/.

Wren, Adam. (2015). "The Week Mike Pence's 2016 Dreams Crumbled." *Politico Magazine*, April 1. https://www.politico.com/magazine/story/2015/04/mike-pence-indiana-2016-116569.

Zezima, Katie, and Matea Gold. (2015). "Cruz's Quiet Fundraising Strength: A Network of Wealthy Donors." *Washington Post*, October 27.

Chapter 5

Abcarian, Robin. (2015). "Kevin McCarthy's Radical Honesty: 'Benghazi' Was about Hurting Hillary." *Los Angeles Times*, October 2. https://www.google.com/url?sa=t &rct=j&q=&esrc=s&source=web&cd=3&cad=rja&uact=8&ved=0ahUKEwi4rKS D9v7YAhUM5mMKHcImCAQQFgg1MAI&url=http%3A%2F%2Fwww.latimes. com%2Flocal%2Fabcarian%2Fla-me-ra-kevin-mccarthy-radical-honesty-20151001-column.html&usg=AOvVaw2A79KNNeFwWLkRJlqF1hQ6.

Adelson, Sheldon. (2016). "Sheldon Adelson: I Endorse Donald Trump for President." *Washington Post*, May 13. https://www.washingtonpost.com/opinions/sheldon-adelson-i-endorse-donald-trump-for-president/2016/05/12/ea89d7f0-17a0-11e6-aa55-670cabef46e0_story.html.

Alberta, Tim. (2017). "John Boehner Unchained." *Politico Magazine*, November/ December. http://politi.co/2zhDZXN.

———. (2018). "The Tragedy of Paul Ryan." *Politico Magazine*, April 12. Available at https://politi.co/2HdjHlA.

———. (2019). *American Carnage: On the Front Lines of the Republican Civil War and the Rise of President Trump*. New York: Harper Collins.

Allen, Bob. (2016). "Advocates Fault New SBC President's Record on Child Sex Abuse." *Baptist News Global*, June 17. https://baptistnews.com/article/advocates-fault-sbc-presidents-record-on-child-sex-abuse/#.X01LlC05RGw.

Allen, Jonathan, and Amie Parnes. (2017). *Shattered: Inside Hillary Clinton's Doomed Campaign*. New York: Crown.

Allison, Bill, Michael Keller, and Blacki Migliozzi. (2016). "The Millions Trump's Businesses Made from His Campaign." Bloomberg, December 9. https://www. bloomberg.com/graphics/2016-trump-campaign-millions/.

Andrews, Wilson. (2015). "Donations to the Clinton Foundation, and a Russian Uranium Takeover." *New York Times*, April 22. https://www.nytimes.com/in-teractive/2015/04/23/us/clinton-foundation-donations-uranium-investors. html?searchResultPosition=3.

Arizona Republic. (2016). "Endorsement: Hillary Clinton Is the Only Choice to Move America Ahead." *Arizona Republic*, September 27. http://www.azcentral.com/story/ opinion/editorial/2016/09/27/hillary-clinton-endorsement/91198668/.

Bailey, Sarah Pulliam. (2016). "The Deep Disgust for Hillary Clinton That Drives So Many Evangelicals to Support Trump." *Washington Post*, October 9. https://www. washingtonpost.com/news/acts-of-faith/wp/2016/10/09/the-deep-disgust-for-hillary-clinton-that-drives-so-many-evangelicals-to-support-trump/.

Ballhaus, Rebecca, and Brady Mullins. (2016). "No Fortune 100 CEOs Back Republican Donald Trump." *Wall Street Journal*, September 24.

Balz, Dan, and Philip Rucker. (2016). "How Donald Trump Won: The Insiders Tell Their Story." *Washington Post*, November 9. https://www.washingtonpost.com/classic-apps/ how-donald-trump-won-the-insiders-tell-their-story/2016/11/09/c2e5558c-a641-11e6-8fc0-7be8f848c492_story.html.

Barbour, Haley, and Eric Westervelt. (2016). "GOP Grapples with a Possible Trump Nomination." NPR, *All Things Considered*, August 10. http://www.npr.org/2016/02/28/ 468483873/gop-grapples-with-a-possible-trump-nomination.

Barrett, Wayne. (2015). "Behind the Seventies-Era Deals That Made Donald Trump." *Village Voice*, July 20. https://www.villagevoice.com/2015/07/20/behind-the-seventies-era-deals-that-made-donald-trump/.

Bazelon, Emily. (2017). "Department of Justification." *New York Times*, February 28. https://www.nytimes.com/2017/02/28/magazine/jeff-sessions-stephen-bannon-justice-department.html.

Becker, Jo, and Mike McIntire. (2015). "Cash Flowed to Clinton Foundation Amid Russian Uranium Deal." *New York Times*, April 23. https://www.nytimes.com/2015/04/24/us/cash-flowed-to-clinton-foundation-as-russians-pressed-for-control-of-uranium-company.html.

Begley, Sarah. (2016). "Arnold Schwarzenegger Calls Judge in Trump U Case an 'American Hero.'" *Time*, June 6.

Brennan Center Staff. (2016). "Voting Restrictions in Place for First Time in Presidential Election in 2016." New York: Brennan Center for Justice, April 4.

Brenner, Marie. (1990). "After the Gold Rush." *Vanity Fair*, September 1.

Brownstein, Ronald. (2016). "Republicans Need to Get Ready for the Trump Aftershock." *Atlantic*, August 11. http://www.theatlantic.com/politics/archive/2016/08/what-will-the-trump-aftershock-look-like/495359/.

———. (2019). "Will Trump's Racist Attacks Help Him? Ask Blue-Collar White Women." *Atlantic*, July 25. https://www.theatlantic.com/politics/archive/2019/07/trumps-go-back-attacks-white-working-class-women/594805/.

Burgis, Tom. (2016). "Dirty Money: Trump and the Kazakh Connection." *Financial Times*, October 19. https://www.ft.com/content/33285dfa-9231-11e6-8df8-d3778b55a923.

Burns, Alexander. (2016). "Donald Trump Seeks Republican Unity but Finds Rejection." *New York Times*, May 6. http://www.nytimes.com/2016/05/07/us/politics/donald-trump-seeks-republican-unity-but-finds-rejection.html.

Burns, Alexander, and Maggie Haberman. (2016a). "Donald Trump Hints He May Fund Race Himself." *New York Times*, June 21. http://www.nytimes.com/2016/06/22/politics/donald-trump-fund-raising-republicans.html.

———. (2016b). "Inside the Failing Mission to Save Donald Trump from Himself." *New York Times*, August 13.

Cheney, Kyle, and Sarah Wheaton. (2016). The Most Revealing Clinton Campaign Emails in WikiLeaks Release. *Politico*, October 7. http://politi.co/2dBOoRl.

Chozick, Amy. (2016). "Hillary Clinton Targets Republicans Turned Off by Donald Trump." *New York Times*, May 6. http://www.nytimes.com/2016/05/07/us/politics/hillary-clinton-republican-party.html.

Cillizza, Chris. (2017). "Paul Ryan's Latest Line in the Sand on Trump? Firing Mueller." CNN, November 6. https://www.cnn.com/2017/11/06/politics/ryan-trump-mueller/index.html.

Cirilli, Kevin, Michael C. Bender, and Jennifer Jacobs. (2016). "Trump Orders Surrogates to Intensify Criticism of Judge and Journalists." Bloomberg, June 12.

Cohn, Nate. (2016a). "There Are More White Voters Than People Think. That's Good News for Trump." *New York Times*, June 9.

———. (2016b). "Why the Election Is Close, and What Trump and Obama Have in Common." *New York Times*, November 6.

Colpaert, Pieter. (2016). "Trump Continues Epic Alienation of Women, Calls for Punishment for Abortions." *New York Times*, March 30.

Confessore, Nicholas. (2016). "How the G.O.P. Elite Lost Its Voters to Donald Trump." *New York Times*, March 28.

Coppins, McKay. (2018). "God's Plan for Mike Pence." *Atlantic*, January/February. https://www.theatlantic.com/magazine/archive/2018/01/gods-plan-for-mike-pence/546569/

Costa, Robert, Jose A. Delreal, and Jenna Johnson. (2016). "Trump Shakes Up Campaign, Demotes Top Adviser." *Washington Post*, August 17. https://www.washingtonpost.com/news/post-politics/wp/2016/08/17/trump-reshuffles-staff-in-his-own-image/.

Date, S. V. (2016). "Donald Trump Jacked Up His Campaign's Trump Tower Rent Once Somebody Else Was Paying It." *Huffington Post*, August 22. http://www.huffingtonpost.com/entry/trump-campaign-rent_us_57bba424e4b03d51368a82b9.

Draper, Robert. (2016a). "How Donald Trump Picked His Running Mate." *New York Times*, July 20. https://www.nytimes.com/2016/07/20/magazine/how-donald-trump-picked-his-running-mate.html.

———. (2016b). "Mr. Trump's Wild Ride." *New York Times*, May 18. http://www.nytimes.com/2016/05/22/magazine/donald-trump-primary-win.html

Drew, Elizabth. (2016). "Trump: The Haunting Question." *New York Review of Books*, June 9. http://www.nybooks.com/daily/2016/06/09/trump-hidden-psychology-election-crisis/.

Edsall, Thomas B. (2015a). "Trump, Obama and the Assault on Political Correctness." *New York Times*, December 23.

———. (2015b). "What Donald Trump Understands about Republicans." *New York Times*, September 2.

Enten, Harry. (2016). "It's Not All About Clinton—the Midwest Was Getting Redder before 2016." FiveThirtyEight, December 9. Available at https://fivethirtyeight.com/features/its-not-all-about-clinton-the-midwest-was-getting-redder-before-2016/.

Entous, Adam. (2017). "House Majority Leader to Colleagues in 2016: 'I Think Putin Pays' Trump." *Washington Post*, May 17. https://www.washingtonpost.com/world/national-security/house-majority-leader-to-colleagues-in-2016-i-think-putin-pays-trump/2017/05/17/515f6f8a-3aff-11e7-8854-21f359183e8c_story.html.

Faris, Robert, Hal Roberts, Bruce Etling, Nikki Bourassa, et al. (2017). "Partisanship, Propaganda, and Disinformation: Online Media and the 2016 U.S. Presidential Election." Cambridge, MA: Berkman Klein Center, August 16.

Fineman, Howard. (2016). "Donald Trump's Top Adviser: 'This Is Not a Hard Race.'" *Huffington Post*, May 25.

Fisher, Marc. (2015). "Seeking America's 'Lost' Greatness and Finding Trump Most Appealing." *Washington Post*, November 1.

Garrett, Major. (2016). "Tweet: Trump on Free Trade." Twitter, May 2. https://twitter.com/majorcbs/status/727291460337410049?lang=en.

Gerson, Michael. (2016). "Buying into Trump's Fake Pivot Would Ruin the GOP." *Washington Post*, April 25. https://www.washingtonpost.com/opinions/buying-into-trumps-fake-pivot-would-ruin-the-gop/2016/04/25/bba290ce-0b13-11e6-a6b6-2e6de3695b0e_story.html.

Glasser, Susan B. (2019). "The Secretary of Trump: How Mike Pompeo Became a Heartland Evangelical—and the President's Most Loyal Soldier." *New Yorker*, August 26, 50–59.

Gold, Matea. (2016). "Koch Network Seeks to Defuse Donor Frustration over Trump Rebuff." *Washington Post*, August 1. https://www.washingtonpost.com/politics/

koch-network-seeks-to-defuse-donor-frustration-over-trump-rebuff/2016/08/01/
7247b8c2-579a-11e6-831d-0324760ca856_story.html.

Goldmacher, Shane. (2016a). "Inside the GOP's Shadow Convention." *Politico*, July 19.
https://www.politico.com/magazine/story/2016/07/rnc-2016-gop-republican-party-
leaders-future-donald-trump-214065.

———. (2016b). "Trump Shatters the Republican Party." *Politico*, February 24.

Green, Joshua. (2016). "How to Get Trump Elected When He's Wrecking Everything
You Built." Bloomberg, May 26. Available at http://www.bloomberg.com/features/
2016-reince-priebus/

———. (2017). *Devil's Bargain: Steve Bannon, Donald Trump, and the Storming of the
Presidency*. New York: Penguin Press.

Green, Joshua, and Sasha Issenberg. (2016). "Inside the Trump Bunker, with Days to Go."
Bloomberg Politics, October 27. http://www.bloomberg.com/news/articles/2016-10-
27/inside-the-trump-bunker-with-12-days-to-go.

Greenfield, Jeff. (2016). "Is Trump Losing the GOP?" *Politico*, June 14.

Grynbaum, Michael M., and Rachel Abrams. (2016). "'Apprentice' Producer Denounces
Trump but Won't Release Possibly Damning Tapes." *New York Times*, October 13.

Haberman, Maggie. (2016a). "Bob Dole Warns of 'Cataclysmic' Losses with Ted Cruz, and
Says Donald Trump Would Do Better." *New York Times*, January 20.

———. (2016b). "Donald Trump Warns of 'Riots' If Party Blocks Him at Convention."
New York Times, March 16. https://www.nytimes.com/politics/first-draft/2016/03/16/
donald-trump-warns-of-riots-if-party-blocks-him-at-convention/.

Haberman, Maggie, Alexander Burns, and Ashley Parker. (2016). "Donald Trump Fires
Corey Lewandowski, His Campaign Manager." *New York Times*, June 20.

Helderman, Rosalind S., Matt Zapotosky, and Sari Horwitz. (2016). "Computer Seized in
Weiner Probe Prompts FBI to Take New Steps in Clinton Email Inquiry." *Washington
Post*, October 28. https://www.washingtonpost.com/politics/fbi-to-conduct-new-
investigation-of-emails-from-clintons-private-server/2016/10/28/0b1e9468-9d31-
11e6-9980-50913d68eacb_story.html.

Hessler, Peter. (2017). "Follow the Leader: How Residents of a Rural Area Started Copying
the President." *New Yorker*, July 24, 21–27.

Hewitt, Hugh. (2016a). "It's the Supreme Court, Stupid." *Washington Examiner*, July 31.
https://www.washingtonexaminer.com/its-the-supreme-court-stupid.

———. (2016b). "Senate Majority Leader Mitch McConnell on 'the Long Game'
(Transcript)." *Hugh Hewitt Show*, May 30. https://www.hughhewitt.com/senate-
majority-leader-mitch-mcconnell-long-game/.

Hohmann, James. (2016a). "The Daily 202: GOP Establishment Offers Lukewarm
Endorsement of Trump." *Washington Post*, July 20. https://www.washingtonpost.com/
news/powerpost/paloma/daily-202/2016/07/20/daily-202-gop-establishment-offers-
lukewarm-endorsement-of-trump/578eb6e3cd96926bdf539f9d/.

———. (2016b). "The Daily 202: Why Trump Sounded More Like a Strongman
Than a Movement Conservative." *Washington Post*, July 22. https://www.
washingtonpost.com/news/powerpost/paloma/daily-202/2016/07/22/daily-202-
why-trump-sounded-more-like-a-strongman-than-a-movement-conservative/
57916dc84acce20505087cdf/?wpisrc=nl_most&wpmm=1.

———. (2016c). "Trump's Attacks on the GOP's Most Prominent Latina, Susana Martinez,
Should Alarm Republicans." *Washington Post*, May 25.

Homans, Charles. (2019). "Mitch McConnell Got Everything He Wanted. But at What Cost?" *New York Times*, January 22. https://www.nytimes.com/2019/01/22/magazine/mcconnell-senate-trump.html.

Hulse, Carl. (2016). "Donald Trump's Advice to Panicked Republicans: Man Up." *New York Times*, June 8. http://mobile.nytimes.com/2016/06/09/us/politics/donald-trump-republicans.html

Kapur, Sahil. (2015). "How Donald Trump Is Winning Over Anti-Wall Street Republicans." *Bloomberg Politics*, September 1.

Kim, Seung Min, and Burgess Everett. (2016). "Hill Republicans Despondent over Trump." *Politico*, June 14.

Kolbert, Elizabeth. (2005). "Firebrand." *New Yorker*, November 7, 134–38. http://www.newyorker.com/magazine/2005/11/07/firebrand.

Kotsko, Adam. (2019). "The Evangelical Mind." *n+1* 35 (Fall). https://nplusonemag.com/issue-35/politics/the-evangelical-mind/.

Kranish, Michael, and Marc Fisher. (2016). *Trump Revealed: An American Journey of Ambition, Ego, Money, and Power*. New York: Scribner.

Kruse, Michael. (2018). "Trump Has No Fear: 'Makes Nixon Look Like a Cream Puff.'" *Politico*, September 5. https://www.politico.com/magazine/story/2018/09/05/donald-trump-nixon-presidency-219639.

Leibovich, Mark. (2016). "Will Trump Swallow the G.O.P. Whole?" *New York Times*, June 21. http://www.nytimes.com/2016/06/26/magazine/will-trump-swallow-the-gop-whole.html.

Letourneau, Nancy. (2016). "Ryan's Dance with Trump." *Washington Monthly*, May 26. https://washingtonmonthly.com/2016/05/26/ryans-dance-with-trump/.

Linskey, Annie. (2016). "Trump, Sessions Struck a Beneficial Relationship." *Boston Globe*, December 12. https://www.bostonglobe.com/news/nation/2016/12/12/trump-and-sessions-two-outsiders-struck-mutually-beneficial-relationship/l4FiPFlyypCcCqEBdMQLCN/story.html.

Lizza, Ryan. (2016). "Taming Trump: A New Campaign Manager Tries to Reform an Unreformable Candidate." *New Yorker*, October 17.

Maguire, Robert. (2018). "GOP Donors Too 'Embarrassed' to Publicly Support Trump Gave Millions to Dark Money Group." *Open Secrets*. March 6. https://www.opensecrets.org/news/2018/03/big-revenues-for-group-providing-cover-for-gop-donors-too-embarrassed-to-publicly-support-trump-in-2016/.

Mak, Tim, and Alexa Corse. (2016). "Trump Campaign Changed Ukraine Platform, Lied about It." *Daily Beast*, August 3. http://www.thedailybeast.com/articles/2016/08/03/trump-campaign-changed-ukraine-platform-lied-about-it.html.

Marshall, John. (2017). "The March Meeting." *Talking Points Memo*, March 3. http://talkingpointsmemo.com/edblog/the-march-meeting.

Martin, Jonathan. (2016). "Blaming Muslims after Attack, Donald Trump Tosses Pluralism Aside." *New York Times*, June 14.

Martin, Jonathan, and Alexander Burns. (2016a). "Key G.O.P. Donors Still Deeply Resist Donald Trump's Candidacy." *New York Times*, May 21. http://www.nytimes.com/2016/05/22/us/politics/donald-trump-republican-fundraising.html.

———. (2016b). "Trump, Waking a 'Sleeping Giant,' Helps Clinton Build an Unlikely Firewall." *New York Times*, November 2. http://nyti.ms/2e4f5AJ.

Martin, Jonathan and Maggie Haberman. (2016). "Corporations Grow Nervous About Participating in Republican Convention." *New York Times*, March 31.

Mayer, Jane. (2018). "Trump vs. Koch Is a Custody Battle over Congress." *New Yorker*, August 1. https://www.newyorker.com/news/news-desk/trump-vs-koch-is-a-custody-battle-over-congress.

McCaskill, Nolan D. (2016). "Trump Tells GOP Leaders to 'Get Tougher.'" *Politico*, June 15.

McCaskill, Nolan D., and Nick Gass. (2016). "Trump Camp Suggests Ryan Unfit to Be Speaker." *Politico*, May 6. http://www.politico.com/blogs/2016-gop-primary-live-updates-and-results/2016/05/trump-paul-ryan-speaker-222890.

Merevick, Tony. (2014). "Exclusive: 9 Former Ex-Gay Leaders Join Movement to Ban Gay Conversion Therapy." BuzzFeed, July 31. https://www.buzzfeed.com/tonymerevick/exclusive-9-former-ex-gay-leaders-join-movement-to-ban-gay-c.

Nakashima, Ellen. (2016). "Russian Government Hackers Penetrated DNC, Stole Opposition Research on Trump." *Washington Post*, June 14. https://www.washingtonpost.com/world/national-security/russian-government-hackers-penetrated-dnc-stole-opposition-research-on-trump/2016/06/14/cf006cb4-316e-11e6-8ff7-7b6c1998b7a0_story.html?utm_term=.fd9dc846ab48.

Neidig, Harper. (2016). "Major Companies Decline to Fund 2016 GOP Convention." The Hill, June 16. https://thehill.com/blogs/ballot-box/presidential-races/283832-

Nemtsova, Anna. (2016). "Trump Is Already Helping Putin Consolidate Control of Ukraine." *Politico*, August 23. http://www.politico.com/magazine/story/2016/08/donald-trump-russia-ukraine-vladimir-putin-214180.

Neumann, William. (2016). "For Trump and Bloomberg, Cordial Ties Have Soured." *New York Times*, July 28.

New York Times. (2016). "Million-Dollar Donors in the 2016 Presidential Race." *New York Times*, February 9. https://www.nytimes.com/interactive/2016/us/elections/top-presidential-donors-campaign-money.html.

Palmer, Anna, and Jake Sherman. (2016). "Targets of Trump's Attacks Fight Back in D.C." *Politico*, March 31.

Palmeri, Tara. (2017). "Subway Sandwiches and U.N. Talk: Inside Sessions' First Meeting with Trump." *Politico*, September 16. http://politi.co/2h6K696.

Parker, Ashley. (2016). "Donald Trump Frowns on Idea of 'Toning It Down,' Despite Aide's Comments." *New York Times*, April 23.

Parker, Ashley, Alexander Burns, and Maggie Haberman. (2016). "A Grounded Plane and Anti-Clinton Passion: How Mike Pence Swayed the Trumps." *New York Times*, July 16. http://www.nytimes.com/2016/07/17/us/politics/donald-trump-mike-pence.html.

Peisner, David. (2013). "The Man behind the Historic Implosion of the Ex-Gay Movement." BuzzFeed, August 22. https://www.buzzfeed.com/djpeisner/the-man-behind-the-historic-implosion-of-the-ex-gay-movement.

Peters, Jeremy. (2016). "'I Can Watch It on TV': Excuses for Republicans Skipping a Donald Trump Convention." *New York Times*, June 1. http://www.nytimes.com/2016/06/02/us/politics/donald-trump-republican-convention.html?ribbon-ad-idx=2&rref=politics&module=ArrowsNav&contentCollection=Politics&action=swipe&region=FixedRight&pgtype=article.

Phillips, Amber. (2016). "John McCain Wins His Primary, Promptly Gives Up on Donald Trump." *Washington Post*, September 2.

Pierce, Charles. (2011). "Paul Ryan Is Living in a Fantasy Land Older Than Ayn Rand." *Esquire*, October 26. https://www.esquire.com/news-politics/politics/a11398/paul-ryan-heritage-foundation-speech-6530510/.

Plaskin, Glenn. (1990). "Playboy Interview: Donald Trump." *Playboy*, March.

Quinnipiac. (2015). "Bump for Trump as Carson Fades in Republican Race, Quinnipiac University National Poll Finds; Clinton, Sanders Surge in Matchups with GOP Leaders." Washington, DC: Pew Research Center, November 30.

Raju, Manu, Deirdre Walsh, and Tal Kopan. (2015). "House Republicans Repudiate Kevin McCarthy Comments." *Politico*, October 1. https://www.cnn.com/2015/09/30/politics/kevin-mccarthy-benghazi-committee-speaker/index.html.

Rappeport, Alan. (2015). "Donald Trump Returns Vladimir Putin's Admiration, Looking Past His Darker Side." *New York Times*, December 18. https://www.nytimes.com//www.nytimes.com/politics/first-draft/2015/12/18/donald-trump-returns-vladimir-putins-admiration-looking-past-his-darker-side/.

———. (2016a). "Donald Trump's Self-Funding Includes Payments to Family and His Companies." *New York Times*, June 21. http://www.nytimes.com/2016/06/22/us/politics/donald-trump-self-funding-payments.html.

———. (2016b). "Judge Faulted by Trump Has Faced a Lot Worse." *New York Times*, June 4.

Real Clear Politics. (2016). General Election: Trump vs. Clinton. Real Clear Politics, November 7. https://www.realclearpolitics.com/epolls/2016/president/us/general_election_trump_vs_clinton-5491.html.

Reilly, Katie. (2016). "Read Paul Ryan's Interview on Not Yet Endorsing Donald Trump." *Time*, May 6. Available at https://time.com/4320476/paul-ryan-interview-transcript-donald-trump-endorsement/.

Rogers, Ed. (2016). "GOP Unity Is Dead." *Washington Post*, July 8.

Rucker, Philip. (2016). "Romney Loyalists' Divisions over Trump Spill Out into the Open at Utah Summit." *Washington Post*, June 11.

Rucker, Philip, and Dan Balz. (2016). "At Romney Summit, Anti-Trump Republicans in Exile Ponder Their Party's Future." *Washington Post*, June 9.

Rucker, Philip, and Robert Costa. (2017). "Trump's Hard-Line Actions Have an Intellectual Godfather." *Washington Post*, January 30. https://www.washingtonpost.com/politics/trumps-hard-line-actions-have-an-intellectual-godfather-jeff-sessions/2017/01/30/ac393f66-e4d4-11e6-ba11-63c4b4fb5a63_story.html.

Saad, Lydia. (2016). "Trump and Clinton Finish with Historically Poor Images." Gallup, November 8. https://news.gallup.com/poll/197231/trump-clinton-finish-historically-poor-images.aspx.

Samuelsohn, Darren. (2016). "Clinton's Tech Team Stumbles toward Trump." *Politico*, May 19. http://www.politico.com/story/2016/05/clintons-tech-team-stumbles-toward-trump-223347.

Sargent, Greg. (2019). "New Disclosures About Lewd Trump Video Reveal His Mastery of the GOP." *Washington Post*, July 10. https://www.washingtonpost.com/opinions/2019/07/10/new-disclosures-about-lewd-trump-video-reveal-his-mastery-gop/.

Seib, Gerald F., and Patrick O'Connor. (2016). "Republicans Rode Waves of Populism Until They Crashed the Party." *Wall Street Journal*, October 26. http://www.wsj.com/articles/republicans-rode-waves-of-populism-until-it-crashed-the-party-1477492356.

Shane, Scott, and Michael S. Schmidt. (2015). "Hillary Clinton Emails Take Long Path to Controversy." *New York Times*, August 8. https://www.nytimes.com/2015/08/09/us/hillary-clinton-emails-take-long-path-to-controversy.html?action=click&module=RelatedLinks&pgtype=Article.

Sherman, Jake. (2016). "Paul Ryan Lays It on the Line." *Politico*, March 23.

Silver, Nate. (2016a). "Election Update: Comey or Not, Trump Continues to Narrow Gap with Clinton." FiveThirtyEight, October 31. https://fivethirtyeight.com/features/election-update-comey-or-not-trump-continues-to-narrow-gap-with-clinton/.

———. (2016b). "Election Update: How Big Is Hillary Clinton's Lead?" FiveThirtyEight, October 3.

———. (2016c). "Election Update: Is the Presidential Race Tightening?" FiveThirtyEight, October 26. https://fivethirtyeight.com/features/election-update-is-the-presidential-race-tightening/.

Smith, Samantha. (2016). "Trump Supporters Differ from Other GOP Voters on Foreign Policy, Immigration Issues." Washington, DC: Pew Research Center, May 11. http://www.pewresearch.org/fact-tank/2016/05/11/trump-supporters-differ-from-other-gop-voters-on-foreign-policy-immigration-issues/.

Solotaroff, Paul. (2015). "Trump Seriously: On the Trail with the GOP's Tough Guy." Rolling Stone, September 9.

Sonenshein, Julia (2016). "Revenge of the White Working-Class Woman." Politico, October 14. http://politi.co/2em8aDi.

Stein, Sam. (2016). "Sad! These Three Campaign Gurus for Jeb Bush, Ted Cruz and Marco Rubio Have Had Some Time to Reflect on Their Loss to the Donald. And Do They Ever Have Stories to Tell." Huffington Post Highline, June 14. https://highline.huffingtonpost.com/articles/en/sad/.

Steinhauer, Jennifer. (2016). "Ryan-Trump Breach May Be Beyond Repair." New York Times, May 6. http://www.nytimes.com/2016/05/07/us/politics/paul-ryan-donald-trump.html.

Stone, Peter. (2016). "Sheldon Adelson to Give $25m Boost to Trump Super PAC." Guardian, September 23. https://www.theguardian.com/us-news/2016/sep/23/sheldon-adelson-trump-super-pac-donation-25-million.

Tartar, Andre, and Kendall Breitman. (2016). "The Donald Trump GOP Unity Tracker." Bloomberg Politics, May 31. http://www.bloomberg.com/politics/features/2016-05-31/the-donald-trump-gop-unity-tracker.

Thrush, Glenn. (2016). "Jill Abramson on Hillary Clinton: 'She Does Get More Scrutiny' Than Men." Politico, March 21. https://www.politico.com/story/2016/03/jill-abramson-hillary-clinton-2016-221017.

———. (2017). "To Charm Trump, Paul Manafort Sold Himself as an Affordable Outsider." New York Times, April 8. https://www.nytimes.com/2017/04/08/us/to-charm-trump-paul-manafort-sold-himself-as-an-affordable-outsider.html?_r=0.

Totenberg, Nina. (2017). "Jeff Sessions Previously Denied Federal Judgeship amid Racism Controversy." National Public Radio, All Things Considered, March 6. https://www.npr.org/2017/01/09/509001314/jeff-sessions-previously-denied-federal-judgeship-amid-racism-controversy.

Unger, Craig. (2017). "Trump's Russian Laundromat." New Republic, August-September. https://newrepublic.com/article/143586/trumps-russian-laundromat-trump-tower-luxury-high-rises-dirty-money-international-crime-syndicate.

Vogel, Kenneth P., and Cate Martel. (2015). "The Kochs Freeze out Donald Trump." Politico, July 29 https://www.politico.com/story/2015/07/kochs-freeze-out-trump-120752.

Vogel, Kenneth P., and Eli Stokols. (2016). "Trump Rejects New Adviser's Push to Make Him 'Presidential.'" Politico, April 26.

Von Drehle, David. (2017). "Trump's Continued Attacks on Clinton Tell Us Why the Democrats Lost." Washington Post, August 4. https://www.washingtonpost.com/

opinions/trumps-continued-attacks-on-clinton-tell-us-why-the-democrats-lost/
2017/08/04/fd654456-793b-11e7-8f39-eeb7d3a2d304_story.html.

Waldman, Paul. (2016a). "Donald Trump and His Aides Admit That It's All an Act." *Washington Post*, April 22. https://www.washingtonpost.com/blogs/plum-line/wp/2016/04/22/donald-trump-and-his-aides-admit-that-its-all-an-act/.

———. (2016b). "Paul Ryan to Tea Party: You Are the Problem." *Washington Post*, February 3. https://www.washingtonpost.com/blogs/plum-line/wp/2016/02/03/paul-ryan-to-tea-party-you-are-the-problem/.

Warzel, Charlie, and Lam Thuy Vo. (2016). "Here's Where Donald Trump Gets His News." BuzzFeed, December 3. https://www.buzzfeed.com/charliewarzel/the-new-york-times-cant-figure-out-where-nazis-come-from-in.

Werner, Erica. (2016). "Senate Republicans on the Spot over Trump Comments on Khan." Associated Press, August 2. https://apnews.com/7d1c7d00f61b4fd299dc48a8b20ae332/senate-republicans-spot-over-trump-comments-khan.

Williams, Joan C. (2016). "What So Many People Don't Get About the U.S. Working Class." *Harvard Business Review*, November 10.

Yoon, Robert. (2016). "$153 Million in Bill and Hillary Clinton Speaking Fees, Documented." CNN, February 6. Available at https://www.cnn.com/2016/02/05/politics/hillary-clinton-bill-clinton-paid-speeches/index.html.

Chapter 6

Abramson, Alana. (2017). "Paul Ryan on ACHA Failure: Transcript." *Time*, March 24. https://time.com/4713114/paul-ryan-ahca-health-care-failure-transcript/.

Abutaleb, Yasmeen, Ashley Parker, and Josh Dawsey. (2020). "Inside Trump's Frantic Attempts to Minimize the Coronavirus Crisis." *Washington Post*, February 29. https://www.washingtonpost.com/politics/inside-trumps-frantic-attempts-to-minimize-the-coronavirus-crisis/2020/02/29/7ebc882a-5b25-11ea-9b35-def5a027d470_story.html?utm_campaign=wp_politics_am&utm_medium=email&utm_source=newsletter&wpisrc=nl_politics.

Alberta, Tim. (2017). "Inside the GOP's Health Care Debacle." *Politico*, March 24. http://politi.co/2n2x2QA.

———. (2019). *American Carnage: On the Front Lines of the Republican Civil War and the Rise of President Trump.* New York: Harper Collins.

Alemany, Jaquline. (2020). "Trump Is Emboldened after Impeachment Acquittal. Here's a Timeline of the Last 16 Days." *Washington Post*, February 21. https://www.washingtonpost.com/news/powerpost/paloma/powerup/2020/02/21/powerup-trump-is-emboldened-after-impeachment-acquittal-here-s-a-timeline-of-the-last-16-days/5e4ef55d602ff16b163b3d72/?itid=sf_powerpost.

Almasy, Steve, and Darran Simon. (2017). "A Timeline of President Trump's Travel Bans." CNN, March 30. https://www.cnn.com/2017/02/10/us/trump-travel-ban-timeline/index.html.

Amiti, Mary, Sebastian Heise, and Noah Kwicklis. (2018). "Will New Steel Tariffs Protect U.S. Jobs?" *Liberty Street Economics*, April 18. http://libertystreeteconomics.newyorkfed.org/2018/04/will-new-steel-tariffs-protect-us-jobs.html.

Associated Press. (2020). "Stock Markets Sell Off as Coronavirus Spread Threatens Global Economy." CBC, February 24. https://www.cbc.ca/news/business/markets-monday-coronavirus-1.5473520.

Autor, D. H., D. Dorn, and G. H. Hanson. (2016). "The China Shock: Learning from Labor-Market Adjustment to Large Changes in Trade." Annual Review of Economics 8: 205–40.

Ayer, Donald. (2019). "Why Bill Barr Is So Dangerous." Atlantic, June 30. https://www.theatlantic.com/ideas/archive/2019/06/bill-barrs-dangerous-pursuit-executive-power/592951/.

Bade, Rachael, Josh Dawsey, and Jennifer Haberkorn. (2017). "How a Secret Freedom Caucus Pact Brought Down Obamacare Repeal." Politico, March 26. http://www.politico.com/story/2017/03/trump-freedom-caucus-obamacare-repeal-replace-secret-pact-236507.

Bade, Rachel. (2017). "Pity Paul Ryan: Moderates Adopt Freedom Caucus Tactics." Politico, July 27. http://politi.co/2tFv3ox.

Baker, Peter, and Annie Karni. (2019). "To Defend against a Mercurial Boss, Trump Aides Wield the Pen as Shield." New York Times, April 21. https://www.nytimes.com/2019/04/21/us/politics/trump-mueller-note-taking.html.

Barabak, Mark Z. (2016). "Analysis: Raw, Angry and Aggrieved, President Trump's Inaugural Speech Does Little to Heal Political Wounds." Los Angeles Times, January 20. https://www.latimes.com/politics/la-na-pol-trump-inauguration-speech-analysis-20170120-story.html.

Barnes, Julian E., and Matthew Rosenberg. (2019). "Charges of Ukrainian Meddling? A Russian Operation, U.S. Intelligence Says." New York Times, November 22. https://www.nytimes.com/2019/11/22/us/politics/ukraine-russia-interference.html?smid=nytcore-ios-share.

Barro, Josh. (2017). "The Republican Healthcare Plan Is Failing Because Trump Is Bad at Making Deals." Business Insider, March 24. http://www.businessinsider.com/republican-healthcare-plan-trump-deals-2017-3.

Bazelon, Emily. (2019a). "What Happens When a President and Congress Go to War?" New York Times, November 5. https://www.nytimes.com/2019/11/05/magazine/congress-president-impeachment.html?searchResultPosition=1.

———. (2019b). "Who Is Bill Barr?" New York Times, October 26. https://www.nytimes.com/interactive/2019/10/26/opinion/william-barr-trump.html.

Beauchamp, Zack. (2016). "Alex Jones, America's Most Famous Conspiracy Theorist, Explained." Vox, October 28. http://www.vox.com/policy-and-politics/2016/10/28/13424848/alex-jones-infowars-prisonplanet.

Beaver, David, and Jason Stanley. (2017). "Unlike All Previous U.S. Presidents, Trump Almost Never Mentions Democratic Ideals." Washington Post, February 7. https://www.washingtonpost.com/news/monkey-cage/wp/2017/02/07/unlike-all-previous-u-s-presidents-trump-almost-never-mentions-democratic-ideals/?utm_term=.fe9b987bbdaf.

Bender, Michael C., and Carole E. Lee. (2016). "RNC Chair Reince Priebus Is Named Donald Trump's Chief of Staff." Wall Street Journal, November 13. http://www.wsj.com/articles/leading-contender-for-donald-trump-s-chief-of-staff-is-rnc-chairman-reince-priebus-1479069597.

Bender, Michael C., Peter Nicholas, and Siobhan Hughes. (2018). "Inside Trump's Trade War: How Tariff Backers Beat Free Traders." Wall Street Journal, March 9.

https://www.wsj.com/articles/inside-trumps-trade-war-how-the-protectionists-beat-the-free-traders-1520611990.

Bernstein, Carl. (2020). "From Pandering to Putin to Abusing Allies and Ignoring His Own Advisers, Trump's Phone Calls Alarm US Officials." *CNN*, June 30. https://www.cnn.com/2020/06/29/politics/trump-phone-calls-national-security-concerns/index.html

Bertrand, Natasha. (2019). "Andrew McCabe Couldn't Believe the Things Trump Said About Putin." *Atlantic*, February 19. Available at https://www.theatlantic.com/politics/archive/2019/02/mccabe-warns-trump-mueller-undeterred/583000/.

Bierman, Noah. (2018). "Trump's High-Risk Strategy Puts Him on the Midterm Ballot Like No One Else." *Los Angeles Times*, November 5. https://www.latimes.com/politics/la-na-pol-trump-ballot-20181105-story.html.

Binder, Sarah. (2019). "Congress in 2019 Was a Rollercoaster." *Washington Post*, December 30. https://www.washingtonpost.com/politics/2019/12/30/congresss-was-rollercoaster-remember-these-highlights/.

Boburg, Shawn. (2017). "Trump Seeks Sharp Cuts to Housing Aid, except for Program That Brings Him Millions." *Washington Post*, June 20. https://www.washingtonpost.com/investigations/trump-seeks-sharp-cuts-to-housing-aid-except-for-program-that-brings-him-millions/2017/06/20/bf1fb2b8-5531-11e7-ba90-f5875b7d1876_story.html.

Bolton, Alexander (2018). "McConnell Urges GOP Senators to Call Trump about Tariffs." *The Hill*, April 10. http://thehill.com/homenews/senate/382531-mcconnell-urges-gop-senators-to-call-trump-about-tariffs.

Bolton, John. (2020). *The Room Where It Happened*. New York: Simon & Schuster.

Bouchard, Mikayla. (2018). "We've Heard It All Before. Shutdown Talk in 2013 Compared to Today." *New York Times*, January 19. https://www.nytimes.com/2018/01/19/us/politics/government-shutdown-trump-obama.html.

Bowden, John. (2020). "Collins: Trump Has Learned 'a Pretty Big Lesson' from Impeachment." *The Hill*, February 4. https://thehill.com/homenews/senate/481486-collins-trump-has-learned-a-pretty-big-lesson-from-impeachment.

Browning, Lynnley, and Benjamin Bain. (2017). "Trump, Real Estate Investors Get Late-Added Perk in Tax Bill." *Bloomberg*, December 17. https://www.bloomberg.com/news/articles/2017-12-18/trump-real-estate-investors-get-last-minute-perk-in-tax-bill?wpmm=1&wpisrc=nl_daily202&sref=I2I6qZII.

Bump, Philip. (2017). "House Republicans Have Spent 378 Hours on Votes to Undercut Obamacare That Went Nowhere." *Washington Post*, July 31. https://www.washingtonpost.com/news/politics/wp/2017/07/31/house-republicans-have-spent-378-hours-on-votes-to-undercut-obamacare-that-went-nowhere/.

Burns, Alexander. (2017). "How Governors from Both Parties Plotted to Derail the Senate Health Bill." *New York Times*, June 27. https://www.nytimes.com/2017/06/27/us/politics/affordable-care-act-governors.html.

Burns, Alexander, Jonathan Martin, and Maggie Haberman. (2020). "As Trump Ignores Virus Crisis, Republicans Start to Break Ranks." *New York Times*, July 19. https://www.nytimes.com/2020/07/19/us/politics/republicans-contradict-trump-coronavirus.html.

Caldwell, Christopher. (2017a). "How to Think about Vladimir Putin." *Imprimis*, March.

———. (2017b). "What Does Steve Bannon Want?" *New York Times*, February 25. https://www.nytimes.com/2017/02/25/opinion/what-does-steve-bannon-want.html.

Campaign Finance Institute. (2017). "President Trump, with RNC Help, Raised More Small Donor Money Than President Obama; as Much as Clinton and Sanders Combined." Washington, DC: Campaign Finance Institute, February 21. http://www.cfinst.org/Press/PReleases/17-02-21/President_Trump_with_RNC_Help_Raised_More_Small_Donor_Money_than_President_Obama_As_Much_As_Clinton_and_Sanders_Combined.aspx.

Caralle, Katelyn. (2018). "Lindsey Graham: Troop Withdrawal in Syria, Afghanistan Paving Way to 'Second 9/11.'" Washington Examiner, December 21. https://www.washingtonexaminer.com/policy/defense-national-security/lindsey-graham-troop-withdrawal-in-middle-east-paving-way-to-second-9-11.

Cheney, Kyle. (2018). "Trump's GOP 'Warriors' Lead Charge against Mueller." Politico, May 7. https://www.politico.com/story/2018/05/07/trump-mueller-republican-warriors-congress-571562.

Chenoweth, Erica, and Jeremy Pressman. (2017). "This Is What We Learned by Counting the Women's Marches." Washington Post, February 7. https://www.washingtonpost.com/news/monkey-cage/wp/2017/02/07/this-is-what-we-learned-by-counting-the-womens-marches/.

Christie, Chris. (2019). Let Me Finish: Trump, the Kushners, Bannon, New Jersey, and the Power of In-Your-Face Politics. New York: Hachette Books.

CNN News. (2019). "McConnell Slams Trump Administration for Syria Withdrawal." KPAX, October 19. https://www.kpax.com/news/national-news/mcconnell-slams-trump-administration-for-syria-withdrawal.

Colvin, Geoff. (2019). "Why Trump Is Bad for Business." Fortune, November 18. https://fortune.com/longform/trump-policies-bad-for-business-trade-immigration-taxes-regulations-us-economy/.

Colvin, Jill. (2019). "White House Aides Try Disappearing Act Amid Impeachment Talk." Associated Press, October 10. https://apnews.com/63a2cabb2a54492591165fe0fcc20214.

Confessore, Nicholas. (2017). "How to Get Rich in Trump's Washington." New York Times, August 30. https://www.nytimes.com/2017/08/30/magazine/how-to-get-rich-in-trumps-washington.htmls.

Cooper, Helene, Peter Baker, Eric Schmitt, and Mitchell Ferman. (2018). "Two Years In, Trump Struggles to Master Role of Military Commander." New York Times, November 16. https://www.nytimes.com/2018/11/16/us/politics/president-trump-military.html.

Coppins, McKay. (2017). "The Prince of Oversight." Atlantic, March 31. https://www.theatlantic.com/politics/archive/2017/03/jason-chaffetz-oversight/521271/.

———. (2018). "The Outrage over Family Separation Is Exactly What Stephen Miller Wants." Atlantic, June 18. https://www.theatlantic.com/politics/archive/2018/06/stephen-miller-family-separation/563132/.

Cormier, Anthony, and Jason Leopold. (2018a). "The Definitive Story of How Trump's Team Worked the Trump Moscow Deal During the Campaign." BuzzFeed, May 17. https://www.buzzfeed.com/anthonycormier/trump-moscow-micheal-cohen-felix-sater-campaign.

———. (2018b). "The Trump Organization Planned to Give Vladimir Putin the $50 Million Penthouse in Trump Tower Moscow." BuzzFeed, November 29. https://www.buzzfeednews.com/article/anthonycormier/the-trump-organization-planned-to-give-vladimir-putin-the.

Costa, Robert, and Sean Sullivan. (2018). "Trump Feud with Koch Network Exposes Rift between Populist Forces and Establishment GOP." *Washington Post*, August 2. https://www.washingtonpost.com/politics/trump-feud-with-koch-network-exposes-rift-between-populist-forces-and-establishment-gop/2018/07/31/2e5fd874-94d3-11e8-80e1-00e80e1fdf43_story.html?utm_term=.b64e0fd5715d&wpisrc=nl_politics&wpmm=1.

Craig, Tim. (2019). "Republican Governors Walk Tightrope between Building Chinese Trade Relationship and Offending Trump." *Washington Post*, May 23. https://www.washingtonpost.com/national/republican-governors-walk-tightrope-between-building-chinese-trade-relationship-and-offending-trump/2019/05/23/97814d04-7d55-11e9-8ede-f4abf521ef17_story.html.

Council on Foreign Relations. (2019). "A Conversation with House Speaker Nancy Pelosi." Washington, DC: Council on Foreign Relations, June 13. https://www.cfr.org/event/conversation-house-speaker-nancy-pelosi.

Dale, Daniel. (2020). "Fact Check: McConnell Claims Obama Didn't Leave Trump a Pandemic 'Game Plan.' Obama Left a 69-Page Playbook." CNN, May 12. https://www.cnn.com/2020/05/12/politics/fact-check-mcconnell-obama-trump-game-plan/index.html.

Davidson, Adam. (2017). "The Iran Business Ties Trump Didn't Disclose." *New Yorker*, October 20. https://www.newyorker.com/news/news-desk/the-iran-business-ties-trump-didnt-disclose.

Davis, Julie Hirschfeld, and Maggie Haberman. (2018). "A President Not Sure of What He Wants Complicates the Shutdown Impasse." *New York Times*, January 21. https://www.nytimes.com/2018/01/21/us/politics/trump-government-shutdown.html.

De Rugy, Veronique. (2019). "What Trump's Aggressive Trade Tactics Have Achieved." *New York Times*, October 7. https://www.nytimes.com/2019/10/07/opinion/trump-trade.html.

Debonis, Mike. (2017). "Capitol Hill Throws up Red Flags as Trump Moves on Sessions and Possibly Mueller." *Washington Post*, July 25. https://www.washingtonpost.com/powerpost/capitol-hill-throws-up-red-flags-as-trump-moves-on-sessions-and-possibly-mueller/2017/07/25/e1e3e05e-715a-11e7-9eac-d56bd5568db8_story.html.

Demirjian, Karoun, Ed O'Keefe, and Abby Phillip. (2017). "Top Republicans Call on Sessions to Recuse Himself from Russia Investigation." *Washington Post*, March 2. https://www.washingtonpost.com/powerpost/top-gop-lawmaker-calls-on-sessions-to-recuse-himself-from-russia-investigation/2017/03/02/148c07ac-ff46-11e6-8ebe-6e0dbe4f2bca_story.html.

Demirjian, Karoun, Sean Sullivan, and Ed O'Keefe. (2017). "Cornyn's Own GOP Colleagues Are Less Than Enthusiastic about His Candidacy for FBI Director." *Washington Post*, May 15. https://www.washingtonpost.com/powerpost/cornyns-own-gop-colleagues-are-less-than-enthusiastic-about-his-candidacy-for-fbi-director/2017/05/15/cdf7097c-3997-11e7-9e48-c4f199710b69_story.html.

Dennis, Steven T. (2018). "Republican Senators Warn Trump Not to Obstruct Justice or Pardon Himself." Bloomberg, June 5. Available at https://www.bloomberg.com/news/articles/2018-06-05/key-senate-republicans-warn-trump-on-obstruction-pardon-powers.

Dent, Wendy, Ed Pilkington, and Shaun Walker. (2017). "Jared Kushner Sealed Real Estate Deal with Oligarch's Firm Cited in Money-Laundering Case." *Guardian*, July 24. http://www.theguardian.com/us-news/2017/jul/24/jared-kushner-new-york-russia-money-laundering.

Dovere, Edward-Isaac. (2017a). "Nancy Pelosi Has Trump Right Where She Wants Him." *Politico Magazine*, November/December. http://politi.co/2gVZr9l.

———. (2017b). "Trump's Threat to Take Down the GOP Still Stands." *Politico*, December 5. http://politi.co/2BzmyPk.

Dowd, Maureen. (2019a). "It's Nancy Pelosi's Parade." *New York Times*, July 7. https://www.nytimes.com/2019/07/06/opinion/sunday/nancy-pelosi-pride-parade.html?action=click&module=Opinion&pgtype=Homepage.

———. (2019b). "Matt Tyrnauer: Chronicler of Trump's Mentor Roy Cohn." *New York Times*, September 1. https://www.nytimes.com/2019/09/01/style/roy-cohn-movie.html.

Eban, Katherine. (2020). "How Jared Kushner's Secret Testing Plan 'Went Poof into Thin Air." *Vanity Fair*, July 30. https://www.vanityfair.com/news/2020/07/how-jared-kushners-secret-testing-plan-went-poof-into-thin-air.

Edsall, Thomas B. (2017). "You Cannot Be Too Cynical About the Republican Tax Bill." *New York Times*, December 21. https://www.nytimes.com/2017/12/21/opinion/republican-tax-bill-trump-corker.html.

———. (2018). "The Robots Have Descended on Trump Country." *The New York Times*, December 13. https://www.nytimes.com/2018/12/13/opinion/robots-trump-country-jobs.html?action=click&module=Opinion&pgtype=Homepage.

Edwards-Levy, Ariel. (2018). Trump's Core Voters Stand Out for Their Support of Family Separation. *Huffington Post*, June 19. https://www.huffingtonpost.com/entry/trump-voters-family-separation-poll_us_5b293726e4b0f0b9e9a5d72e.

Elving, Ron. (2017). "Trump Puts a Twist on the Meaning of 'Bully Pulpit." National Public Radio, July 4. https://www.npr.org/2017/07/04/535429508/trump-s-weekend-gives-twist-to-meaning-of-bully-pulpit.

Entous, Adam. (2017). "House Majority Leader to Colleagues in 2016: 'I Think Putin Pays' Trump." *Washington Post*, May 17. https://www.washingtonpost.com/world/national-security/house-majority-leader-to-colleagues-in-2016-i-think-putin-pays-trump/2017/05/17/515f6f8a-3aff-11e7-8854-21f359183e8c_story.html.

Entous, Adam, and Evan Osnos. (2018). "Jared Kushner Is China's Trump Card." *New Yorker*, January 29. https://www.newyorker.com/magazine/2018/01/29/jared-kushner-is-chinas-trump-card.

Everett, Burgess. (2017). "Conservatives Near Revolt on Senate Health Care Negotiations." *Politico*, June 9. http://politi.co/2rVsIWm.

———. (2018). Republicans Wage Trade War against Trump. *Politico*, June 6. https://www.politico.com/story/2018/06/06/trump-tariffs-bob-corker-bill-629124.

Fallows, James. (2020a). "The Media Learned Nothing from 2016." *Atlantic*, September 15. https://www.theatlantic.com/ideas/archive/2020/09/media-mistakes/616222/.

———. (2020b). "The 3 Weeks That Changed Everything." *Atlantic*, July 2. https://www.theatlantic.com/politics/archive/2020/06/how-white-house-coronavirus-response-went-wrong/613591/.

Fang, Lee, and Nick Surgey. (2018). "Koch Document Reveals Laundry List of Policy Victories Extracted from the Trump Administration." *The Intercept*, February 25. Available at https://theintercept.com/2018/02/25/koch-brothers-trump-administration/.

Fed Staff. (2020). "Share of Corporate Equities and Mutual Fund Shares Held by the Top 1%." Federal Reserve Bank of Saint Louis (FRED).

Filkins, Dexter. (2016). "Turkey's Thirty-Year Coup." *New Yorker*, October 17. https://www.newyorker.com/magazine/2016/10/17/turkeys-thirty-year-coup.

Flaaen, Aaron, and Justin Pierce. (2019). "Disentangling the Effects of the 2018–2019 Tarriffs on a Globally Connected U.S. Manufacturing Sector." Finance and Economics Discussion Series. Washington, DC: Federal Reserve Board, December 23. https://www.federalreserve.gov/econres/feds/files/2019086pap.pdf.

Forsythe, Michael, Eric Lipton, Keith Bradsher, and Sui-Lee Wee. (2019). "A 'Bridge' to China, and Her Family's Business, in the Trump Cabinet." *New York Times*, June 2. https://www.nytimes.com/2019/06/02/us/politics/elaine-chao-china.html.

Frum, David. (2017). "How to Build an Autocracy." *Atlantic*, March. https://www.theatlantic.com/magazine/archive/2017/03/how-to-build-an-autocracy/513872/.

Frum, David. (2018). Trumpocracy: The Corruption of the American Republic. New York: Harper.

Gamm, Gerald, and Renée M. Smith. (1998). "Presidents, Parties and the Public: Evolving Patterns of Interaction, 1877–1929." *Speaking to the People: The Rhetorical Presidency in Historical Perspective*, edited by Richard Ellis, 87–111. Amherst: University of Massachusetts Press.

Gardner, Page, and Stan Greenberg. (2017). "Women Trump Voters Are Starting to Doubt Him." *Time*, April 21. https://time.com/4750602/trump-women-voters-doubts/?ct=t%28Time+op-ed+on+March+WV+FGs%29.

Garrett, Laurie. (2020). "Trump Has Sabotaged America's Coronavirus Response." *Foreign Policy*, January 31. https://foreignpolicy.com/2020/01/31/coronavirus-china-trump-united-states-public-health-emergency-response/.

Geraghty, Jim. (2017). "The Outsider Enters Boldly and Trips over His Own Shoelaces." *National Review*, March 27. http://www.nationalreview.com/corner/446127/outsider-enters-boldly-and-trips-over-his-own-shoelaces.

Gerstein, Josh. (2017). "3 Key Trump Mistakes That Led to the Travel Ban Court Defeat." *Politico*, February 9. http://politi.co/2k9RhJO.

Glasser, Susan. (2018). "Trump Insists on a Putin Summit." *New Yorker*, June 15. https://www.newyorker.com/news/letter-from-trumps-washington/theres-no-stopping-him-trump-insists-on-a-russia-summit.

Global Strategy Group Staff. (2020). "Communicating in Crisis: Coronavirus No. 41." *GSG Navigator*, September 16. https://navigatorresearch.org/public-opinion-on-coronavirus-navigator-update-41/.

Goldberg, Jeffrey. (2019). "The Man Who Couldn't Take It Anymore." *Atlantic*, October. https://www.theatlantic.com/magazine/archive/2019/10/james-mattis-trump/596665/.

Gravelle, Jane G., and Donald J. Marples. (2019). "The Economic Effects of the 2017 Tax Revision: Preliminary Observations." CRS Report R44762. Washington, DC: Congressional Research Service.

Greif, Mark (2019). "On the Mueller Report, Vol. 1: How They Got Away with It." *n+1* 35. https://nplusonemag.com/online-only/online-only/on-the-mueller-report-vol-1/.

Grimaldi, James V., Shane Harris, and Aruna Viswanatha. (2017). "Mueller Probes Flynn's Role in Alleged Plan to Deliver Cleric to Turkey." *Wall Street Journal*, November 10. https://www.wsj.com/articles/mueller-probes-flynns-role-in-alleged-plan-to-deliver-cleric-to-turkey-1510309982.

Grimaldi, James V., Dion Nissenbaum, and Margaret Coker. (2017). "Ex-CIA Director: Mike Flynn and Turkish Officials Discussed Removal of Erdogan Foe from

U.S." *Wall Street Journal*, March 24. https://www.wsj.com/articles/ex-cia-director-mike-flynn-and-turkish-officials-discussed-removal-of-erdogan-foe-from-u-s-1490380426.

Grynbaum, Michael M., and Edmund Lee. (2019). "Trump Suggests a Boycott of AT&T to Punish CNN." *New York Times*, June 3. https://www.nytimes.com/2019/06/03/business/media/trump-att-boycott-cnn.html.

Haberman, Maggie, and Nicholas Fandos. (2019). "In Combating Democratic Investigations, Trump Borrows from an Old Playbook." *New York Times*, May 1. https://www.nytimes.com/2019/05/01/us/politics/trump-democrats-investigations.html.

Harris, Shane, and Carol E. Lee. (2017). "Comey's Firing Came as Investigators Stepped up Russia Probe." *Wall Street Journal*, May 10. https://www.wsj.com/articles/james-comey-had-requested-more-money-for-fbi-s-russia-investigation-before-being-fired-u-s-official-1494433061.

Harris, Shane, Carol D. Leonnig, Greg Jaffe, and Josh Dawsey. (2018). "Kushner's Overseas Contacts Raise Concerns as Foreign Officials Seek Leverage." *Washington Post*, February 27. https://www.washingtonpost.com/world/national-security/kushners-overseas-contacts-raise-concerns-as-foreign-officials-seek-leverage/2018/02/27/16bbc052-18c3-11e8-942d-16a950029788_story.html?utm_term=.9c12fd1fa2a7.

Harris, Shane, Josh Dawsey, and Carol D. Leonnig. (2019). "Former White House Officials Say They Feared Putin Influenced the President's Views on Ukraine and 2016 Campaign." *Washington Post*, December 19. https://www.washingtonpost.com/national-security/former-white-house-officials-say-they-feared-putin-influenced-the-presidents-views-on-ukraine-and-2016-campaign/2019/12/19/af0fdbf6-20e9-11ea-bed5-880264cc91a9_story.html?utm_campaign=politics_am&utm_medium=Email&utm_source=Newsletter&wpisrc=nl_politics&wpmm=1.

Hennesy-Fiske, Molly. (2020). "Sacrifice the Old to Help the Economy? Texas Official's Remark Prompts Backlash." *Los Angeles Times*, March 24. https://www.latimes.com/world-nation/story/2020-03-24/coronavirus-texas-dan-patrick.

Hofman, Mike. (2019). "As the Steel Industry Falters, Will Trump Pay a Political Price?" *Fortune*, October 10. https://fortune.com/2019/10/10/us-steel-industry-trump-tariffs-china/.

Hohmann, James. (2017a). "The Daily 202: Did Mike Pence Get Burned by Michael Flynn?" *Washington Post*, February 10. https://www.washingtonpost.com/news/powerpost/paloma/daily-202/2017/02/10/daily-202-did-mike-pence-get-burned-by-michael-flynn/589d13ffe9b69b1406c75ca2/.

———. (2017b). "Why the Markets Shrugged Off Trump's Threat to Break up the Big Banks." *Washington Post*, May 2. https://www.washingtonpost.com/news/powerpost/paloma/daily-202/2017/05/02/daily-202-why-the-markets-shrugged-off-trump-s-threat-to-break-up-the-big-banks/5907d78de9b69b3a72331f11/.

———. (2018a). "The Daily 202: More Memos Are Coming. Here Are Six Questions About 'Phase Two' of the Nunes Investigation." *Washington Post*, February 5. https://s2.washingtonpost.com/3e9193/5a78595afe1ff634eb13a73e/c3BvcGtpbkB1Y3NkLmVkdQ%3D%3D/9/133/a44efa691cb926719c1d55f5d9ba146e.

———. (2018b). "The Daily 202: Trump Has No Nominees for 245 Important Jobs, Including an Ambassador to South Korea." *Washington Post*, January 12. https://www.washingtonpost.com/news/powerpost/paloma/daily-202/2018/01/12/daily-202-trump-has-no-nominees-for-245-important-jobs-including-an-ambassador-to-south-korea/5a57cce830fb0469e8840085/?wpisrc=nl_daily202&wpmm=1.

———. (2018c). "The Daily 202: Trump Hands the Russians More Victories with Syria Withdrawal, Sanctions Relief and Ukraine Inaction." *Washington Post*, December 20. https://www.washingtonpost.com/news/powerpost/paloma/daily-202/2018/12/20/daily-202-trump-hands-the-russians-more-victories-with-syria-withdrawal-sanctions-relief-and-ukraine-inaction/5c1b248e1b326b6a59d7b207/?wpisrc=nl_daily202&wpmm=1.

Homans, Charles. (2019). "Mitch McConnell Got Everything He Wanted. But at What Cost?" *New York Times*, January 22. https://www.nytimes.com/2019/01/22/magazine/mcconnell-senate-trump.html.

House, Billy, and Steven T. Dennis. (2017). "GOP Splits on Need to Scrap Obamacare Taxes in Swift Repeal." Bloomberg, January 6. https://www.bloomberg.com/politics/articles/2017-01-06/gop-splits-on-need-to-scrap-obamacare-taxes-in-fast-track-repeal.

Hsu, Tiffany. (2018). "G.M. Says New Wave of Trump Tariffs Could Force U.S. Job Cuts." *New York Times*, June 29. https://www.nytimes.com/2018/06/29/business/automakers-tariffs-job-cuts.html.

Hulse, Carl, Nicholas Fandos, and Emily Cochrane. (2020). "How Mitch McConnell Delivered Acquittal for Trump." *New York Times*, February 6. https://www.nytimes.com/2020/02/06/us/trump-impeachment.html?searchResultPosition=1.

Ioffe, Julia, and Franklin Foer. (2017). "Did Manafort Use Trump to Curry Favor with a Putin Ally?" *Atlantic*, October 2. https://www.theatlantic.com/politics/archive/2017/10/emails-suggest-manafort-sought-approval-from-putin-ally-deripaska/541677/.

Isikoff, Michael. (2017). "How the Trump Administration's Secret Efforts to Ease Russia Sanctions Fell Short." Yahoo News, June 2. https://www.yahoo.com/news/trump-administrations-secret-efforts-ease-russia-sanctions-fell-short-231301145.html.

Jacobs, Jennifer, and Alex Wayne. (2020). "In Zeal to Urge U.S. Reopening, Pence Sets Virus Worries Aside." Bloomberg, May 20. https://www.bloomberg.com/news/articles/2020-05-09/in-zeal-to-urge-u-s-reopening-pence-sets-virus-worries-aside?sref=I2I6qZII.

Jacobson, Gary C. (2019). "Extreme Referendum: Donald Trump and the 2018 Midterm Elections." *Political Science Quarterly* 134(1): 9–38.

Jacobson, Gary C., and Huchen Liu. (2020). "Dealing with Disruption: Congressional Republicans' Responses to Donald Trump's Behavior and Agenda." *Presidential Studies Quarterly* 50(1): 4–29.

Jalonick, Mary Clare. (2018). "As GOP Balks, McConnell Shuts Down Bill to Protect Mueller." *Washington Post*, April 17. https://www.washingtonpost.com/politics/congress/mcconnell-wont-allow-vote-to-bill-to-protect-mueller/2018/04/17/7c53ad0c-4281-11e8-b2dc-b0a403e4720a_story.html.

Kaiser, Robert G. (2020). "Fear and Loathing and the FBI." *New York Review of Books*, February 27. https://www.nybooks.com/articles/2020/02/27/fear-loathing-fbi/.

Kamin, David, David Gamage, Ari D. Glogower, Rebecca M. Kysar, et al. (2018). "The Games They Will Play: Tax Games, Roadblocks, and Glitches under the 2017 Tax Legislation." *Minnesota Law Review* 103: 1439–521.

Kane, Paul. (2017). "A New Dynamic May Be Emerging in the House: A Right and Left Flank within the GOP Willing to Buck Leadership." *Washington Post*, March 25. https://www.washingtonpost.com/powerpost/a-new-dynamic-may-be-emerging-in-the-house-a-right-and-left-flank-within-the-gop-willing-to-buck-leadership/2017/03/24/f0f2602a-10b6-11e7-9b0d-d27c98455440_story.html.

Kaplan, Thomas. (2017). "Health Bill Would Raise Uninsured by 24 Million but Save $337 Billion, Report Says." *New York Times*, March 13. https://www.nytimes.com/2017/03/13/us/politics/affordable-care-act-health-congressional-budget-office.html.

Kelly, Kate, and Mark Mazzetti. (2020). "As Coronavirus Spread, Reports of Trump Administration's Private Briefings Fueled Stock Sell-Off." *New York Times*, October 14. https://www.nytimes.com/2020/10/14/us/politics/stock-market-coronavirus-trump.html?action=click&module=Top%20Stories&pgtype=Homepage

Kim, Seung Min. (2020). "These Republicans Said They Hope Trump Has Learned a Lesson from Impeachment. He Said He Hasn't." *Washington Post*, February 5. https://www.washingtonpost.com/politics/these-republicans-said-they-hope-trump-has-learned-a-lesson-from-impeachment-he-said-he-hasnt/2020/02/04/fa68c18c-478e-11ea-ab15-b5df3261b710_story.html.

Kirkpatrick, David D. (2017). "Trump's Business Ties in Persian Gulf Raise Questions about His Allegiances." *New York Times*, June 17. https://www.nytimes.com/2017/06/17/world/middleeast/trumps-business-ties-in-persian-gulf-raise-questions-about-his-allegiances.html?hp&action=click&pgtype=Homepage&clickSource=story-heading&module=first-column-region&region=top-news&WT.nav=top-news&_r=0.

Klein, Charlotte. (2020). "Trump Ally DeSantis Forced to Walk Back COVID Mission-Accomplished as Florida, Other States, See Steep New Spikes." *Vanity Fair*, June 27. https://www.vanityfair.com/news/2020/06/trump-ally-desantis-forced-to-walk-back-covid-mission-accomplished-as-florida-other-states-see-steep-new-spikes.

Krugman, Paul. (2019a). "Manufacturing Ain't Great Again. Why?" *New York Times*, October 31. https://www.nytimes.com/2019/10/31/opinion/manufacturing-trump.html?action=click&module=Opinion&pgtype=Homepage.

———. (2019b). "What Economists (Including Me) Got Wrong about Globalization." *Bloomberg*, October 10. https://www.bloomberg.com/opinion/articles/2019-10-10/inequality-globalization-and-the-missteps-of-1990s-economics.

Kruse, Michael. (2019a). "The 5 People Who Could Have Stopped Trump." *Politico*, November 1. https://www.politico.com/magazine/story/2019/11/01/the-five-people-who-could-have-stopped-trump-229894.

———. (2019b). "'If He's Not in a Fight, He Looks for One': Trump's Ukraine Scandal Reflects His Lifelong Craving for a Fresh Enemy." *Politico*, September 23. https://www.politico.com/magazine/story/2019/09/23/trump-ukraine-scandal-enemy-228152.

Labaton, Stephen. (2007). "Congress Passes Increase in the Minimum Wage." *New York Times*, May 24. https://www.nytimes.com/2007/05/25/washington/25wage.html.

Landler, Mark. (2019). "A White House Correspondent Departs the Jaw-Dropping Trump Beat." *New York Times*, July 12. https://www.nytimes.com/2019/07/12/us/politics/trump-white-house-.html?action=click&module=RelatedLinks&pgtype=Article.

Laporta, James, and Chantal Dasilva. (2018). "Immigrant Caravan Troop Deployment Could Cost U.S. $50 Million Despite No Evidence of Terrorists, Major Criminal Gang Presence." *Newsweek*, October 31. https://www.newsweek.com/trump-administration-migrant-caravan-border-troops-1194215.

Lee, Michelle Ye Hee, and John Wagner. (2018). "'A Total Joke': Trump Lashes out at Koch Brothers after Political Network Slams White House." *Washington Post*, July 31. https://www.washingtonpost.com/politics/a-total-joke-trump-lashes-out-at-koch-brothers-after-political-network-slams-white-house/2018/07/31/063a28ae-94ab-11e8-80e1-00e80e1fdf43_story.html.

Leibovich, Mark. (2019). "How Lindsey Graham Went from Trump Skeptic to Trump Sidekick." *New York Times*, February 25. https://www.nytimes.com/2019/02/25/magazine/lindsey-graham-what-happened-trump.html.

Lind, Dara. (2017). "It's Becoming Increasingly Clear That Jared Kushner Is Part of Trump's Russia Problem." *Vox*, May 20. https://www.vox.com/2017/5/20/15668162/kushner-trump-russia-corruption.

Lizza, Ryan. (2017). "How Democrats Rolled Trump on the Debt Ceiling." *New Yorker*, September 6. https://www.newyorker.com/news/ryan-lizza/how-democrats-rolled-trump-on-the-debt-ceiling.

Lowry, Rich. (2018). "The Republican High-Water Mark." *Politico Magazine*, April 18. https://www.politico.com/magazine/story/2018/04/18/republicans-trump-lowry-218054.

Lynch, David J., and Heather Long. (2018). "Harley-Davidson Moves Work Offshore to Limit Blow from Trump's Trade War." *Washington Post*, June 25. https://www.washingtonpost.com/news/business/wp/2018/06/25/harley-davidson-moves-work-offshore-to-limit-blow-from-trumps-trade-war/.

MacGillis, Alec. (2012). "How Paul Ryan Convinced Washington of His Genius." *New Republic*, September 14.

Mak, Tim. (2020). "Weeks before Virus Panic, Intelligence Chairman Privately Raised Alarm, Sold Stocks." National Public Radio, March 19. https://www.npr.org/2020/03/19/818192535/burr-recording-sparks-questions-about-private-comments-on-covid-19.

Marshall, John (2018). "Nunes Dirty Hands—Part Two?" *Talking Points Memo*, January 31. https://talkingpointsmemo.com/edblog/nunes-dirty-hands-part-two.

Martin, Jonathan, and Alexander Burns. (2017). "Republican Governors' 2018 Dilemma: What to Do about Trump?" *New York Times*, November 19. https://mobile.nytimes.com/2017/11/18/us/politics/republican-governors-trump-backlash-2018.html?_r=0&referer=.

Martin, Jonathan, Maggie Haberman, and Alexander Burns. (2017). "Trump Pressed Top Republicans to End Senate Russia Inquiry." *New York Times*, November 30. https://www.nytimes.com/2017/11/30/us/politics/trump-russia-senate-intel.html?hp&action=click&pgtype=Homepage&clickSource=story-heading&module=first-column-region&region=top-news&WT.nav=top-news.

Massoglia, Anna, and Karl Evers-Hillstrom. (2019). "World of Influence: A Guide to Trump's Foreign Business Interests." *Open Secrets*, June 4. https://www.opensecrets.org/news/2019/06/trump-foreign-business-interests/.

Mayer, Jane. (2019). "Trump TV: Fox News Has Always Been Partisan. But Has It Become Propaganda?" *New Yorker*, March 11, 40–53. https://www.newyorker.com/news/news-desk/is-kris-kobachs-defeat-in-kansas-a-model-for-how-to-beat-trumpism.

———. (2020). "How Mitch McConnell Became Trump's Enabler-in-Chief." *New Yorker*, April 12. https://www.newyorker.com/magazine/2020/04/20/how-mitch-mcconnell-became-trumps-enabler-in-chief.

McCubbins, Mathew D., Roger G. Noll, and Barry R. Weingast. (1987). "Administrative Procedures as Instruments of Political Control." *Journal of Law, Economics, & Organization* 3(2): 243–77.

McIntire, Mike. (2017). "Russia Renewed Unused Trump Trademarks in 2016." *New York Times*, June 18. https://www.nytimes.com/2017/06/18/us/politics/russia-trump-trademarks.html.

Melber, Ari, Meredith Mandell, and Mirjam Lablans. (2017). "Putin Rival Ties Kushner Meeting to Kremlin Bankers." NBC News, October 17. https://www.nbcnews.com/politics/white-house/putin-rival-ties-kushner-meeting-kremlin-bankers-n811631.

Memoli, Mike. (2017). "Whistleblower: Flynn Told Ex-Partner Russia Sanctions Would Be Ripped Up." NBC News, December 6. https://www.nbcnews.com/news/us-news/amp/whistleblower-flynn-told-ex-partner-russia-sanctions-would-be-ripped-n827031?__twitter_impression=true.

Milbank, Dana. (2019). "Poof! There Goes Another Infrastructure Week." *Washington Post*, April 30. https://www.washingtonpost.com/opinions/for-trump-its-always-infrastructure-week/2019/04/30/0e9888a2-6b8c-11e9-be3a-33217240a539_story.html.

———. (2020). "What 11 Republican Senators Had to Say About Trump's Racism." *Washington Post*, July 6. https://www.washingtonpost.com/opinions/2020/07/06/silent-republican-lawmakers-are-handmaidens-white-supremacy/.

Miller, Greg, Adam Entous, and Ellen Nakashima. (2017). "National Security Adviser Flynn Discussed Sanctions with Russian Ambassador, Despite Denials, Officials Say." *Washington Post*, February 9. https://www.washingtonpost.com/world/national-security/national-security-adviser-flynn-discussed-sanctions-with-russian-ambassador-despite-denials-officials-say/2017/02/09/f85b29d6-ee11-11e6-b4ff-ac2cf509efe5_story.html?hpid=hp_hp-top-table-main_usrussia-%3Ahomepage%2Fstory.

Morris, Edmund. (2001). *Theodore Rex*. New York: Random House.

Nakashima, Ellen, Adam Entous, and Greg Miller. (2017). "Russian Ambassador Told Moscow That Kushner Wanted Secret Communications Channel with Kremlin." *Washington Post*, May 26. https://www.washingtonpost.com/world/national-security/russian-ambassador-told-moscow-that-kushner-wanted-secret-communications-channel-with-kremlin/2017/05/26/520a14b4-422d-11e7-9869-bac8b446820a_story.html.

Newman, Jesse, and Heather Haddon. (2018). "U.S. To Pay Farmers $4.7 Billion to Offset Trade-Conflict Losses." *Wall Street Journal*, August 27. https://www.wsj.com/articles/u-s-to-pay-farmers-up-to-4-7-billion-to-offset-trade-conflict-losses-1535396442.

Newman, Jesse, and Jacob Bunge. (2019). " 'This One Here Is Gonna Kick My Butt'—Farm Belt Bankruptcies Are Soaring." *Wall Street Journal*, February 6.

Newman, Omarosa Manigault. (2018). *Unhinged: An Insider's Account of the Trump White House*. New York: Gallery Books.

New York Times. (2020). "Trump Calls to 'Liberate' States Where People Are Protesting Social Distancing Restrictions." *New York Times*, April 17. https://www.nytimes.com/2020/04/17/us/coronavirus-cases-news-update.html#link-12bb7c5e.

Nguyen, Tina. (2015). "Donald Trump to Prominent Conspiracy Theorist: 'Your Reputation Is Amazing.' " *Vanity Fair*, December 2. https://www.vanityfair.com/news/2015/12/donald-trump-alex-jones-interview.

Nicholas, Peter, Rebecca Ballhaus, and Siobhan Hughes. (2017). "Frustration with Republicans Drove Donald Trump to Deal with Democrats." *Wall Street Journal*, September 15. https://www.wsj.com/articles/frustration-with-republicans-drove-donald-trump-to-deal-with-democrats-1505517354.

Niemietz, Brian. (2020). "Fox News Pundit Pushed 'Herd Immunity' during the Pandemic." *New York Daily News*, May 7. https://www.nydailynews.com/news/

national/ny-fox-news-pete-hegseth-coronavirus-courage-herd-immunity-20200507-hqotaclizne77kvgm3cdmh537q-story.html.

Norman, Jim. (2017). "Majority in US No Longer Thinks Trump Keeps His Promises." Gallup, April 18.

Ollstein, Alice Miranda. (2016). "There Is a Lot More to the Trump Argentina Story." Think Progress. November 23. https://thinkprogress.org/there-is-a-lot-more-to-the-trump-argentina-story-e4a5026a959c/.

Orden, Erica, and Kara Scannell. (2020). "William Barr's Actions Spark Unease among US Prosecutors." CNN, February 15. https://www.cnn.com/2020/02/15/politics/william-barr-roger-stone-prosecutors-outrage/index.html.

Packer, George. (2020). "How to Destroy a Government." *Atlantic*, April. https://www.theatlantic.com/magazine/archive/2020/04/how-to-destroy-a-government/606793/.

Parker, Ashley, Rosalind S. Helderman, Josh Dawsey, and Carol D. Leonnig. (2018). "Trump Sought Release of Classified Russia Memo, Putting Him at Odds with Justice Department." *Washington Post*, January 27. https://www.washingtonpost.com/politics/trump-sought-release-of-classified-russia-memo-putting-him-at-odds-with-justice-department/2018/01/27/a00f2a4c-02bb-11e8-9d31-d72cf78dbeee_story.html.

Parker, Ashley, and Josh Dawsey. (2019). "Trump and His Allies Plan to Use Barr's Summary of Mueller Report as a Cudgel against Critics." *Washington Post*, March 25. https://www.washingtonpost.com/politics/trump-and-his-allies-plan-to-use-barrs-summary-of-mueller-report-as-a-cudgel-against-critics/2019/03/25/a22a52f4-4f25-11e9-a3f7-78b7525a8d5f_story.html?wpisrc=nl_daily202&wpmm=1.

Parker, Ashley. (2020). "Trump Uses Pandemic Briefing to Focus on Himself." *Washington Post*, April 13. https://www.washingtonpost.com/politics/trump-pandemic-briefing-focus-himself/2020/04/13/1dc94992-7dd8-11ea-9040-68981f488eed_story.html?utm_campaign=wp_politics_am&utm_medium=email&utm_source=newsletter&wpisrc=nl_politics.

Parker, Ashley, Yasmeen Abutaleb, and Josh Dawsey. (2020). "Trump Administration Has Many Coronavirus Task Forces, but Still No Plan for Beating the Pandemic." *Washington Post*, April 11. https://www.washingtonpost.com/politics/trump-task-forces-coronavirus-pandemic/2020/04/11/5cc5a30c-7a77-11ea-a130-df573469f094_story.html.

Parlapiano, Alicia, and Wilson Andrews. (2018). "These Factions in Congress, Split over 'Dreamers,' Could Lead to Government Shutdown." *New York Times*, January 18. https://www.nytimes.com/interactive/2018/01/18/us/politics/government-shutdown-congress.html?action=click&module=Top%20Stories&pgtype=Homepage.

Peker, Emre, Paul Vieira, and Bojan Pancevski. (2018). "After Steel and Aluminum Tariffs, U.S. Allies Move to Coordinate Retaliation Efforts." *Wall Street Journal*, June 6. https://www.wsj.com/articles/after-steel-and-aluminum-tariffs-u-s-allies-move-to-coordinate-retaliation-efforts-1528313629.

Peterson, Kristina, Peter Nicholas, and Sadie Gurman. (2018). "Some Republicans Urge Attorney General to Remain in Job." *Wall Street Journal*, August 28. https://www.wsj.com/articles/some-republicans-urge-attorney-general-to-remain-in-job-as-elections-loom-1535487332.

Popkin, Samuel L. (2007). "Changing Media and Changing Political Organization: Delegation, Representation and News." *Japanese Journal of Political Science* 8(1): 71–93.

———. (2012). *The Candidate: What It Takes to Win—and Hold—the White House.* Oxford: Oxford University Press

Prokop, Andrew. (2016). "Donald Trump's History of Corruption: A Comprehensive Review." *Vox*, October 31. https://www.vox.com/policy-and-politics/2016/9/28/12904136/donald-trump-corrupt.

Radden Keefe, Patrick. (2017). "Trump's Favorite Tycoon: The Washington Misadventures of Carl Icahn." *New Yorker*, August 28. http://www.newyorker.com/magazine/2017/08/28/carl-icahns-failed-raid-on-washington.

Rago, Joseph. (2016). "Inside Paul Ryan's Congress Rescue Mission." *Wall Street Journal*, October 22.

Riga, Kate. (2018). "Corker: GOP in 'Cult-Like Situation' in Refusal to Stand Up to Trump." *Politico*, June 13. https://talkingpointsmemo.com/livewire/corker-gop-is-in-cultlike-situation.

Rohde, David. (2020). "Sword and Shield: The Attorney General's Mission to Maximize Executive Power and Protect the Presidency." *New Yorker*, January 20. https://www.newyorker.com/magazine/2020/01/20/william-barr-trumps-sword-and-shield.

Rosenberg, Matthew, and Mark Mazzetti. (2017). "Trump Team Knew Flynn Was under Investigation before He Came to White House." *New York Times*, May 17. https://www.nytimes.com/2017/05/17/us/politics/michael-flynn-donald-trump-national-security-adviser.html.

Rove, Karl. (2017). "The 30 Republicans Holding Up Tax Reform." *Wall Street Journal*, September 13. https://www.wsj.com/articles/the-30-republicans-holding-up-tax-reform-1505343197.

Rucker, Philip, and Carol Leonnig. (2020). *A Very Stable Genius: Donald J. Trump's Testing of America.* New York: Penguin Press.

Rucker, Phillip, Robert Costa, and Josh Dawsey. (2018). "'A Tailspin': Under Siege, Trump Propels the Government and Markets into Crisis." *Washington Post*, December 20. https://www.washingtonpost.com/politics/a-tailspin-under-siege-trump-propels-the-government-and-markets-into-crisis/2018/12/20/e30347e0-046b-11e9-b6a9-0aa5c2fcc9e4_story.html.

Rudalevige, Andrew. (2018). "Regulation beyond Structure and Process." *National Affairs* 34 (Winter).

Rupar, Aaron. (2020). "Ted Cruz Now: Quid Pro Quo 'Doesn't Matter.' Ted Cruz Before: Quid Pro Quo Talk Is 'Hearsay.'" *Vox*, January 29. https://www.vox.com/2020/1/29/21113331/republicans-quid-pro-quo-ted-cruz-does-not-matter.

Safire, William. (2008). *Safire's Political Dictionary.* New York: Oxford University Press.

Sanger, David E., and Steven Erlanger. (2018). "Hacked European Cables Reveal a World of Anxiety about Trump, Russia and Iran." *New York Times*, December 18. https://www.nytimes.com/2018/12/18/us/politics/european-diplomats-cables-hacked.html.

Sanger-Katz, Margot. (2019). "For Trump Administration, It Has Been Hard to Follow the Rules on Rules." *New York Times*, January 22. https://www.nytimes.com/2019/01/22/upshot/for-trump-administration-it-has-been-hard-to-follow-the-rules-on-rules.html?em_pos=small&emc=edit_up_20190122&nl=upshot&nl_art=0&nlid=7641649emc%3Dedit_up_20190122&ref=headline&te=1.

Savage, Charlie. (2017). "How a Special Counsel Alters the Russia Investigation." *New York Times*, May 17. https://www.nytimes.com/2017/05/17/us/politics/special-counsel-in-russia-investigation-raises-stakes-for-trump.html.

Schleifer, Theodore. (2017). "Kochs Pledge Millions to GOPers in 2018—If They Vote No on Health Care Bill." CNN, March 23. https://www.cnn.com/2017/03/22/politics/kochs-reserve-fund-health-care/index.html.

Schmidt, Michael S. (2017). "In a Private Dinner, Trump Demanded Loyalty. Comey Demurred." New York Times, May 11. https://www.nytimes.com/2017/05/11/us/politics/trump-comey-firing.html.

———. (2020). Donald Trump v. The United States. New York: Random House.

Schneider, Elena. (2017). "Democrats' Early Money Haul Stuns GOP." Politico, October 23. http://politi.co/2hYnjt5.

Schor, Elana. (2017). "McCain: If Trump Lifts Sanctions, Congress Will Restore Them." Politico, January 27. http://politi.co/2jFx1jw.

Sellers, Frances Stead, and David Farenthold. (2017). "'Why Even Let 'Em In?': Understanding Bannon's Worldview and the Policies That Follow." Washington Post February 25. https://www.washingtonpost.com/politics/bannon-explained-his-worldview-well-before-it-became-official-us-policy/2017/01/31/2f4102ac-e7ca-11e6-80c2-30e57e57e05d_story.html.

Sells, Heather. (2018). "'It's Disgraceful': Franklin Graham Rebukes Immigration Policy on CBN Drawing National Attention." Christian Broadcasting Network, June 14. http://www1.cbn.com/cbnnews/us/2018/june/its-disgraceful-franklin-graham-rebukes-immigration-policy-on-drawing-national-attention.

Senate Select Committee on Intelligence. (2019). Report of the Select Committee on Intelligence, United States Senate on Russian Active Measures Campaigns and Interference in the 2016 U.S. Election. Volume 2: Russia's Use of Social Media with Additional Views. Washington, DC: Senate Select Committee on Intelligence.

Severns, Maggie, and Lorraine Woellert. (2018). "Business Lobbyists Dial Back Efforts to Prop up GOP Establishment." Politico, October 31. https://www.politico.com/story/2018/10/31/business-lobby-primary-spending-gop-952158.

Severns, Maggie. (2020). "The Koch Network, Avatar of the Tea Party, Rejects Shutdown Protests." Politico, April 22. https://www.politico.com/story/2018/09/19/simon-sisters-donations-democrats-828606.

Shane, Scott. (2016). "Combative, Populist Steve Bannon Found His Man in Donald Trump." New York Times, November 27. http://www.nytimes.com/2016/11/27/us/politics/steve-bannon-white-house.html.

Shapiro, Robert Y., and Greg M. Shaw. (2017). "Why Can't the Senate Repeal Obamacare? Because Its Policies Are Actually Popular." Monkey Cage (blog). Washington Post, July 19. https://www.washingtonpost.com/news/monkey-cage/wp/2017/07/19/why-cant-the-senate-repeal-obamacare-because-its-actual-policies-are-popular/.

Shear, Michael D. (2020). "Inside the Failure: 5 Takeaways on Trump's Effort to Shift Responsibility." New York Times, July 18. https://www.nytimes.com/2020/07/18/us/politics/trump-coronavirus-failure-takeaways.html.

Shear, Michael D., Sheri Fink, and Noah Weiland. (2020). "Inside Trump Administration, Debate Raged over What to Tell Public." New York Times, March 8. https://www.nytimes.com/2020/03/07/us/politics/trump-coronavirus.html?referringSource=articleShare.

Shear, Michael D., Noah Welland, Eric Lipton, Maggie Haberman, et al. (2020). "Inside Trump's Failure: The Rush to Abandon Leadership Role on the Virus." New York Times, July 18. https://www.nytimes.com/2020/07/18/us/politics/trump-coronavirus-response-failure-leadership.html.

Shephard, Alex, and Theodore Ross. (2016). " 'There's No Check on Trump Except Reality': A Q&A with Wayne Barrett." *New Republic*, December 1. https://newrepublic. com/article/139094/theres-no-check-trump-except-reality-qa-wayne-barrett.

Sherman, Gabriel. (2018a). " 'No One Is in Charge": Inside Trump's New Fox Takeover." *Vanity Fair*, October 28. https://www.vanityfair.com/news/2018/10/ inside-trumps-new-fox-takeover.

———. (2018b). " 'Stephen Actually Enjoys Seeing Those Pictures at the Border': The West Wing Is Fracturing over Trump's Callous Migrant-Family Policy." *Vanity Fair*, June 20. https:// www.vanityfair.com/news/2018/06/stephen-miller-family-separation-white-house.

———. (2020a). "Inside Donald Trump and Jared Kushner's Two Months of Magical Thinking." *Vanity Fair*, April 28. https://www.vanityfair.com/news/2020/04/ donald-trump-jared-kushners-two-months-of-magical-thinking.

———. (2020b). "Trump Desperate, Despondent as Numbers Crater, 'Loser' Label Looms." *Vanity Fair*, July 2. https://www.vanityfair.com/news/2020/07/ trump-despondent-as-numbers-crater-loser-label-looms.

Sherman, Jake, Anna Palmer, and Daniel Lippman. (2018). "Politico Playbook: Shutdown Negotiations Stalled." *Politico Playbook*, December 23. https://www.politico.com/ newsletters/playbook/2018/12/23/shutdown-negotiations-stalled-368632.

Shin, Youjin, Chiqui Esteban, and Dan Keating. (2019). "Timeline: The Who, What, Where of the Sprawling Mueller Investigation [Russian Interference]." *Washington Post*, April 19. https://www.washingtonpost.com/graphics/2019/politics/mueller-investigations-plots/.

Silver, Nate. (2018). "Trump's Base Isn't Enough." *FiveThirtyEight*, November 20. https:// fivethirtyeight.com/features/trumps-base-isnt-enough/.

Smith, Greg B. (2017). "President Trump Chooses Inexperienced Woman Who Planned His Son Eric's Wedding to Run N.Y. Federal Housing Programs." *New York Daily News*, June 15. http://www.nydailynews.com/news/politics/ trump-chooses-family-event-planner-run-n-y-housing-programs-article-1.3251314.

Sommer, Will, Maxwell Tani, and Andrew Kirell. (2020). "Fox News Internal Document Bashes Pro-Trump Fox Regulars for Spreading 'Disinformation.' " *Daily Beast*, February 6. https://www.thedailybeast.com/fox-news-internal-document-bashes-john-solomon-joe-digenova-and-rudy-giuliani-for-spreading-disinformation.

Stanley-Becker, Isaac. (2018). "Devin Nunes, in Secretly Recorded Tape, Tells Donors GOP Majority Is Necessary to Protect Trump: 'We're the Only Ones.' " *Washington Post*, August 9. https://www.washingtonpost.com/news/morning-mix/wp/2018/08/09/ devin-nunes-in-secretly-recorded-tape-tells-donors-gop-majority-is-necessary-to-protect-trump-were-the-only-ones/.

Stolberg, Sheryl Gay, and Carl Hulse. (2020). "Alexander Says Convicting Trump Would 'Pour Gasoline on Cultural Fires.' " *New York Times*, January 31. https://www.nytimes. com/2020/01/31/us/politics/alexander-impeachment-witnesses.html?action=click& module=Spotlight&pgtype=Homepage.

Stone, Peter, and Greg Gordon. (2017). "Exclusive: Manafort Flight Records Show Deeper Kremlin Ties Than Previously Known." McClatchy, November 23. http://www. mcclatchydc.com/news/nation-world/article186102003.html.

Suebsaeng, Asawin, and Lachlan Markay. (2018). "Trump on Coming Debt Crisis: 'I Won't Be Here' When It Blows Up." *Daily Beast*, December 5. https://www.thedailybeast.com/ trump-on-coming-debt-crisis-i-wont-be-here-when-it-blows-up.

Swisher, Kara. (2020). "Bonus: Kara and Maggie Haberman Debrief on Brad Raffensperger." *The New York Times*, December 15, Available at https://www.nytimes.com/2020/12/15/opinion/sway-kara-swisher-maggie-haberman.html?searchResultPosition=10&showTranscript=1.

Tax Reform Task Force. (2016). "A Better Way: Our Vision for a Confident America." Better.GOP, June. https://www.novoco.com/sites/default/files/atoms/files/ryan_a_better_way_policy_paper_062416.pdf.

Tenpas, Kathryn Dunn. (2018). "Why Is Trump's Staff Turnover Higher Than the 5 Most Recent Presidents?" Washington, DC: Brookings Institution, January 19. https://www.brookings.edu/research/why-is-trumps-staff-turnover-higher-than-the-5-most-recent-presidents/.

Thielman, Sam, and Tierney Sneed. (2017). "Emails Show Manafort's Involvement in Op-Ed." *Talking Points Memo*, December 9. http://talkingpointsmemo.com/muckraker/new-filing-and-tpm-exclusive-emails-show-manaforts-involvement-in-op-ed.

Thrush, Glenn. (2019). "Matt Gaetz Is a Congressman Liberals Love to Loathe. It's All Part of the Plan." *New York Times*, March 30. https://www.nytimes.com/2019/03/30/us/politics/matt-gaetz-trump.html.

Thrush, Glenn, and Maggie Haberman. (2017). "Trump's 'Great National Infrastructure Program'? Stalled." *New York Times*, July 23. https://www.nytimes.com/2017/07/23/us/trump-infrastructure-program.html?src=twr&_r=0.

Thrush, Glenn, Maggie Haberman, and Sharon Lafraniere. (2017). "Jared Kushner's Role Is Tested as Russia Case Grows." *New York Times*, May 28. https://www.nytimes.com/2017/05/28/us/kushner-trump-relationship-russia-investigation.html.

Tilove, Jonathan. (2016a). "Austin's Alex Jones: The Voice in Donald Trump's Head." *Austin American Statesman*, October 24. https://www.statesman.com/news/20161024/austins-alex-jones-the-voice-in-donald-trumps-head.

———. (2016b). "First Reading: Donald Trump Thanks Alex Jones: 'I Just Called the King of Saudi Arabia, Queen of England, Now I'm Moving on To You.'" *Austin American Statesman*, November 14.

———. (2018). "Why Beto O'Rourke May Be Headed toward Run for President." *Austin American-Statesman*, November 1. https://www.statesman.com/news/20181101/cruz-amplifies-trumps-caravan-warnings.

Toobin, Jeffrey. (2020). "Why the Mueller Investigation Failed." *New Yorker*, July 6–13, 46–55.

Tracy, Abilgail. (2019). "Two Days in the Life of Nancy Pelosi, Political Grandmaster." *Vanity Fair*, October 9. https://www.vanityfair.com/news/2019/10/in-the-life-of-nancy-pelosi.

———. (2020). "'If You Aren't Making News, You Aren't Governing': Matt Gaetz on Media Mastery, Influence Peddling, and Dating in Trump's Swamp." *Vanity Fair*, September 14. https://www.vanityfair.com/news/2020/09/matt-gaetz-donald-trump-firebrand.

Traister, Rebecca. (2017). "Hillary Clinton Is Furious. And Resigned. And Funny. And Worried." *New York Magazine*, May 26. http://nymag.com/daily/intelligencer/2017/05/hillary-clinton-life-after-election.html.

Tsebelis, George. (2017). "This Is Why Trump's 'Art of the Deal' Doesn't Work in Politics." *Washington Post*, March 29. https://www.washingtonpost.com/news/monkey-cage/wp/2017/03/29/this-is-why-trumps-art-of-the-deal-doesnt-apply-to-politics/.

Vazquez, Maegan. (2020). "GOP Sens. Cornyn and Cruz Say They Don't Understand Why Federal Funds Are Being Pulled from Coronavirus Testing Sites." CNN, June 25.

https://www.cnn.com/2020/06/25/politics/texas-coronavirus-testing-trump-funding/index.html.

Von Hoffman, Nicholas. (1988). *Citizen Cohn*. New York: Doubleday.

Wagner, John. (2017). "Trump Takes Issue with McConnell's Accusation That He Had 'Excessive Expectations' for Congress." *Washington Post*, August 9. https://www.washingtonpost.com/news/post-politics/wp/2017/08/09/trump-takes-issue-with-mcconnells-accusation-that-he-had-excessive-expectations-for-congress/.

———. (2018). "'He's Just Trolling People': Ryan Plays Down Trump's Threat to Revoke Security Clearances." *Washington Post*, July 24. https://www.washingtonpost.com/powerpost/hes-just-trolling-people-ryan-downplays-trumps-threat-to-revoke-security-clearances/2018/07/24/3af53254-8f48-11e8-bcd5-9d911c784c38_story.html.

———. (2019). "Pelosi Rules Out a Censure of Trump: 'If the Goods Are There, You Must Impeach.'" *The Washington Post*, June 19. https://www.washingtonpost.com/powerpost/pelosi-rules-out-a-censure-of-trump-saying-if-the-goods-are-there-you-just-impeach/2019/06/19/6ddf2192-9295-11e9-aadb-74e6b2b46f6a_story.html.

Wall Street Journal. (2017). "Man Up, Mr. Meadows." *Wall Street Journal*, September 8. https://www.wsj.com/articles/man-up-mr-meadows-1504910703.

Watkins, Eli. (2018). "Republican Rep. Jim Jordan: Paul Ryan Has 'Got Problems.'" CNN, February 12. https://www.cnn.com/2018/02/11/politics/jim-jordan-paul-ryan-house/index.html.

Wattles, Jackie. (2017). "Preet Bharara Reveals Why He Made President Trump Fire Him." CNN, April 6. http://money.cnn.com/2017/04/06/news/preet-bharara-donald-trump-cooper-union/index.html.

Weigel, David. (2018). "No, Conor Lamb Didn't Run as 'Republican-Lite.'" *Washington Post*, March 15. https://www.washingtonpost.com/news/powerpost/wp/2018/03/15/no-conor-lamb-didnt-run-as-republican-lite/.

Werner, Erica, Damian Paletta, and David J. Lynch. (2018). "Ryan Splits with Trump on Trade as GOP Lawmakers Move to Block Planned Tariffs." *Washington Post*, March 5. https://www.washingtonpost.com/business/economy/ryan-splits-with-trump-as-gop-lawmakers-move-to-block-planned-tariffs/2018/03/05/cbb5c786-2094-11e8-94da-ebf9d112159c_story.html.

Werner, Erica, Yasmeen Abutaleb, Lena H. Sun, and Lenny Bernstein. (2020). "Trump Officials Warn of Inevitable Spread of Coronavirus across the United States." *Washington Post*, February 28. https://www.washingtonpost.com/us-policy/2020/02/25/cdc-coronavirus-inevitable/?utm_campaign=wp_the_daily_202&utm_medium=email&utm_source=newsletter&wpisrc=nl_daily202.

Widdicombe, Lizzie. (2016). "Family First." *New Yorker*, August 22.

Williams, Jason. (2017). "McConnell's Delicate Dance When It Comes to Donald Trump." *Cincinnati.Com*, August 7.

Wittes, Benjamin. (2017). "Malevolence Tempered by Incompetence: Trump's Horrifying Executive Order on Refugees and Visas." *Lawfare*, January 28. https://www.lawfareblog.com/malevolence-tempered-incompetence-trumps-horrifying-executive-order-refugees-and-visas.

Wolff, Michael. (2016). "Steve Bannon Trump Tower Interview: Trump's Strategist Plots 'New Political Movement.'" *Hollywood Reporter*, November 18. http://www.hollywoodreporter.com/news/steve-bannon-trump-tower-interview-trumps-strategist-plots-new-political-movement-948747.

———. (2018). *Fire and Fury: Inside the Trump White House*. New York: Henry Holt.

Woodward, Bob. (2018). *Fear: Trump in the White House*. London: Simon & Schuster.

———. (2020). *Rage*. New York: Simon & Schuster.

Zaitchik, Alexander. (2011). "Meet Alex Jones." *Rolling Stone*, March 2. http://www.rollingstone.com/politics/news/talk-radios-alex-jones-the-most-paranoid-man-in-america-20110302.

Zapotosky, Matt. (2019). "Trump Would Have Been Charged with Obstruction Were He Not President, Hundreds of Former Federal Prosecutors Assert." *Washington Post*, May 6. https://www.washingtonpost.com/world/national-security/trump-would-have-been-charged-with-obstruction-were-he-not-president-hundreds-of-former-federal-prosecutors-assert/2019/05/06/e4946a1a-7006-11e9-9f06-5fc2ee80027a_story.html.

Zengerle, Jason. (2018). "How Devin Nunes Turned the House Intelligence Committee Inside Out." *New York Times*, April 24. https://www.nytimes.com/2018/04/24/magazine/how-devin-nunes-turned-the-house-intelligence-committee-inside-out.html.

Zhang, Jiakun Jack. (2020). "The U.S. And China Finally Signed a Trade Agreement. Who Won?" *Washington Post*, January 21. https://www.washingtonpost.com/politics/2020/01/21/us-china-finally-signed-trade-agreement-who-won/.

Zimmerman, Neetzan. (2016). "Omarosa: Trump's Haters Will Be Forced to 'Bow Down' to Him." *The Hill*, September 23. https://thehill.com/blogs/in-the-know/in-the-know/297430-omarosa-trumps-haters-will-be-forced-to-bow-down-to-him.

Chapter 7

116th Congress (2019a). H. Res. 6 Rules of the One Hundred Sixteenth Congress. Washington, DC: US House of Representatives.

———. (2019b). H.R.1: For the People Act of 2019. Washington, DC: US House of Representatives.

Adrian, Charles R. (1952). "Some General Characteristics of Nonpartisan Elections." *American Political Science Review* 46(3): 766–76.

Alberta, Tim. (2019). *American Carnage: On the Front Lines of the Republican Civil War and the Rise of President Trump*. New York: Harper Collins

Andersen, Hans Christian ([1837] 1959). "The Emperor's New Clothes." In *Hans Christian Andersen's Fairy Tales: A Selection*. Oxford: Oxford University Press.

Bade, Rachael. (2020). "House's Most Liberal Caucus Divided over How to Use Its Political Clout." *Washington Post*, November 1, https://www.washingtonpost.com/politics/house-democrats-liberals-biden/2020/11/01/0d7a527c-1abb-11eb-aeec-b93bcc29a01b_story.html.

Bade, Rachael, and Erica Werner. (2020). "Centrist House Democrats Lash out at Liberal Colleagues, Blame Far-Left Views for Costing the Party Seats." *Washington Post*, November 5. https://www.washingtonpost.com/politics/house-democrats-pelosi-election/2020/11/05/1ddae5ca-1f6e-11eb-90dd-abd0f7086a91_story.html.

Barker, Kim, and Theodoric Meyer. (2014). "Who Controls the Kochs' Political Network? ASMI, SLAH and TOHE." ProPublica, March 17. https://www.propublica.org/article/who-controls-koch-political-network-asmi-slah-tohe.

Berelson, Bernard, Paul Lazarsfeld, and William McPhee. (1954). *Voting: A Study of Opinion Formation in a Presidential Campaign*. Chicago: University of Chicago Press.

Berman, Russell. (2020). "How Ed Markey Defeated Joe Kennedy." *Atlantic*, September 1. https://www.theatlantic.com/politics/archive/2020/09/ed-markey-defeats-joe-kennedy-massachusetts-senate/615937/.

Blake, Aaron. (2021). "'Let's Have Trial by Combat': How Trump and Allies Egged on the Violent Scenes Wednesday." The Washington Post, January 6, https://www.washingtonpost.com/politics/2021/01/06/lets-have-trial-by-combat-how-trump-allies-egged-violent-scenes-wednesday/?utm_campaign=wp_the_5_minute_fix&utm_medium=email&utm_source=newsletter&wpisrc=nl_fix&carta-url=https%3A%2F%2Fs2.washingtonpost.com%2Fcar-ln-tr%2F2e3830e%2F5ff6407d9d2fda0efba2495e%2F596b90caae7e8a44e7d9cacd%2F26%2F47%2F5ff6407d9d2fda0efba2495e.

Blake, David Haven. (2016). *Liking Ike: How Mad Men and Celebrities Remade Politics in the 1950s*. New York: Oxford University Press.

Bollen, Peter. (2006). *Frank Talk: The Wit and Wisdom of Barney Frank*. iUniverse.

Bone, Hugh A. (1952). "Campaign Methods of Today." *Annals of the American Academy of Political and Social Science* 283: 127–40.

Boyd, James. (1970). "Nixon's Southern Strategy: 'It's All in the Charts.'" *New York Times*, May 17.

Brenan, Megan. (2019). "Americans' Trust in Government to Handle Problems at New Low." Gallup, January 31. https://news.gallup.com/poll/246371/americans-trust-government-handle-problems-new-low.aspx.

Brennan Center. (2019). "A Guide to Emergency Powers and Their Use." Washington, DC: Brennan Center for Justice, September 4.

Bump, Philip. (2017). "Another Day, Another Poll Showing How Deeply Unpopular the GOP Health-Care Bill Is." *Washington Post*, June 22. https://www.washingtonpost.com/news/politics/wp/2017/06/22/another-day-another-poll-showing-how-deeply-unpopular-the-gop-health-care-bill-is/.

Calmes, Jackie. (2016). "Left-Leaning Economists Question Cost of Bernie Sanders's Plans." *New York Times*, February 15.

Carter, Ashton, Dick Cheney, William Cohen, Mark Esper, et al. (2021). "10 Former Defense Secretaries: Involving Military in Election Disputes Would Be Dangerous, Unlawful." *The Washington Post*, January 3, https://www.washingtonpost.com/opinions/10-former-defense-secretaries-military-peaceful-transfer-of-power/2021/01/03/2a23d52e-4c4d-11eb-a9f4-0e668b9772ba_story.html.

Clymer, Adam. (1978). "Carter's Clash with Kennedy." *New York Times*, December 12. https://www.nytimes.com/1978/12/13/archives/carters-clash-with-kennedy-contest-for-leadership-seen-in-budget.html.

CNN (2021). Transcript of President Trump's Audio Call with Georgia Secretary of State. *CNN*. January 4. https://www.cnn.com/2021/01/03/politics/trump-brad-raffensperger-phone-call-transcript/index.html.

Corasaniti, Nick, Reid J. Epstein, and Jim Rutenberg. (2020). "The Times Called Officials in Every State: No Evidence of Voter Fraud." *New York Times*, November 10. https://www.nytimes.com/2020/11/10/us/politics/voting-fraud.html.

Cottle, Michelle. (2017). "The Congressional War on Expertise." *Atlantic*, July 2. https://www.theatlantic.com/politics/archive/2017/07/why-lawmakers-need-the-congressional-budget-office/532929/.

Cox, Gary W. (2009). "The Organization of Democratic Legislatures." In *The Oxford Handbook of Comparative Politics*, edited by Carles Boix and Susan C. Stokes, 141–61. Oxford: Oxford University Press.

Cruz, Ted. (2021). Ted Cruz Senate Speech on Election Certification (Transcript). *Rev.com*. January 6. https://www.rev.com/blog/transcripts/ted-cruz-senate-speech-on-election-certification-transcript-january-6.

Davis, Julie Hirschfeld. (2019). "Tensions between Pelosi and Progressive Democrats of 'the Squad' Burst into Flame." *New York Times*, July 9. https://www.nytimes.com/2019/07/09/us/politics/nancy-pelosi-ocasio-cortez.html?searchResultPosition=1.

Davis, Julie Hirschfeld, and Emily Cochrane. (2019). "House Democrats Move to Rein in Trump's Immigration Crackdown." *New York Times*, June 25.

Del Valle, Gabby. (2019). "Chick-Fil-A's Many Controversies, Explained." *Vox*, November 19. https://www.vox.com/the-goods/2019/5/29/18644354/chick-fil-a-anti-gay-donations-homophobia-dan-cathy.

Dietrich, Eric. (2019). "SCOTUS Won't Hear Challenge to Montana Disclose Act." *Montana Free Press*, February 19. https://montanafreepress.org/2019/02/19/scotus-wont-hear-challenge-to-montana-disclose-act/.

Dorman, Sam (2021). Mitt Romney Accuses Trump of Inciting an Insurrection. *Fox News*. January 6. https://www.foxnews.com/politics/romney-trump-insurrection-gop-obejctors.

Douthat, Ross Gregory and Reihan Salam. (2008). Grand New Party: How Republicans Can Win the Working Class and Save the American Dream. New York: Doubleday.

Douthat, Ross. (2015). "Searching for Richard Nixon." *New York Times*, November 22.

Druckman, J. N., and A. Lupia. (2000). "Preference Formation." *Annual Review of Political Science* 3: 1–24.

Dyche, John David. (2009). *Republican Leader: A Political Biography of Senator Mitch McConnell*. Wilmington, DE: ISI Books.

Easley, Jonathan. (2012). "Sen. Graham: 'We Were Too Hard' on Newt Gingrich in 1997 Coup Attempt." *The Hill*, February 2. http://thehill.com/blogs/blog-briefing-room/news/208293-sen-graham-we-were-too-hard-on-newt-in-1997-coup-attempt.

Edmondson, Catie, Emily Cochrane, and Lisa Friedman. (2019). "Liberal Freshmen Are Shaking the Capitol Just Days into the New Congress." *New York Times*, January 6. https://www.nytimes.com/2019/01/06/us/politics/tlaib-aoc-new-congress.html.

Edsall, Thomas B. (2014). "The Demise of the White Democratic Voter." *New York Times*, November 11.

———. (2015). "Losing the Tea Party Baggage." *New York Times*, January 6. http://www.nytimes.com/2015/01/07/opinion/cory-gardner-losing-the-tea-party-baggage.html.

Fadulu, Lola, and Abby Goodnough. (2020). "Amid a Pandemic, Trump Moves Forward with Safety Net Cuts." *New York Times*, March 13. https://www.nytimes.com/2020/03/13/us/politics/coronavirus-food-stamps-medicaid.html?action=click&module=Latest&pgtype=Homepage.

Fang, Lee. (2020). "Foreign-Funded Dark-Money Groups Lobby IRS to Repeal Remaining Reporting Requirements." *The Intercept*, February 15. https://theintercept.com/2020/02/15/dark-money-irs-reporting-501c/.

Ferris, Sarah and Heather Caygle. (2020). "Kathleen Rice Beats out Aoc for Spot on Coveted House Committee." *Politico*. December 17. https://www.politico.com/news/2020/12/17/kathleen-rice-aoc-house-committee-448001.

Frank, Barney. (2016). "Three Reasons Why Things Will Get Harder for Bernie Sanders." *Politico*, February 3. https://www.politico.com/magazine/story/2016/02/three-reasons-why-things-will-get-harder-for-bernie-sanders-213591.

Freedlander, David. (2019). "'There Is Going to Be a War within the Party. We Are Going to Lean into It.'" *Politico Magazine*, February 4. https://www.politico.com/magazine/story/2019/02/04/the-insurgents-behind-alexandria-ocasio-cortez-224542.

———. (2020). "One Year in Washington." *New York Magazine*, January 6. https://nymag.com/intelligencer/2020/01/aoc-first-year-in-washington.html.

From, Al, and Alice McKeon. (2013). *The New Democrats and the Return to Power*. New York: Palgrave Macmillan.

Frymer, Paul, and John David Skrentny. (1998). "Coalition-Building and the Politics of Electoral Capture during the Nixon Administration: African Americans, Labor, Latinos." *Studies in American Political Development* 12: 131–61.

Galston, William, and Elaine Kamarck. (1989). "The Politics of Evasion: Democrats and the Presidency." Washington, DC: Progressive Policy Institute.

Gerson, Michael. (2020). "The Big Lie That Won't Die: How Trump and His Allies' Favorite Bogus Fraud Claim Keeps Surviving." *Washington Post*, December 14, https://www.washingtonpost.com/opinions/the-moral-hypocrisy-of-conservative-leaders-is-stunning/2020/12/14/35e62f16-3e2d-11eb-8bc0-ae155bee4aff_story.html.

Gold, Matea, and Tom Hamburger. (2013). "California Donor Disclosure Case Exposes How Nonprofit Groups Can Play in Politics." *Washington Post*, November 4. https://www.washingtonpost.com/politics/california-donor-disclosure-case-exposes-how-nonprofits-play-in-politics/2013/11/04/70e0b7ac-4246-11e3-a624-41d661b0bb78_story.html.

Gold, Matea, and Ed O'Keeffe. (2015). "Never Before Have So Many People with So Much Money Run for President." *Washington Post*, April 27. https://www.washingtonpost.com/politics/why-the-2016-gop-race-may-be-more-like-2012-than-the-party-hoped/2015/04/26/fff662c8-e9f9-11e4-9767-6276fc9b0ada_story.html?utm_term=.ac9fd8b38b09.

Goodnough, Abby. (2015). "In Vermont, Frustrations Mount over Affordable Care Act." *New York Times*, June 4. https://www.nytimes.com/2015/06/05/us/in-vermont-frustrations-mount-over-affordable-care-act.html.

Greenberg, Stanley B. (2020). "Race War: Will Trump's Use of Bigotry to Rally Anxious White Voters End with His Term of Office?" *American Prospect*, December 10 https://prospect.org/politics/race-war-will-trumps-use-of-bigotry-end-with-his-term/.

Greenhouse, Linda. (1980). "Byrd Says Carter's Remarks on Budget Cost Him." *New York Times*, June 1.

Griffith, Robert. (1982). "Dwight D. Eisenhower and the Corporate Commonwealth." *American Historical Review* 87(1): 87–122.

Haberman, Maggie. (2021). "Trump Told Crowd 'You Will Never Take Back Our Country with Weakness.'" *The New York Times*, January 6, https://www.nytimes.com/2021/01/06/us/politics/trump-speech-capitol.html?action=click&module=Top%20Stories&pgtype=Homepage.

Hasan, Mahan. (2020). "'A Car Crash between Nicholas Sparks and Mein Kampf': In the Tangled World of Far-Right Chat Rooms, White Supremacists Are Getting Organized." *Vanity Fair*, October 13. https://www.vanityfair.com/news/2020/10/talia-lavin-in-the-tangled-world-of-far-right-chatrooms.

Healy, Andrew, and Neil Malhotra. (2009). "Myopic Voters and Natural Disaster Policy." *American Political Science Review* 103(3): 387–406.

Herndon, Astead W. (2020a). "Alexandria Ocasio-Cortez on Biden's Win, House Losses, and What's Next for the Left." *New York Times*, November 7. https://www.nytimes.com/2020/11/07/us/politics/aoc-biden-progressives.html.

———. (2020b). "Conor Lamb, House Moderate, on Biden's Win, 'the Squad' and the Future of the Democratic Party." *New York Times*, November 8. https://www.nytimes.com/2020/11/08/us/politics/conor-lamb-democrats-biden.html?searchResultPosition=1.

Hess, Stephen, and David S. Broder. (1967). *The Republican Establishment: The Present and Future of the G.O.P.* New York: Harper & Row.

Hohmann, James. (2016). "The Daily 202: Trump's Romp in Nevada Shows Why Conventional Wisdom about His Ceiling May Be Wrong." *Washington Post*, February 24.

Hohmann, James. (2021a). "The Daily 202: Freshman Senators Backing Trump's Baseless Election Challenge Showcase Republican Radicalization." *The Washington Post*, January 4, https://www.washingtonpost.com/politics/2021/01/04/daily-202-freshman-senators-backing-trumps-baseless-election-challenge-showcase-republican-radicalization/?utm_campaign=wp_the_daily_202&utm_medium=email&utm_source=newsletter&wpisrc=nl_daily202.

Hohmann, James. (2021b). "The Daily 202: Conservatives Fear Trump's Plot to Overturn Loss Will 'Imperil the Electoral College.'" *Washington Post*, January 5, https://www.washingtonpost.com/politics/2021/01/05/daily-202-conservatives-fear-trumps-plot-overturn-loss-will-imperil-electoral-college/.

Huntington, Samuel P. (2004). "Dead Souls: The Denationalization of the American Elite." *The National Interest* 75 (Spring): 5–18.

Itkowitz, Colby and Mike Debonis. (2021). "Cruz, Cadre of Other GOP Senators Vow Not to Certify Biden Win without Probe of Baseless Voter Fraud Claims." *The Washington Post*, January 2, https://www.washingtonpost.com/politics/2021/01/02/cruz-johnson-9-other-gop-senators-say-they-will-not-vote-certify-electors-unless-audit-is-conducted/.

Jakes, Lara. (2020). "Pompeo Backs Trump's Actions to Contest Election Results, and Biden Calls Them 'an Embarrassment.'" *New York Times*, November 10. https://www.nytimes.com/2020/11/10/us/politics/pompeo-backs-trumps-actions-to-contest-election-results-and-biden-calls-them-an-embarrassment.html?searchResultPosition=3.

Janson, Donald. (1964a). "Extremist Book Sales Soar Despite Criticism in G.O.P." *New York Times*, October 4.

———. (1964b). "Rightists Buoyed by the Election." *New York Times*, November 23.

Kabaservice, Geoffrey. (2016). "What Establishment?" *Wall Street Journal*, May 13.

Kansas City Star. (2021). "Assault on Democracy Sen. Josh Hawley Has Blood on His Hands in Capitol Coup Attempt." *Kansas City Star*. January 6. Available at https://www.kansascity.com/opinion/editorials/article248317375.html.

Karabell, Zachary. (2000). *The Last Campaign: How Harry Truman Won the 1948 Election.* New York, Knopf.

Kopan, Tal. (2020). "Nancy Pelosi Declares She Will Run Again for House Speaker as Dems Quarrel About Messaging." *San Francisco Chronicle*, November 6. https://www.sfchronicle.com/politics/article/Nancy-Pelosi-declares-she-will-run-again-for-15707513.php.

Krugman, Paul. (2019). "Don't Make Health Care a Purity Test." *New York Times*, March 21. https://www.nytimes.com/2019/03/21/opinion/medicare-for-all-democrats.html?action=click&module=Opinion&pgtype=Homepage.

Lawrence, W. H. (1948). "Victory Sweeping: President Wins, 9471/2 to 263, over Russell on First Ballot." *New York Times*, July 15.

Lee, R. Alton. (1966). "Army Mutiny of 1946." *Journal of American History* 53(3): 555–71.

———. (1970). "The Truman–80th Congress Struggle over Tax Policy." *The Historian* 33(1): 68–82.

Lithwick, Dahlia. (2016). "Resolved: Ted Cruz Was His Worst Self as a Presidential Candidate." *Slate*, May 4. https://slate.com/news-and-politics/2016/05/i-was-on-the-college-debate-circuit-with-ted-cruz.html.

Lupia, Arthur. (1994). "Shortcuts versus Encyclopedias—Information and Voting-Behavior in California Insurance Reform Elections." *American Political Science Review* 88(1): 63–76.

———. (2016). *Uninformed: Why People Know So Little About Politics and What We Can Do about It*. New York: Oxford University Press.

Lupia, Arthur, and Mathew D. McCubbins. (1998). *The Democratic Dilemma: Can Citizens Learn What They Need to Know?* Cambridge: Cambridge University Press.

———. (2019). "Democracy's Continuing Dilemma: How to Build Credibility in Chaotic Times." *PS: Political Science & Politics* 52(4): 654–58.

Masket, Seth E. (2009). *No Middle Ground: How Informal Party Organizations Control Nominations and Polarize Legislatures*. Ann Arbor: University of Michigan Press.

Massoglia, Anna. (2015). "Could Criminal Complaints Be a New Way to Tackle Dark Money?" *Open Secrets*, December 3. https://www.opensecrets.org/news/2015/12/could-criminal-complaints-be-a-new-way-to-tackle-dark-money/.

Mayer, Jane. (2020). "How Mitch McConnell Became Trump's Enabler-in-Chief." *New Yorker*, April 12. https://www.newyorker.com/magazine/2020/04/20/how-mitch-mcconnell-became-trumps-enabler-in-chief.

McGrane, Victoria. (2020). "Ed Markey Beats Joe Kennedy in Senate Primary." *Boston Globe*, September 2. https://www.bostonglobe.com/2020/09/01/metro/voters-have-their-say-senate-race-between-ed-markey-joe-kennedy/.

Miroff, Nick, and Josh Dawsey. (2020). "Chad Wolf Emerges as Trump's Favorite Department of Homeland Security Chief." *Washington Post*, August 3. https://www.washingtonpost.com/national/chad-wolf-dhs-trump/2020/08/03/38b6adf8-d1d4-11ea-af07-1d058ca137ae_story.html?utm_campaign=wp_politics_am&utm_medium=email&utm_source=newsletter&wpisrc=nl_politics.

New York Times. (1964). "G.O.P. Nominee's Views, in His Own Words, on Major Issues of Campaign." *New York Times*, July 18. http://www.nytimes.com/1964/07/18/gop-nominees-views-in-his-own-words-on-major-issues-of-campaign.html.

Noonan, Peggy. (2020). "The Week It Went South for Trump." *Wall Street Journal*, June 25. https://www.wsj.com/articles/the-week-it-went-south-for-trump-11593127733?mod=searchresults&page=1&pos=1.

Perlstein, Rick. (2001). *Before the Storm: Barry Goldwater and the Unmaking of the American Consensus*. New York: Hill and Wang.

Peters, Cameron. (2021). "A GOP Plan to Challenge Election Results Is Splintering the Republican Conference." *Vox*. January 3. https://www.vox.com/2021/1/3/22211315/electoral-college-vote-gop-senators-debate.

Phillips, Morgan. (2021). "Sen. Tom Cotton Calls on Trump to 'Quit Misleading' Supporters." *Fox News*. January 6.

Pildes, Richard H. (2019). "Small-Donor-Based Campaign-Finance Reform and Political Polarization." *Yale Law Journal Forum*, November 18. https://www.yalelawjournal.org/pdf/Pildes_SmallDonorBasedCampaignFinanceReformandPoliticalPolarization_1nbukg72.pdf.

Plotke, David. (1997). "Representation Is Democracy." *Constellations* 4(1): 19–34.

Popkin, Samuel L. (1984). "The Donkey's Dilemma: White Men Don't Vote Democratic." *Washington Post*, November 11.

———. (2007). "Public Opinion and Collective Obligations." *Society* 44(5): 37–44.

Popkin, Samuel L. (2012). *The Candidate: What It Takes to Win—and Hold—the White House*. Oxford: Oxford University Press.

Popkin, Samuel L., and Henry A. Kim. (2007). "It's Uphill for the Democrats: Winning the White House? History's against Them." *Washington Post*, March 11.

Porter, Representative Katie. (2020). "Rep. Porter, Joined by House Committee Chairs, Introduces Bill to Crack Down on Unconfirmed Agency Officials." Press Release. Office of Representative Katie Porter. https://porter.house.gov/news/documentsingle.aspx?DocumentID=130.

Reedy, George E. (1987). *The Twilight of the Presidency: From Johnson to Reagan*. New York: New American Library.

Robbins, Hollis (2003). "The Emperor's New Critique." *New Literary History* 34(4): 659–75.

Romo, Vanessa. (2012). *NPR*. January 6. https://www.npr.org/sections/congress-electoral-college-tally-live-updates/2021/01/06/954218720/after-chaos-insurrection-and-death-pro-trump-rioters-defy-d-c-curfew.

Rothschild, Neal, and Mike Allen. (2019). "Alexandria Ocasio-Cortez Has More Twitter Power Than Media, Establishment." *Axios*, January 19. https://www.axios.com/ocasio-cortez-dominates-twitter-6a997938-b8a5-4a8b-a895-0a1bcd073fea.html.

Rovere, Richard. (1964a). "The Campaign: Goldwater." *New Yorker*, October 3.

———. (1964b). "On the Trail with George Wallace." *New Yorker*, May 16.

Ryan, Erica. (2013). "Hastert: Primary Challenges Making Congress 'Kind of Neurotic." *NPR*, October 8. http://www.npr.org/sections/itsallpolitics/2013/10/08/230256554/hastert-primary-challenges-making-congress-kind-of-neurotic.

Shapiro, Robert Y., and Greg M. Shaw. (2017). "Why Can't the Senate Repeal Obamacare? Because Its Policies Are Actually Popular." *Monkey Cage* (blog). *Washington Post*, July 19. https://www.washingtonpost.com/news/monkey-cage/wp/2017/07/19/why-cant-the-senate-repeal-obamacare-because-its-actual-policies-are-popular/.

Smith, Ben. (2020). "The Trump Presidency Is Ending. So Is Maggie Haberman's Wild Ride." *New York Times*, November 8, https://www.nytimes.com/2020/11/08/business/media/trump-maggie-haberman.html.

Smith, Richard Norton. (1982). *Thomas E. Dewey and His Times*. New York: Simon Schuster.

Sonmez, Felicia and Sarah Pulliam Bailey. (2020). "Televangelist Pat Robertson Says It's Time for Trump to Accept Biden's Win and 'Move On." *The Washington Post*, December 21, https://www.washingtonpost.com/politics/televangelist-pat-robertson-says-its-time-for-trump-to-accept-bidens-win-and-move-on/2020/12/21/83143262-43df-11eb-a277-49a6d1f9dff1_story.html.

Stein, Sam. (2012). "David Axelrod: Todd Akin's Comments Are 'Inconvenient' for Romney-Ryan, 'Not Inconsistent.'" *Huffington Post*, August 20. http://www.huffingtonpost.com/2012/08/20/david-axelrod-todd-akin_n_1811693.html?utm_hp_ref=elections-2012.

Steinhauer, Jennifer. (2020). "Why Democrats Are Still Not the Party of Alexandria Ocasio-Cortez." *New York Times*, March 8. https://www.nytimes.com/2020/03/05/sunday-review/democratic-party-ocasio-cortez.html.

Steinhauer, Jennifer, Katie Benner, Eric Schmitt and Helene Cooper. (2021). "D.C. Braces for Two Days of Protests as the Leader of the Proud Boys, a Far-Right Group, Is Arrested." *New York Times*, January 5, https://www.nytimes.com/2021/01/05/us/politics/dc-braces-for-two-days-of-protests-as-the-leader-of-the-proud-boys-a-far-right-group-is-arrested.html?searchResultPosition=1.

Stevens, Stuart. (2020). "We Lost the Battle for the Republican Party's Soul Long Ago." *New York Times*, July 29. https://www.nytimes.com/2020/07/29/opinion/trump-republican-party-racism.html?action=click&module=Opinion&pgtype=Homepage.

Stone, I. F. (1964). "Review: *The Collected Works of Barry Goldwater.*" *New York Review of Books*, August 20.

Sullivan, Amy. (2008). *The Party Faithful: How and Why Democrats Are Closing the God Gap.* New York: Scribner.

Swisher, Kara. (2020). "Bonus: Kara and Maggie Haberman Debrief on Brad Raffensperger." *The New York Times*, December 15, Available at https://www.nytimes.com/2020/12/15/opinion/sway-kara-swisher-maggie-haberman.html?searchResultPosition=10&showTranscript=1.Tabarrok, Alex. (2016). "Former Dem CEAs Write Open Letter to Sanders." *Marginal Revolution*, February 17. http://marginalrevolution.com/marginalrevolution/2016/02/ceas-open-letter-to-sanders.html.

Tavits, Margit. (2007). "Clarity of Responsibility and Corruption." *American Journal of Political Science* 51(1): 218–29.

Thebault, Reis. (2019). "Ocasio-Cortez's Chief of Staff Accuses Moderate Democrats of Enabling a 'Racist System.'" *Washington Post*, June 28. https://www.washingtonpost.com/politics/ocasio-cortezs-chief-of-staff-accuses-moderate-democrats-of-enabling-a-racist-system/2019/06/28/5ef787a0-993e-11e9-916d-9c61607d8190_story.html.

Tumulty, Karen, and Sean Sullivan. (2018). "'That's the Model': Republican Cory Gardner Stands up to President Trump." *Washington Post*, January 5. https://www.washingtonpost.com/powerpost/thats-the-model-cory-gardner-stands-up-to-president-trump/2018/01/05/b3b9b2b6-f17b-11e7-b3bf-ab90a706e175_story.html.

Vandehei, Jim, and Mike Allen. (2012). "The Right Drops a Bomb on Newt." *Politico*, January 26. https://www.politico.com/story/2012/01/the-right-drops-a-bomb-on-newt-072000.

Weiner, Daniel I. (2015). "*Citizens United* Five Years Later." Washington, DC: Brennan Center for Justice, January 14.

Weisman, Jonathan. (2012). "Tax-Exempt Group's Election Activity Highlights Limits of Campaign Finance Rules." *New York Times*, July 17. https://www.nytimes.com/2012/07/17/us/politics/hope-growth-and-opportunity-shows-limits-of-disclosure-rules.html.

Wilkins, Roger. (1984). "Bad Advice on Blacks." *New York Times*, November 18.

WBUR Newsroom. (2021). "'Go Home': Trump Tells Supporters Who Mobbed Capitol to Leave, Again Falsely Claiming Election Victory (Transcript)." *WBUR*. January 6. https://www.wbur.org/news/2021/01/06/go-home-trump-supporters-us-capitol-transcript.

Will, George F. (2021). "Hawley, Cruz and Their Senate Cohort Are the Constitution's Most Dangerous Domestic Enemies" *The Washington Post*, June 4, Available at https://www.washingtonpost.com/opinions/hawley-cruz-and-their-senate-cohort-are-the-constitutions-most-dangerous-domestic-enemies/2021/01/04/912d2530-4ebf-11eb-83e3-322644d82356_story.html.

Index

For the benefit of digital users, indexed terms that span two pages (e.g., 52–53) may, on occasion, appear on only one of those pages.